Toward a Radical Therapy

S O C I A L   C H A N G E   S E R I E S   edited by Victor Gioscia

This series of books is published in tandem with an international journal entitled Social Change, edited by Victor Gioscia and Philip Slater, and published by Gordon and Breach

VARIETIES OF TEMPORAL EXPERIENCE   (in four volumes)
    by Victor Gioscia

BETWEEN PARADIGMS   The Mood and its Purpose
    by Frank Gillette

HOW BEHAVIOR MEANS
    by Albert E. Scheflen

FOOTHOLDS
    by Philip Slater

EARTHCHILD
    by Warren Brodey

BIRTH AND DEATH AND CYBERNATION   Cybernetics of the Sacred
    by Paul Ryan

GALAXIES OF LIFE   The Human Aura in Acupuncture and Kirlian Photography
    edited by Stanley Krippner and Daniel Rubin

TOWARD A RADICAL THERAPY   Alternate Services for Personal and Social Change
    by Ted Clark and Dennis T. Jaffe

Other books in this series will be announced as they approach their completion

0 677 04730 4 (hardback edition)

0 677 04735 5 (paperback edition)

TOWARD A RADICAL THERAPY

Alternate Services for Personal and Social Change

by

TED CLARK and DENNIS T. JAFFE

AN INTERfACE BOOK

An INTERFACE book, published by Gordon and Breach, New York

Copyright ⓒ 1973 by:

    Gordon and Breach, Science Publishers, Inc.
    One Park Avenue, New York
    New York, N.Y. 10016

Editorial office for the United Kingdom:

    Gordon and Breach Science Publishers, Ltd.
    41/42 William IV Street
    London, W.C.2

Editorial office for France:

    Gordon & Breach
    7-9 rue Emile Dubois
    Paris 14e

Library of Congress catalog card number: 73-78296

Man is an endangered species.

We think the separation of fact from value is the principal illusion responsible for the nearly terminal condition of species man on planet earth. This series is an attempt to share the facts and values of intelligent people who know valuable things that might help us find, live, and experience in ways that are species-enhancing, not species-destructive.

We think sharing information of this kind is as vital to humans as water is to fish.

We think we can depollute our information environment by introducing life-enhancing values into the changing currents of our lives.

We think the series should serve as a critical information resource for people who are seriously trying to enhance the life of species man.

We will publish hard science only when we think it will help us do that. We will publish opinion, analysis, exhortation, review, speculation, experiment, criticism, poetry, and/or denunciations if we think it is of critical human benefit.

We are not naive. We do not think publishing a few truths will set us free. We are not optimists. We do not think the chances for human survival are very good. We are not elitists. We do not think that showers of wisdom from Olympus will illuminate the simple man's darkened awareness.

We believe that human consciousness both guides and responds to human interaction, and that most contemporary interaction proceeds from and perpetuates assumptions about human life that are no longer valid. We believe that these assumptions can be changed if/when we want to.

Some of our fondest assumptions have already been unmasked by changes, unleashed by blind commitments to short run values. The most glaring example---we once believed technology made interaction "easier." Now we know that when our technologies violate ecological laws, we murder each other.

Some new forms of interaction (and some old ones) are currently being touted as the way. We do not think there is, or can be, any one way. How to sort out the promising ones from the blind alleys constitutes our principal aim.

We therefore deliberately adopt a post-disciplinary stance, believing that no one view, be it philosophical, scientific, aesthetic, political, clinical, what have you, has the answer.

We intend to be a sort of whole earth idea catalogue for people who think that thinking about the human predicament might help us to live as one self-aware species, deliberately guiding its own evolution for the first time.

As editors, we will select and publish things we value as attempts to foster that kind of voluntary humanity.

Therefore, we invite anyone, whether clinical, social, behavioral scientist (or fan), student, faculty (or interested person), young or old (or in the middle) to join us in the attempt to make a joyful human future not only possible but likely.

So---if you think "Science" is the way, we're not for you, and you probably won't like us. If you think radicals are mad (nee crazy, disturbed, insane, deviant, misguided, etc.), we're not for you, and you'll probably loathe us. If you think the world will not be safe till sociologists are kings, we think you're mad. Ditto for politicians.

Every day, changes race into our world like mad floodwaters, undermining all we hold sacred and sure.

Change is called for.

Yet, change is crisis.

What to do in such times. How to live. Feel. Know. Experience.

That's what this Series is all about.

                                             Victor Gioscia
                                             Series Editor

CONTENTS

Introduction   1

1. The Destruction of Youth   7

2. Deviance and Delinquency as Frustrated Rebellion   27
    A. Fundamentals   27
    B. A New Theory of Deviance   40

3. The Counter-Culture as a Process of Social Change   53

4. The Repression and Support of Psychedelic Experience   73

5. Number Nine: Crisis and Growth Center for Youth   99
    A. Creating a Counter-Institution   99
    B. The Battle for "Free Space" at a Drop-in Center   109

6. The Structure and Function of Alternate Services   121
    A. The Development of Alternate Services   121
    B. Two Models of Youth Crisis Centers   134

7. Radical Counseling Programs   151
    A. Crisis Phone Lines   151
    B. An Alternate System for Counseling   171

8. Three Experimental Therapeutic Communities   203
    A. Diary of a Residential Crisis Center   205
    B. A Halfway House Community   225
    C. Kingsley Hall: "The Floodgates of My Soul Are
        Open . . . "   237

9. The "Foreign Policy" of Number Nine   249
    A. Dynamics of Funding and Legitimacy   251
    B. Psychiatry and Social Welfare   262
    C. Intervention in High Schools   272

    Bibliography   285

ACKNOWLEDGMENTS

Numerous people were involved in the total experience of creating Number Nine. Many of them were critical to Nine's survival. It is impossible to mention them all, so it is better not to single out a few at the expense of slighting or overlooking other contributions. They include staff members, people who came for help and helped us learn, friends and lovers, supporters and even opponents. All added parts of their vision to this growing community.

Two people have been intimately involved with the writing process. Yvonne Durchfort Jaffe, who was also a co-founder of Nine, has been a continual source of moral confrontation, support, encouragement and criticism. She was constantly with us during the writing of the book, and her spirit pervades the entire attempt at setting down our experiences and reflections (although she has reservations about some parts of it). Boris Astrachan, who has been the only person to read and comment on the entire manuscript during preparation, offered encouragement and the perspective of a professional.

The W. Clement and Jessie V. Stone Foundation provided us with a grant which supported us, in part, during the writing of this book. The two earliest sources of financial support for Number Nine, without whom none of the last three years would have been possible, were the United Church on the Green, particularly Dr. David Weinland, and the New Haven Foundation, directed by Norman Harrower. Other contributors to Number Nine include the Hazen Foundation, the Carolyn Foundation, and the Drug Dependence Institute at Yale.

Portions of this book have been published previously in The American Journal of Orthopsychiatry (42 (4), July 1972), The Radical Therapist, Psychotherapy: Theory, Research, Practice (8 (3), Fall 1971) and Going Crazy (Bantam, 1972), and are reprinted with permission.

INTRODUCTION

In 1969 we started a youth crisis center, which we called Number Nine
(after a Beatles' song). Each of the founders — Yvonne Durchfort (now
Yvonne Jaffe), Ted Clark, and Dennis Jaffe — was in the midst of intense
personal changes and had been involved in the civil rights movement and
community organizing. Collectively our experiences ranged from movement activities, use of psychedelic drugs, and communal living, to teaching in a Headstart program, social work, claims adjusting, attending
graduate school, and organizational consulting. All of us had reached
a point where we could no longer work for traditional institutions. Independently each of us had arranged to get support for organizing vaguely
defined innovative youth projects. We knew each other only slightly, but
in September we agreed to occupy a donated storefront, put in a crisis
phone line, and start a new program.

We tried to make the values and priorities of our program fit other
experiments in what has been described as a counter-culture, new consciousness and alternate society. Initially we merely listened to the phone
calls and the people who visited Number Nine, so as to identify their
needs and find out what kind of program they would support. Their responses suggested that they were basically at odds with the services
which already existed, and that their experiences led them to demand a
service which operated according to new norms. As we built Number
Nine, we began to see connections between broad social changes and personal crises and the difficulties which this circumstance would present
to a growing alternative project.

Our work placed us in a unique position to learn about both large-
scale and personal transitions. Number Nine's openness put us in contact
with the kind of information which traditional services are structured to
avoid. We saw how institutions affect young people; we joined their rebellion against them. We also saw many experiments in new styles of
community, behavior, and work, and we helped casualties who ran into
trouble along the way. Many of the young people who were in the midst
of these change processes made up Number Nine's staff. When they took
on this chore, we saw the previously untapped capacity to take responsibility and help others in people who were at the same time creating
disturbances and filling the case loads of traditional services.

1

We saw young people act crazy on a hospital ward and use drugs regularly, but turn around and help their friends when they were on bad trips or freaking out. In rebelling against the institutions of the dominant culture, young people had informally developed skills and methods which reflected their new values.

Number Nine tried to create an institution based on these values and experiences. We formed a community which lived together and made contact with other communities around the country. From our vantage point we came to see more clearly how the dominant society contributes to the social problems it felt powerless to solve and how it prevents itself from acting in obvious ways to alleviate personal distress and dissent. For example, the myth that only professionals are qualified to provide help has kept schools and social services from utilizing the energy of their students and clients to help each other and from improvising creative new ways for the institutions to help them grow. To escape at least partially from the constriction and irrationality of the existing order, some of us opted for the formation of new services which were more honest, more helpful, and more joyous.

This book is about crises and transitions in personal life and society and about building communities and alternate services to help people live through these crises. It is about difficulties and complications along the path of forming a new culture. For an individual, this path involves shedding the skin he or she was raised with, as reflected in family, school, community, and government, and developing a new one in company with others who share the task. This change process includes pain, confusion, frustration, violence, and risk. Rejected values and structures do not cooperate by withering away, disappearing, or welcoming the new. They resist, and they conflict with new directions by a network of overt and covert means. The personal choices and desires of those who choose alternative values are thus the object of a social conflict. This conflict is fought in the area of defining and treating deviants, by systems of social sanction and control, and through economic and community efforts at cooption of new directions. Chapters 1, 2, 3, 6, and 9 deal with society's response to change and personal experimentation, and with the dominant institutions' efforts to confuse and complicate moves to form alternatives.

We are activists, working to promote the new values we describe. Our intention in this book is to facilitate social change, not to write social commentary. The bulk of it is about the experience of creating communities and social services to help young people who are caught in this social and personal process of transition. The external conflict of values is reflected and internalized in the struggles of young people to grow and change. As they see traditional communities and services not only not responding to them but fundamentally opposing their interests and goals, they are forced to build new ones. Our experiences in this effort at Number Nine and a number of other communities is the substance of chapters 4, 5, 7, and 8. They relate young people's internal struggles and conflicts concerning living together, responding to injustice, dealing with the powerful revelations of drug use and other pathways to inner experience,

helping others with issues the helpers themselves have not solved, and
dealing with some of the unintended consequences of trying to actualize
counter-cultural values in everyday life.

We call our work therapy because we begin our work by concentrating
on a difficulty an individual is experiencing, but it could as well be called
education, growth, or community organizing. People come to Number
Nine for help in resolving a crisis or conflict or to work on some basic
issue surrounding their experience of the world, themselves, and their
relations to others. Our style of responding further defines us as radical
therapists for two reasons. The first (and least important) is that we are
not tied to individual, psychodynamically oriented treatment. We are
aware that other means — such as encounter groups, Gestalt therapy,
bioenergetics, psychosynthesis, meditation, psychedelic therapy, direct
analysis, psychodrama and energy sharing — all make sense at times and
for some people. But they alone do not constitute all that is therapy; most
people use other means to resolve transition crises. They change the
structure of their lives by living differently or by changing their relationships with their families or lovers, or they find support from friends
or from groups during the period of change. Therapy is anything which
supports or initiates a growth process. As radical therapists at Number Nine and in other helping communities, we are concerned with
remaining open to the many modes which therapy includes, rather than
falling into a narrowly defined particular technique which may be out of
the context of the broad process.

The second reason why we consider ourselves radical therapists is that
our work is rooted in a critique of the major institutions and structures
of our society and is associated with a broad movement to change them.
We cannot advocate humanistic and counter-cultural values within our new
communities without confronting institutions which we experience as being
oppressive and denying these values. We reject the traditional therapeutic
goals of adjustment to the status quo and independence from the therapist.
We want to liberate individuals from such constraints and to open them to
new experiences and possibilities for change. In order to liberate individuals, we must evolve structures and relationships in our own lives which
support these new values and are not repressive. We strive to make our
work processes and projects reflect our values, and when we deal with
institutions which do not, we keep our differences loud and clear, as is
detailed in Chapter 9. Radical therapy thus helps individuals to change,
then supports these changes by helping the formation of new communities
and alternatives and finally confronts the contradictions in established
institutions as well as its own.

The movement for basic social change, of which radical therapy is a
part, is at the stage of developing alternate communities and communication networks. Basic alternate services and change oriented communities,
as described here, are crucial to this goal. Service groups help those in
transition from the old to the new culture to overcome their personal conflicts and to live according to the values they choose, help individuals and
communities to grow and develop human potentials, intervene in crises

or difficulties, and work with casualties who sink into self-defeating drug use, alienation, or confusion. The old culture relies on drug use, confinement, coercion, and punitive conditioning to force people out of deviance, drug use, depression, or confusion. Thus, when a person in transition comes under the control of a conventional therapy center, the results are apt to be brutalizing and to aggravate the initial anger and confusion as a result of the conflict of values and goals between the individual and the treatment center. Alternate services are needed because support for personal growth, temporary shelter, and alternative living and working arrangements are a means of avoiding such dehumanizing treatment.

The collective for alternate service, crisis intervention, or radical therapy is important not only to the people who come for help. The structure and process of the alternate group also act as a laboratory for the basic issues of how a new culture deals with its day-to-day business of working and living. Staff members can use their personal sensitivity and experience of crises to help in defining and establishing guidelines for relationships within a new culture. The social change movement received its earliest lessons in the structure of our society and government by confronting them directly, and now we have turned some of our energies to defining and practicing fair and human relationships among ourselves. Psychedelics and new therapies have led to a new psychological sophistication, to go with the movement's economic and structural critique of our culture. Communes, group marriages, consciousness-raising groups, extended family living, and great mobility under extreme pressure have also exposed problems, even created some new ones, as well as building new methods for dealing with them as they arise. Intimacy and openness elicit fears and conflicts which traditional families rarely experience, and our upbringing in such families has given us few tools with which to face these situations. Radical therapists are called on to help communities learn to incorporate such experiences into their lives.

Although radical therapists may only be a half a step ahead of their brothers and sisters, that half-step may be crucial to a new community racked with personal pain. The role of a radical therapist or alternate service is thus to be both explorer and educator, seeker and helper.

Our experience at Number Nine and in other communities taught us much about the nature of change in individuals and society, ways to facilitate it, and the resistance of society. As we made sense out of our learning, we began to write essays to clarify where we were and to communicate with our friends about our work. This process helped to create a dialogue with others. Rather than write about what we would like to happen, we wrote about what was happening and what we made of it. We saw ourselves, not as a complete and final model of how to do things, but as a growing community, taking risks, opening up new territory, and working out new assumptions and procedures. We have experiences to share about what happens when one attempts to implement new values. These essays are for others who want to take a similar path. Our aim is not to prove or stand for some one method or program, but to encourage others to experiment and act. We feel that descriptions of new ways are more important right now than statements of what is wrong, catalogues of ideals, or studies of results which leave out a description of the process which is so precise that others can cover the same ground independently. The essays, written between 1970 and 1972, by no means offer an orderly development. In creating social change, it seems important to maintain and examine inconsistencies and to develop several theoretical frameworks.

The first three essays develop some basic frameworks for understanding the changes young people are going through and society's repressive reaction to them. Chapter 1 discusses the ways in which the basic institutions of our society — 'family, school, and community' — act together to limit and mystify attempts at independence or change. Chapter 2 develops a new framework for looking at deviance and delinquency and at adults' projections of the basic social problems which youth pose for society. The new model looks at deviance as the first awareness of oppression and as personal steps to change or strike out at it, and suggests a developmental model for moving from self-destructive gestures toward meaningful social change. The control of deviance and the facilitation of social change are conflicting goals for youth services. The third chapter talks about the changes which young people participated in during the 1960's and suggests a model of a process of counter-cultural change. The values and the strategy of this process are articulated, and some examples of the development of new communities follow.

Chapter 4 is a compilation of several presentations we have developed to explain the spread of psychedelic drugs among youth. Our thesis is that the use of drugs can be enormously educational under the proper conditions, and that the fear of these drugs by society represents a backlash against some of the basic positive impulses of the counter-culture. In the context of the social conflict concerning psychedelic experience, some guidelines for a helping service dealing with bad trips are presented, along with a particularly vivid case study.

The next two chapters deal with the issues facing an alternate service in defining its program and developing a structure. Chapter 5 begins with an essay written after Number Nine's first year, in which some of the basic issues in starting an alternative service are explored. This article, previously published, has evoked a wide response, in part because it deals concretely with issues as they affect a growing community. The second part of the chapter deals with the difficulties concerning the "free space" at Number Nine's drop-in center. These difficulties, which exposed a basic weakness of participatory group processes, have been duplicated in the experience of many other programs around the country. Chapter 6 contains two essays on some of the basic structural issues in new services. The first part is a historical account of the development of alternate services while the second part attempts to differentiate between two very different types of alternate service, one which accepts the basic professional model of providing service and another which tries to go beyond that limited concept toward a new structure and set of values. The growth of alternate services is seen as movement from the first to the second model.

Chapter 7 looks at two kinds of radical counseling services — crisis

phone lines and an alternate counseling model. Both examinations try to
move beyond a recital of techniques to expose the context and goals of
such services and the ways in which the counseling style provides an
alternative to the traditional values and style. Each essay contains several case studies which illustrate the theory's application in practice.
Chapter 8 contains accounts of three very different residential therapeutic
communities. Each formed in reaction to traditional practice, and each
evolved unique solutions to the difficulties of a change-oriented community.
The communities are Number Nine's residential crisis center, the New
Haven Halfway House, and Kingsley Hall in London.

   The final chapter discusses the interaction of the alternate service
with the community. The values of the community and the new service
are somewhat in conflict, and yet the service depends on the outside
world for survival and legitimacy. This conflict as it relates to funding,
legitimization, psychiatric and social welfare institutions, and high
schools is detailed through description of Number Nine's experience.

   Each of the essays is a working paper, in the sense that all consist
of thoughts and examples set down in the process of work, and not as
isolated tests of a well-developed theory of action. The development of
an action science — where experiment and reflection are part of a continuous cycle and where a support group provides the energy for constant
reevaluation and development — is our goal. These essays are therefore
presented with their temporal discontinuity, divergent and even self-
contradictory frameworks, and unevenness and vagueness when the vivid-
ness of the experience defies our efforts to capture it on paper. This
book represents an experiment in communication, as well as an experiment in our own discovery of where we are and what strategy we can use
to work more consistently toward our ideals. In spirit this book represents a dialogue among ourselves — and now with you, the readers — about
our collective next step.

                                        Ted Clark and Dennis T. Jaffe

Chapter 1

THE DESTRUCTION OF YOUTH

We have often been asked to speak to adult groups about the problems of young people because of our experiences in a crisis intervention center. Yet we are never asked to define these problems, a relatively basic starting point. Adults assume that they know what the problem with kids is, and they use such terms as "drugs," "communication breakdown," "having it too soft," and "overpermissive parents". Making the judgment that someone's behavior is a problem he has is essentially a moral stance — what the person making the judgment believes to be right and wrong. Since most adults feel certain about what is right and wrong with young people's behavior, they do not need to ask what the problems are, just what to do about them. The point here is that the judgments, in the form of labels placed on certain kinds of behavior, are imposed on the young people, disregarding their own point of view. Furthermore, the judgments are prescriptive in the sense that, once they are made, they imply that the individual must change his behavior to correspond to the judge's view of right or correct behavior. Treatment and rehabilitative programs are often methods of imposing (or at least attempting to impose) moral judgments on the individual, so as to make his behavior more appropriate and acceptable.

This discussion is based on the presentation by various young people of what they consider as their problems in their attempts to get help from Number Nine. Another difference between our approaches and many others is the fact that we do not find the usual distinctions between adolescents and various other groups within the society useful or meaningful. None of the dilemmas faced by young people (or any strategies devised by young people to resolve these dilemmas) are unique to youth. In fact, one of the difficulties in presenting even a superficial overview of young people's problems is that the youth class is just one locus among many where the problems endemic to the society and the culture can be examined. The question for discussion is not so much the particular problems of adolescents as young people's reflection of the basic unresolved dilemmas facing every individual in Western culture.

A classic example of the way young people become the focus of society's hostility in the family, the school, and the community is furnished by the issue of drugs. Drug use pervades the entire society, yet officials and the general public act as if it is unique (or at least especially dangerous) among young people and blacks living in ghettoes. Almost all the attention is given to youths and to ghetto inhabitants, while middle-class housewives and their addiction to barbiturates and abuse of amphetamines merely receive lip service. Society attempts to displace its failures onto various minority groups — adolescents, blacks, women, the poor, the foreign, the institutionalized, and so forth. In this sense the moral culpability and corruption of the entire social system (the root of most of the "problems" that occupy people) goes unnoticed and unexamined, except by a few easily disregarded critics. The lack of integrity or corruption of the social system can be examined in the attitude toward drugs.

On the dubious, and totally unsupported, assumption that marijuana is dangerous — an assumption reached out of fear rather than from evidence or reasoned argument — young people are lied to, terrorized by false threats (marijuana leads to heroin), made into criminals, harrassed by authorities, diagnosed as emotionally disturbed ("drug problem") and often institutionalized and subjected to infiltration of their social groups by undercover agents (a euphemism for secret police). Parents, more susceptible to threats and fears generated through the authority of government officials, scientists, and psychiatrists, have subjected their children's rooms to searches, informed on them to the police, or attempted to have them hospitalized for treatment. School officials have allowed specially trained police dogs into their schools to smell out marijuana in lockers (these are the same school officials who have often used amphetimines in the lower grades to keep troublesome — "hyperkinetic" — kids quiet and well-behaved) and have encouraged young people to report drug use among their friends. And the community as a whole is reacting punitively through unrealistic legislation. This is a clear paradigm of the hysterical, punitive, controlling, and corrupted process of socialization young people are continually subjected to.

If we begin where the problems for young people begin, we must focus on the family. The family is a social institution; its form and purpose is defined by the society. Put simply, its purpose is to make the individual fit into the society — that is, to teach him how to behave according to socially acceptable standards. The family functions almost independently of the individuals who comprise it, since the role of parent is inculcated in the father and mother from the time of their birth. The family becomes the "family," an internalization of various norms, and this "family" creates strong feelings of shame and guilt if the father and mother fail to be "good parents" — in other words, when their children misbehave. The social standing (face) of the parents is lowered when the child fails to adjust to the demands of the family.

This pressure from the family is quite intense and is applied on all levels of behavior. In order to discuss the fundamental difficulties presented by the family, we have to isolate the specific areas of social interest in the individual's behavior: authority, aggression, sexuality, and

individual relation to the social system. When the directives of the society are incomplete, contradictory, or irrelevant to the young person's
experience, they will be resisted. Yet the directives are internalized
as well, reinforced by external authorities (such as the political-
economic system and its representatives). The enemy is the self
and the society; the family is the first and most significant battle-
ground.

Parents have a difficult task as the central authority figures within
the family. They have the responsibility for making sure the behavior
and attitudes of their children correspond to socially acceptable standards,
even though these standards are never explicitly stated, are interpreted
differently by different families, and are often self-contradictory. Without clear guidelines, and with their own interests leading them in directions other than enforcing social standards on their children — a
generally stressful activity — parents are experiencing feelings of failure, helplessness, and powerlessness. These reactions are within the
context of their socially defined roles as parents, although the feelings
are clearly reinforced by the social system itself. At any rate, parents
know their role is unfulfilled when their child's behavior departs from
appropriate standards, or they think it does, and they try to find solutions. This brings them into contact with surrogate parents — school
administrators, psychiatrists, juvenile courts, and the like.

Despite the general breakdown in the effectiveness of the socializing
function of the family, there is still ample reason to be concerned about
the harmful effect of the institution on young people. Of particular concern is the most effective weapon used by parents to manipulate the
behavior of their children: dependency. Dependency begins as a natural
reliance on the parents for protection and nourishment in infancy. As the
child matures, he ordinarily becomes more self-reliant and independent.
The family is the first social institution with a vested interest in frustrating the maturation process. Adolescence itself is the period in a young
person's life when his "growing up" is rigorously defined by the family
(as well as the school). It is essentially a time of artificial childishness.
The family attempts to reinforce the assumption of dependency — that is,
that the needs of the individual will be fulfilled by others — by attempting
to meet the young person's every imaginable need. The surfeit of material wealth imposed on young people — a college education and braces,
even a car of their own — all imply that at least the family would like to
do everything possible to make the individual healthy, happy, and as much
like others in his peer group as possible, so that he will not be unloved
or lonely.

There is only one catch. Meeting the needs of the individual becomes
conditional on his behavior's conforming to acceptable standards. Inappropriate behavior is therefore associated with the withdrawal of love,
the absence of protection, the undermining of support, and the creation
of loneliness. Underlying dependency is a feeling of helplessness,
powerlessness, and vulnerability. The individual is caught in a bind,
where any direction except obedience to his parents' expectations opens

up terrifying and destructive possibilities. The manipulation of behavior
through the threatened or actual frustration of the youth's felt needs,
coupled with the constant reinforcement of his sense of helplessness,
inadequacy, and lack of confidence, occurs in almost every family as a
result of the task the family feels compelled to fulfill: the socialization
of the child. Of course the cycle of dependency, threat, frustration, and
partial fulfillment works; the young person learns to conform to at least
the basic norms of his society. But there are destructive consequences.

Young people relate to other authority figures in much the same way
they do to their parents. They seek fulfillment, or they turn toward
authority all the resentment and sense of disillusionment engendered by
the failure of their parents to meet their needs. The choice is often one
of dependency or counterdependency. Counterdependency is a counterfeit
form of rebellion, but the generalizations inherent in the basic underlying
dependency, albeit a frustrated one, demonstrate that the posture is
spurious. The anger, even rage, underlying the hostility is disproportionate
to the situation, and the condemnation of authority per se demonstrates
a basic distrust of the internal desire for fulfillment of the dependency
needs.

The latent hope that one will after all be taken care of by someone
persists independently of contradictory experiences. It is a seductive wish.
The basically frustrated person turns his energy into dependent or counter-
dependent (resistive) strategies, creating more frustration and greater
feelings of helplessness, loneliness, and vulnerability. Eventually, the
the energy drain creates a feeling of imminent collapse, of weakness.
The sense of hopelessness and helplessness, as well as deep frustration,
creates depression and leads to feelings of isolation, often to suicide
attempts. Even in the depression the individual seeks to create a child-
like image, so that people will love and nourish him without expecting
a responsible (ability to respond) individual. Despite its inherent frustration of the individual's sense of being, the dependency assumption
prevails.

The internalization of the family — that is, the child's inner recreation of the parents' values — and the consequent structuring of individual
consciousness around the dependency assumption, with its attendant
fears and resentments, create a sense of imprisonment without indicating
the source. The incredible rage and violence of many young people,
turned against their bodies or those of others, occasionally against such
structures as schools and empty buildings, reflect this dynamic. Anyone in authority and any structure representing limits on the individual
may be hurt in the attempt to destructure the conscious, to free the
individual from the internal constraints his dependency forces upon him.

This construction — that the individual rages against himself and
authority in an attempt to break down his own internalizations of the
family — may seem rather vague. An example may help clarify the
process. John had liberal and well-educated parents, relatively permissive, who allowed him to establish his own limits while being quite
judgmental. He always knew what they disapproved of, despite their
refusal to stop him from behaving in ways they censured. He learned

their values, and they occur within his mind as voices telling him what he should and should not do. If he were to act out these voices, he would be imitating his parents. His own voice, determined to represent what he wants, argues with his internalized parents. Despite the failure of the real parents to establish limits, the internalized parents still succeed in making their judgments known. John cannot rebel against his internalization (which he confuses with his "self") without externalizing it. Since his father in particular fails to establish any limits — since the father is, in fact, unknowingly expressing contempt for his son — John accumulates anger, rage, and frustration at his own failure to live up to his internalized father's expectations or at his guilt for doing something he should not have done, without being able to share this anger with his father.

Yet the voices continue. And to the extent that John fails to live up to the inner demands (representing his parent's values) he finds it difficult to live with himself. He therefore seeks an escape from the demanding and punitive "father", from his real father, and from any persons or structures representing more or similar demands. In this case John's father, being very reasonable, resists setting any limits, taking any stand, presumably unaware of the son's confusion between his internalization and his real father. Without his father's telling him to stop — using drugs, for example — John has only the voice telling him to stop. The voice continues to berate John for using heroin while at the same time expressing contempt for John. John's father of course professes to love John, making John feel that the contempt he feels is his own, he cannot live with himself. Eventually he looses sight of who he is, having already lost sight of who his father is behind his reasonableness, and becomes "psychotic." The confinement of the hospital at least provides a clear limit, although it is not imposed by John's father. He is able to release some of his rage and become more balanced. Medication (prescribed drugs) helps in the same way heroin (self-medication) did. Until John can come to grips with his punitive and contemptuous "father," a person his real father would never allow himself to be (which explains his camouflage behind reasonability and permissiveness), John will always experience contempt for himself.

Finally we can understand how dependent John is on his father's acceptance and respect and how much this was withheld. The father's unwillingness to fight, to set limits, to declare a value prevents John from ever experiencing his father as a whole person. Acceptance and respect are not words but attitudes, and John's father's attitude is one of contempt for his son. But he does not acknowledge this fact directly. John is told one thing, experiences another, internalizes both (he "knows" his father likes him, he "hates" himself for what he does "wrong") and suffers from a "divided self." He feels helpless, unsafe, and alone and searches pathetically for someone to take care of him. His father, through his concern, has the son institutionalized as a "last resort," knowing he cannot provide what his son wants: a father who is real. There is probably no more significant issue in therapy than coming to terms with the internalization of one's family and the resulting dependency.

The young person is an object within his own family, since he must be controlled if the parents are to feel that they have done a good job. A mother recently said to me, in discussing the problems she was having with her daughter, "Won't people think I have failed if she gets into trouble?" The mother, acting out of fear that the girl will become involved in dangerous activities, wanted to control her daughter; she even had fantasies of locking the girl up to keep her out of trouble. The daughter, struggling against her own desires to let her mother take care of her, fought her mother's every effort to control her. A typical counter-dependent, she reacted to her mother's rule that she may not stay out after ten, for example, by lying, running away, or whatever was necessary just to stay out after ten. This behavior established, in some ways, that if she is not actually independent (her behavior is precisely, if inversely, related to her mother's directives), she is at least not being controlled.

As is usually the case, the mother was reacting out of her worst fears rather than acting from any moral objection to what she actually knew her daughter to be doing. And as usual, the daughter underneath her disobedience was actually frightened, insecure, and feeling helpless enough to avoid potentially dangerous activities. (In general, a parent's repeated warning to the child about a particular danger, acts as a message to the child to keep involving himself in this activity and eventually to become addicted, pregnant, or whatever.) Although nothing more was occurring than the normal mother-daughter power struggle, the worst fears of both allowed them to justify their battle by predicting what would happen if they stopped fighting. The mother would never let her do anything, according to the daugher, while the mother was sure her daughter would take up hard drugs. Eventually such battles do evolve to precisely these extremes. The daughter will eventually get into drugs abusively, while the mother will try to have her daughter institutionalized. The self-fulfilling prophesy.

Power struggles characterize most families, and because the children must deal with both the real and the internalized family, they are often the victims of the struggle. In this case the girl used concealment, lying, and her friendship with another girl as her strategies, while her mother tried to use the courts, a psychiatric clinic, threats, withdrawal of privileges, and her own suffering (inducement of guilt). This kind of overkill is terribly oppressive to young people, and they tend to identify with other oppressed groups. Youth as a class is in fact oppressed, and the overwhelming weaponry on the side of parents merely compounds the destruction rather than providing relief. One is inclined to note the parallels between the United States government's attempts to bring a small, underdeveloped country into line with our political beliefs through an overwhelming superiority of arms and parents struggling to make their children conform to the parents' ideology. Neither attempt succeeds both wreak destruction on the enemy, and both enemies are inclined to distinguish the oppressor from the individual caught up in that role. J. Anthony Lucas' recent book, Don't Shoot, We Are Your Children noted this war against young people.

The failure of the family is not the failure of the individuals who make up the family. Parents have learned ways of behaving which do not meet their personal goals, do not give their role as parents meaning, and are ineffective in their own terms. Parents are as helpless, dependent, and confused as their children. Parents do tend to rely on their roles and the social structure of the society for support, while young people, struggling against the same basic issues, tend to defy authority and distrust the structures of the social system (even when they behave as if they accepted their situation). Because youth must resort to strategies which are by definition illegitimate, young people tend to attract more attention. But this fact must not continue to obscure the underlying similarity between the emotional dilemmas of the child and the parent.

The destructive consequences of the family are, in fact, often minimized through the strengths of the individual members of the family. Some parents resist their role as authority figures, or at least emphasize genuine support and trust of their children. Rather than trying to control their children, they understand the youth's needs to experiment and take risks. They wisely do not pry into their children's privacy nor stress the need of the child to conform to their standards instead of the youth's own vision of self. But power struggles are still present, even if counterbalanced by more humanized and less role-oriented behavior. And the fact that many young people survive their families — with the help of their parents or without it — cannot be used to avoid acknowledging the destructive consequences of this social institution.

Dependency, frustration, helplessness, rage, a deep-seated suspicion of authority, a fear of vulnerability, a reliance on indirection, manipulation, concealment, and rigid psychological defenses are characteristic of most young people. Tied deeply into the "family," many young people recapitulate the family environment wherever they go. But if the family treats its young people by rewarding dependency, stimulating the basic underlying feelings which reinforce the dependency assumptions, and providing for the continuance of this dynamic through the internalization of the parental authority; and if the family continues, as a social institution, to struggle against its children because of a need to control them, then the real harmfulness to young people occurs in the surrogate parent, the school system. Families do not provide their children with any really effective means for gaining what they want: love, respect for themselves as persons, excitement, growth experiences, fun and enjoyment, a sense of purpose. Families do not even succeed in giving their children adequate means for surviving in a society which is becoming more and more hostile to life. No longer does a good home protect the youth against a life of crime, or even against becoming a victim of crime. No longer does the advantage of a middle- or upper-middle-class background insure the individual's ability to remain upwardly mobile. The sudden economic reversals of the recent recession prove as much to many high-income families who suddenly find themselves in reduced circumstances regardless of their own backgrounds, education, training, and successful job performance. Finally, in failure and confusion, the family is more and more likely to turn the socializing (preparing) function over to the schools. This is perhaps their worst mistake of all.

It is regrettable that schools mystify the socialization process by calling it education. American high schools prepare young people to take their place in society by making certain that their behavior and attitudes fit narrowly defined social norms. The essential task for a student is learning to cope with authority. If he can also acquire some knowledge — usually factual material the student has only to make intelligible (facts and numbers; items easily committed to memory, and even more easily evaluated on exams, since facts can be quantified with little effort — how many correct answers?) — that is really incidental to the process. Most intelligent students quickly learn that the effort they expend and the grades they receive are not correlated. It is the image they create, the efficacy with which they form personal relationships with the teachers, and their ability to be articulate in expressing the ideas of the teacher that are directly related to their grade averages and recommendations.

Educational critiques are plentiful, and in some ways they are easy to make. There is too much wrong with our schools. Here we want to develop those themes that originate in the family: dependency, internalized authority figures, power struggles over values and moral ideas, and the oppression of youth. The school picks up children directly from home and has the most consistent effect on them during the formative years. The school shares the family's purpose — the socialization of the individual — but because of the clearly institutional nature of the process, the school can be more direct. It has, after all, a relatively captive audience.

The school emphasizes the comparative helplessness of the individual from the beginning. This is especially true of high schools, since most high schools are very large — they have literally thousands of students. The student's role is clearly at the bottom of a confusing hierarchy. He is answerable to administrators and to teachers, both of whom share a disciplinary function, rationalized by the population density of the school and the obvious need for order if the school is to function properly. The disciplinary function exploits the dependency tendency in every young person.

Though the youth feels dependent on his parents, at least certain areas of his life are under his own control from infancy on. For example, after toilet training, the child is expected to take care of his own excretory functions. Not so in school; he is expected to forego immediate relief in the interest of the school's schedule. "Can't you wait until after class?" is a familiar refrain. The impatient student must raise his hand, get the teacher's attention, ask for permission, get a pass for the corridor, and go to the john within a specified period of time. The embarrassment to boys and girls is acute. In some schools a teacher is assigned lavatory duty; he stands outside the bathrooms to make sure that no one abuses the privilege by smoking, talking to friends, reading,

or loitering. After a certain period of time, the monitor knocks on the
door and occasionally enters the bathroom.

The dependency of the individual on the whims of many different
authority figures is developed further. Students are held accountable for
everything they do. One local school principal went so far as to measure
girls' skirts personally to make sure they met his rigid dress code;
only an unusual student strike forced him to drop the dress code. Even
so, there are many high schools where the student's appearance is made
the business of the school. Besides appearance, presence is also under
the jurisdiction of the school officials. Anywhere, anytime, the student
may be stopped and asked to account for his whereabouts. Corridor
passes, hastily concocted excuses (usually overlooked because they
implicitly accept the authority of the school to demand an accounting), and
so forth, are normal parts of the school system's daily existence for students. The control of the school over the individual student is often complete. He can be given low marks for behavior and attitudes, he can even
be expelled for them. Some schools provide both a letter grade (for academic work) and a number grade (for behavior). Tardiness, "insolence,"
talking in class, being at the wrong place at the wrong time, violation of
countless rules concerning noise, smoking, or even reading, all can result in expulsion regardless of the academic grade.

The student is graded as much on his opinions and beliefs as on any
academic performance. Teachers often find themselves unknowingly
penalizing young people for heretical ideas, political beliefs, and so forth.
One young girl, for example, was constantly ridiculed by several of her
teachers for her religious beliefs (she was a Seventh Day Adventist).
Constant exposure to petty, often poorly educated, and even stupid, pedan-
tic, and boring teachers, with their power to discipline the student in
many painful ways (low grades on a report card are said to follow the
student the rest of his life, and the benefit of the doubt is rarely given to
the student), creates a cynical and detached attitude on the part of most
students. They feign the role, playing the teacher's ego against him in
order to pass the course with a decent letter grade. Integrity is the first
victim in our school systems.

Going further with the carefully institutionalized control of the student
through dependency, we can note that even the thoughts of the individual
are managed by teachers and administrators. Students are expected to
think on demand and to learn on schedules, despite individual differences.
Besides being graded on their opinions, ability to memorize information,
ability to recite the teacher's own opinions back (sometimes word for
word), students find that all their thinking is suspect. At no time in the
average school system is a young person given the opportunity to talk
about himself, his experiences, his dreams, his worries. For the entire
school day the student exists solely in terms of his role. His self is
completely suppressed.

Schools set limits on the individual in both directions. Below a certain level, he fails. This failure is interpreted as involving the whole
person, since the student is expected to invest his "self" in his studies.

Those who fail are often given (or it is suggested that they get) psychiatric help or counseling. Otherwise they are merely expelled, held back, ridiculed, or just disregarded completely. The real crime, however, is to demonstrate great ability and be unwilling to use it to secure good grades; this "problem" is labeled underachieving. The underachiever has a high IQ but gets low grades. Rather than speculating on the failure of the school to provide stimulating, meaningful, relevant, and interesting educational experiences, the authorities consider the individual in some sense inadequate. His parents often communicate their shame (he has failed them as well), speculate (along with everyone else) on what is wrong with the student, and anxiously seek help from the school. A great deal of attention is given to the failures, and they gain a self-image that can last many years, since success in school is such an important expectation for young people. But firm limits are set also on how well the student may do.

The ceiling is easily seen in the numerical equivalents for most grades. A is given when 90 to 100 percent of the test material is answered correctly, while an F is usually given to any result below 60 percent. In other words, a person's achievement is restricted to the material he is assigned and tested on, and the test forms are the only criterion for evaluating exceptional scholarship, aside from papers, which are unpopular with high school teachers, who may have well over a hundred students to examine. The ability to pursue one's own intuition to its logical conclusions, to experiment freely with materials, to study one's own interests, to set one's own space and speed, meditation or contemplation, the ability to fail continually without penalty — these are all vital to the education of man, and they have all been almost solely responsible for important scientific studies, fine novels, and so forth. Yet they are made virtually impossible for the average student.

The average student — what a terrible constriction on the individual! Average people may never succeed gloriously (but how many brilliant students do?), but they are responsible for vital research, for most of our school's teaching staffs, and so forth. The necessity for getting A's limits the brilliant, confining them to work which is established and created in terms of the average student — who is then devalued, since average is not exceptional, noteworthy, or successful. The dependency engendered toward the school for one's own sense of self-worth is shattered by the "gentleman's C." It gets a person nowhere. Where is there to go? The successful get the right to continue within America's educational system. The very successful may never leave, staying in colleges and universities as teachers. It is becoming a commonplace in our society that, despite the value placed on degrees, with rare exceptions they do not prepare a person for anything, they do not guarantee competence, they do not give the slightest idea of what the person really knows, except how to play the academic game well.

There are, then, two terrible fates awaiting those who are successful in the school system. Their true abilities will be measured and limited by the average (even the average of the exceptional is terribly confining), and their only means of being successful is to continue within the school system indefinitely. Very few bright students are ever pushed anywhere near their capabilities, just as it is only one kind of student who can even demonstrate that he has capabilities — the one who can get good grades. Those who fail can merely subsist in our society; there is little economic space for them. If they learn a skill, they will still carry a basic image of themselves as not quite good enough. Anti-intellectualism in this country is basically a reaction against the fact that most self-images (good and bad) are determined by the school and by one's success within it. The most tragic are the exceptionally intelligent individuals who cannot or will not put their abilities at the service of good grades but suffer a profound sense of failure despite the fact that they retain their integrity. At present the only good news in education is the fact that many fine colleges are disregarding high-school performances and accepting students on the basis of who they are as people. The most tragic cost schools extract from their students is human qualities.

Students resist school. They know they are imprisoned, and their references to school as a place where they are doing time, waiting to get out, and the like, reflect this sense of entrapment. They also know that the lesson material is irrelevant to their concerns, and they therefore feel little guilt about fantasizing, taking drugs, being tardy, cutting school, or eventually dropping out. They are willing to consider themselves failures rather than sustain the indignity and lack of respect created by schools. They know that the teachers have even more power than do their parents, if only because parents react so angrily to the school's implications of incorrect behavior or lack of concentration on studies. Furthermore, teachers can threaten expulsion, being kept back, being sent to the office (there are vice-principals specializing in disciplining students), and so forth. Ridicule or scoldings in front of other students is another weapon teachers have at their disposal. But the most effective means of control is the basic authority of the school system and the respect accorded administrators by the legal and political systems.

Students resort to stronger measures than just fantasizing during class or using drugs for escape or quick energy. Violence in schools is depressingly common. Vandalism is just one form; many schools show the suppressed hostility of their students in the form of deep etchings in desks, gum all over chairs, holes in tables, broken windows. School disturbances (called riots when they occur in prisons) are common, as are attacks on teachers or other students. In one local high school all the teachers at one meeting agreed that they only had one problem: corridor passing. It seems that students rushing by (ten minutes to cover up to a quarter of a mile) took swings at teachers. Teachers, terrified by the suppressed hostility and potential for violence, often resort to strict controls out of just such fears.

Though schools do not ordinarily directly relate to internalizations of parental figures, they do indirectly reinforce them by awarding behavior which corresponds to the values held by the parents (socially acceptable norms) and suppressing dissent, resistance, and even critical

evaluations of these norms. The suppression of young people contributes
to their sense of weakness, helplessness, and essential wrongness. Everything they are is against the rules here, too. When the individual's integrity and sense of self-worth are undermined by the competition for
acceptance, nourishment, love, respect, prestige, and all the other
needs represented by good grades (the premise which creates or reinforces the assumption that the school can meet the individual's needs
if the student will only do what is expected of him — here at least students
find the expectations are relatively clear), the internalized parents are
strengthened, and reinforced. What the individual should do always seems
to be what everyone expects him to do. But what about the person herself?

Schools and families, which are close to the student, are therefore
likely to represent society's most ambivalent responses. The pervasive
hatred of the society toward youth expressed through individual representatives of the system is ameliorated by personal liking for the young
person. But as the distance from young people increases, the adults in
the community are able to treat them more objectively. When the position of the young person in the community is examined, the true intensity of the hatred for young people as a class becomes clear, and the
oppression of the young found in the institutions of the family and the
school systems is concretized.

Oppression is the frustration of being, the prevention of selfhood.
Political oppression is the creation of a class which has no power, is
economically dependent on the oppressor, is stereotyped by the oppressor,
and is typically disorganized, discriminated against, and treated with
contempt. The first indication of young people's oppression is their identification with other oppressed groups such as women, blacks (for example, during the New Haven demonstrations for the Panthers over 75
percent of the supporters appeared to be white adolescents), the poor
(witness the poverty-level life styles young people adopt for comfort),
and the elderly (young people relate very warmly to old people).

Oppression is practiced on one level by economic leverage — both to
reinforce dependency and to commercially exploit youth's needs. Young
people depend largely on their parents for money, and they have a lot of
it to spend. Part of the family's control is economic, making the affluence of family life difficult to reject. When young people take to the
streets, declaring themselves part of the mysterious, dangerous underground life of our cities, they adopt poverty as a way of eliminating the
economic dependency they associate with affluence. The common irony
is that, despite the life style, many are still tied to their parents through
money; affluent habits die hard. In the community, youth are exploited
economically. The record industry — and its younger cousin, pop concerts
— with artificially high prices, demonstrate the willingness of society to
profit from the boredom and emptiness of adolescent lives. The community does little to change this underlying desperation. Many young
people find themselves welcome in stores and restaurants only as long

as their presence is profitable. Larger stores have policemen whose
basic job it is to kick teenagers out, preventing them from simply drift-
ing, loitering to talk to friends, or just "looking for something to do."
Because the economic exploitation is resented and young people feel
"ripped off," they act on the theory that turnabout is fair play, and shoplifting is a common sport. Records, clothes, and other merchandise
appealing to young people's conditioned appetites, are taken to redress
the profit the stores clearly make off young people. This sense of fair-
ness inherent in most shoplifters can only be explained by a basic sense
of exploitation.

The economic sphere, however, is not the only locus of exploitation;
it also exists in the sexual sphere. Though young people are derided for
their nonconformist ways of living, teenage girls are often lured into
prostitution, and the same long-haired boy who is jeered at from a passing car may be propositioned by the driver of the next. And the same
older men who deplore the lack of morality in the younger generation
exploit young women.

Because youth has become an oppressed class, the society fears
it — fears its potential for violent revolt, and envies its occasional ability
to slide out from under the authority of the society. To prevent such
feared outcomes, the community can apply a number of strategies to
keep youth powerless.

Besides exploitation, ridicule is a powerful weapon. Young people's
life styles, appearance, mannerisms, vocabulary, all are objects of hostile comment. In this way they are deprived of any legitimacy and prevented from spreading into wider segments of society. Another weapon
is contained in the old divide-and-conquer strategy. There are very
few places where young people can gather that are approved of by the
community.

The basic needs of young people are commonly perceived in terms
of recreation. Keep them off the streets and out of trouble, the philosophy goes, with pool tables and gymnasiums. The old cliché of "natural
athletes" comes to mind. Youth are thought of in terms of their bodies,
not their minds or their potential for meaningful involvement in the
community.

Another basic reason for keeping gathering places for young people
severely limited in number and size is that the obvious desperation and
frustration of kids leads adults to fear that gatherings will lead to violence. Woodstock came as a shock. Despite the evidence that young
people prefer peace (the hippies, the peaceniks, the desire to study
religions of the East, and so forth), adults presumed that violence was
inevitable. Eventually, with the stress on drug arrests and the corresponding increase in the use of alcohol, violence did increase. Young
people, particularly those called "freaks," are often beaten up by motor-
cycle gangs (usually men over thirty) with tacit acceptance by the police.
Violence toward young people is common, and violence from young people
is expected. But the anticipation of trouble is a camouflage for the fear
that youth will organize into political groups which will turn against the

the social system and dismantle the prevailing structure. This is the de-
structuring adults fear under their rhetoric of "trouble."

Youth is a fragmented class. Those closely identified with authority
figures are alienated from those identified with dissent and resistance.
Counterdependent individuals tend to emphasize physical powers and
their potentially violent nature, which intimidates those other young
people who basically empathize with their position and respect their ability to stand up to authority figures. This splintering along specious boundaries (torks — straight-arrow types — wear one kind of clothes, hippies
and greasers another kind; torks drive regular cars, hippies Volkswagens,
greasers hotrods or motorcycles) is another characteristic of oppressed
groups. The unwillingness of the community to provide areas where these
groups can get together to find out how much they have in common is based
on young people's potential for organizing themselves for change. At a
local community-run coffee house (records and pool tables for over
three hundred suburban youths each Friday and Saturday night) the three
groups were present, but the adult supervisor carefully avoided any
direct confrontations between them and managed to insinuate his presence
in any intergroup conversations. Despite his subtle, and essentially well-
meaning, attempts to be helpful, his own political naiveté helped to obscure his community-reinforced role — keeping order.

Young people threaten the status quo, the cherished order. They are
likely to try new alternatives given half a chance, they do not allow tradition to tie their hands, and they are ready for a struggle. Their dependency is frustrating, but their power as a social group has yet to be
tested. The community generates a number of difficulties that individual
young people must overcome in order to keep them confused and disoriented and to minimize their self-confidence. Since young people pose the
greatest threat to the society in the area of sexuality, the mystification
and obfuscation of the basic issues for young people is most intense in
this sphere. Consequently sexuality keeps young people busy, detracts
them from political perspectives which might generate difficulties for
the social system, and undermines their self-confidence. Sex is set up
in such a way as to reinforce the individual's sense of frustration, helplessness, and isolation. The myths surrounding sex promote isolation
and feelings of competition (mutual threats between young people), which
the schools also insist upon as a condition for maintaining a sense of
order and control.

The most pervasive myth about sexuality is the romantic ideal of one
love, analogous to the Judaeo-Christian belief in one God. Polygamy,
like polytheism, is a moral heresy (except for discreet men). So many
rules are connected with this ideal — to the effect that for each person
there is only one love, and that perfect sex must wait until this one love
is discovered — that many young people find themselves lonely, afraid of
intimacy ("how do I know he/she is the one"), withholding themselves
("until I'm sure you're the one"), frustrated, and therefore ripe for a
dependent relationship with its resentments, frustrations, and ultimate

disillusionment and hurt. The one-love myth prepares a person for the assumption that the one person will protect and nourish him completely, and it therefore follows that he will feel fulfilled and complete when he finds her. The dependency assumption, and its corollary — good behavior insures that all needs will be met — reinforce the sexist roles women's groups have so accurately noted. If, the girl reasons, I'm everything I'm supposed to be and give everything I have, then all my needs will be met. Women learn how to apply the dependency strategies they learned at home and in school to their relationships with men, men are also applying what they learned: take what you can get, because it may be withdrawn at any time for misbehavior. The fear that the need for dependency may be partially met and then frustrated completely derives from the experience of many men of being punished by the withdrawal of love and support. Love (and therefore sex) is offered by the family, as are acceptance and respect by the school, in return for good behavior and withdrawn for bad behavior (or simply a change in mood). When a young woman implies, by sexual consent, that she is giving something, the man learns to withhold his feelings so as to avoid the hurt of rejection. This defensiveness creates a distance between the man, who ends up dominating and exploiting the woman, and the woman, who ends up with her illusions shattered and her own feelings brutalized.

The myth legitimizes a dependent relationship. The easily impassioned teenager initially finds emotional rewards in the single-minded romantic relationship, but it turns out to be destructive to real intimacy and genuine sexual satisfaction. Sexuality is for all practical purposes turned into a religious rite, too idealized to be accepted for what it really is. Everyone seems to be searching for the idealized relationship, the elusive completeness promised by the dependency assumption, at the expense of real relationships. "I did everything he wanted, but he still didn't love me," is the usual outcome. Cynicism, coldness, a lack of feeling, and a defensiveness against intimacy characterize increasing numbers of sexual liaisons. They tend to be ritualistic and matter-of-fact as young people try to compensate for their disillusionment with an attitude of "realism." Sex as recreation is the opposite of sex as the union of two people deeply in love. Having been exalted far too much, sex is now often too much belittled. The emotional aspects of sexuality are distorted, trivialized, and even disregarded as young men and women learn how brutalizing the experience of demystification can be when sex becomes a physical reality instead of a metaphysical ideal.

If the outdated myth of one true love is dying a hard and painful death through the experiences of lonely teenagers searching for the fulfillment of their needs by that certain someone, as promised implicitly in their religious background, their family experiences, and their school systems, the scientific myth which is replacing religion as the answer to the mysteries of life is equally destructive. To be sure, science legitimates experimentation (the word is commonly used to refer to risk taking with sex and drugs), which in itself has led many young people to try out sex, but it also dehumanizes it. Science as myth suggests that sex involves an

expertise, presumably acquired by mastering such skills as sexual techniques. Consequently popular literature is filled with how-to manuals.
Furthermore, the science myth assumes quantifiability, which becomes
a goal. Experience is converted into numbers, sexual experiences into
conquests. This move also makes sexuality profitable, since there can be
a market in equipment which implies the likelihood of more — anything
from a sports car to a stereo to toothpaste, deodorant, and vaginal sprays.
Sexuality becomes technical and profitable, even prestigious. Because
science, as everyone knows, is a specialty requiring experts and authorities, what you don't know can hurt you, or at least make you appear
stupid. Perhaps this is why people are afraid to ask. Sexuality has been
obscured by the assumption that knowledge about sexuality improves the
meaning and enjoyment of sex. There is a further belief that this knowledge is in the hands of authorities, who can therefore pass judgment on
the appropriateness of anyone's sexual behavior. From Ann Landers to
Masters and Johnson, people look for the solutions to the problems — a
typical formulation based on the science mythology. Because everything
is a problem, it is only a matter of research and time until the solution
is found. Unfortunately the information often passed on to young people,
and everyone else, is technical, and though it is of general interest, it is
usually not generally relevant.

The substantial dilemmas created by the interface between the one-
love myth and the science myth obscure and mystify the essential dilemma
surrounding sexuality. It is an area fraught with moral dilemmas, which
create myriads of choices and alternatives, undermined with potential
guilts and shame, always involving questions of right or wrong rather
than good or bad (the ethical questions raised by the personal approximation to the dependency myth of one fulfilling love), and success or
failure (the scientific questions relating to the technical proficiency of
the performers). All the factual information in the world will not guarantee satisfaction, any more than all the worrying and struggling to find
the right person promises fulfillment and happiness. The avoidance of
the moral issues frustrates the real need of young people to evaluate
their choices based on the understanding, perspectives, and values of
others compared with their own experiences.

The avoidance of the moral questions in the area of sexuality, or the
equally punitive and frustrating reliance on absolute moral platitudes
based on religious or mythological standards considered irrelevant or
meaningless by young people, destroys their belief in their own experiences and understanding. They fall back on the myths, experience endless and confusing contradictions, and are brutalized and dehumanized
in the process. Young people are experiencing sexual relations with
apparently increasing frequency, but they are not exploring the issues
morally. They need and want to compare their experiences with one
another, to evaluate their own choices in the light of others' perspectives, and to arrive at basic principles which will give their personalities
a sense of coherence and relation to others. Yet there are few if any
such possibilities, except on a limited and informal (often excessively

anxious) basis between a few boys here, a few girls there. Moral issues
are difficult to discuss when the vocabulary is a blend of science and
romanticism and when the individual must reveal either stupidity and
ignorance or loneliness and inadequacy.

The mystification of sexuality as a domain of science, psychology,
and biology, instead of an area of complex moral choices to be made
individually, functions defensively for the community. The various institutionalized churches are spared from having to expose their cherished
beliefs to critical appraisal by young people. Young people, in turn, are
forced to rely on experts who provide little or no help or understanding,
and who themselves depend on facts, norms, and averages. The exploitation of human resources in the name of profit and objectivity continues
unexamined on even so fundamental a level as intercourse. Sexism
flourishes, along with the commercialization of sexuality. Truly satisfying sexual relations are prevented, and the frustration forms the basis
for various economically profitable ventures in films, magazine foldouts,
and so forth. Young people remain ignorant about the true nature of
their problems — that they are without a morality, without a cogent
framework to give their choices meaning, significance, and consistency.
Strong supportive networks among young people, the basis for political
organization on a radical perspective, are prevented by the emphasis
of the competitive nature of sexual relationships (only one to a customer,
better get there first, and how many have you made lately).

Sexuality has a strong and vital hold on young people. Communities
hate young people, fear them, and envy them. It is beyond the scope of
this essay to suggest why this situation has arisen; but any accurate
description and the destructive consequences of the society on youth
allows no other conclusion. The mystification of sexuality and the obfuscation of the basic moral dilemmas experienced by young people
through two very prevalent cultural myths serve as paradigms for the
community's obscuring of the basic dilemmas and problems of youth
under such clichés as "the drug problem," "communication breakdown,"
or "generation gap." The increasing numbers of young people filling
every pejorative category adults have devised (drug addicts, vandals,
shoplifters, dropouts, emotionally disturbed, institutionalized, suicidal,
and many more) indicates that the time has come to stop asking what is
wrong with the individual that he does not fit in, and instead ask what is
wrong with the social system to make the individual not want to fit in.
Sexuality is increasingly an unpleasant experience for young people because the basic moral dilemmas have been pushed aside — not forgotten,
but ignored. The community reinforces this state of affairs out of the
fear that the hostility it directs toward youth will be returned if young
people are allowed to organize.

The community hates and fears young people because their frustrations create in them a potential for growth, for real learning. Though
the school system tends to perpetuate the myth that learning takes place
only when the individual has goals to strive for, people essentially learn

to minimize discomfort. We can easily understand that a young person
who goes home every night to a color TV only to be bored by it might
find unimpressive the goal of obtaining a degree so that middle-class
affluence can eventually be his and he can buy his own TV. The goal does
not promise resolution of any frustration or sense of incompleteness. If
young people were to organize, to begin questioning the basic moral
assumptions or the myths which surround moral dilemmas for them in
this society, the social institutions will give way. Some young people are
doing this, and they have rejected traditional social structures.

The myth of one love for example, forms the basis for such mono-
gamous systems as marriage and going steady. It is also a metaphor for
the basic dependent relationship, where appropriate behavior by one leads
to the fulfillment of all needs by the other. To question this myth, to
assert that there can be many loves, or at least a few, perhaps even simultaneously, and that a dependent relationship is unnecessary and ultimately frustrating, implies that marriages are unnecessary, even
undesirable. Living with someone, or living alone, even the raising of
children by one parent instead of two or in a small communal situation, all
become viable alternatives. Whatever the counter-culture is, it is a discussion of the moral issues of our time, and the search for new alternative modalities for self-expression.

As the individual examines the social obstacles to moral growth, the
relationship between personal and social changes will become evident.
Young people are close to the truth. To question the dependency assumption, to challenge the internalized authority-parent figures, to violate
the social authority of the family and school in an attempt to survive —
these actions threaten the viability of the entire social system at its
roots. Economics, the political structure, attempts to remove moral
examination of the self and to institutionalize morality through laws and
the legal system are all extensions of the basic structure of the society,
the family.

The usefulness of therapy to young people must come through its
ability to assist in their struggles for liberation. When therapists accept
young people as their clients, they are making a political move. To view
their problems from the fragmented and incoherent perspective of the
society — that is, as problems of the individual, who must have some
basic deficiency or inadequacy — is to do them an injustice. Granted,
young people's behavior (strategies) may be self-defeating and destructive, and the first step may be to help the youth regain some sense of
self and personal power and responsibility; this is no more than helping
him regain what the society is trying to take away. But if therapy stops
with the attempt to help a person adjust his behavior to his social situation as it is, then the root of the problem will persist, and more young
people will appear with "problems." Eventually this minimal treatment
will fail of its own impoverishment. Young people will find it meaningless and irrelevant, just as they have many other forms of mystification
and obfuscation. Therapy must make radical social changes, as well as
radical personal ones. Support groups must be developed, consciousness

raising processes for the young must be started, alternative institutions must be examined carefully and thoughtfully for their potential contributions and detractions to the gradual development of political and economic bases for young people.

Effective therapy will move the individual beyond the narrow confines of his own internalizations toward new alternatives in his life style and new possibilities in the social institutions he will help to form. The internalization of the family and dependency assumptions will be the two issues confronting psychotherapists working with adolescents. The de-mystification of love, sexuality, and aggression will only come about when the internalized punishment-and-reward system is destructured; other-wise the individual will not "understand" what is meant. Avoiding the tendency to atomize adolescents and their problems will make the thera-pist aware that , as with members of other politically oppressed groups in therapy, successful change implies radical social change as a nec-essary outcome, and that the problems of young people are indeed the unresolved moral questions of the entire society — the questions of what is right, and what is wrong.

Chapter 2

DEVIANCE AND DELINQUENCY AS FRUSTRATED REBELLION

A. Fundamentals

A radical analysis of deviance and delinquency by its nature departs from
conclusions reached by established theories. Such an analysis questions
the basic values, assumptions, or premises behind these theories and
offers an alternative conceptual framework for understanding the phenomenon of unconforming behavior. Two basic questions demand a reevaluation of deviance in American society — how society can remain
flexible in dealing with internal changes and how it can deal with deviant
behavior in ways which protect and develop human potential.

Kai Erikson (1966), studying deviance among the Puritans, argues
that deviance functions as a means for the society to define its boundaries and limits.

> The deviant is a person whose activities have moved outside the
> margins of the group, and when the community calls him to ac-
> count for that vagrancy it is making a statement about the nature
> and placement of its boundaries. It is declaring how much vari-
> ability and diversity can be tolerated within the group before it
> begins to lose its distinctive shape, its unique identity. [p.11]*

To limit deviant behavior, society uses social control mechanisms, primarily the legal system and mental health organizations.

Questioning the universal claim that the almost exclusive reliance on
social control to limit deviance is justified by the harmfulness of deviant
or delinquent behavior, Erikson refers to others who are skeptical of
this assumption:

> As both Emile Durkheim and George Herbert Mead pointed out
> long ago, it is by no means evident that all acts considered devi-
> ant in society are in fact (or even in principle) harmful to group
> life ... for instance, we might well ask why prostitution or mari-
> juana smoking or homosexuality are thought to endanger the
> health of the social order. Perhaps these activities are danger-
> ous, but to accept this conclusion without a thoughtful review of

*All works cited can be found in the Bibliography.

27

the situation is apt to blind us to the important fact that people in every corner of the world manage to survive handsomely while engaged in practices which their neighbors regard as extremely abhorrent. [p.8]

Social control is ineffective, is often self-defeating, and has destructive consequences to both deviants and the community as a whole as judged by its own standards. The widespread use of drugs among middle-class youth, despite its illegality and consequent stiff punishments (drug use, which was once controlled by and limited to black poor in ghettoes, is now a problem for white upper-middle-class suburbia), is the most obvious of the recent failures of this strategy. Erikson writes:

It is by now a thoroughly familiar argument that many of the institutions designed to discourage deviant behavior actually operate in such a way as to perpetuate it. For one thing, prisons, hospitals, and other similar agencies provide aid and shelter to large numbers of deviant persons, sometimes giving them a certain advantage in the competition for social resources. But beyond this, such institutions gather marginal people into tightly segregated groups, give them an opportunity to teach one another the skills and attitudes of a deviant career, and even provoke them into using these skills by reinforcing their sense of alienation from the rest of society. [p.14]

Consequently any theory which accepts the harmfulness of deviant behavior without question, and assumes the necessity for social control without offering alternatives (that assume alternative goals), will contribute to an ineffective, alienating, and often self-defeating process of dealing with deviance.

Nevertheless, the use of social control is a basic assumption in many sociological theories on deviance and delinquency. Cloward and Ohlin's 1960 work is representative of this kind of approach. In justifying their study of differences in subcultural delinquent groups, they mention that these differences have "not only very different styles of life for their members, but also very different problems for social control and prevention" (pp.1-2). It is interesting to examine their conception of "harmfulness" in order to understand how in a theory of delinquency they can assume as a basic premise the appropriateness of social controls.

"Law-violating ways of life" — as they refer to delinquency — are a potential threat to society because " 'The hallmark of the delinquent subculture,' according to Cohen, 'is the explicit and wholesale repudiation of middle-class standards and the adoption of their very antithesis' " (p.133). Anyone who identifies with the values of the middle class will therefore perceive deviance and delinquency as threats to the society, whether there are actual victims or not.

Although Cloward and Ohlin maintain that their theory will have "both theoretical and practical significance" presumably for social control, they disclaim any interest in how their study will be applied. "The research scientist must develop classifications that enable him to

understand and explain the events he is investigating without regard to
their immediate implications for action, official or otherwise" (p. 9).
Their obviously unintentional bias in favor of social control mechanisms
— in addition to the absence of critical discussion of possible alternatives
to the goals of control, prevention, or elimination of deviant behavior —
endorses these goals. Since their study begins with these goals as un-
questioned premises, it can be assumed that the content of this theory
will support arguments in favor of preventing, controlling, or eliminating
deviant behavior.

Spergel (1967) also exhibits this bias in favor of social control mechanisms, though he defines control more narrowly, leaving the impression of
a wider choice of strategies in dealing with deviant behavior. "The major
objectives are control of delinquent behavior, rehabilitation or treatment
of group members, the provision of limited access to opportunities, value
change, and the prevention of delinquent activity" (p.28). The goal of
social control over deviant and delinquent behavior is obvious in each
item. Spergel's idea of the goal of treatment seems to "modify delinquent activity and attitudes by developing socially appropriate behavior
and values" (p.xiii). The criterion of success for control strategies is
the adjustment of the deviant to socially acceptable forms of behavior,
with no mention of agreement as to the efficacy of these procedures by
the deviant or deviant group in question.

Essentially strategies which have as their goal the suppression or
elimination of deviance are reactive and defensive. Although the harmfulness of deviance or delinquency is more significant in terms of the
society's self-interest than in its effects on individuals or property, social control mechanisms are often justified to society as a means of
protecting the interests of the individual taxpayer.

> For example, the rules that protect persons, reputation, property,
> and contractual agreements regulate interests of both individuals
> and groups which are regarded as important to the maintenance
> and stability of the existing social order. [Cloward and Ohlin,
> p. 3]

The nature of the threat offers new insights into the nature of deviant and
delinquent behavior and a new perspective on social control goals within a society.

> For the social control of such deviant conduct [violations of so-
> cial rules coming under the heading of "bad manners"] various
> types of informal sanction, such as ridicule, criticism, or scorn,
> are customarily invoked. It is a different matter, however, if an
> act interferes with the achievement of the general welfare as de-
> fined by the controlling interest groups in a society. [Cloward
> and Ohlin, p. 3]

In a simple word, the "wholesale repudiation of middle-class standards,"
the "adoption of their very antithesis," and the interference with the
"controlling interest groups" system is rebellion, an act which implies
radical social change.

The attempt to see deviants as people fundamentally different from

others conceals the possible legitimacy of their alienation from their social situation. By assuming that deviant individuals are different from
others in a negative and unattractive way (disturbed, maladjusted, socio-
pathic, deviant, criminal), the potential role model of the rebel is negated
or minimized for any other discontented individuals within the society
who still manage to conform to socially acceptable standards of behavior.
People assume that a deviant is basically different "from those of his
fellows who manage to conform, but years of research into the problem
have not yielded any important evidence as to what, if anything, this difference might be" (Erikson, p. 5).

The individual often colludes with the assumption that there is a basic
difference between himself and others, even if, at first glance, such a
view appears to be against his self-interest. He will accept the designa-
tion, and will even conform to the role, of a mentally ill individual, a
sociopath, or a victim of his economic background, of cultural deprivation, of maladjustment, of sociopathology, and the like. Closer examination reveals that each "difference" has two common elements: the category continues to negate the behavior but detaches the individual from
his own behavior, thereby assuming that the act was neither willful nor
intentional, but that the individual was a victim of his own behavior.

The more successfully the individual assumes the role which corresponds to each category (drug dependency is a recent example), the less
he will be punished and the better he will be treated. This outcome is
explained by the contention that deviant behavior is a form of rebellion;
by denying the intentionality of the action, the <u>validity</u> of the behavior is
actually denied. Thus the potential for the behavior to serve as a role
model for other discontents is again lessened. A close examination of
the concept of deviance reveals no reason to assume that deviant acts
are not willful and intentional and that the deviant individual is not fully
responsible for his actions, regardless of how immoral or repugnant
the goals and consequences of the behavior appear to most people.

Deviance, Cloward and Ohlin write, "involves the violation of social
rules that regulate the behavior of participants in a social system". Such
an act, they admit, "challenges the legitimacy and authority of these
rules" (p.2). Deviance which can also be seen as experimentation with
alternative strategies and alternative value goals, takes in a wide range
of behavior. Yet sociologists studying deviance invariably focus on behavior which society strongly condemns. Drug use extends into socially
adjusted and successful individual life styles as well as into those groups
society might judge as marginal in adjustment or successfulness. Often
individuals who are productive and successful and who appear intelligent,
critical, and educated maintain that drug use is constructive and leads
to growth. Yet the emphasis of present studies on the negative and harmful aspects of drug use seems severely out of proportion and perspective.

Deviance as a noun has no specific referent. The basic adjective,
<u>deviant</u> expresses an attitude toward certain kinds of behavior which the
society has determined to be negative and harmful. As Erikson puts it,
"Deviancy is not a property inherent in any particular kind of behavior;

it is a property conferred upon that behavior by the people who come into
direct or indirect contact with it" (p. 6). What is deviant behavior at one
time becomes socially acceptable action at another, as society's needs
change or its values expand to include a greater variety of alternative
behavior patterns. But the most significant fact about deviance is its use
as a negative judgment about particular behavior rather than as a description. The pejorative connotations attached to most of the terms
used to describe boundary-extending (or-breaking) behavior conceal the
possibility that deviance might be valuable, worthwhile, and helpful in itself. The reevaluation of deviant behavior from the point of view of expanding constrictive and rigid boundaries (which exist primarily to insure
the continuation of a social system that may have become unviable) suggests that many forms of deviant behavior need to be supported, rather
than controlled or limited.

It is still possible, of course, to devalue certain activities — such as
murder — as immoral, and other forms of behavior — such as vandalism
in high schools — may be perceived as self-defeating and ineffective. But
the underlying rage and frustration at the school system may be valid,
justifiable, and not expressible through legitimated channels. This underlying fury may result from an oppressive and constrictive system, and
the usefulness of this energy as a potential source for social change from
within the system cannot be ignored without insuring a continuance of
vandalism. Changes within a high school will always be met with defensive and controlling strategies if they challenge the legitimacy and authority of the system, and they will therefore be invalidated by people
identified with the system as it stands. The alternative to a total nega-
tion of deviance is to advocate social change through effective, yet often
equally threatening, strategies. The validation of the deviant's feelings
and perceptions concerning the social system assumes a willingness to
work for fundamental realignments of power within the social system.
In order to understand this point of view, the underlying causes of deviance must be addressed.

Cloward and Ohlin, following Durkheim, write: "Anomie results from
a breakdown in the regulation of goals such that men's aspirations become unlimited. Unlimited aspirations create a constant pressure for
deviant behavior — that is, for behavior that departs from social norms"
(p. 78). Young people have experienced the goals middle-class society
offers them, and they find the attainment of these goals a meaningless
procedure. Before rejecting the values of the middle-class, a deviant
individual explores alternative means of achieving these goals. When
even minor forms of deviance result in community pressures to return
to conforming standards, the individual's inclination is to explore more
forms of deviance as a means of maintaining a sense of power over their
own behavior.

Middle-class youth rebel out of a sense of meaninglessness, cynicism,
and unmet needs. Anomie is caused by a social system which deprives
the individual of a sense of power over his own destiny yet offers few
inducements to conform to socially acceptable standards that satisfy his

wants and desires. When almost everything is possible, the task is to
decide what one really wants and then to find ways to achieve these ends.
Generally strategies may have high risks, or unpleasant secondary consequences, but still achieve an approximation of the goal. Experimentation, however, is often not goal-oriented but rather serves as a means of
satisfying desires and wants which may not even be articulated. The individual desires satisfaction, and self-expression, sometimes at the expense of achieving other purposes or goals. The social order generally
defines experimentation as dangerous and seeks to minimize all risks;
alternately it ritualizes risk-taking activities in order to control and
limit them, as a roller-coaster ride, where thrills and enjoyment come
from the sensation of risk while comparatively safe — stories about accidents heighten the thrills; or in movies where vicarious risk-taking
becomes a form of escapism from ritualized and routinized role-deter-
mined behavior. Under such circumstances any experimentation is deviant, and many forms become illegal.

The sense of powerlessness in youth is characteristic of the society,
but young people find it easier to believe in the possibility of alternatives,
though they may be risky or unapproved of by the society. Daniel Ellsberg, speaking about the American people, comments:

> they've been told they're powerless, for a long time, all their
> lives ... but they're indoctrinated along these lines by people
> who protect their own power that way. Because there are two
> parts to that message they hear: one part is, by yourself, you're
> powerless. The other side is: if you join up, you can share in
> this power, you can plug in. The power will flow through you; at
> least you'll be a part of it. [Terkel 1972]

When the goals regulating their behavior become meaningless, or are
more easily obtained through illegitimate strategies, young people turn
to deviance. They are motivated by a sense of powerlessness, an inability to influence their own destinies through legitimate avenues, because society controls and determines so much of their behavior in the
family, the school and the community. Deviance in its more acceptable
forms is the first stage of rebellion, but lacking a conceptual framework,
the deviance is often without any point except the satisfaction of personal
needs, rather than the changing of an unviable social structure. The
overresponse (extreme and unreasoned attempts) through social control
mechanisms to eliminate deviance, or to ridicule and embarrass deviants
through widespread presentations of their actions as meaningless or
hopelessly naive and idealistic, undermines the authority as much as the
existence of the deviance itself.

A major, if unintended, consequence of social control mechanisms in
dealing with social change is the exposure of the irrational, reactionary,
and defensive nature of the legal or mental health system. The reliance
on fear and intimidation, the creation of paranoia through the use of undercover agents and informers (in effect, secret police), the unsupported
claims of "experts," the total confusion and misunderstanding about what

is happening, all undermine the social fabric and cause young people to isolate and alienate themselves from the system even further. The consistent and interlocking support of the social system (the cooperation between police and psychiatry in dealing with drugs, for example) defines for young people the need for peer-group support, and alternative social systems become more desirable. Finally, control systems are generally most ineffective against organized and entrenched deviance, such as heroin use, and tend to suppress less dangerous drugs (such as psychedelics) while increasing the despair of young people when no social changes of any significance are possible; this in turn leads to increases in the most self-destructive forms of deviant behavior to express contempt, resentment, and failure.

Immaturity, lack of skills, and absence of a radical ideological framework defeat most deviant strategies among young people; the ultimate expression of social rebellion, radical social change, is actually the least evident outcome. When Cloward and Ohlin describe deviant strategies as "senseless and self-defeating," they are speaking in terms of the deviant's unachieved goals. But deviant and delinquent behavior as a form of rebellion is self-satisfying. Rebellion is resistance to external authority — that is, external controls over an individual's behavior. As such it is almost heroic and always interesting. Our society affirms this fact by vicariously identifying with deviants in films and novels — though often only until the last reel or chapter, when they are punished for their social transgressions. Recently movies have used the antihero, a deviant above or beyond retribution (almost always a violent individual), while a Charles Manson is in reality an object of ambivalence: horror and fascination.

Young people often avoid goal-directed behavior because of the inability (or unwillingness) to defer gratification; carried to its logical extreme this facet of adolescence suggests that the deviant or delinquent act is in itself meaningful. As a form of rebellion it is a means of asserting autonomy while expressing hostility and resentment toward authority, which is perceived by the deviant as oppressive. Erikson hints at this quality of deviance: "There are people in any society who appear to 'choose' a deviant style exactly because it offends an important value of the group" (p. 20).

From the point of view of deviance and delinquency as rebellion, the active and intrusive (into private lives) reactions of social control systems can be understood as repressive in intent and behavior. This repression, partially successful, wreaks havoc among deviants and delinquents. The victims of any repressive action are always the most visible, the role models and leaders, but they also belong to either of two groups: the incompetents or the most honest. Either way the more successful (in terms of survival) deviant is secretive, paranoid, distrusting, and withdrawn. This individual, by his success at avoiding the police or the psychiatrist, becomes the role model for other deviants; total concealment and alienation from the social system become primary values. The result is not the relinquishing of deviant behavior, but an adoption of deviant patterns which amount to subversion and sabotage of the social system; if this kind of deviance had a conceptual framework, such as addiction has, typical behavior would be the bombing of buildings. Both indicate a deviance devoted to survival in completely hostile and untrustworthy environments. The more open, or out-front, deviant, who is most likely to conform to society in other ways, becomes the victim of repression. As a result, the positive potentials for social change inherent in such deviant behavior as school demonstrations, controlled drug use and experimentation, and open exploration of sexuality become suppressed. The result is a rigidification and suppression of society: drugs become random and uncontrolled and are often used self-destructively; resistance to the high school takes the form of vandalism or rioting; and sexuality becomes exploitive and irresponsible. The individual himself is often radicalized (and made more extreme) by the confrontation with overreactive authority figures.

The process by which deviance becomes delinquency and by which delinquency becomes characteristic of a group offers further clarification about how deviance and delinquency function as stages in the process of social change. The delinquent act "interferes with the achievement of the general welfare as defined by the controlling interest groups in a society" (Cloward and Ohlin, p. 3). The delinquent act, Cloward and Ohlin point out, is defined by two aspects (though nothing intrinsic in the act determines that it becomes delinquent): "(1) it is behavior that violates basic norms of the society, and (2) when officially known, it evokes a judgment by agents of criminal justice that such norms have been violated" (p. 3). Delinquency is whatever the authorities determine is delinquent.

"Delinquent acts are distinguished from other deviant acts by the fact that they result, or are likely to result, in the initiation of official proceedings by agents of criminal justice" (Cloward and Ohlin, p. 4). Such a description is, in fact prescriptive and evaluative; unbiased social scientists may want to avoid such terms or at least to acknowledge these inherent functions. Furthermore, this categorization — along with the multitude of "scientific" research which supports social assumptions about the relationship between deviance and delinquency by incorporating the assumptions into the premises underlying the theories — legitimizes and justifies the prescriptive and evaluative functions. Social science, then, contributes to the process of social control. It precludes the likelihood of studies based on alternative values or minimizes their usefulness through preconceived notions.

Cloward and Ohlin, while not remarking on the arbitrary nature of categories of delinquency (they note the arbitrary qualities, but after limiting their definition of delinquency to behavior characteristic of gangs, they proceed) do state the fact clearly: "The law confers broad discretion upon officials to define many types of youthful activity as delinquent .... In fact, statutory definitions of delinquency are so broad that all children at one time or another are likely to engage in behavior that could be defined as delinquent" (p. 4). This is a rather astounding statement. By replacing the abstraction, "law," with the concept of "men in authority, representing vested interest groups and controlling interest groups," a tautology results: men in authority or power to limit behavior confer legitimacy onto others in power to limit behavior when it is in the interests of these two groups to limit the behavior. The myth that law-makers represent the people, rather than controlling vested-interest groups, sustains the illusion that the process is an open one. Only those persons, closely identified with the preservation of the established social system's status quo, who are not interested in social changes (particu-larly radical social changes) which challenge the system's authority and responsiveness (or capability of responsiveness) do not see that the cycle is closed. The deviant and delinquent is a person without power or access to power who finds himself a threat to the established social order. When a corporate executive is discovered stealing millions of dollars, he may be jailed for a total of five days — if he is jailed at all; this is only one distinction made between the delinquent in reform school for petty theft and his counterpart within the system.

Flexibility contributes to the gradual change in the function of the social control process, from limiting to active repression of social changes considered too threatening. Cloward and Ohlin do not pursue the consequences of prejudice, uninformed and reactionary responses, and of the pressure from private interest groups on the decisions made by the judicial system concerning what behavior will be punishable by "law." Yet this might have a bearing on both the formation of delinquent groups — as a protection against repressive forces or as a means of supporting the individual against anxiety over arbitrary, varying, and often indes-criminate, picayune, and punitive legalized responses to deviance, for example. The arbitrary nature of the adjudication of youth underlines the powerlessness of young people when confronted by the judicial system's concept of society's best interests.

Finally, this statement implies that childish and adolescent behavior per se is within the court's jurisdiction. It becomes an adjunct to the socialization process and emerges as a support to the authority of par-ents and teachers. Courts, then, can operate to socialize an individual; for example, a girl whose parents bring her to the attention of the court because they do not know what to do about her can be adjudicated a de-linquent because she is in "manifest danger of falling into vice" and can be placed in a reform school "for her own good." The interaction be-tween a delinquent and school officials and parents adopting their role as authority figures in the socialization process will be colored by their ability to receive support from social control systems. Supporters of deviant behavior (as a frustrated form of social rebellion or as a social change strategy) will find themselves confronting alliances among par-ents, teachers, principals, and mental health professionals, who are de termined to protect their power and authority over young people ("for their own good").

Because of the arbitrary nature of delinquent status, young persons must experience fear and anxiety (or fear internalized as guilt) whenever

they go beyond the boundaries of the normal. Any deviant act becomes a
rejection of the authority of legal norms and of the legal system's relevance to behavior. Marijuana smokers begin to see all illegal behavior
in a different light since their own indiscretion, and any other illegal action on their own part becomes easier. The arbitrary nature of legal
statutes concerning youth contribute to the development of deviance and
delinquency and to the spread of deviant behavior among youth. This is
particularly true when young people share the conceptual realization that
the social system is unviable, against their own interests, and resistant
to meaningful changes. Up to this point, deviance and delinquency remain
limited forms of rebellion, and the young person often fixates in this
stage, unable to grow beyond the ineffectual and often self-destructive
strategies which deviance and delinquency usually offer the unskilled,
inarticulate, and poorly educated individuals. When society is not in
transition, deviance and delinquency remain isolated, idiosyncratic, and
often ritualized forms by which the deprived individual can vent frustration and overcome to some extent his alienation from legitimate opportunities; but, with one important qualification, they are still forms of
rebellion and therefore a denial of society, resistant to the social control system's manipulation toward the goal of adjustment.

> Most of the behavior of delinquents conforms to conventional ex-
> pectations; their violations of official norms are selective, con-
> fined to certain areas of interest. [Cloward and Ohlin, p.19]

This view implies that the delinquent chooses his strategies and is
therefore intentionally deviant. Yet he is defined by society as a delinquent, which suggests that delinquency is not in his self-interest as he
perceives it. Treatment oriented toward changing an individual against
his will is called brainwashing when it happens in other countries. The
effectiveness of psychotherapy and rehabilitation is often assumed to be
based on the cooperation of the client; but despite the resistance of deviants to such efforts, they are still subjected to programs which have
as their goal his adjustment to a society which he rejects, and which
has no validity for him. The perception of deviance as rebellion raises
the question of whether the deviant or rebel is right. A reevaluation of
the family or school from the perspective of the individual (instead of the
reverse process) might lead to the conclusion that the individual is the
victim of society, rather than a victim of himself. Rather than adjustment, effective rebellion as a strategy might be a "treatment goal" when
the treatment is based on the individual's own desire for "help."

The right of society to confine harmful individuals is not being questioned. Whether this right includes the freedom to subject youth to treatment and rehabilitation is another question, as is the authority to determine what is truly harmful, to whom, and under what conditions. Our
argument is that a redefinition of deviant or delinquent behavior opens up
greater possibilities than do the established perspectives of relating to
deviance and delinquency. A reevaluation of deviant behavior, coupled
with an exhaustive analysis of the system to which the deviant behavior

responds, might generate (we believe it must) strategies of response other than control. Present theories have still other inadequacies. They fail to account for the spread of deviant behavior among classes (such as drugs among young people, vandalism in high schools, or shoplifting among affluent youth). They fail to understand how deviant behavior can provide the basis of an alternative society, rather than just a subculture. And they fail to generate a theory of social revolution and an understanding of how this end result relates to other forms of deviant and delinquent behavior.

The basic difference between a delinquent act and a self-consciously rebellious one is in the conceptual awareness of the individual of the source of his problem. Many individuals have internalized a negative self-image based on their failure to adjust to a society most other people appear to find meaningful and acceptable. This feeling of inadequacy is augmented by the fact that most individuals internalize social values even if they act out of their own experience and the values this experience generates. This internal conflict creates anxiety and guilt and results in an ambivalence toward deviance. Society interprets the individual's ambivalence as a basic desire to conform and therefore as a sign of the fundamental invalidity of the deviant act. Of course someone's response to support an opportunity to conform depends on whether he has learned deviant values and behavior as part of a socialization process or out of his own personal experience. The former would create a potential for adjustment to other values; the latter would minimize the potential, since it would be analogous to a person's rejecting parts of his self which have proved their significance to his existence (survival).

In his autobiography, Soul On Ice, Eldridge Cleaver gives a clear example of the transition from delinquency to rebellion through a self-education effort.

> Through reading I was amazed to discover how confused people were. I had thought that, out there beyond the horizon of my own ignorance, unanimity existed, that even though I myself didn't know what was happening in the universe, other people certainly did. Yet here I was discovering that the whole USA was in a chaos of disagreement ... In these circumstances I decided that the only safe thing for me to do was go for myself. It became clear that it was possible for me to take the initiative: instead of reacting I could act. [p.5]

The movement is from a passive state to an active one, from struggling against an internalization of powerlessness within the context of a system socializing individuals into dependent and passive behavior patterns to moving toward self-determination. The brutal rape of a white woman, coming after his realization of his own potency is a revolutionary act, an attack on the white man's objective symbol of power and supremacy over others. It is the white man who turns his women into sexual (desired) objects, then creates a society which deprives individuals of sexual satisfaction. Beauty becomes a marketable quality, insuring that

the most attractive are also the possessions of the most famous, rich,
and powerful. Cleaver, who was idolized by many young people, overcomes his powerlessness with violence — a violence closely identified
with sexuality.

This transition from delinquency to conscious forms of rebellion requires a conceptual framework. The transition of delinquent subcultures
into larger social groups, even counter-cultures, is facilitated by the
nature of groups. Cloward and Ohlin give a good account of this process,
although they intend to describe the delinquent group as static, even
fixated, with the potential neither for facilitating individual growth nor
for development toward the rudimentary beginnings of an alternative
society through a subculture network.

> The new member encounters and learns ways of describing the
> world about him which equip him to engage in these prescribed
> activities, enabling him to understand, discriminate, predict,
> and interpret the actions of others in relation to himself as a
> member of the subculture. [p.13]

Such a group may be characterized by deviant or delinquent behavior at
some stage in its development; but when it has among its values personal growth or change, or when the prevailing pattern of deviance creates the experience of personal growth (as is often the case with the use
of drugs — for example, the psychedelics which alter perceptions and
create intense emotional and symbolic experiences), individuals find
that the supportive function of the peer group facilitates this potential
for growth. Unless society interferes, the group's period of self-limit-
ing and destructive behavior will change of its own accord as its members find the natural limits for themselves and look for ways to transcend them.

A deviant or delinquent peer group may also become rigidified, either
because its members lack the skills and abilities to go beyond this kind
of adaptation to their environment or because the intervention of the
society creates a defensive response.

> Acts of delinquency that reflect subcultural support are likely to
> recur with great frequency ... the delinquent subculture imparts
> to the conduct of its members a high degree of stability and re-
> sistance to control or change. [Cloward and Ohlin, pp.10-11]

The solidification of a peer group is always a possibility. When a society
fails to respond to proposals for non-violent social change, the individual
has the choice of either giving up, withdrawing and admitting failure or
resorting to more violent and forceful methods of social change; a strong
peer group or subculture reinforces any of these choices. As did Cleaver,
a person turns to rebellion because it is the only viable alternative and
to violence because it is the only way to insure survival. Either experience is not a matter for argument; countering it requires the creation of
experiences which offer alternatives to violence or withdrawal.

The peer group is formed around the need for support in characteristic

activities the members feel a common need to engage in; it offers the
opportunity for a shared consciousness, or perspective. Eventually an
ideology emerges. "The beliefs and values that the subculture provides
are in turn mobilized to support its prescriptions, which become elab-
orated as a set of norms for directing and controlling the behavior of its
members" (Cloward and Ohlin, p.13). The development of an ideology
offers a coherent strategy for rebellion or, if the group is deviant or
delinquent, a way of moving out of the stage where the deviance is merely
reinforced and the individual only grows by alienating himself from the
peer-group situation.

The strategy assumed by deviance/delinquency/rebellion-oriented
peer groups depends on the nature of the deviant pattern the individuals
have adopted. Cloward and Ohlin list three major groupings of delinquent gangs. Here are the rudimentary strategies a deviant group can
follow and eventually utilize as a coherent ideologically supported form
of rebellion.

> The "criminal gang" — devoted to theft, extortion, and other il-
> legal means of securing an income; some of whose members may
> graduate into the ranks of organized or professional crime.
>
> The "conflict gang" — where the participation in acts of violence
> becomes an important means of securing status.
>
> The "retreatist gang" — the enigmatic group, where the consump-
> tion of drugs is stressed, and addiction is prevalent. [p.1]

In other words, deviance with revolution as a goal may adopt three
different strategies, extending them beyond their more limited forms as
frustrated forms of rebellion. Subversion and sabotage — devoted to
undermining the system by involving oneself within it, then engaging in
actions designed to break the system down — is the most insidious, ranging from bombings and arson (particularly in connection with the military draft) to the rebel within the system, concealed behind an obstensibly
conforming exterior but working toward fundamental change of the entire
social system. Open warfare — ranging from vandalism, rioting, and
street fighting to full-scale violent revolution — is particularly attractive
to racially oppressed and exploited groups with poor socially imposed
self-images, although any group with a low tolerance to frustration and
with experiences of having been brutalized (as for example in Chicago
during the 1968 Democratic Convention) may experience violence as the
only satisfactory (satisfying) strategy.

Finally, the withdrawal-oriented group seeks to deal with reality
through the alteration of internal experience. On the one hand, when
this kind of group is composed of despairing, highly frustrated, and oppressed individuals, the withdrawal can be extreme, as in the development of addiction, the ultimate high being death, the ultimate drug experience before death being the use of such highly potent heroin that
others have overdosed upon it. But altering of internal experiences by
drugs, other manufactured experiences, such as communals, and other

forms of withdrawal, can be helpful and meaningful to the individual. In a supportive peer group even the self-destructive and abusive use of drugs becomes a stage that individuals can outgrow in time. This is particularly true of the use of psychedelics among the youth culture. This group can go for either total apathy concerning social change (it has been observed that addicts lose their "addiction" during riots) or it can be the fundamental resource for the development of an alternative society, offering new forms and institutions to replace the older versions which have been experienced as too constraining. The significant factor may be the response of the society to deviance and delinquency and their implication for social change.

There is the possibility of a fourth one, which is presently emerging in certain areas of the country. This black-magic cult, organized around sacrifices of animals and evil acts, is the negative version of the trend toward astrology, mysticism, Eastern religions, and the like, a denial of and rebellion against institutionalized religions and against science (which removes the mystery from life, reducing everything to quantities).

The use of the word "retreatist," with its connotations of cowardice and weakness, reveals the negative bias of such books as Cloward and Ohlin's. It is important to see the nature of deviance from a less pejorative perspective. Deviance lies on a continuum of behavior ranging from extremes of blind conformity and chauvinism to counter-dependent over-reactions to any authority or limitation. Oversimplification or total avoidance of moral issues underlying the issues of deviance, delinquency, and emotional disturbance; the tendency to reify deviance rather than recognizing the term as pejorative description of one kind of solution to social-interpersonal-personal-environmental conflicts and frustrations which may have much to offer society, and the use of social control in shaping the relationship between society and the individual who does not conform — all these have proven destructive and limiting approaches. Hopefully recognition that deviance, delinquency, and emotional disturbances are in fact experiments with solutions to the underlying contradictions inherent in the established social system will facilitate a more complete discussion of the issues involved, as well as suggest alternative strategies for responding to deviance.

B. A New Model of Deviance

Some changes in deviance and delinquency among young people have apparently taken place since the 1950's. At that time, for example, deviant and delinquent populations remained relatively constant numerically, were largely confined to lower classes, and existed within clear territorial boundaries. Now deviant and illegal behavior is common among young people in virtually every community, regardless of class distinctions; furthermore, the amount of deviant and illegal behavior among white middle-class youth has increased dramatically. Deviants and delinquents used to be easy to deal with because they stayed together in groups or acted individually and were highly visible. Now almost all

young people are engaged in some form of deviant or illegal behavior
(such as smoking marijuana, sexual experimentation, or draft avoidance), and many young people have organized support groups around
deviant behavior. As a result, a recent full-scale arrest of over 100
drug users created a movement within the deviant population to provide
support, bail, and defense funds and to call attention to the nature of the
arrests, even identifying some of the undercover agents involved. Consequently there were no convictions, and some charges were brought
against the police for illegal procedures and harassment.

Lobby groups for deviant causes have begun attempts to force legal
acceptance of homosexuality, penal reforms for alleged and convicted
felons, civil rights for inmates of mental institutions, and the like. Other
support activities among the deviant population are the rise of self-help
programs, the development of intentional communities which accept deviance or illegal behavior, and the attempt at developing such alternative
institutions as extended families and free schools. Despite the fact that
these groups often result in arrests or confinement in treatment facilities,
the underlying organizing myth proclaims that a counter-culture is emerging which will be more sensitive to the felt needs of individuals. In other
words, deviant and delinquent activities have become behavior patterns
supported by sophisticated cognitive processes; they are part of an ideology
which aims at radical social change.

Certainly something is going on which is, at best, only partially understood. Often people attempt to use concepts which may have been useful in the 1950s to deal with behavior patterns in the 1970s. The attitude
toward drug pushers is an excellent example. The trend toward the le-
galization of marijuana (using the Prohibition era as a precedent) promotes the idea that use itself is acceptable but that anyone who sells
marijuana should continue to be punished. In fact, almost everyone who
uses drugs either gives some away to friends or — if he has an abundant
supply — sells the dope at cost. The original source for most drugs used
by adolescents in the middle-class is not the figure in a black raincoat
seducing innocent, naive, and uninformed children, but young people who
obtain the drug through others who grow, synthesize, or steal dope
(raiding relatives' medicine cabinets for amphetamines and barbiturates).

Not only have established conceptual frameworks failed to clarify
the changes in deviant behavior patterns, or the creation of a youth
culture which promotes the illegal or deviant behavior in a variety of
ways; they have also failed to generate explanations for the recent increases in deviant behavior among young people. Vandalism in the high
schools costs almost $40 million a year, according to an editorial in
Life magazine; Newsweek reports over a million runaways; the Gallup
poll notes that up to 75 percent of college students are using illegal
drugs (principally marijuana); stores have invested thousands of dollars
in protection against shoplifting; school riots (disturbances) have broken
out in every major city school system and in many suburban ones as
well; and there is an increase in suicides among the young.

What is needed is a fundamental reexamination of the nature of deviant and delinquent behavior. A radical analysis must begin with a new
conception of deviance, should demonstrate how this phenomenon becomes
widespread, and might generate a frame of reference both for reevaluat-
ing deviant and delinquent behavior and for suggesting strategies for
responding to delinquents.

Society is in a period of transition, with many conflicts in values.
Many young people are trying to establish life styles to meet needs and
desires that the present social system is at best irrelevant to. In this
context the importance of deviance cannot be overestimated. If someone feels that his needs are not being met, he can either accept a state
of permanent frustration or try to develop new strategies which offer the
promise of satisfaction. Since the society uses norms and laws to limit
behavior to what is acceptable within current middle-class standards,
any form of experimentation with alternative strategies will be perceived
as deviant, even delinquent (in violation of the law). Yet social change
begins with individuals who change their behavior to meet their needs.
Deviance is the cutting edge of social change.

Existentialism asserts that the first act of rebellion consists of saying No! to authorities; sociology defines deviance as any individual behavior that violates a norm, limit, or law sanctioned by a person, or
persons, in positions of authority. Both concur, then, in seeing deviance
as a form of rebellion. Understanding deviance this way suggests basic
similarities between various kinds of social revolutionary activities, and
the misbehavior of a child. Based on this perspective a developmental
model of deviance (including disturbance and delinquency) can be created.

Five types of deviance can be described, ranging in development from
a random act to the complex social phenomenon of revolution.

Level I. The person knowingly or unknowingly breaks a rule, transgresses
    a limit, or — more rarely — violates a law out of impulse, curiosity,
    or desire. A young person may, for example, stay out too late;
    smoke grass; expose himself; hit someone; break an object; or stay
    out of school or be tardy.

Level II. The person clearly and often enough goes beyond those limits
    strongly sanctioned by authority to develop a self-image as a deviant.
    This level implies an acceptance of deviance in disregard of potential
    consequences, even though the behavior itself may conflict with the
    person's standards and values. Thus he may be homosexual, a drug
    user, a genius, a thief, a delinquent, or emotionally disturbed.

Level III. The person discovers others who share the same form of de-
    viant behavior, and he develops a sense of belonging to a group. The
    group, in turn, supports and reinforces the deviant behavior. Exam-
    ples are associations of delinquents, hippies, neurotic kids, drug
    users, thieves, and homosexuals.

Level IV. The person defines his role in society, creates a life style,
    and enters into a subculture, accepting for himself the legitimacy
    of his deviant patterns. In this group belong professional criminals

or the policeman who chose his work because he has a taste for
brutality.

Level V. The person purposely sets out to institutionalize his deviant
patterns, to seek legitimacy for them through organizations or social movements. If he encounters any systematic attempt by the
authorities to use repression or suppression to eradicate his pattern,
he may, jointly with his fellow deviants, form a revolutionary consciousness which seeks the removal of this authority and aims at
profound (radical) changes in the entire society to render it less
oppressive to certain minorities. Such visible manifestations as SDS,
women's liberation associations, and crisis centers, as well as such
milder forms as extended families, communes, and military coffee
houses belong in this category.

Deviance is a one-way street. Once someone has become defined by
himself and society as deviant, it is difficult if not impossible to become
"normal" through personal change. A particular form of deviance may,
of course, become socially acceptable over time. But personal changes
from deviance to socially acceptable behavior would mean a change in
values, a disregard of one's own experience and history, and a significant risk that what one gives up is worth more than what is gained by
conforming behavior.

But the primary reason for the inability to retrace one's steps down
our model from Type V to Type I is the necessary reversal in cognitive
complexity. In fact, the movement into greater deviance involves growing awareness and increasing cognitive complexity. In the same way,
the five types of deviance correspond to the individual maturation process. This maturing and cognitive development can also be divided into
five phases, analogous to the deviance types.

Phase I: immaturity. Random activity, often naive and unaware, ranging
from a child's exploration of the sensations in his own body to a
young person's experimenting with drugs to discover the quality of
the experience. Behavior is motivated by pleasure, curiosity, or
impulsiveness. There is no plan, often no awareness of negative
consequences; at best there is an assumption that unpleasant results
can be avoided through caution and/or secrecy.

Phase II: identity formation. Insight, awareness of self, and the distinction between what is purposeful activity and what is accidental are
necessary for the development of a concept of self. In this phase the
the person must decide to be responsible for his own behavior in order to gain a sense of self — an identity.

Phase III: membership in a peer group. This level calls for the development of social skills, learning how to relate to others and conform
behavior within acceptable channels, to be responsible to someone
out of choice rather than necessity (as is required in the family unit).

Phase IV: young adulthood. The person develops a life style, a view of
the world he lives in, a sense of direction and purpose in his actions.

If a person cannot develop a life style which supports his deviance,
he must develop and maintain a conscious mask or camouflage.

Phase V: the exceptional case. The person's self-interest must be identified with that of others whose behavior and values are like his own,
and he must be willing to work to organize and institutionalize his
particular values and life style. This effort often calls for commitment and sacrifice, the development of an ideology, and the assumption of personal risks.

Within each phase there are various degrees of success at achieving
personal potential. Occasionally an individual can become fixated at a
particular level because of a lack of personal or material resources,
social isolation, institutionalization, or the like. Many people find enough
gratification on one level to want to stop developing or maturing, others
simply never understand the implications of their behavior or their role.
Under extreme circumstances a personal crisis may make the individual
return to an earlier level of development for security or support, but he
moves on easily if this is forthcoming.

Within the individual, the development of deviant behavior patterns
can coexist with the development of normal behavior patterns, although
conflicts usually result. When parents, teachers, or others overreact to
deviant patterns, these will tend to be overemphasized defensively, as a
means of protecting the individual's sense of autonomy. A typical parallel can be seen in the common juxtaposition of thumbsucking and masturbation, when both occur in a home situation where the parents accept the
first but are uncomfortable with and made distraught by the idea of the
second.

Socially Acceptable	Deviant
Phase I	
Child learns to suck his thumb for pleasure; parents ignore the behavior.	Child learns that playing with himself is pleasurable, but parents interact around the behavior in disapproving ways.
Phase II	
Child's self-image: "normal kid".	Child's self-image: "naughty, dirty."
Phase III	
Child sees other kids doing the same thing; must be all right. Gradual awareness dawns that some kids are stopping; parents encourage him to stop as well.	Child never sees other kids doing it. Child stops of own accord until much older, when group of close friends secretly have "circle jerk"; young person feels

guilty, ashamed, afraid of being
caught, but continues on his own
— first act of independence, supported by knowledge that others
are doing it too.

Phase IV

Child adopts role of middle-class
conformist.

Child accepts social identity as
someone who masturbates, but
conceals behavior to avoid embarrassment at being caught
doing something others might
disapprove of.

Phase V

Parent tells child to stop sucking
thumb but doesn't become too
alarmed about continuance.

Parent tells child directly or
indirectly that masturbation is
okay.

Teacher tells students that sucking thumbs is normal at a certain age but cannot be allowed to
go beyond a certain age or ex-
ceed a set amount.

Teacher tells students that masturbation is normal and per-
missible within the same boundaries as thumb sucking (age
and extent). Young person becomes radicalized, as an alternative, and states that masturbation might even be useful,
necessary, and important to
society.

Though an individual may turn to deviance for a number of reasons,
its roots are in childhood. All children are deviant to some degree, although they are quite unaware of the negative impression made on others
by such behavior (nose picking, for example). "Normal" behavior is
learned through socialization. If this process is incomplete, deviant
traits may remain or come to replace confusion. Alternately, if the process of socialization is aimed at goals uncongenial to an individual, he
may use deviant behavior as a means of pursuing his own goals.

Thus at any given moment in time a certain percentage of the population, subjected to inadequate or misdirected socialization, will be
"guilty"of deviant behavior to some degree. Society is well able to accom-
modate to this phenomenon by identifying a certain select number of
these deviants as criminal and/or disturbed and treating them in ways
designed to demonstrate social disapproval of their actions. By this
definition the number of deviants must remain stable, since the size of
the institutional case load must conform to the fact that most institutions do not grow to keep pace with the population. Furthermore, society
needs the deviant and the potential for social change and liberation his
existence provides. Even if the individual sought to change, he would

find the social system conspiring to ignore the change, to devalue its significance. A rather amusing example is provided by the psychotic who, once he has been institutionalized, claims to be sane but who is told that his claim and "imitation" of sanity are still further signs of his insanity.

Still another source of deviance is in situations when the process of socialization is in itself experienced as undesirable, boring, punitive, or repressive and suppressive; under these conditions large numbers of young people will turn to deviance as a search for alternatives. Though it is rare for the processes of socialization to break down altogether, this is exactly what is happening at the present time. As a result hundreds of thousands, perhaps millions, of young people are engaging in various deviant patterns as a normal fact of their experience. Because the family, the school, and the community are losing their authority, becoming ineffective, unpleasant, meaningless, and punitive or restrictive, young people as a class are becoming more radicalized. Deviance is increasing among youth and is coalescing as a social movement: the Counter-Culture.

If the individual is allowed to develop freely, sophistication concerning his own behavior and his relationships to others will change without intervention. His behavior will still be deviant, however, even if it becomes less sporadic, more consistent, and more controlled or contained. While inherently self-defeating deviant patterns can be, and often are, out-grown in the normal course of events, there is another movement or growth pattern which can be maximized or focused by intervention — the move from self-destructive deviance to constructive deviance. This transition is more easily achieved than the change from deviance to conformity, and in the long run it may profit society more. Yet it is precisely this transition (or potential for change) which is not perceived when the perspective is automatically set against all forms of deviance as a matter of personal judgment or taste.

Drug use may serve as an example. Drug use can be perceived as totally negative: illegal, self-destructive, dangerous to others, tending to produce insanity or immoral behavior, at best a stepping stone to drug abuse or addiction. This moralistic position (regardless of whether the rationalizations can be defended by evidence) precludes the possibility that society may benefit from drug use, even from drug abuse in certain quantities (it helps to define the limits of useful drug use). Even if this hypothesis were to prove untrue, certainly differentiations can be made between clearly destructive drugs and those which may or may not be harmful. A move from destructive to neutral seems preferable for a person beginning on or persisting in a dangerous drug pattern because (for economic reasons) society is more successful at limiting LSD or marijuana than heroin. Social intervention which assumes as a goal the elimination or control of all drug use will find any limit helpful and will be blind to the obvious fact young people will use drugs, do use drugs, and will take the more dangerous drugs when less dangerous drugs are in short supply or unavailable.

Charting this discussion so far:

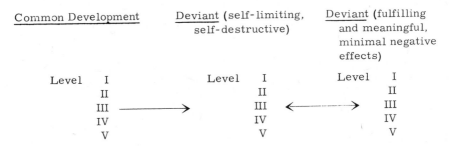

| Common Development | Deviant (self-limiting, self-destructive) | Deviant (fulfilling and meaningful, minimal negative effects) |

The two-way arrow indicates fairly easy movement between constructive and destructive deviant behavior. The one-way arrow indicates changes which almost always go in one direction, for a variety of factors. By putting those deviant patterns which are self-destructive and threatening in the middle, we can see how easily the potential usefulness (to the individual and the society) of deviance can be obscured. The following chart on drug use gives a more detailed example of the differences between destructive and constructive deviant patterns.

Drug Use

Level	Negative	Positive
I	Uses drugs to hurt his parents, withdraws on drugs from school or family, ceases to be interested in anything but drugs; makes exaggerated claims.	Acts out of knowledge of the effects of drugs, uses them for particular purposes and occasions, avoids seeing drugs as excluding other interests; avoids having parents know about drug use.
II	Sees self as drug abuser or is unconcerned; takes drugs randomly, without discrimination; builds identity around drug experiences.	Sees self as drug user, has balanced perspective of pros and cons, accepts drug use as a part of his development, but avoids making it central.
III	Has friends who use drugs, avoids non-drug users, tends to proselytize, depends on drugs for social contact and avoids non-drug use experiences, develops contacts for other drugs.	Shares drugs with friends, relates to non-drug users although may prefer others of similar experiences; respects right of an individual to choose for himself, builds group bonds around many different experiences besides drugs.
IV	Role as drug addict, drug dependent; sees self as one	Role as drug user; sees drugs as having a useful part in his

who either must contend with police as antagonist or needs but "can't ask for" help; role of victim.	life for recreation, personal growth, peak experiences; feels in control of drugs, not victimized.
V Often becomes anti-drugs with a passion or creates elaborate social system around dealing in addictive drugs; is periodically institutionalized.	Wants drugs legalized, takes balanced position, accepts drugs as part of social experiences, but recognizes negative aspects; possibly sees drugs as revolutionary activity, particularly LSD.

Each type of deviance is substantially different from all the others. Therefore a person or society who confronts a deviant act reacts differently, based on different intensities of response. A hierarchy of fears in turn elicits an escalating set of defenses. These can be charted roughly as being equivalent to each type of deviance as it develops into a form of revolution.

Type of Reaction

Level of Deviance	Form of Fear	Form of Defense
I	Personal irritation, frustration, anger.	Yelling, scolding, confinement to room, withholding of affection, restrictions, low grades, detentions.
II	Fear of personal harm (to self or people one is close to), loss, failure.	Expulsion, psychiatric treatment, reform school, residential treatment center, hospitalization, economic reprisals.
III	Fear of loss of control, loss of authority, loss of legitimacy, prestige, job.	Intervention by social workers, police harassment, depriving youth of meeting places by closing down areas where young congregate on grounds that they are "causing a disturbance" or using drugs.
IV	Fear of destruction (literally de-structuring), loss of structure or support, leaving everyone stranded and alone, fear of physical de-	Severe harassment and arrest, with an occasional killing, widespread use of force, systems intervene to vilify behavior in the

	struction, psychological and moral degradation, insanity, chaos, anarchy.	press, use of under- cover agents for federal interventions; massive funding for projects de- signed to control and limit movements of in- dividuals and subculture.
V	Fear of dissolution, the end of everything in- cluding consciousness, absolute annihilation of "everything worth liv- ing for", loss of values, ideals, social dissolution.	Use of army, open dis- play of authority's force, mass imprison- ment.

Somewhere between phase III and IV all the social systems combine to defeat the growing social movements which portend revolution. Schools, churches, families, government, psychiatric institutions run by the state and the government, the court and police systems, the army, all wage an all-out war against the potential for social revolution. The biggest enemy continues to be fear, particularly in terms of hatred and over- reaction movements for social change. Events during this phase of de- velopment are often perceived out of perspective, and a mutually danger- ous situation is created. Desperately needed social change may be completely eliminated, individuals may be needlessly injured or killed, the society may become more totalitarian. Such a move necessitates either violent revolution or total stagnation and decay.

Vandalism can be charted as an example of the development of almost totally destructive deviance patterns in a frustrating yet virtually com- pletely oppressive situation.

The Phenomenon: Vandalism; the destruction of property.
The Value: Private property.
The Rule: Be careful you don't break anything.
The Limit: Don't break anything, or you'll suffer the consequences.
The Law: The destruction of property is a criminal offense, punishable under the law by a fine and/or imprisonment.
Phase I: Carelessness. The young person accidentally or in rage destroys something belonging to his family as an alternative to expressing rage toward another who might either be hurt or retaliate by causing hurt.
Phase II: "Fun is more important than the rule." The youth destroys or mutilates any object at random, acting out of frustration, boredom, or maliciousness.
Phase III: Gratification is more important than obeying the law. The peer group enters a school and vandalizes it or breaks into a home and destroys its contents.

Phase IV: "Ownership of things is unimportant." The person recognizes
   the legitimacy of his anger at the family, school, or community because it is oppressive and restrictive, creating meaningless situations for useless purposes. Vandalism is viewed as a legitimate —
   though not necessarily mature — expression of hostility. The person
   looks for ways to de-structure the family, school, or business experience in less obvious — less physical — ways.
Phase V: Private property is at the root of a corrupt system which exploits people for the limited materialistic gain of a few, leaving
   many people poor and deprived of what is rightfully theirs. Sabotage
   and controlled and purposeful destruction of property are used as
   revolutionary activity after less direct means have failed and the
   person is repressed in his attempts at the social change of structures.

In short, vandalism occurs when the individual is alienated from
property. In an oppressive environment, where he is constricted and
restricted — such as the home or the school — destruction is a means of
expressing fury and rage. When the rage is intense enough, the possibility of punishment will not act as a deterrent. Without alternatives to
the rage-producing environments which do not include adjustment and
accommodation to those very situations, it is unlikely that young people
will be less destructive. Someone may internalize the destructiveness,
turning his rage upon himself, or he may generate the rage at whoever,
or whatever, is insisting that he adapt himself to a situation he experiences as untenable.

The task of the radical is to transform the potential for revolution
latent in every deviant act into a coherent strategy for profound social
change. The issues are complex, involving inner conflicts, situational
oppression and repression, and interaction between the individual and
impressively large social institutions with enormous power. The natural
trend in the development of deviant behavior is toward an expansion of the
limits within a society, but the interference (intervention) of social
control systems devastates the natural, reducing individuals to helpless,
dependent (or counter-dependent) victims of their own social system.
What is happening to young people seeking new solutions to old, largely
unanswered dilemmas of survival and happiness is a travesty on humanity.
   Moving away from the developmental model, recognizing the frustrating tendency of people to become fixated at one or another level out
of fear or personal satisfaction, far short of fulfilling their promise to
society, or even to themselves, is a risky proposition. Essentially the
support of deviance which would encourage development, rather than
adjustment and accommodation to an outmoded, self-destructive social
system, into deviant life styles and social systems requires a program
which in itself is deviant. Furthermore, as our model implies, a deviant
program is more threatening to more people than any small group of
deviants without organization. How to provide a real alternative and
survive becomes an issue for any radical program.

Programs which intend to support growth, encourage experimentation with minimal risks, and create support groups for individuals making a transition from one level of consciousness to another will generally follow certain guidelines.

1. The program will be completely in the control of the young people running it. This is important for the integrity and freedom of the program.
2. The decision-making process will be consensual rather than arbitrary and hierarchical whenever possible.
3. Staff members will have the same values, experiences, life styles, and interests as the clients. Furthermore role distinctions will be minimized as much as possible, hopefully to conform to behavior differences rather than abstract conceptual frameworks.
4. Clients will be self-selected. No coercion or pressure will be placed on those coming into the program.
5. Setting of limits will be dealt with as individual cases as much as possible, and general rules, limits, and structures will therefore be held down. Structure must facilitate experimentation, not shape it or contain it.
6. Besides being a program, an organization should be a small community. While individuals may be kept out of certain service roles because they are inadequate helpers at the time, they cannot be excluded from the community unless they are actually dangerous. This community should be developed with the same intensity as any service program, since in the long run most service programs are temporary protection for the dilemmas our society is facing as communities dissolve.
7. Funding should be shaped to meet the needs of the program, rather than programs being shaped to meet the needs of those who fund them.
8. Services must be provided to the clients without cost in an economic sense, but also free from demands to change and to get better (which is common), and from collusion with the strategies of the staff.
9. The program's major interventions must be with the institutions and systems shaping the lives of young people — the family, the school, and the local community. Alternatives must be developed as often as possible. Focusing on the individual is often a cop-out, more often merely a stopgap with no real benefits to anyone.

These nine points are basically different from similar assumptions in professional social service programs. Each one is fraught with contradictions and experiential dilemmas whenever they are conscientiously applied. Many alternative programs have become nonprofessional imitations of professional organizations, rather than social change agencies. The form appears different, but the content and end result appear to be substantially the same (see Chapter 6). This situation is a basic consequence of trying to create a deviant program in a society committed to coopting or destroying viable alternatives. To some degree the shaping

of a program to conform to the social context is necessary and unavoid-
able. However, every alternative program which is eventually coopted
becomes another example of the failure of society to allow change, another
reason for cynicism and despair among young people.

A program aimed toward radical change through the support of deviant individuals must in itself be deviant in theory, in structure, and in
function. The success of the program as a strategy of social change will
depend on its success in being radically changed on all three levels.

Chapter 3

THE COUNTER-CULTURE AS A PROCESS
FOR SOCIAL CHANGE

The members of the generation growing up in the 1960s have had a series
of powerful, direct learning experiences which have profoundly altered
the way they perceive, set priorities, and act. In their attempts to do
something about the inequities, injustices, and violence they saw around
them, they stumbled on the realization that these evils were deeply
present and structurally rooted in every person and every institution in
America. Even they themselves were implicated. Their search for
direct solutions led to a highly sophisticated understanding of the ways
in which our society blocks change and social reform. In response, they
have begun a series of experiments with change in personal consciousness
and community relationships.

These experiments have led to marked differences in the way young
people relate to change. Their style, goals, and way of ordering reality
are so different from those of the generation that preceded theirs that
some see the shift as being as profound as the development of technology
and industry. This "New Copernican Revolution,"as futurist Willis Harman (1963) calls it, has distinguished intellectual roots in the work of
such humanistic psychologists as Abraham Maslow, such holistic plan-
ners as Buckminster Fuller, and such Third World political theorists as
Mao and Fanon. It is a turning inward to neglected potentialities of the
psyche with acceptance rather than fear, and outward to traditions, myths,
and processes which have been ignored by our mechanistic culture.

This new force goes beyond theorizing (to which it gives low priority)
and tackles tasks which need doing but which the dominant culture has
neglected. It includes a practical strategy for action. It is not a traditional pressure group, religion, mass movement, or political force;
rather, it represents a change process shared by many individuals and
groups. It has been reified (mainly by such writers as Roszak and Reich
who aro not in tho aotion but otraining to maotor it by intolloctual work)
into a counter-culture, alternate society, or Consciousness III. These
terms are used interchangeably to unify various pursuits which spring
from experiences and processes which contradict the dominant modes of
action in our culture.

Form and Style

The new force consists of more than simply new ideas or programs;
rather, it is a new method and style of action which contrasts so highly with
conventional modes that it can legitimately be called a counter-culture.
Outlining these contrasts sets the stage for a full typology of the new
values and for a history and description of the counter-culture's manifestations. Similarities in style and form result from the intuitive unity
which different groups within the new culture feel and which is the source
of this metaphor's great reductive power to capture the energy and imag-
inations of so many. The medium, the form, the style is the message and
the ideology of the counter-culture. The new culture is refreshing because
it is one of the few movements whose means are its ideals and whose
process is its product.

The new culture goes far beyond traditional liberal reform in identifying the problems and specifying the depth of necessary change. Rather
than seeking a few adjustments and refinements in an otherwise service-
able and open system, the counter-culture sees every action as potentially destructive to social good and consequently in need of reevaluation
and transformation according to new values. Rather than focusing on
new programs and legislation, it focuses on new behavior and styles of
living and relating. The pervasiveness of the concern is shown in the
terse typology of Philip Slater (1970), who wrote about the changes he
saw as chairman of the sociology department at Brandeis and then resigned his post to participate in these changes personally.

> The old culture, when forced to choose, tends to give pre-
> ference to property rights over personal rights, technological
> requirements over human needs, competition over cooperation,
> violence over sexuality, concentration over distribution, the
> producer over the consumer, means over ends, secrecy over
> personal openness, social forms over personal expression,
> striving over gratification, Oedipal love over communal love,
> and so on. The counter-culture tends to reverse all these pri-
> orities. [P.100]

The counter-culture in its many mainfestations represents a reversal not only of the priorities of the dominant culture, but also of the
strategic starting point of traditional social reform. Rather than aiming
at the mass or legislative level, young people have learned that it makes
more sense to begin with the individual person. Only after an extensive
process of personal change is an individual competent to dictate what
programs are feasible for larger numbers. Young people perceived a
contradiction between the actions of political reformers and their goals.
There seemed to be no clear connection in practice between the two;
mass movements and legislation, for example, did not alter rascism and
inequality. The reformist goal — to alter basic values and the way institutions and behavior reflect these values — is unchanged. The counter-
culture offers a more comprehensive and sophisticated strategy for

moving toward this goal on many levels, starting with the person. Emile
Capouya (1970) writes:

> The idea that much can be accomplished by changing "condi-
> tions" is useful only insofar as we remember that we are our
> conditions, that we embody them in our thoughts and our actions.
> Customary movements of reform proceed on the assumption that
> conditions are objective and persons subjective, which amounts
> to regarding things as real and people as fictitious. For that
> reason the usual patterns of reform, insofar as they are effective,
> achieve more ingenuously tyrannical forms of the abuses they
> set out to correct. [P.172]

The new force among young people, the counter-culture, arrives at a
more direct, more integrated, and presumably more effective strategy
for realizing old goals, as well as a clearer perception of what that
would mean and look like. The ancient criticism leveled at radical pro-
testers — What is your program? How would you accomplish things? —
is answered by young people who wish to embody their program and live
out their changes, rather than hoping that the next generation does better.
They experiment with drug use, communes, craft cooperatives, encounter
groups, nutrition, farming, new media and art, human use of technology,
direct politics, free schools, and services. Young people's anger and
impatience, like Thomas Edison's laziness, is a seeming deficiency which
is turned to positive use. That, and the decision to practice justice by
treating each other fairly, whatever the law or custom, are the earmarks
of this new style of action. The outlines are recognizable all the way back
in 1966, in this statement by a white girl who became a SNCC organizer:

> Finally it all boils down to human relationships. It has nothing
> to do with governments. It is the question of whether we ... wheth-
> er I shall go on living in isolation or whether there shall be a we.
> The student movement is not a cause ... it is a collision between
> this one person and that one person. It is a "I am going to sit
> beside you ... " Love alone is radical. Political statements are
> not; programs are not; even going to jail is not . [In Zinn, 1966,
> p. 7].

While in the 1950s young people had responded to the bankruptcy of
America's values and priorities with apathy, withdrawal, and alienation,
the 1960s began with a positive response. SNCC and the peace movement relate directly to the drug and hippie movement which followed. An
early statement by the Diggers of San Francisco, who see a new life
style as a powerful political statement, clarifies the debts and connections:

> We ... stare at the preposterousness of doing our thing within
> the frame of a reality that can incorporate and market anyone,
> anything, anytime. And then we begin to understand that if some
> attempt is not made to manage the world with love, it will run
> mad and overwhelm everything, including the woods.
> And so we stay dropped out. We won't, simply won't play the

> game any longer. We return to the preposterous consumer society
> and refuse to consume .... And we do our thing for nothing. In
> truth, we live our protest. Everything we do is free because we
> are failures. [In Kornbluth, 1968, p.66−67]

Diggers, yippies, hippies, and other dropouts realize that unlearning
and relearning how to live together cannot be a partial process, because
partialness can contradict the goal and undermine the vision. This is not
an attitude of apathy or withdrawal, but a beginning of alternative possibilities and renewed creativity. While many young people have followed
this path with varying degrees of failure and destructive personal effects,
in this account we are only dealing with the vanguard, the relatively few
people whose creative energy develops paths and widens possibilities.

A Short History

The civil-rights and peace movements led to political activity which,
because it was direct and personal, was able to capture the imagination
of people frustrated by conventional political channels. The new elements
stressed basic moral expressions and personal statements, such as
turning in draft cards, refusal to serve, sitting in, boycotting, marching,
leaking secret papers, burning draft records, "levitating" the Pentagon,
and drafting a new constitution. Much of this was a discovery of the tactics of nonviolence and a reaction to reformist strategies which counseled
patience and compromise of basic values in the name of effectiveness.

On campuses protest grew into activities more central to the new
style of the counter-culture. The paradigmic schools are Berkeley and
San Francisco State, where political protest concerning civil liberties
grew to reevaluation of the structure of a learning institution (see Rossman, 1971, for personal accounts of this process). Out of this came a
series of learning experiments, side by side with large-scale disruption,
which were simultaneous and interrelated with strategies for university
reformation. Free universities and experimental programs were born;
they were negotiated into existence by traditional reformist compromise,
but they also represented direct alternatives to the abuses which earlier
protests reflected. At San Francisco State the tragic final act was the
backlash of the administration and political leaders who resisted the
growing energy for structural and educational reform. They fought back
with the characteristic weapons of the <u>counter</u> counter-culture — police,
expulsion, and rigid social control, making a New Right folk hero out of
President Hayakawa, previously a liberal reformer. While educational
reform in larger institutions may be temporarily frustrated, small experiments in creating new schools and learning communities are the
counter-cultural response to the same impulse which began by trying to
"stop the university machine."

Psychic exploration through psychedelic drugs, encounter groups,
communes, and religious experience are another strand of the new strategy. Art, the media, literature, music, the environment, and consciousness, were all harnessed to the exploration of the limits of personal

expression. The search for new ordering principles and new forms of space which would bring relief from the valuelessness and confusion among which the young people grew up led them to every possible permutation of extreme experience, from madness to Zen Buddhist satori. Encounter groups, growth centers, and sensitivity training create time- and space-limited microcosms of a new culture, with new norms focusing on relating, expression of feelings, and exploration. This limited creation of an alternative community has been attempted in organizations and institutions with partial success. Young people cite the use of such experiments by a large number of conventional people as a validation of their experiences and explain the equivocal results of such groups as owing to their limited nature and lack of complete commitment by participants.

For young people drugs are a riskier means of producing a free space than encounter groups. The difference is that drug experiences take place within the individual (See Chapter 4). In living groups and communes, drugs and high-intensity experiments with sexuality, encounter, and religion pushed participants to tremendous redefinitions of personality, behavior, and interpersonal relations, as well as to new insights into the nature of politics and communities. Out of these came first urban, then rural, counter-communities, where groups and loose confederations created a network and barter system of basic services and goods, which keep them almost totally out of the consumer, work, and economic spheres of the dominant culture. Social services, newspapers, meeting places, homes, schools, crafts and farms are the products of the new communities. These also experience first-hand the dominant culture's tolerance of change — just barely. While managing to survive, they also faced the man-made hazards of building codes, violence, drug arrests, and lack of public funds to support innovations. Those who remain in the city end up with the high degree of political sophistication and practical skill necessary for survival.

Crafts, organic truck farming, and rural self-sufficiency relate the person to the objects of his or her labor and to the earth. The influence of Eastern thought — the Tao, Yoga, Buddhism, the I Ching (Book of Change) — led to a renewed sensitivity to the earth and to man's delicate balance with the environment. It also freed many from the middle-classness of their families, which had left them without skills and knowledge for basic survival work. Such activity directly deals with alienation by rediscovering ancient but relevant truths about personal balance and unity with the earth.

While the counter-culture is no longer recruiting at such a tremendous rate, the groups which constitute this process are developing a commitment to long-term work. They include many dissenting, deviant, alienated, exploratory, and innovative groups and individuals. They share a desire to relate personal consciousness and interpersonal behavior to political values and eventual liberation from a constricting and oppressive social system. They do not see this task as one of moving society wholly from one set of values to another; rather they wish to help rediscover a

balance and harmony among opposites and to live with duality rather than
singlemindedness. They want to be a balancing force in society rather
than an opposition. The tendency of the society, however, is to announce
its intolerance and incapacity for change by treating these innovators
as its opposition. But as individuals move freely among new projects and
more conventional groups, they recognize within their experiences common roots and directions, and they become interdependent with the wider
culture. For the sake of survival they have learned to depolarize conflict,
stay out of jail, wait patiently, and gently infect those they meet who are
beginning to feel the need for changes in the new direction. The task now
is to stabilize the learning, to build way stations for others in their
progress toward new living and work styles, and to coexist with violent
and evil forces without being destroyed or ignored.

Elements of the Counter-Cultural Process

In the learning experiences which define the new culture, there is a
recognizable progression of steps. This core process over and over
again results in the separation of an individual from the dominant values
which he has learned, turning him toward a search for new ways.

The first step is the awareness of a source of injustice or of a social
problem. While looking simultaneously for the cause and for the termination of the abuse, the individuals or group gradually come to realize that
even they themselves are not blameless, since they contribute to the
situation. In the early days of the civil-rights movement, this recognition
took the form of realizing that racism was not something practiced only
by the Southern power structure but was part of a system in which blacks,
Northerners, and even young people also took part.

The second stage is an awareness of how deeply our society is rooted
in structural injustice and how violently and powerfully our society fights
against attempts to change it. Southern blacks, Northern hippies and
college students, all learned that once they had made the public aware of
a problem, a backlash in turn placed blame on them and punished them.

In reaction to this process each protest or social change group turned
inward for support, establishing the basic structures of the counter-community. The result was a small community based on deep personal ties
of love, shared economy, common work, and great hardship.

Through the pressures of their work, or its failures, members of the
counter-community eventually turned in on themselves. They discovered
drugs and other forms of personal exploration which, though available
for many years, had awaited a consciousness ready and prepared for the
insights which they could provide. The need for personal change was
also bolstered by the consciousness of shared culpability and participation in the injustices which they sought to end. It was a process of personal growth and personal purification.

The final step occurs when the counter-community reforms and re-
defines itself, synthesizing the personal knowledge of its members and
the political understanding of its previous change efforts. As a result

the group selects a portion of the whole which it is uniquely qualified or committed to deal with, and develops the skills and capacity to accomplish limited goals. Its members also work to stabilize and expand the possibilities in their own small community and in their relations to other communities. This is the highest development of the counter-culture, the outcome of all previous personal and political exploration and experiment. People can enter at this level and — through drugs, reading, limited forms of past lessons (such as a drug bust or political action in one's high school or college) or sharing with others — quickly go through the learning process of the other stages.

The flowering of the search for alternatives seems badly needed to reverse the dangerously rigid and one-sided nature of our dominant culture. In the Middle Ages a similarly rigid and obsessive devotion to virtue and religious purity led to a counter-culture of witchcraft and heresy and a repressive reaction by the dominant culture. The current counter-culture similarly rediscovers qualities which have been suppressed by our dominant culture. Such reactions usually come when they are needed to rejuvenate a culture. Young people are most in touch with this need for new experience because they are among the first to know that their education and family experience are of little use given the new social conditions they find, and they have the freedom and energy to look for new ways. They clearly perceive the crisis and prepare a response.

Once started, it is difficult to repress the reactive counter-culture. Eventually the counter-modes become incorporated in the dominant culture, producing a new emphasis and greater balance. One generation's deviance and nonconformity become the new norm. To illustrate how the counter-culture represents a reaction to extreme positions by a dominant culture, the dominant values and the counter-culture's reaction to them can be listed. The new culture represents not the opposite extreme from the dominant culture, but an equilibrium between the two polar opposites. This balance represents the ideal outcome of the change process. Less desirable possibilities include an extreme reaction against the new ways and a swing overboard in the opposite direction. Today the repressive reaction is the more likely.

Topography of Our Current Value Conflict

Dominant value	moving toward a	Counter-value
	Ordering Experience	
conceptual, cognitive, abstract	Knowledge	experiential, concrete, feeling
reduction of experience to exclusive categories		unity of self and experience, nonjudgmental, nonevaluative
division of situations into abstractions, using fragments to represent the whole		synergy, gestalt focus, taking things as a whole

	Focus	
look for differences past/future, historical prefer the familiar		look for similarities here/now change for its own sake, experimental, risk-taking
external experience, avoid feelings, use of "down" drugs		interest in inner experience, expansion of consciousness to include repressed material, use of psychedelic drugs, expression of strong emotions, fantasies, myths

Formation of Self

	Identity	
prefer maturity and consistency static end product, advancement of self personal identity paramount		prefer regression, childlike state, evolving, self-process growth within and with group collective identity
individual performance, productivity	Goals	group experiences, rituals, attainment of feeling state
treated as object	Person	treated as human being
life is for work, achievement, leisure is incentive reward		life is to play and create, identity of work and play

Morality

	Laws	
punitive, controlling		laissez-faire, inner-direction
traditional, set norms prescribed social games	Order	ideals, evolving ways game-playing for its own sake
something to achieve	Ideals	something to be
rational, scientific, technological	Beliefs	the absurd, mysterious, paradox, magic as meaningful activity

Roles

	Relationships	
structured, formal		intimate, shared, flexible, role-free
fragmented, rational separations		continuity, work-play fusion, integration
professionalization, specialization	Skills	shared basic skills, generalizations
to conform and control others to basic norms	Education	exploratory, expressive, personal growth experience

	Norms	negotiable, ascribed authority
fixed or prescribed authority	Norms	negotiable, ascribed authority

Interaction

content	Group Focus	process, then content
structural solutions	Problem-Solving	direct personal confrontation, negotiation of solutions
leadership initiates	Change	self-initiated, risk-taking
conversation, formal rules	Speech	free-associative, unrestricted rapping
violent aggressive solutions to pain and frustration, projection and blaming, criticism as a rejection	Conflict	gentleness, openness, warmth, facilitation of responses, sharing responsibility for outcomes, introspection
rejection, isolation, punishment	Deviance	acceptance and toleration
win-lose, outcome crucial	Games	win-win, process

Organization

graded, hierarchical	Authority	consensual decisions, shared
closed, exclusionary groups	Definition	inclusive gatherings
crisis-oriented, one-sided planning	Planning	global view of planning, end-oriented, synergistic

Culture

fear-oriented, defensive, concealment for protection		supportive, open, risk-taking
centralized, accumulated	Resources	distributed according to need
coercive, punitive, law and order	Social Control	positive reinforcement, supportive, civil liberties
delegated, top-down decisions	Responsibility	decide for self, accept it for your decisions
competition due to scarcity, real or artificial		sharing based on plentitude and work according to shared goals
neutral, nonarousing	Environments	spontaneity, sexuality, stimulation
rational, rule-oriented	Consciousness	tribal, mythic structures, rhythmic
norms and procedures	Cement	shared emotional bonds

nuclear family, small units   L i v i n g   extended families, peer
                                                                                     groups
war, violence   P r o t e c t i o n   peace, understanding
                                     *   *   *
                          C o u n t e r - C o m m u n i t i e s

     The interface between personal or life style changes and institu-
tional or social change consists of the new living-working-learning communities. These may be called transition groups because they consist of
individuals going through personal change and learning experiences together and connecting their personal task with the need to interact with,
survive, and facilitate change toward new priorities in the wider community. They are the basic structural unit of the new culture, dealing
with all levels of transition along the continuum toward counter-values,
forms, and behaviors. Such groups usually combine living together with
work on a specific task which is economically viable in dealings with
other groups and society. The counter-community allows intense personal bonds with each other member, while also serving as a mechanism for social and political consequences for more than its immediate membership. In what Herbert Marcuse calls a repressively-tol-
erant society (which allows freedom but exerts social control over deviance by covert and increasingly violent measures) the collective or
commune is a unit which can maintain its integrity as different from the
cultural norm. It gives all its members the kind of personal and social
support within, which they need to maintain a deviant stance outside it.
     The small group is the smallest social unit which can support new
norms of behavior and thus allow them to be stabilized as new patterns
and habits. At the small-group level a person can evaluate and receive
feedback about personal changes and receive support, validation, and
love as a changing self. Similar support groups formed the underground
organization of Communist cells and of the thought-reform groups which
changed the values and culture of China. Robert Lifton (1963) sees such
groups as the most powerful force for large-scale personality change.
The fear and negative associations felt by Americans toward these
processes is another aspect of our fear of change and loss of willpower;
such groups are merely tools, ideologically neutral, which are helpful
for change of any kind. In America, less effective therapy and sensitivity groups have the same goals.
     In the process of evolving, transition groups usually create several
norms characteristic of the style of the new culture. Learning, change,
and personal growth are seen as identical processes, relevant to all
aspects of life and the justification for the community. People are there
to change in certain directions, and the process must facilitate that aim.
Mike Rossman (1972) writes: "In the conversation of a [new] learning
group as much emphasis is given to the process of the group's learning
and to the cultivation of the appropriate skills and meta-skills as to the
nominal content of the learning" (Part III, p.4). The group constantly
investigates and questions the way it works, whether it is meeting its
needs and working toward its goals. Each person asks the same questions

of himself, and the reflective process enables each member to focus on his or her own, as well as the community's, changes.

Counter-communities learn from encounter and sensitivity groups techniques and ways to focus on personal expressiveness and to explore obstacles to openness among people. In many communities the focus on emotional learning and expressiveness practiced by encounter groups is a necessary remedial measure, to compensate for the lack of such activity elsewhere. As new communities begin to deal with collective tasks, the differentiation between cognitive and emotional learning breaks down. The group by that time has structures, metaprocesses, which allow it to stop, look at itself, evaluate its progress, and institute new norms. It is important that every aspect of communal life be dealt with openly and out front within the group; new communities run into trouble when issues between people are not discussed and resolved. Because the pressures and tensions of change are immense, a process group is almost a necessity for working through changes, dealing with conflicts and difficulties, and evaluating progress.

The counter-community's striving for personal integration at all levels is one source of its strength. It is not possible to have one set of values for political action and another for one's family; if someone is deliberately oppressive in one area, he is likely to be inadvertently oppressive in the other. One reason why organizational and institutional renewal strategies usually fail is that the people in the program strive for new values, but when they go home or relate to people outside the renewed area, they do not receive support for new norms, experience a conflict of values, and often opt for the old and traditional norms once the program ends. New values must be internalized and supported by each person's closest, most relevant people. The effectiveness of such political strategies as nonviolence stems from their integrity; for example, the power of Gandhi as a political leader came from his drive to reformulate himself at every level, by living simply, making his own clothes, and having a community of like-minded people working with him. His ashram was an early counter-community.

The lack of integration across different levels may be the chief flaw in liberal reform political action. The inability of legislation to produce change in our national racism or to curb crime is quite obviously due to the lack of support for such behavior on family, economic, social, and personal levels. For a social change to "take" permanently in a society, it must be integrated into enough levels for all the relevant social structures to support a given value. While we think we abhor crime, for example, our competitive ethic supports a kind of lawless acquisitiveness in business which is reflected in the entrepreneurial efforts of petty criminals. They are deviant only in the level of their aspiration.

Further, action on one level may be prompted by a need or cause at another level. Fear as a personal experience may contribute to hoarding of resources on a national level. Global military domination does little to erase inner fears because the action is taken on the wrong level; but some people still go on seeking military protection from themselves.

Much of our political activity and our social controls result from partially misplaced levels of causality. People in the counter-culture, by becoming sensitive to themselves, are able to cut such misperceptions to a minimum, producing fewer fear-motivated, defensive behavior patterns. The new culture attempts to implement change on the level where it is needed. For example, members of a new community tend to deal with fear and threat by looking within and understanding its roots, looking realistically at the sources of threat outside, and acting on that balanced understanding. Essentially they add a personal and psychological sophistication to their political and social actions, which keeps the personal and the political in better relationship.

Working through basic values at each level — from individual consciousness to couple to family to living unit to community to economic and political system — is a basic task of the counter-community. The realization of inconsistency across levels came when "movement" people looked at their own organizations, families, and personal relations and saw that they themselves committed acts which they would not condone in governments; at this point they implicated themselves. Many political radicals go through a period when their interest shifts to more internal levels; for example, they begin to use psychedelics or go to live on a farm. Conversely, those whose predominant interest has been personal growth see their experiments and communities fail because of economics or as a result of pressure from the police or building authorities. When they experience the political consequences of their private behavior, they widen their interests.

Consciousness-raising groups are a tool for such changes. These groups which began as self-critical sessions for members of political organizations, were adopted by liberation groups of women, gay people, veterans, and young people. A group of people, without an appointed leader or format, support each other in making the changes each wants — usually in a direction given little social support outside the group. This form of people's therapy tackles the basic issues of liberation from a puritanical and repressive morality supported by economic sanction, social control, and custom; many people have received enough support from such groups to make major changes in their living and working environments. Further collaboration often results; members of women's groups, for example, put out literature, counsel others, and create day-care and cooperative child-rearing communities to facilitate change.

A great deal of movement takes place among counter-communities. Mike Rossman (1972) lived through the last decade in the Berkeley area and followed the changes from the Berkeley Free Speech movement to the experimental college at San Francisco State to use of psychedelics to establishing a living-working community. He writes: "In the six months following the sit-in [at Berkeley] literally everyone I knew who had been deeply involved with the movement accomplished some major and long-delayed change in their personal lives." While there is conflict as personal risks multiply, the need to grow and survive in the areas where new consciousness is developed leads to decisive and creative

resolutions in practice. Rossman and others relate this spontaneous
learning and growing process to the liberation of energy which was blocked
by precarious and rigid patterns. Through experience of only one part of
the new movement, energy is released creating a free space with others
to grow in the newly liberated zone.

People move on to other activities within the counter-community because of an experience of incompleteness at one level. Ray Mungo was
a founder of Liberation News Service and a participant-observer of
many significant political events. But at the start of his second book,
Total Loss Farm, he announces a move to a stage where he is more concerned with the total living system.

> But I woke up in the spring of 1968 and said, "This is not what I
> had in mind," because the movement had become my enemy; the
> movement was not flowers and doves and spontaneity, but another
> vicious system, the seed of a heartless bureaucracy, a minority
> party vying for power rather than peace. It was then that we put
> away the schedule for the revolution, gathered together our dear
> ones and all our resources, and set off to Vermont in search of
> the New Age. [P.11]

Many who welcomed the new politics see this move as a withdrawal or
cop-out, but those in the midst of similar changes see such a search not
as an end, but as another stage in a process. Mungo has not lost interest
in activism or change; he merely regards his previous activity as incomplete and imperfect. He seeks ways to make his politics more con-
gruent with other, possibly higher, truths; when he works on his farm,
he carries his politics with him as an assumption, which leads him to
constantly relate his action to a wider system of others — society and the
earth.

The small group or the counter-community has become the basic
unit of the change movement because solitary experiments ended in isolation or self-destruction, and mass movements have ended up by defeating themselves or being defeated by backlash from their culture. In
groups, individual change joins social process in a transformation which
no longer connotes merely political change but also involves analysis and
change of personal behavior toward new values. The "work" of such
groups is both the creation of a new culture and survival within the old
one. The basic difficulty is the continuous differentiation between what
is rejected in the old culture and the personal and group change technologies. To show how such communities work, we will focus on urban
and rural communities. Through several examples we will show how
counter-communities deal with personal integration and change, community conflict and growth, and relations and survival in the wider repressive society. Urban and rural groups have quite different focuses and
adjustment problems, though their goals may be similar.

The rural transitional community. Rural groups tend to be self-con-
tained in that a member's commitment to the group commands much of

his time. Such communities include growth centers, farms, small manufacturing groups (domes, crafts, and the like), Syanon and other therapeutic communities, religious communites (ashrams, meditation centers,
Zen monasteries), and simple families or groups of people living in the
country. While it is impossible to gauge the number of such settlements,
oppression and the general distaste for city life have swelled them enormously, and thousands of them exist in Vermont, New Mexico, Colorado,
and Northern California; many of them are several years (and generations) old.

While studies, such as that by Rosabeth Moss Kantor (1970), and
personal accounts tend to judge the success or failure of such communities by their longevity, it should be remembered that people join such
communities chiefly to rediscover certain basic values inherent either
in working on the land or in personal relationships. These explorations
are not ends in themselves, but rather part of a growth process that may
take people to many communities, both urban and rural, as well as to
schools and to more traditional work experiences.

Ray Mungo describes a visit to Mendecino County in Northern California, which may now have a hippie majority; as people flee urban repression in and around Berkeley.

> The friends I had come to see, who I did not know before I got
> there, were artists, too, but in the absolute sense of my age-
> group: in which everybody (it seems) is an artist, one and all
> re-create life and we never ask each other "what do you do?"
> in the sense of "how do you make money?" Many of us make
> no money at all, others do but it is something less than inciden-
> tal to our lives, which are really about a million forces having
> nothing to do with career, profession, or money; we fish, farm,
> draw, paint, write, love, drive about in cars, cook, bake, give
> birth, redecorate, build, destroy, you name it; and reserve the
> right to stop whatever we're doing and do something else, just
> for the hell of it. [P.103]

In the areas where counter-cultural rural communities flourish,
every town is likely to have its "head shop" (selling general counter-
cultural goods, such as posters and incense sticks), bookstore (stock-
ing, among others, the writings of members of the counter-culture), a
craft shop (selling both supplies to and the works of local craftspeople),
and a natural-foods store. These small-business outlets for counter-
culture tradesmen also serve as community centers, and when young
people, such as Mungo, travel to new areas, they can meet and find new
friends through these stores.

Newsweek and other publications have reported an increasing aura
of distrust filtering into hippie communities; this is especially true in
urban ghettos, where there is a scarcity of goods and a rise in lawless-
ness as a reaction to exploitation and police repression. In the rural
areas, these pressures are minimized and as a consequence there still
persists an atmosphere of relaxed trust.

While some rural communes feel that they are attracting too many visitors, most of them are willing to share with like-minded people, and they remain open to new members as long as there is room. Transition people in cities or on campuses are usually in touch with one or another rural group and usually spend some time each summer staying in one or several communes.

The outstanding form of rural community — mainly because of its accessibility and its appeal to middle-class and pre-counter-cultural groups — is the growth center. There are roughly a hundred of these throughout the country, available for a fee to outsiders. Such centers are staffed by residents, who stay for about a year, whose prior experiences enable them to create growth experiences for the paying customers. But these staff members use the centers primarily for their own growth and practice their disciplines of personal growth at all times; they see their services mainly as a means of assuring the communities' economic survival.

Kantor (1970) sees such growth centers as the most stable and enduring model of a utopian community and finds that they have many characteristics in common with nineteenth-century Utopian ventures:

> Growth-and-learning communities, in short, tend to create family-like feeling, to use mutual criticism, to provide a strong sense of participation and responsibility, to affirm their bonds through ritual, to organize work communally, to have stringent entrance requirements, and to develop strong values symbolized by charismatic leaders. [P.78]

Tart and Creighton (1966), describe Bridge Mountain Community, a growth center almost twelve years old, which was the model for Esalen. They discuss many methods that its members use for breaking free of the old culture. They include planned experience of new patterns, group sharing and support for change, exploring new patterns of body movement, fantasy, sexuality, and consciousness. The philosophy of the community includes various assumptions:

> We do not discover our answers in life, we create them.
> The Community affirms that every man can realize his own authority in life. That the natural organism contains the ability to know its needs and the creativity to meet them.
> We stress the affirmation and growth of the individual through the group.
> Mutual interaction is characterized by warmth, openness, and an almost total lack of social roles ... informality, empathy, acceptance of the worth of others, shared meals, work and recreation.
> The spirit of these (daily) meetings is that of seeking optimal resolution of whatever problems arise. This is not the same thing as the spirit of compromise, where everyone loses something, nor of one person winning at the expense of others, but rather a genuine attempt to understand the positions of others,

> and the real needs they represent, as well as fully understanding
> one's own needs and how they determine one's position. [pp. 55–
> 56, 58]

Residents and paying guests share in the daily program of necessary
work, relaxation movements, working in various media to liberate
creative potentials. There are music and movement programs, sensory
programs, myth programs, improvised acting program, and a program
for young children stressing the same basic themes.

This center has thought through its relationship to the old culture
and sees itself as a transitional state and oasis for those who must deal
with the old culture more intimately:

> While the Bridge Mountain Community does not share many of
> the goals, values, and mores of contemporary society, it does
> not advocate an escape from society through avoidance of con-
> tact with it, but rather maintains that as the individual begins to
> realize his own potentialities more completely, he is able to
> move in the society or in the Community with equal ease. At
> this point in his growth the choice not to accept the values of
> society is not negative resistance to society but a positive affir-
> mation of values which he chooses, having the freedom to move
> in many new directions.
>
> The role of guests in bring aspects of society into the Com-
> munity has been of great value . . . . Increasingly other residents
> are moving out into society more with a sense that they can give
> without having to react to the negative aspects of society . . . .
>
> On the other hand, the response of different elements of so-
> ciety to the Community has been varied and uneven . . . . We do
> not suffer unduly from the attacks of an active opposition [P. 61].

People have come to this community from political work, and those who
return to the cities from this center attempt to express their newly
heightened awareness of the existing culture through productive work
toward its reform and rejuvenation.

Urban transitional communities. Because urban communities spend a
good deal of time dealing with the outside community, they are less en-
closed and total than rural settlements. They include small businesses
— food and art cooperatives; service groups, such as hotlines, free
clinics, legal help, and runaway shelters; educational groups, usually
structured around a university program political and organizing collec-
tives; and finally the complete urban counter-community, such as Project One in San Francisco. Each of these represents an attempt to create
an area of free space where the transitional group can learn and grow
in new ways, while also dealing meaningfully with an outside issue or
problem caused by social oppression or lack of a crucial service.

Each group very clearly relates to a need, which must be satisfied
in a new way according to the new values of the counter-culture. Food

coops grew up to deal with the new interest in health foods or with a
need for lower prices. Service groups came into being to deal with the
stresses and strains on young people who were faced with competing sets
of priorities and demands and who sensed that traditional helpers, such
as psychiatrists, were not working in their clients interests or were
simply inefficient. Free universities and, subsequently, smaller experiments (often part of a regular college program) grew out of the recognition that traditional education was structured in such a way to frustrate most creative learning, while the environment was increasingly
demanding creative solutions to the problems of simply living. Each
program represents an attempt at the redefinition of a need and the
structure of appropriate response.

These experiments represent an entirely different approach to organizational development than that used by reform movements within
institutions. Traditional innovation saw the need for change only in the
way the service was provided. For example, when faced with irrelevance, psychiatrists began seeing families and going out in the community; but traditional innovation rarely questions the ways in which the
structure of the organization, and the personal values of the members of
the system, relate directly to the way they treat the people they serve.
The hierarchy of the mental hospital is reflected in the treatment of
patients, who are the lowest, oppressed class. Only a redefinition of the
class relationships can make a difference in how clients' needs are met
by a service group. Transitional communities begin by understanding
that everything is relevant to the service, and they therefore throw open
the whole question of structure and relationships. Such groups are almost universally small enough to permit face-to-face communal decision-
making, where all the participants share in creating a structure that relates directly and flows out of the nature of the task.

An example comes from Robert Lefcourt (1971) of the New York Law
Commune. This group was engaged in the traditional and time-consum-
ing task of defending clients whose cases were political in nature — chief
among these the New York case of the Panther 13 (who were acquitted).
The group's success may be due both to its new structure and its traditional
competence. These law associates are committed to being up-front with
issues created by their treatment of each other, which are political in
that they maintain the social structure. They have had to redefine roles
so that such traditionally subservient positions as secretary or woman
lawyer were no longer excluded from direct influence on decisions and
responsible tasks, and they have created new roles for political aspects
of their work, such as organizing law students, writing, and working
with groups around recognizing and capitalizing on their legal rights.

Lefcourt's description of meetings is more reminiscent of personal
growth or consciousness-changing groups than of a business meeting
in a law firm. The experience of working there would probably be closer
to Bridge Mountain than to a traditional firm. He writes:

As frustrating and bitter as some of the Commune meetings have

been, they are the one place where the drama and boredom of
human relationships are played out unsparingly. These are not
"group encounters." They are work sessions involving people engaged in the politics of transformation — both of decadent institutions like the legal profession, and of unequal roles such as
those that exist between men and women, professional and worker.

In fact, the issues of encounter groups are crucial to the working of a
counter-institution and to the development of a viable radical response
to political oppression.

   The most ambitious form of counter-community grows in two and a
half acres of space in an old candy factory in downtown San Francisco
and is called Project One. The building was renovated by about 200 young
professionals, trained in post-industrial skills which they feel are
rapidly growing obsolete or self-destructive unless humanized. Inside
Project One space is shared and governed cooperatively by community
meetings. Groups include the Women's Center, the Medical Committee
on Human Rights, a switchboard, two free schools, an education-
switchboard-exchange community, a counseling center, media and crafts
coops, political groups, a computer group, a Body Room, and an alter-
nate-employment service. Many people live there, and communal meals,
the sharing of tasks and needs, and fluid boundaries break down distinctions between groups, work, living, and play.

   Jud Jerome (1970), a radical educator who visited Project One after
much experience with educational reform, wrote:

> The economy of the place, once you catch on, is simple. In every
> way possible the cash nexus has been replaced with an energy
> nexus. People talk about "energy ripoffs" as for example, when
> someone dominates a meeting with an ego trip. . . . Moral force
> pervades every meeting, every encounter; but one shouldn't get
> the impression that it is a negative or oppressive force. The
> point is replacement of one kind of gratification (profit) by anoth-
> er (love) . . . . The principle is what Robert Theobold has called
> "sapiential authority." One's ability to command derives exactly
> from his knowledge of how to do — and extends no further I
> was interested in the community meeting to watch the members
> who were older and more knowledgeable (some in their early or
> mid-forties) back off from leadership functions. In order to
> maintain their usefulness and authority as accountants or lawyers
> or architects, it was important that they withhold, to some ex-
> tent, their participation in areas in which their authority as a
> person did not exceed that of others present. [P.2]

Jerome writes of the process in a community meeting, and how people
struggle with issues of purpose and goals, on the pressure of deciding
whether to expel someone who is a confessed informer:

> Earlier a member whose mental disturbance had made him

violent had been sent to an institution — and a number of people
in the community felt that that was the wrong response. To fall
back on institutions, particularly those of the straight world,
represents a failure of community. The question arises whether
the community itself does not have, or should not have, the
therapeutic power to help people with problems, no matter how
severe. (For example, it is impossible to imagine this community calling on the police or FBI for help under any circumstances.)
[P.6]

Such projects are more stable and solve more basic issues than do
many of the more visible or highly publicized aspects of the new culture.
The activities represent the convergence of a new class of young people,
who respond to the increasing threat and irrationality of the world around
them by constructing new contexts, restructuring consciousness, and
recreating relationships which go beyond some of the paradoxes in the
old culture. As they are adaptive, as they deal with more aspects of our
environment and technology, as they relax and liberate people from repressive structures, they will survive.

It should be apparent that the present changes, while remarkable in
their diversity and their multifaceted, multileveled grasp of issues and
problems, represent a movement unified in intent. The people in one
project identify with those in other groups as their brothers and sisters,
as part of their nation. While there is friction and vacillation in their
support of each other, pain in the growth process each person undergoes,
and casualties as young people are almost literally torn apart by the
conflicts between new and old priorities, the outcome is more and more
positive. It is now not simply a hollow and self-defeating rebellion
against old structures, but a movement toward integrating technology,
psychology, and personal values into a new society.

Chapter 4

THE REPRESSION AND SUPPORT OF PSYCHEDELIC EXPERIENCE

Basic Issues

A 1972 Gallup Poll reports that 20 percent of the nation's college students have tried psychedelic drugs — an increase of 1800 percent in the past four years — at a time when the government has halted most research on the uses of these drugs as too dangerous and spends millions of dollars to control their use. In the controversy that has lasted a decade, the powerful interests which have led to these policies effectively counter the demands of well over a million young people to use these drugs. The debate concerns the usefulness and validity of the experiences reported with these drugs and whether American society will allow change in the area of personal experience. Psychedelic drugs are powerful and unpredictable, and sometimes result in difficulties which need medical or crisis intervention. Help must be offered within the value context of the drug user if the helper is not to run the risk of reflecting the prejudices and fears of current drug policies, an attitude which is plainly against the interests of those who use the drugs. The nature of this conflict of interests is the theme of this chapter.

Willis Harman, an engineering professor turned psychedelic researcher (and now turned futurecaster), clearly defined the gap between policy and reality as early as 1963:

> The consciousness-expanding drugs LSD and psilocybin have been hailed, in some quarters at least, as having fantastic potentialities for aiding man to know himself, for helping him release his creative powers, for contributing toward reducing his alienation from himself and his fellow man and toward the discovery and creation of meaning in his life. Yet LSD was recently banned in Canada, along with thalidomide, as a "dangerous drug," and in general it is harder to get than heroin or cyanide... Dr. Sidney Cohen, who has made what are no doubt the most detailed studies of adverse reactions to LSD, recently summarized his findings in the statement,"Considering the enormous scope of the psychic responses it induces, LSD is an astonishingly safe drug." Physiologically, it is less dangerous than aspirin or penicillin, and certainly far less deleterious than alcohol or tobacco. Yet

a recent editorial in the psychiatric organ of the AMA warns that
"greater sickness and even death is in store ... unless controls
are developed against the unwise use of LSD," and expresses
alarm that the public has heard of the claimed benefits from LSD
and "is looking for psychiatrists who specialize in its administration." [P.5]

In 1966 Harman's center at Stanford University, which was engaged in
detailed studies of therapy and creativity with LSD which initially showed
highly promising results, had its license to use LSD terminated along
with all but two other research centers.

Evidently the threat of LSD arouses some powerful defensive reactions in society. While professional judgment is invoked to justify each
step of social policy, the issues raised by psychedelics involve matters
of values and ethics. Against this background, therapists must intervene
with individual users in difficulty. Even these interventions are colored
by the helper's stand on these issues. Someone who considers the experience of psychedelics as potentially useful helps out in a different
way than someone who believes the effects to be harmful and aims only
at stopping them. Crisis intervention therefore depends on an understanding of the nature of psychedelics and the controversy surrounding
their use.

The sudden shift of young people from alcohol to marijuana (a mild
psychedelic), LSD, mescaline, peyote, psilocybin and other psychedelics
can only be explained by the drugs' unique nature. Since young people
value these drugs enough to risk criminal penalties and poisonous im-
purities, their effects must be different or better than that of alcohol.
Drug policies try to account for the shift with simplistic theories of
peer-group pressure and rebellion, excluding the possibility that use of
psychedelics may in some ways represent positive and useful activity.

Drug use is a form of the search to change the self and to form new
kinds of relationships with oneself, with others, and with society. The
growing use of psychedelics would be explained if experiences with these
drugs help young people to reach their goals. The best way to explain the
shift from alcohol to psychedelics by a large number of intelligent and
aware young people is that drug use helped them to get where they wanted
to go. Psychedelics seem to catalyze experiences which are at times
quite valuable and useful; these are not peculiar to the drug but are
characteristic of a more general class of growth experiences.

Psychedelics and Personal Change

Psychedelic use by young people has powerful positive and negative
effects. Since such experimentation is done without the safeguards and
controls of research settings, it can also be expected that dangers which
are avoided in clinical situations will crop up in nonsanctioned use. But
to the extent that use is informed by the conditions for safe and proper
experiences, the results can also be highly positive. The frequency of
positive reports by young people, and the similarity in accounts of psychedelic therapy with certain aspects of the youth culture, suggest that

positive results of psychedelic use are causes as well as results of the development of a new culture by youth.

I am presently part of a research team* collecting life histories from young psychedelic users in five parts of the country. Two-hour interviews focus on their experiences with drugs, how each came to use them, and the ways that drug use affected the users' relations to themselves, family, friends, lovers, school, society, and basic values. The accounts throw much doubt on the hysterical and negative stories which dot medical journals and media outlets. With full knowledge of the risks, young people choose to use psychedelics for the same reasons that researchers study them. They rarely seem disappointed. Further, they rarely use psychedelics more often than weekly during an initial stage of not more than a few months, and then taper off to either no use or more likely, use once every few months. Temperance and moderation are the rule because the drugs are regarded as learning tools, not as escapist fare or pleasure drugs, and they are treated with great respect. Ironically, youthful psychedelic users exhibit the good judgment, awareness of both sides of the issue, utilization of real data and others' experiences, reflection on the experience, and desire for corroboration and exchange that are the earmarks of the scientific method, completely lacking in some of the more professional accounts and opinions on drug use.

Our 150 respondents represent a cross section of youth by age, present drug use (present or past users) and positive and negative effects (many have been hospitalized or arrested because of drug use, and almost all report bad trips). Most of them assess their experiences with psychedelics as positive, and they detail specific stages of learning and growth through them. They see such changes as leading in the direction of their personal goals, and they assess their values as different from the dominant culture and shared with other young people around them. They report great pain and struggle in their attempts to change, and they believe that misuse or overuse of psychedelics can be disastrous. They respond positively to marijuana and hashish, which they use frequently, and to the stronger psychedelics, which are used less often; they associate them with personality and value changes. Alcohol, amphetamines, barbiturates, and tranquillizers are used by some of them for more traditional results, such as tension release, avoidance of negative feelings, and relaxation; they are mentioned as being quite different from psychedelics.

The following anecdotes are an almost random sample of the literally thousands which document the richness, variety, and creativity that attend use of psychedelics by young people. The positive experiences and the people who have grown greatly outnumber the few who use drugs self-destructively. Much of our data also suggests that self-destructive drug use is generally an isolated episode, a stage of growth which leads

* Contract Number HEW-OS-72-12, "A Field Study of Drug Use and the Youth Culture." Available from the Office of Field Evaluation, U.S. Dept. HEW.

to so much pain that it eventually transcends itself, usually to a level of greater insight and more productive use of energies. There is a great deal of accumulated learning among young people concerning themselves, personal change, and change experiences such as drugs and new communities, but its underground nature has kept this data from most professional circles.

People turn to psychedelics for several reasons:

1. To get into the here and now. This goal is shared by sensitivity groups and Gestalt therapy. It is considered a corrective to the cognitive, detached, patterned way in which people are taught to deal with the world. The process is usually connected with a discovery of the body and sensual and sensory pleasures. Patterns break down, and free flowing consciousness dazzles with creative new patterns.

2. To see something real, vivid, novel, exciting. The major educational experience reported by young people is boredom and sensory deprivation. They feel a need to blast themselves into experience, to saturate themselves with something new, as compensation. This can be an end in itself, or it can be a spur to new kinds of experiencing and activity.

3. To explore consciousness and the inner self. This is the journey associated with psychoanalysis, madness, and artistic creation. The change is that archetypal and repressed experience is experienced in fantasy and lived through, and eventually loses its fearsomeness. Jung, Laing(1967) and Norman O. Brown (1966) are much better guides on this trip than Freud. Along with a growing interest in rituals, other cultures, and extraordinary states of consciousness, there is a renewed or more vivid experience of feelings and a sensitivity to the ambivalence characteristic of all relationships.

4. To end anxiety and boundaries between people and parts of the self. The goal is to achieve unity and to end alienation induced by the culture. Communities and relationships are organic wholes and, being natural, are not to be feared. The fear and anxiety which accompany this trip are a culturally determined defense which can be systematically reduced as wholeness is achieved.

5. To achieve transcendence, satori, peak experience. The search for higher states of consciousness usually starts with psychedelics but eventually leads to one of the older traditional religious disciplines, such as meditation, Tai Chi, or yoga. The goal is to get high and to maintain the state, which cannot be done for long with drugs.

Psychedelics seem useful as part of a process of conscious growth which extends to the time before and after the trip. One girl tells of her most significant psychedelic experience:

> One that was by myself. I don't think consciously of working on something when I trip, but that one time I did, and that was right after I had moved out from living with A. I went to the beach. I

remember feeling alone at first, but then it was really good. I like
to be out in nature. That one time was the only time I ever did it
specifically to work on something. I find that things usually work
out in my head anyway, but I don't do it deliberately. I do it in the
process of watching an ant. I trip to play and for a kind of spiritual enlightenment, and as a vacation kind of thing. With drugs,
it is a kind of religious experience out in the woods to have a
feeling of oneness, to feel a part of life and life processes. It
doesn't seem supernatural. It's just natural and awesome. Being
humbled. I don't think that consciously about it, but it has something to do with putting things in perspective. It's standing back
from all that and realizing that our world's not going to fall apart
if you don't get to the grocery store today. You can have that
experience just by getting away and taking a vacation, but drugs
seem to heighten that for me.

Another girl reports a lack of learning and change from scores of
experiences with many drugs, until:

I never conceptualized any of my drug use until last year. The
first one which we really planned was with B. We got real close
and played music, and then we went to a plastic shopping center
and realized that it was just that, a plastic bourgeois shopping
center. I reached a whole new level. I was coming from thinking
of things in a linear and culturally determined fashion to a much
more intuitive way. I realized that I didn't have to think all the
time and read. I could rely on my intuition. I had gotten into a
pattern or trap, and the acid destroyed me so I could build up
things again.

That too is a stage, and also unstable. The same girl later returns to the
school she had left:

I had started an intentional process to de-intellectualize myself,
but I got caught in all kinds of clichés and couldn't express myself articulately, so I'm back in school and getting my mind to
work again.

Young people have a tremendous psychological sophistication, stemming largely from reading combined with their familiarity with inner
experience. When a bad experience occurs, the person often knows himself well enough to work on correcting it, so that the next experience will
be better. The concepts of therapeutic working through are in everyday
use among young people:

I first had mescaline in a country gathering. It wasn't a great
trip. My girl friend and I dropped, and all this stuff we'd been
repressing came out. My visual image of it was this violent
stranglehold on each other, and we couldn't let go, we were frozen
there. Getting stoned made the whole thing come out in high relief. It's now my conviction that either it's a mistake to do

psychedelics wanting something, or one has to be very careful
about how one sets one's mind to want something. Or else what
the trip is about is the thing that you want tortures you.

     After I started doing psychedelics I was really relentless
about trying to make it work. My first good trip happened when
I dropped mescaline in the airport. It was like every trip before
had been a resistance which wasn't going with the flow. And then
I had this amazing experience while I was eating breakfast of
hearing this beautiful music. At first I thought it was coming
from the headset, but it was coming out of my head. It was taking
the sounds of the engine and transforming them into a musical
score. And then I found that I could transform the music, high-
lighting the brass section, etcetera. And it really made me ecstatic, a bona fide ecstatic experience! And then I looked out the
window and noticed the earth was breathing. That had a profound
effect on me. I've since been empowered by the practice of
"facing things." I guess I learned that I had this emotional body
I had to liberate, and the only way to liberate it was by facing
reality. Drugs played a big part by putting me in touch with ecstasy. And it was also manifest to me that ecstasy and pain exist
along the same vector of sensation. And if you've got pain stored
up in your body, then the only way to experience ecstasy is to experience it through the pain.

Another subject reports working through a conflict by fantasy:

     It was about that time that I got eaten by this big red mouth. I
     was making love on acid and got eaten. At first it was horrible,
     but then I got eaten and that was that. It felt like some kind of
     symbolic turning point. But drugs were taking the lid off of a
     sexual repression among a whole group of people that I was with
     all the time.

He speaks of drugs as accentuating the sense of communal sharing, and
others report instances of telepathic union of a couple or group. This
young man expressed his discovery of the social basis of mankind through
work in a form of myth-oriented theater troupe.

     On the negative side, the increased sensitivity to others and the en-
vironment also produces heightened perception of fears. Since drug use
is illegal, many subjects report paranoia, and fears of getting caught are
accentuated. To escape this state, and to move toward the union with the
earth and nature which many psychedelic users desire, many people
eventually move to the country for a period of their lives:

     We were all outlaws and the paranoia levels were rampant. But
     most of the time you knew who your friends were because of the
     solidarity of drugs. In the mountains there was less paranoia
     and drugs were different. You could consume less and still stay
     on top of ordinary reality. I went from feeling I had no roots to
     seeing them everywhere and feeling caught in them   Things were

no longer flat to me any more. It gave a dimension to my existence and liberated energy.

Another account is from a middle-aged architect who went through
a period of great change with psychedelics:

> I've never taken them as uppers or downers. I've taken them to
> play, but it always is an experiment because I never know what's
> going to happen. Mostly I take them as an edge, to break patterns.
> I don't ever take them when I don't feel good. A couple of years
> ago I was going through a lot of ambivalence about commitment
> to women, and I lived up here alone for a month. I'd smoke a lot
> of dope and it bummed me all the time. Bummers were being
> afraid of just about everything; machines, hating everything I'd
> designed, hating myself for ever having cut down a tree, being
> afraid of people. I think that dope blasted me out of roles and
> perceptions that were keeping me tied in. It was catalytic, it
> changed motivation, my whole future orientation. All those things
> I used to worry about.

Sometimes people report changes which might be regarded as negative even though they are reported as positive:

> Another thing that has happened is that I am very inarticulate
> most of the time. I am just not able to think and talk in a linear
> way any more. I am not able to make complex plans any more.
> That's right on for me.

Prolonged or frequent use seems to result in negative changes which
are not reported in the research literature. These include confusion,
disorientation, and a general dullness caused by the overstimulation of
the trips. Material which comes up is defended against, and the subject
seems to develop all the defenses to psychedelic experience which are a
characteristic of everyday experience.

At this point the person either chooses to stop using drugs, cut down
drastically, or switch to a more alienating type of drug, such as heroin,
speed, or barbituates. The intensity and vitality of psychedelics soon
fade:

> I thought, hey, wait a minute man, I'm never going to get my shit
> together if I don't stop this for a while. For one thing my memory
> was getting really fucked up. I couldn't remember anything. My
> world was just always on a trip, you know. My life was just one
> long trip, it seemed. I wasn't living in the real world at all. My
> world was all fantasy. I couldn't hold on to anything — everything
> was just slipping through my fingers and I felt that I had to stop
> tripping so much. That whole period of my life is a haze now.

Like many others, this user found a community that would offer the
support she needed, and she began to be more involved with others. She
found that she could explore experience and express herself much better
as a member of a community than through drugs. She now feels that she

understands the door-opening qualities of psychedelics, and she uses
them only infrequently, when she knows she can handle them and has the
time to deal with what comes up.

Peak Experience and Value Change

Some experiences are so profound and impressive that they result in
new orientations toward basic values and in changed relations with others
and the self. Such remarkable and historically rare events are called
religious, mystical, transcendental, or mad and are not typically seen as
having great practical or social significance unless they lead to religious
communities, as with the conversion of St. Paul. Abraham Maslow (1962),
one of the few psychologists to look at healthy rather than pathological
human functioning, reports that such events have much in common with
the aesthetic, oceanic, creative, loving, therapeutic, parental, orgasmic,
athletic, or intellectual experiences during which, his respondents report,
they are most themselves, most in touch with who they are, and most
alive and productive in terms of their basic values. Exceptionally healthy
people report these peak experiences more commonly and frequently than
the norm. Such experiences are

> an episode, or a spurt in which the powers of the person come
> together in a particularly efficient and intensely enjoyable way,
> and in which he is more integrated and less split, more open for
> experience, more idiosyncratic, more perfectly expressive or
> spontaneous, or fully functioning, more creative, more humorous,
> more ego-transcending, more independent of his lower needs,
> etc. He becomes in these episodes more truly himself, more
> perfectly actualizing his potentialities, closer to the core of his
> Being. [P.91]

The cumulative evidence of research is that when psychedelics are
used under carefully supervised conditions, they enormously increase
the probability and frequency of such peak experiences. Wilson Van
Dusen (1961), who has given LSD to chronic alcoholics, reports:

> There is a central human experience which alters all other ex-
> periences ... it is the very heart of human experience. It is the
> center that gives understanding to the whole. It has been called
> Satori in Japanese Zen, moksha in Hinduism, religious enlight-
> enment or cosmic consciousness in the West ... LSD appears to
> facilitate the discovery of this central human experience. [P.11]

Stanislav Grof (1972), a psychoanalyst in Prague, used small
doses of LSD in repeated sessions (up to eighty in all, at weekly inter-
vals) with his most disturbed neurotic and psychotic patients. In data
gathered over a decade of work, he details how psychedelics enormously
increase the range and depth of therapy, while decreasing the time needed
for it, in cases which had not previously responded to any kind of treatment. According to Grof, psychedelics magnify whatever happens to the
person: his perceptions, fears, expectations, and inner feelings. By

placing the person in touch with repressed and primitive material of consciousness, psychedelics can be quite frightening.

Initially many therapists were confused and unsettled by the strange
and novel reactions to this new class of drugs. Unger, one of the few ac-
credited LSD researchers in the United States, reports that this was
particularly true of those who did not themselves use LSD. He points
out that peak experiences could easily be described, and devalued, by
psychoanalysts as "delusionary escapes from unresolved infantile or
Oedipal conflicts." The description of LSD as primarily anxiety or psychosis producing was based on observations not balanced by personal
experiences. Savage and Stolaroff (1965), suggest some reasons why
professionals would resist the usefulness of psychedelics:

> The hallucinogens (more properly called psychedelic agents when
> used to explore new understanding of the mind) open up dimen-
> sions of consciousness with which few therapists are familiar.
> The heightened sensitivity and enhancement of sensory modalities,
> the reliving of events in time and other dimensionless phenomena,
> and the oft-reported profound philosophic and universal experi-
> ences, tend to lie outside the therapists' conceptual frame of
> reference .... Contrary to the belief of many investigators, the
> hallucinogens do not produce experiences but inhibit repressive
> mechanisms that ordinarily allow subjects to explore the con-
> tents of their own minds. [P.218]

The extent and direction of the changes in patients reported by Grof
go far beyond the outcome of traditional therapeutic procedures, and
thus are another source of the uneasiness which has accompanied reports of psychedelic research. A few of the outcomes he mentions are:

> The patients who have reported deep experiences of melted ec-
> stacy in these advanced sessions showed very specific changes
> in perception of themselves and the world, in their behavior and
> their hierarchy of values. As a rule, psychopathological symp-
> toms were greatly reduced — depression dissolved, anxiety and
> tension disappeared, guilt feelings were lifted. Deep feelings of
> relaxation, serenity, tranquility and inner peace seemed to be the
> rule .... The self image was greatly improved and an en-
> hanced feeling of health and smooth physiological functioning
> was very common .... They became more understanding, more
> empathetic and loving toward their fellowman and perceived the
> world as a fascinating and basically friendly place .... The
> subjects were discovering meaning and beauty in ordinary things
> of their everyday environment .... There was a more definite
> need for personal freedom and the antiauthoritarian tendencies
> were definitely increased. The previously all-important values
> seemed trivial (striving for power, status, money, fame, etc.)
> and a deep wisdom was discovered in simplicity of life .... These
> true values (sense of beauty, love, justice, etc.) were accepted
> readily and joyfully as part of the universal order rather than

because of fear of punishment. There seems to be a striking
parallel here with Maslow's findings in people who had spontaneous peak experiences. Many of the mentioned attitudes can be
found in an extreme form in the hippie movement, sometimes
exaggerated to the point of caricature.

Grof's work suggests some fascinating connections. LSD therapy
has produced results in mental patients in Prague which correspond
almost precisely to Maslow's values of Being (which he considers basic,
natural, human, and good as reported by healthy, fully functioning people),
and to the values of hippies and other young people. Grof's results could
not have been produced as a consequence of his expectation, since he
only learned of Maslow, Jung, and other depth psychologists when his
traditional psychoanalytic formulations could no longer account for what
he was seeing. Now that he is director of one of the two extant psychedelic therapy centers in the United States, he ironically works under
much greater restrictions than he faced in Prague.

There have been over a thousand studies of supervised use of psychedelics, most of which suggest positive effects following its use. The
evidence of research teams all over the world is that LSD not only helps
alleviate traditional symptoms, but also tends to lead to a change in
values and goals. It can effect a total personality reorganization, even
in a single dose. Studies of single massive doses with alcoholics, terminal cancer patients, and neurotics have all shown positive results
after other interventions had proven ineffective or, in the case of cancer
patients, nonexistent. There is clearly a tremendous disparity between
the research results and government accounts claiming lack of data and
ascribing dangerous consequences to supervised psychedelic use.

Society's Defense Against Psychedelic Learning

Evidence of the relative safety and potential good of psychedelics
has been presented from research and the experience of young people.
Why has society reacted so negatively? Simplistic reactions use the
messianic claims and proselytizing of such figures as Timothy Leary
and the extreme cases of supposed "bad trips" and even deaths (which
are largely unrecorded in medical literature) as scapegoats to justify
repressive policies against all use. Since there is no similar reaction
to the thousands of alcohol-caused body deteriorations, violent incidents,
and auto accidents, it is wise to consider alternate explanations for the
powerful negative reaction.

There is evidence that psychedelics greatly increase the frequency
and likelihood of peak experiences which are not only "self-validating,
self-justifying moments which carry their own intrinsic value with them"
(Maslow), but seem to have long-lasting and therapeutic effects and
facilitate personality and value change. Young people use psychedelics
to explore themselves and their world. Maslow points out that those
having frequent peak experiences have different priorities in the basic
values of life. This value system, which is similar to Buddhist and
Eastern philosophy as well as the youth counter-culture, conflicts

with the values of the dominant culture and leads to the backlash directed at young people and their use of psychedelics.

The dominant culture devalues and avoids exploration of inner experience, concentrating on mastery of the external world and control over the self. The dimensions of the conflict are old and well traveled, and the confrontation between culture and the counter-culture is only the most recent manifestation. Today's dominant culture has Freud on its side, since he maintained that civilization is a precarious balance in which creative and ordering forces of the ego must overcome the aggressive and self-destructive forces of the id. Further support comes from Hobbes and Locke, who located the safety of society in contracts which people enter for mutual protection and who saw man as needing rulers and laws to maintain control over his destructive inner self.

The opposite view is that man is naturally in harmony with nature and himself and has nothing to fear from the natural impulses, death, and disorder. This view, which is the cornerstone of Eastern thought, has been formulated in the West by Maslow, Jung, Hesse, Laing, Rousseau, and Plato in his later dialogues.

One view holds that man should strive for greater control over himself and his inner experience, as personified by the order, rigidity, secrecy, drabness, and unresponsiveness of the Nixon administration. The other view maintains that inner experience should flow naturally and should be expressed as unity with nature and that man can thus attain higher ranges of Being and consciousness. Each theory has masses of evidence to support its claims, and the adoption of one or the other seems to be a matter of personal and cultural temperament. The use of psychedelics evidently leads to conversions from the predominant to the alternative viewpoint, thus proving potentially subversive.

Currently great strains are placed on the dominant system of rigid control, which seems on the verge of demonstrating its alienation from nature by destroying it. Advocates of tighter controls aim at separating people even further from experience and natural values. This attempt leads to a self-defeating spiral. Anxiety increases as man is evermore deeply conflicted, and the anxiety results from the gap between man and his inner experience. Psychedelics threaten members of the dominant culture because their fear of themselves, based on their distance from themselves, leads to the fantasy that drugs will release something awful inherent in the soul. Youthful drug users accentuate this fear by their sensitivity to the potential redemptive powers of their experience. They want people to get in touch with basic fears, so that they will recognize their illusory nature and be less destructive. Opponents of this urge cannot see past the implied threat to any potential gains, so that the claims for psychedelics are heard as messianic nonsense. The vehemence and irrationality of the public response can only be explained on the basis of people's fears about themselves.

The mechanisms whereby a culture evades feelings by projecting the cause on others are documented by Kai Erikson (1966 in a study of religious persecution), Thomas Szasz (1970, extending the study of religious persecution to current practices in the treatment of mental illness), and R.D. Laing (1967, 1971, with an approach centering on the objects of these mechanisms). The process extends into a whole society the individual mechanism of psychological projection. When someone encounters in another a feeling or action that he denies or avoids in himself, he experiences embarrassment, discomfort, or anger. In reaction, he denies the validity of such behavior; in reality his sensation is one of ambivalence — part fears the loss of control such behavior would imply within his own value system, and the fear convinces him that the only possible outcome of the action or feeling would be one of violence and damage.

When such reactions are shared throughout a culture, the form of behavior that provokes them is labeled deviant and becomes hedged about with restrictions and enforceable prohibitions. Because deviance calls into question the shared values of a culture, it must be discouraged in order to maintain societal defenses. Szasz has noted that the treatment of homosexuals as sick or criminal beings is a mechanism for dealing with the culture's repressed homosexual feelings; by confining helpless offenders in prisons or mental hospitals, the culture maintains its defenses against releasing such feelings into the society at large.

Less dramatically, the cultural fear of unleashing uncontrollable forces of violence is manifested throughout the educational establishment by a system of rigid controls: regimented classes, strong discipline, and control of free movement (hall passes); that these values are shared throughout the society is interestingly demonstrated by the fact that parents frequently exhort school personnel to impose yet stricter discipline on their children!

Yet when this same fear takes the form of feeling that vague others are out to destroy one, it is labeled paranoia. Fears must have culturally sanctioned objects — the Russians perhaps, or drug pushers. Fear leads to social control, whether or not this fear has a real basis in the behavior of the other. Laing (1971) documents many aspects of mutual projection and the confusing tangle that can result from acting on them. The argument "If drugs are legalized, people will be stoned all the time, and all sorts of horrors will result" is based on fantasy fears. There is no reason to suppose that legalizing an action in which millions are already engaged will result in any sort of increase; certainly it can cause nothing worse than the self-destructiveness of drug users' distrust of each other and fear of getting caught. The crucial issue for sensible social policies is the decision whether deviant behavior causes actual harm to others. Punishment for lateness to class and for dropping acid are similar in that they protect society, not from harm, but from something it might wish to do.

This mechanism is also common in mental hospitals, where people whose actions do not make sense are sent on the assumption that they are really asking for help. Help is offered in the form of aids to control — locking up the mad person, administering electric shocks and drugs to calm him down, and trying to convince him through verbal therapy to

to act differently. Only such heretical therapists as Laing — who understand that madness is also within themselves — look within the reality of
the mad person to learn how he makes sense of the world. Projection of
fears also operates when therapists attempt to stop "bad trips" merely
because the person seems highly emotional, explicably involved or upset.
The societal response is to stop him, to control him with drugs, because
it is immediately assumed that his goal is to terminate the experience.
From the previous discussion, it follows that the person will more probably want to continue the trip with the aid of someone whose interest is
not control.

The dominant culture prefers drugs which either do not affect experience, such as tobacco, or those which cut off the user from feelings
and tension, such as tranquillizers and alcohol. The pressure of living
creates a need to avoid the intensity of built-up negative feelings. In
work and school relations the standard belief is that feelings are not relevant and are counter-productive if not kept under control. The poker face
is a positive value; one does not show pain, anger, sadness, and above all,
fear.

The risks that are encouraged reveal still more about the culture's
orientation to inner experience. The dangers of a flight to the moon —
which call for steel-hard, emotionless, automatons able to keep cool and
to calculate under great pressure, skilled in all manner of control technology — create its heroes. The risk of injury in a football game, which
is almost certain in a scholastic career and usually permanent, is sanctioned and applauded, because it models toughness and coolness under
pressure. The risks which are sanctioned by the creation audiences to
watch and applaud them define the skills valued by the dominant culture
— control, technology, competition, exploitation, power, strength, and
lack of emotion. All feelings other than well-channeled anger at the other
team, the enemy, are considered harmful. The model that has been internalized to deal with all conflicts is one of working together to overcome a common enemy. It might be better to devise games in which at
least part of the enemy is within. Since in reality we are not all good,
and the enemy is not really all bad, win-lose strategies are self-defeating — as our foreign policy has continually shown.

With such an orientation it is easy to see why no value attaches to the
possible gain of self-knowledge through psychedelics when balanced against
the risks of bad feelings and unplesantness. Thousands die from alcohol,
yet LSD is feared. Alcohol seems socially useful because it releases violence while it tranquillizes other feelings, such as closeness to others,
leading to the preferred stance for our culture. When faced with the
difficulty of proving harm to others, policy-makers end up having to
justify their prohibition of psychedelics on the grounds of the user's
possible harm to himself. Such logic could lead to a prohibition of sex
for causing neurosis. By concerning itself with the user — who is jailed
or put in the hospital — society avoids its mixed feelings — fear mingled
with desire — about being seduced by drugs. Worry about chromosomal
damage (decisively disproven), psychosis, falling out of windows (a real

danger, but one which can be prevented by other means) — all are mobilized to support current policies.

The danger of possible psychosis must be clarified further. Originally, the LSD experience was classified as a model psychosis, and therapists were urged to try to experience madness. More recent studies have shown that there are many similarities in language construction and involvement in fantasy-oriented behavior at a symbolic level, particularly when there is an expectation of becoming psychotic; but on other levels the experiences are opposite. For example, genuine psychosis is rarely experienced as pleasant and equally rarely leads to spontaneous personality alteration or growth. Rather psychosis stems from a long-standing inevalidation of the self as a person, so that the sense of self and reaction to ego loss in the two modes are quite different. Psychosis is a defensive strategy against the experience of pain in relation to others, while psychedelic experience is often a de-structuring of defenses. Psychotic episodes have occurred after the use of psychedelics, but in each documented case there were clear pre-psychotic personality features and the psychedelic drug may have precipitated the episode. Previous stability, however, makes such breakdowns highly amenable to even traditional treatments. It has also been suggested that unstable people seem to be attracted to psychedelics, and that therefore statistics on freak-outs reflect this preference rather than the action of the drug. Grof (in press) and Cohen (1960), among others, claim that psychedelics are useful in helping people to recover from breakdowns. Psychedelic therapists do not fear such breaks because they see them as treatable and as positive steps in a natural restructuring of consciousness.

Opposition to psychedelics leads to social policies which confuse moral with medical issues in a mystification of judgments with medical justification. Morally, the issue is whether people are to be free to ingest whatever drugs they choose. American norms and laws take the affirmative for only some drugs with some limits. Social and medical experience is then considered to regulate drug use under conditions which can harm others, such as drunken driving. The traditional, conservative, civil-libertarian, strict-constructionist view, shared by most young people whether or not they use drugs, is that limits should only be set according to the need to protect others.

The rising power of psychiatry raised a further consideration which is the source of a current controversy concerning psychedelics. The moral issue is whether the law should determine — presumably by relying on objective scientific evidence — what is good for the individual and should enforce that decision. Increasingly the conflict of interests and values that such judgments might entail is ignored. Involuntary hospitalization, criminal penalties or enforced treatment for addicts (independently of whatever crimes they may have committed), and the legal ban on cigarette commercials on TV, are all areas where society tries to protect its citizens from themselves; all are ineffective. More importantly, the first two can happen against the will of the individual involved, and involuntary hospitalization may not even require due process.

Medical authorities justify prohibition on the grounds of potential harm to the user. He is defined as being ill and requiring treatment merely because of his use of drugs. Treatment aims at pursuading the patient to stop using illegal drugs, usually in exchange for prescribed ones. This policy in effect substitutes for one group's preferred drugs — psychedelics or heroin — socially acceptable drugs of proven harmfulness, such as tranquillizers, methadone, alcohol and tobacco. Among young people, the result of this policy has usually been that they use both kinds of drugs simultaneously, with nobody profiting except the policy-makers, who stand to gain money and prestige. Because they utilize the coercive methods of the dominant culture and refuse to recognize the existence of a conflict of values, current drug policies not only fail to pursuade young people to cut down on drug use, but also fail to reach and help the obvious casualties of drug use among young people. All conflicts have been resolved in favor of the dominant culture, without so much as a hearing to entertain the interests of young drug users.

Crisis Intervention with "Bad Trips"

The effects of a psychedelic, note Savage and Stolaroff,

> will depend on a) the mental content, the subject's individual personality, conditioning, attitudes, values and beliefs; b) his preparation for the experience, which determines in part how he will use the opportunity; and c) his environment during the experience, which very appreciably affects how he will deal with the material he touches on and the opportunities afforded. Most investigators now agree that preparation and setting profoundly affect the subject's experience, and the presence of supportive, understanding, accepting companions is essential to a comfortable and rewarding session.

Distrust of the experience, lack of a guide, or anxiety induced by companions or a setting which triggers negative feelings are aspects of the set and setting which can produce the intense anxiety which is called a "bad trip." Essentially intervention must aim at helping the person back to a space where the fear is manageable and the person can deal with and integrate the experience afterward without constructing stronger defenses against the revelations released by the trip.

The behavior of a tripper is often highly emotional, exhibiting shifts of mood and sudden bursts of energy which can be strange and fearsome to someone not used to such activity. Humphrey Osmond, the researcher who coined the term "psychedelic," propounded the controversial Golden Rule, which states that anyone dealing with psychedelics should start with himself. Unger points out that researchers who overestimated the harmfulness of the psychic reaction to psychedelics were invariably those who had not tried the drug themselves. He suggests that the anxiety shown by their subjects may have been induced by their similar feelings. Projection of fears operates when therapists label trips "bad" even though they may lead to rewarding, growth-producing personal experiences.

The inexperience and negative setting of most hospitals clearly contributes to the bad tripping experiences which young people report in that environment. Savage and Stolaroff suggest:

> By denying these new dimensions of consciousness, or attempting to restrict the experience to his own theoretical framework, the therapist can produce great conflict in the subject, and cause him to reject important parts of the experience or force him into delusional solutions.

Trips are commonly judged adversely if the tripper was huddled in a corner, crying, screaming, or talking to a nonexistent person. "Bad" connotes the discharge of feelings out of context, which threatens some therapists.

Psychedelic therapists agree that the harmful effects of a trip are negligable if the drug is used in a comfortable setting, with a guide the user knows and trusts, who has experience both with the drug and as a helper. Sidney Cohen, former drug abuse director of the National Institute of Mental Health, found almost no record of permanent harm in a study of 25,000 supervised trips (1960). Grof claims that none of the thousands of trips he has guided — many with the sickest possible people — has led to harm. When a patient had a particularly frightening experience, Grof always found it to be due to unconscious material struggling for recognition. His procedure was to ask the patient to trip again as soon as possible, to face the fear rather than avoid it. Blewett (1969) writes that he gave patients additional psychedelics when they encountered frightening material, thus facilitating the passage of the material into consciousness.

Medical practice tends to devalue the possibilities and to reduce the question of bad trips to one of alleviation of symptoms. This trend is shown in one of the few articles on the subject, by Drs. Taylor, Maurer, and Tinklenberg (1970). A month earlier Pahnke, Kurland, Unger, Savage, and Grof (the only legally approved psychedelic therapy team in the United States) had written about their work. They detailed the special characteristics of LSD, the wide range of possible experiences — psychotic, cognitive, aesthetic, psychodynamic, and mystical — and the possibilities of LSD use for growth and personality change. Evidently without benefit of this earlier article, Taylor and his coworkers define the psychedelic experience only as "producing perceptual and cognitive distortions which, in the majority of instances, are experienced by an individual as strange but tolerable, if not pleasant or even exhilarating."

The article betrays all the prejudices of the dominant culture. The therapeutic goal is managing the bad trip, which is described as "a state of unease, varying from mild apprehension to panic," the exact cause of which is unknown (to the authors, at least). They seek to stop this negative experience, to protect the tripper from himself and others — they apply the standard medical caveat. They suggest two methods — the preferred one of talking the tripper down and sedation. By condoning this second method, the authors betray their total lack of psychological consideration. Therapeutically, sedation of a tripper amounts to no intervention at all. Interrupting someone in mid-trip interrupts the natural process of working on the material which enters consciousness. It leaves the subject confused, detached, and unable to get back in touch with what was happening. Since he has lost access to unconscious material but is left with the mood it produced — sedation introduces great difficulty in working through and understanding the significance of the trip, which is crucial to the outcome. Sedation is not warranted, also because young people themselves have discovered that large doses of niacin bring the tripper down quite gently, without loss of consciousness and the subsequent difficulty in reintegrating and reorienting. Since consciousness is the working part of the tripper, no intervention should deprive him of its use.

An interview with an eighteen-year-old girl suggests the kind of aid which is more desirable:

> Acid can be used in a really good way, I really truly believe.
> What acid does I think is open a lot of doors in your head and
> lets a lot of things out. I just had so many repressed feelings
> that when I did acid it opened these doors and things came out that I
> just wasn't really ready to handle. I was going through heavy
> things with my parents. They were freaked out about the things
> I was doing, really put across the idea that I was bad because I
> was doing them — I was a bad person. That started a long time
> before — it started in fifth grade, so it had really deep root that
> I was a bad person. And when I tripped, it just opened the doors
> — you're bad, no you're not, you're good, you're good — and these
> conflicts would come out. It would've been really good for me, I
> think, if I could have understood the feelings that I was getting
> when I did acid. But I couldn't understand them at all, I had no
> one to guide me. I was just lost in this infinite number of feelings
> and horrible things and good things, just lost. I wish that I had
> had a guide or someone that could have said, "Well, let's look at
> those things that you're getting when you do acid, let's see where
> they're coming from." But I couldn't look at them. I was so con
> fused I couldn't do anything except go "aaah" and freak out.

A few weeks later, she took some powerful acid at home and was unable to come down. Her psychiatrist, whom she considers irrelevant and destructive to the process within her, hospitalized her. She ran away from the hospital when she came down from the trip and moved first to a foster home and then to a communal runaway house, where she found the support she needed and, incidentally, stopped using most drugs.

Alternatives to hospital treatment are the growing number of free clinics, crisis centers, and switchboards, where young people who are experienced with psychedelics themselves help each other. Many hospitals refer psychedelic cases to such groups, which deal with trips without fear and anxiety and with the understanding that the experience should be a positive one. Such groups reflect the values of the counter-culture

and agree to the positive value placed on self-exploration through psychedelics and through other growth experiences, ranging from encounter
groups through meditation to art and service to others. Such centers do
not think that the investigation of inner experience, fantasy and feelings,
or going deep into the self, are "cures" for feelings of personal discomfort or dissatisfaction with the world, or the self. Crisis centers
do not aim at cures or management of bad trips; rather they value the
process of exploration as an end in itself.

The process of intervention with a tripper starts when the person
arrives at the crisis center. Without having to ask questions, the staff
members recognize what is happening. Someone with trip experience
takes the person to an area or room where the setting is peaceful, warm,
and comfortable, often like a womb, in a conscious attempt to legitimate
regressive fantasies. The guide assures the tripper that his feelings
are all right, that he is on acid, and that he should not fear his experience. It is often necessary to reassure the person that he is good, that
his body is good, that sex is good, that whatever he feels guilty of or in
conflict about is a legitimate part of himself. The tripper is encouraged
to explore his feelings as extensively as he wants. If he is crying, he is
told that he can cry more if he wants; the validity of the feelings being
expressed is always reinforced, and the helper is present like a parent,
to comfort and help the tripper physically and emotionally as long as he
needs help. Such interventions last as long as the trip plus time afterward for working through the experience. There are no medical short-
cuts unless the person is perfectly calm and says that he can be left
alone.

The guide is there to support the positive expression of feelings and
to lessen the fear of the experience by reinforcing the positive side of
ambivalences. This attitude usually helps the tripper resolve conflicts
between wishes and fears in favor of the wish for expression. The guide
tries never to tell the person what to do. The tripper should be restrained
only to prevent destruction or physical harm to himself. A good trip area
is soft and durable enough to allow restraint to be held to a minimum.
When the person comes down, a working-through session is the critical
point of the trip. Similar to a regular therapy session, the guide talks
to the tripper about what happened, so that the feelings which came up
are not treated as foreign bodies which possessed him but as valid and
legitimate parts of himself. The session goes over whatever painful but
real feelings are still unresolved. Memory of a trip is acute, but mechanisms of denial and other defenses begin to operate immediately afterward, and if the follow-up sessions are not successful, all gain from
the trip will be lost.

Crisis centers are the most feasible safeguard against the potential
harm of psychedelics to young people. The fact that they are using drugs
is unchangeable, and while social policies dream of control, independent
crisis centers are becoming increasingly valuable as way stations for
young people undergoing crises which may or may not be related to
drugs. The use of psychedelics is a calculated risk by young people — a

healthy and adaptive behavior in the current conflict of values. As it becomes apparent that psychedelics will not be controlled, suggestions such
as one voted down in Canada make more sense — that places be created
where people can have supervised psychedelic experiences.

Sara's Odyssey

The following is a complete account of a psychedelic intervention,
written with Yvonne Jaffe, who was the guide. It illustrates how even a
completely negative set can be transformed into a peak experience. It
also illustrates the possibilities for new styles of therapy — in this case
regression as a way of overcoming conflicts which block completely
positive outcomes. Though the method here used is not a recommended
procedure, it may serve as a model for what life-transition crises can
lead to.

Sara was almost sixteen and needed space to grow. Her confused
feelings and contradictions burst the constricted boundaries of her childhood self. She read about Ché dying in Bolivia, her native land, and about
war and injustice in her new adopted country, yet none of this connected
with her suburban existence. Her family's relating to her as a child;
awakening sexuality, conflicted with Catholic upbringing; and a neutral
school experience; all created feelings of anger and frustration. These
events were not talked about or dealt with in her environment; so one
night she left.

When she arrived in New Haven, she made her way to the Green and
struck up conversations, asking for friendship, help, and shelter. Sara's
fears and doubts about herself were amplified by the pressures of survival in a marginal society, which were expressed to her as "a bed for a
lay." The police-induced paranoia about informers had undermined the
youth culture's desire to be open and to share, further hurting Sara's
chances of making contact. Eventually she was directed to Number Nine,
the social welfare and mental health arm of the new culture. At Number
Nine she felt things out and eventually made her way upstairs to where
counseling, crisis intervention, and bad trip help are offered. The rooms
are curtained off, with old sofas or mattresses covered with fabric, rug
scraps on the floors, and murals on the walls. Sara received shelter for
a few days at Number Nine's crash pad and then moved into a new friend's
apartment. Sex brought her in contact with feelings she had defended
against — fear, guilt, loneliness, and alarm at not having her parents
nearby or finding a place where she felt safe. She was bombarded with
sensation she had no categories to deal with.

Sara felt like hurting herself. She had heard from drug education
classes that with LSD "you have all those bummers," so she took a tab
of acid. The fears she had been holding back overwhelmed her. She
responded by regressing to an earlier stage of growth, when she had
been more comfortable and secure; this defensive maneuver is common
when psychedelics open the lid too fast. She began to cry, moan, and act
afraid and upset. Her friends took her back to Number Nine, for help.

Because most staff members are personally familiar with LSD phenomena, Sara's acting out strong feelings with her whole body was instantly recognized.

Sara's account of what she felt during her trip (taped when she returned two weeks later) shows the importance of the setting in transforming an initial negative set.

> I was feeling very depressed, and I had tried to kill myself, so I thought I'd just become and acid head or speed freak or something. I expected it to be like going crazy and I was surprised it turned out so differently, because of the state of mind I was in. Maybe it was the surroundings. I'll never forget what happened in that room, because it's been so important to me.

Her trip unrolled in three distinct stages in a progression reported by Grof and others. The first stage encompasses the gradual breaking down of ego, and a conflict between guilt and fear, superego and id. The second stage, a death and rebirth, follows on the resolution of this conflict with Yvonne's help. Sara wonders whether she deserves the pleasure she is experiencing; she sees the guides as members of her family. Her Oedipal conflict is resolved symbolically in the manner described by Norman O. Brown (1966), not through identification with one parent but through union with both parents in and through intercourse. The third stage which follows quickly is the peak experience. She talks of white light, starting a new world, milk, and she takes on characteristics of both man and woman, whom she sees as unified. After the trip came a difficult period of working through the experience.

At first Sara huddled in the corner and cried out in Spanish, her native language which she had not used regularly for years, "Mike Samuels I love you. I need you. I want to die." Yvonne was called in because she is Spanish also, and Jerry and Billy, two other staff helpers, also came. Sara repeated those phrases in a common trip sign of a psychic conflict. The repetition is usually an internal dialogue between a wish (in this case for love, closeness, and sexual pleasure) and fears and guilt associated with satisfying it (punishment by dying), which indicates that the conflict is not being resolved. Yvonne encouraged Sara to express the feelings she blocked and work through a fantasy solution, which will then be vividly remembered as the experience which resolved the conflict.

Sara was afraid and in need of support and security. She was on such a regressed level that the most meaningful support would be physical contact with a surrogate mother (of either sex). Yvonne took this role, telling her not to be afraid and bathing her hands and feet with a wet handkerchief. Yvonne saw her withdraw slightly, and took this as a sign that she was working on negative feelings about touching her body. It is easy to build rapport with someone who is tripping, even when the guide and tripper have never met before, because the tripper relates to people mainly as fantasy versions of parents and other important figures in his life.

Mothering is best when it is physical and direct. Words are confusing and often not understood, because the tripper may regress to a period before language. The integrity and self-awareness of the guide in this role is critical. He or she must move with the tripper, not seeking power or advantage over him because people on psychedelics are unusually sensitive to such maneuvers. The work of John Rosen (1953), Margaret Sechehaye (1968), and people who have lived at Kingsley Hall (Chapter 7) — Laing, Joseph Berke, and others — with psychosis supports the contion that a mother surrogate, whose love is more unconditional than the original, can undo some of the damage in people who are much more fearful than Sara. The trip out of psychosis, while much longer, can be similar and demands the same kind of patience from the guide-mother.

Once contact is made, the guide can tune into the conflict the tripper is experiencing. There are only a small number of themes which make up the human condition, though they exhibit infinite variations. Since they involve sexuality, guilt, union with parents, or desire for closeness and intimacy, the guide can test for the relevant theme by suggesting phrases which relate the tripper's words or actions to possible sources of the conflict; he can then judge from the reaction whether the supposition is correct. If the theme suggested by the guide is not relevant, the tripper will simply ignore it, since LSD frees one almost totally from social games and polite conversations. Under acid all relationships relate directly to central needs.

Yvonne began this trial-and-error process from Sara's words. When Yvonne bathed her, Sara asked, "Lesbian?" Yvonne answered, "No, I'm not a Lesbian, I'm Yvonne." This exchange alerted Yvonne to the fact that, while Sara might enjoy contact with a mother, this wish was in conflict with a fear that enjoying such contact was bad. Sara associated this fear with lesbianism as a defense against her desire for contact with women. Sara's contacts were soon resolved in favor of expression of positive feelings, as her words show:

> I remember Billy, he was my father, and Yvonne, she was my mother, and they were welcoming me from all the hardships I had gone through. It was like a trial, and I kept asking them, "Am I deserving of all this pleasure?" I could feel all these tender feelings, as a physical thing. I was free of all inhibitions, and could hug them and do all the things . . . and I could, and I did! I remember kissing my mother on the mouth, which you know I was always told not to do. I really wanted to hug and kiss her and even make love to her. There was music and it was the Spanish setting, and Yvonne had on a purple dress and long skirt, and her breasts were coming out, and she was telling me, "See, breasts are beautiful. You shouldn't be ashamed of them." I wanted milk and I wanted love. I told Yvonne I wanted to be breast-fed.

The infantile themes of union with mother and nourishment are inseparable from sexual themes. Sara told us later that for her the expe-

<u>rience</u> (not the intellectual insight) of food and sex were connected.

When Jerry came into the room, Yvonne asked if he was her friend Mike, trying to incorporate him into the fantasy. Sara said, "No, he's Jerry." Yvonne asked if she loved him, and she said yes. Yvonne asked, "Would you like to fuck him?" tuning in on the sexual implications of her impish grin. Such direct language is commonly used in fantasies but rarely in unself-conscious conversation. Yvonne uses the vocabulary to legitimate such intimate sexual fantasy conversation. Sara, embarrassed at first, tried to ignore the word but then agreed that her need for Mike was sexual. She said that she wanted Mike inside her, but that this would cause her to die. Given a phallic-looking object to play with, she alternately sucked it and moved it between her legs.

Another common theme Sara was working through was rejection of the body. Sara felt guilty about her previous sexual contact with Mike, especially her enjoyment of physical intimacy. She kept repeating, "Do I deserve it?" at every stage of her trip. Whenever she smiled and said that sex was good, the guides reinforced her good feelings by replying that bodies were beautiful, like a Greek chorus underscoring the message. Yvonne felt that Sara would be still more free to express her sexuality and become aware of her body if everyone, including Sara, undressed. She expected that the sight of genitals would focus some of Sara's fantasies.

In the counter-culture nudity is not especially unusual. While this procedure may ignite fears of orgies and of sexuality out of control, even among prominent psychiatrists emerging from the radical sexual tradition of Freud, open expression of sexual feelings and fantasies and baring the body is not particularly dangerous, nor is it that helpful or revolutionary. For someone like Sara, who has been taught to feel guilty about the very existence of her body, the experience of social nakedness can be helpful in making her feel that there is nothing particularly dangerous, fearful, or shameful about genitals. Nudity is best experienced as beautiful and natural, as growth centers such as Esalen demonstrate, and Sara's account of her feelings during the trip bears out this fact.

At first she pulled back in surprise and refused to look. But she was obviously fascinated by the men's genitals, gradually allowing her childish feelings of awe and curiosity to come out on her face. Everybody hugged her and chorused that bodies were nice, and Sara agreed. She began to smile, at first guiltily and then more broadly, saying she didn't deserve it. Her struggle between opposing forces seemed to lessen, and her natural desire to openly express her sexual feelings seemed to overcome guilt and fear. Sara remembers the nudity as

> sort of an Adam and Eve thing, it was so natural. I was so surprised at first, because I knew I had all these inhibitions, like those parts of your body are not to be seen. I went to a nun's school and they really mess you up about that. I remember I wanted to get nude, in my life, in front of everybody. At first I was scared, and felt Yvonne was going to rape me, but then I knew that was what I really wanted. Like these ideas were always

> in back of my head, in my subconscious, but now I realized them.
> Of course I still have bad feelings about myself, but I feel now
> that I want to do something about it.

The dramatic action of the next part of her trip was Sara's death
and rebirth as part of a new culture. It is remarkable that she perceives
symbolic connections which usually accompany only long-term therapy,
and that this occurs without the interpretive mediation of a therapist.
Sara saw her death as a symbolic suicide caused by her guilt about sex.
But in this case the suicide was also revitalizing.

> I can remember that this guy I met, Mike Samuels, was in the
> room, and was saying things like, "I only went out with her a
> couple of times." I was sort of hung up on him. I remember I was
> afraid to make love to him, and I'd like go frigid, and he told me,
> "You're so fucked up it makes me sick." Every day I'd get up and
> think about that, and it was driving me crazy, it was all I'd think
> about.

When she kept repeating his name, the staff telephoned him, not being
sure of his relationship to Sara. He came down to Number Nine but was
obviously too anxious about the incident himself; he stayed only long
enough for Sara to hug him and ask him to make love to her and then
spent the evening talking to Dennis about his own confusions.
Sara's account continues:

> So when I died, I remember calling him on a street corner, all
> hunched up, and there were people around me, saying that I was
> gonna die now. First they took me to an institution, because I had
> gone mad or something. That was here, Number Nine. And I was
> saying I was crazy in Spanish. I went through a lot and I had to
> die in order to be reborn again. My heartbeat started to get
> slower and slower. I remember I'm going to die, there's no
> place to go, it's going to be like when I was born, nothing, and I
> don't want it to be like that. I wanted to be something, not
> nothingness.

Many of these themes take on additional meaning when they are compared
with those Buddhist or Tibetan texts that are guides for people undergoing such experiences in their natural deaths.

> When I was born again it was like paradise, it was so beautiful!
> It's like I came through this light, but they expected it and I
> expected it. I could hear an ambulance, and it was like they were
> bringing me. It was my mother, and I'm coming out to her, and I
> did. Everybody was there to see it, and everybody's eyes were
> tearful with the joy. It was like utopia, I felt feelings that were
> indescribable. There was happiness and joy and I was crying. I
> was born with everything, all this knowledge. I remember the
> press or something was there and they were going to print it. It
> was our world, maybe the whole world had died off and we were

the new culture. My parents were there and I wanted to be part of
them both, to make love to both of them, like I had to have their
approval because I was part of them. There was little colored
twinkling things all around, and it was like we had made this
world, because we were so strong. I remember we were going
out to cut cane, and our hands were so calloused. I remember
putting these boots on, and Yvonne telling me, "But darling, put
these clothes on because tomorrow is another day, and we're
going to start." Now I remember I didn't want to go to sleep, because I wanted to start right now having babies and working for
the new culture.

A subsequent theme was the idealization of her father and masculinity and the realization that male qualities existed in her. She saw the
conflicting elements — maleness and femaleness, yin and yang, childishness and adulthood — not in conflict, but existing simultaneously
within her.

It was this brotherhood feeling and everyone was sharing it. Billy
was sitting in the chair. He was like one of those Indian gurus
also, and I was saying, "Daddy, I want to make love to you, I
don't want to wait anymore." He said that I had to. Then we were
going out to cut cane, and he was Ché Guevara, and he was my
father. I kept thinking about the milk and Yvonne, and then I
remember smoking a cigar, and I was Ché. I was both a man and
a woman. That was the most beautiful thing. I could be both. I
could be gentle and the maternal type of thing, and I could also
be strong and lead. I remember I was with my family, and there
were three guys, brothers or something, and I had to choose
between them. I think it was Jerry who was like the sweetness,
the tender type of part, the shy part. And then Billy, he was the
revolutionary type, and then somebody else, Dennis, represented
wisdom and knowledge and everything. Then they told me that
you have to choose which of your parents you want, and I told
them, "No, I can have both." And I was so happy, and it was so
beautiful.

Toward the end Sara was helped to relax with massage. She talked
about what she wanted to do in her life, about school, writing, and making
the world a better place to live in. She stayed at Number Nine and tried
to make love to everyone, but was gently put off. She was helped to take
a shower, and then she fell asleep. The next day, when Yvonne woke
her, she found her depressed and guilt-ridden. Yvonne reviewed the
trip, explaining that its feelings had been real and that Sara should accept them as part of herself. Sara refused to talk and finally stated that
she wanted to consider the trip as a dream because she saw now that
reality was not really like this. She left soon afterward.
When she came back two weeks later, she was beaming and smiling,
wearing colorful clothes and a bright rainbow shawl. As she thanked us
for the experience, her face was as radiant as it had been during the trip,

in sharp contrast to the subdued demeanor before and immediately after it. Her account validated our impression of the significance of the trip, and of the amount she had uncovered and learned to accept about herself.

She ends her narrative with her conclusions:

> Right after the trip I didn't really know what I had done, but I felt guilty anyway. When I woke up it was so different. Then I started reconstructing things, and I realized it was true, that's your subconscious and that's how you feel. I started feeling that we really have to live to satisfy ourselves. Not be selfish you know, but you can't satisfy anyone if you're not satisfied yourself. That's my main goal now. Before, I was so afraid of being hurt that I built this wall and made myself a prisoner in it. I've changed now. Like before I'd just nod. My feelings have been blocked and sterile. I couldn't communicate with people. Like I wanted to shout "I love you" or "I just want to hold your hand" or something like that, but I couldn't because I was so restrained. We have only one of those things we call lives, and we breathe and walk around and things like that, and poof, it's gone. As far as I'm concerned there's nothing else, as far as positive proof is concerned, so I'd better make sure I make something of it, enjoy myself.

The trip intervention turned what was intended as an act of self-destruction into an opening-up peak experience. Because of her tremendous insight and capacity to integrate learning, Sara has since been freed to trust people more and to express herself without drugs, and she has no desire to trip again. Through counseling and group experience at Number Nine, she continues to relate her insights to her everyday life. She contacted her parents and told them about what she is doing and about some of the feelings she was holding back. She visited home, and her family agreed that she could continue to live in New Haven in a residential job-corps program.

Transitional Communities

Both psychedelic drugs and the support community which helped Sara play critical roles in the development of a new culture. The themes and visions which came to Sara while tripping are a spontaneous personal rediscovery of the central values of the counter-culture. Psychedelics seem to have catalyzed a vision of what can be, and they release enough dammed-up energy to lead many to actualize these values in their other experiences. The convergence in Sara's trip of Maslow's Being values and the themes of the counter-culture leads to speculation about whether this new culture, born of drugs, may have recovered some bedrock truths about the deepest levels of the psyche, of which the dominant culture has lost sight. This is the thesis of Maslow, psychedelic researchers, and youth. Sara's story shows some of the fruits of young people's exploration of the deeper levels of their psyche. The new culture holds the possibility of a nonrepressive culture, which can be developed through communal living, encounter groups, sexual exploration, the study of other cultures and religions, and the restructuring of political institutions.

Sara's journey also demonstrates how the developmental crises which are exposed by drug use can be worked through constructively, without the psychic damage or the destructive effects of an exploitative environment. With the recognition that our culture is in a new form of transition, the Protean Man whom Robert Lifton (1969) describes, provisions should be made so that risks of young people in drugs and new communities do not lead to harm. Alvin Toffler suggests in <u>Future-Shock</u> (1970), that we need transition communities to help us cope with the onslaught of rapid change. Growing up and changing is now a lifetime job. As an adaptive strategy, the experimentation that young people choose through psychedelics and new communities is a healthy survival mechanism. Adaptation is the way to survival during change. The most rapid changes take place in the young, who bring new energy and flexibility to a totally new and threatening situation. Customary education is antithetical to these changes, since it disallows feelings and experiment and promotes conformity to an authority which no longer makes sense. The young must go out and seek learning by taking risks and developing learning opportunities. They use psychedelics as one antidote to their education and environment, as a way of breaking up patterns and enabling them to create new ones. Such communities as Number Nine can develop into the new learning centers, as well as spaces to work through personal crisis on the way.

In a time of confusion, conflict and cultural transition, the best that people can do is to search together for answers and possibilities that do not yet exist. The future of any new culture lies in transition communities which can be formed to support and focus growing attempts at self-definition. New learning tools, such as psychedelic drugs, are being harnessed to help people grow, despite the persecution of drug users by the dominant culture. Because these controls are powerless, exploration goes on, albeit with frustration and occasional harassment. Only a worldview which emphasizes change, risk, openness to inner experience, and exploration can cope with our changing environment. A psychology which emphasizes sickness, man's evil, caution, and self-control is outmoded and self-defeating. Sara — and others like her — should not be adjusted or controlled by the dominant culture which she does not want. She must be free to grow beyond it.

Chapter 5

NUMBER NINE: CRISIS AND GROWTH CENTER FOR YOUTH

A. Creating a Counter-Institution

Number Nine was created in October 1969 as a service to young people
in crisis. Founded by a group of young people, who had found the
frustrations and internal contradictions of working within the existing
mental health system too great, it represents an attempt to create an
alternative model of a service institution which helps people change. In
addition, it is politically relevant in that it hastens the adoption of its
humanistic values by a wider segment of society. We want to discuss several themes in Number Nine's development, not because we have solved
any basic dilemmas, but because our struggles highlight some of the
concrete issues that arise when the attempt is made to apply radical
approaches to personal growth as a service to a specific community.

Getting Started

Before we could open a crisis clinic for young people, we had to
make sure we were on their side. The young people we knew (mainly
white and middle-class, like ourselves) had a basic and massive distrust of their parents, their teachers, their government, and much of
what they saw around them. They had developed a counter-culture of institutions, media, and ways of relating which had the trust, if not the outright allegiance, of a majority of their peers. As a result of the development of this culture, they were sensitive and resistant to efforts to
depersonalize them, adjust them, change them against will, or blackmail
them by withholding achievement. The young people we knew were intro-
spective, self-critical, and idealistic, and they demanded moral honesty
from adults who wished to work with them. When given the chance, they
could define concretely what they wanted. If we were to build up enough
trust to make our venture successful, we had to learn to embody the
values of the counter-culture. It would be presumptuous, for example,
for us to try to "treat" their problems, because the nature of their

dilemma, as they defined it, was to develop new and more meaningful ways to relate. Our service could not take the form of those who had answers helping those who did not, because we ourselves were searching for answers to the same questions and trying to actualize the same values. From the first we had to develop a style of collaboration.

The founders — a small but fairly representative group of young people, most of whom had lived through several stages of the radical movement — had a twofold task. First we had to break free personally from the traditional assumptions about service that would be reflected in behavior if the planning process was not highly self-critical and open to new information at every step of the way. We also had to constantly seek feedback from the community and evaluate our efforts to check whether we were responding to real needs and whether our clients felt helped. We very quickly found that it would be a long time before we could be satisfied with any one type of service. We expected to constantly try new projects and never develop a stable set of procedures and programs; therefore any static concepts of organization would be useless to us.

In order to develop a flexible and responsive service, we decided to concentrate on our own personal growth as a staff, and this has turned out to be one of our chief attractions to volunteers. We felt that if we worked among ourselves to actualize our values in our own relationships, we would be likely to embody these values in our service to others. Concentrating on our own growth and openness as a community also allowed us to become comfortable in criticizing each other, which is crucial to any community which does not want to institutionalize and structure in its own blind spots.

With a vague and ambiguous collaborative structure we set out to offer service to young people in a radically new way. We chose our name, Number Nine, from a Beatles song; it would be easy to remember and would identify us in a way that "mental health clinic" would not. We knew of centers in other cities which operated switchboard, referral, and counseling services twenty-four hours a day, offered emergency housing for runaways, dealt with bad drug trips, and helped in family crises. All of these seemed valid needs, and no other services in New Haven existed to accept responsibility in these areas. We decided that our services should be offered free and that we could build greater trust and respect confidences by not asking names. We felt also that this attitude would be the best defense against police interference with our drug or runaway counseling.

Number Nine opened two weeks after the planning process began, with $100, a storefront donated by the Redevelopment Agency, an apartment-crash pad borrowed from the Free School, and telephones on credit. After a tremendous initial influx of volunteers formed the staff, and after many young people with various problems phoned and came in, we were able to attract donations and $13,000 in foundation funds to buy a condemned house that we could fix up, hire seven full-time staff members, and meet expenses. We now have about ten full-time staff members who are paid around $50 a week, plus often room and board at our house.

There are ten spaces in the house for people who are going through personal or family crises and need a place to stay for a short time; we also had a psychedelic bus and a rock band which used to travel around, give shows and help out at rock festivals, which sometimes brought in money. In 1970 we moved into a three-story building which we use for such new programs as a free school, personal growth center, and community meeting place.

This progress illustrates both the opportunity and the need for creative expansion of current views of social services. All of our activities grew out of our interaction with young people and our dialogue about what they needed for growth in a world which they experienced as largely hostile. While psychotherapy, encounter groups, family counseling, and other social services form a large part of our work, they seem to take on meaning and relevance by their connection with our other activities. All are unified through our growing, and still largely fuzzy, conception of ourselves as a community within a larger alternative culture which is working for broad changes in the fabric of our society.

Making Contact with Our Community

Traditional institutions have a passive idea of offering service: you open for business, perhaps announce your existence to other professionals, and wait for people to come. If they don't like what they get, they can leave. Many such services — court, welfare, or school counseling; mental hospitals — utilize compulsion to obtain their clientele. We believe that a service has to justify itself to its clients and must constantly ask the community it serves whether its service is useful. This cannot be done by bureaucratic means — for example, by a committee — because such means are unlikely to attract those who might be critical or have fresh ideas to offer.

The best way, we found, is to be in the community in as many and as active ways as we can. Our concepts derive from the more active forms of community organization, where the first step is to fight the inertia and apathy of people accustomed to passive acceptance of a status quo they disagree with. In mental health treatment the analogous problem is that people who seem to be in the greatest distress usually have defense mechanisms that keep them from actively seeking help, even if it is available; ironically many mental health institutions take the attitude that people whose problem is an inability to accept their help should be punished. We sought to make our image as broad as possible, so that, whatever someone's problem, he would feel comfortable in at least trying us out. We also wanted to move out into the community and offer many ways to become involved in our program, so that we could reach those very people who are not usually helped because they deny their difficulties, arouse the hostility of service agencies, or just generally alienate others.

We made ourselves visible. (1) We sent staff to places in the community where we expected to find clients (2) we participated in other activities of the counter-culture (3) we advertised in the media that young people responded to (4) we made our staff and our own community open to the point where people could drift into our meetings or office without having the burden of having to relate as a client (5) we created the bus and band, which was not only fun for us but also demonstrated that we were involved in ways that young people respected.

As a byproduct of our openness, one of the greatest problems we have is uncertainty about who is a member of the staff. We have a weekly community meeting, which anyone can attend, and people are free to sit in on any staff meetings. Anyone can help out in such efforts as building our house, fixing up the storefront, or going out with the bus. We found that, while diffuse boundaries cause a lot of confusion, the situation helped those young people to reach us who had difficulty admitting that they wanted help. Often our community or staff meetings became therapy sessions or feedback, where people got the kind of information they would get from therapy, without ever having to put themselves down by asking for it directly. They were able to accept it in that context, because they respected the way we operated. So far this procedure has sufficed to deal with difficult problems of social control, where someone creates a lot of tension in others or is disruptive. We try to get at the meaning of a conflict rather than to resolve it restrictively by creating rules or boundaries.

The greatest problem we had in starting was to create trust in the entire youth community. We found that suspicion of any agency, even a new radical one such as ours, ran almost to paranoia. Several times we found ourselves victimized by rumors that we were informers; these beliefs were not generated out of malice but were due to genuine misunderstandings or foul-ups by our staff. We always dealt with such situations by going to the people we knew to be critical, trying to work things out. We found that young people demanded an almost complete moral purity from an institution and were put off by any dealing that showed us to be less than they wanted us to be.

We tried to maintain informal networks at each local high school and to stay in touch with the "freak" community by sending staff members to hang-outs and by talking to people there. Though aware of our shortcomings and failures, as time goes on, they begin to see our honesty and our pluck in remaining open despite them; we are beginning to outlive our criticism. Our bus at festivals, even if at first we were astonishingly inept showmen, has brought us a visibility and energy in meeting people and learning about their problems that we could not have gotten any other way.

How We Are Helpful

Our help to clients has traveled far beyond the traditional limits of counseling, owing to the incredible range of possibilities offered to us through the new media and forms of growth-self-expression developing within the counter-culture. Aside from a few basic ground rules, our basic principle has been experimentation. Some of the organizers had experience with psychotherapy, as well as with community organizing and

political confrontation, and our style is a blend of these two influences.
We have tried to look critically at each of our preconceptions about
helping others in order to get back in touch with the whole person and his
dilemmas. At first our method was to be available as listeners from the
moment a person came in or phoned. We would try to look as openly as
possible at all aspects of any situation. Through questions we tried to
get our client to look at other aspects of his situation. We responded
naturally out of our own understanding and experience with other situations, often going into some of the seeming contradictions in what the
client was saying or helping him to explore outcomes other than hopelessness.

Some general characteristics of the youth counter-culture are an
emphasis on immediate experience, dealing directly with people, an
awareness of one's feelings, and a willingness to look directly into areas
of anxiety. We tried to incorporate these traits into our counseling style.
In addition, we learned from our clients that one of the primary characteristics of a personal crisis is the storage and inability to discharge
strong feelings. A goal for counseling, then, is to help people to recognize and deal with feelings concerning their situation, for example toward
family or boy friend. We also began to include all the relevant people in
the session because we began to see that resolving a situation required
work by all the main actors. This led us into counseling families and
groups of friends or couples. Now more than one-third of our clients
(about ten new contacts a day) eventually have one to four lengthy family
sessions. We were surprised at our clients' willingness to call in their
families, even in cases that in the past had dealt with parents by rebellion or flight. Parents also cooperated easily; we are coming to
feel that people do not really wish to maintain a generation barrier but
are forced into it by feelings they do not know how to understand. We
have found that our involvement and immediate service has impressed
parents as much as it has our clients.

Another aspect of our method is our involvement in all aspects of the
situation; not merely counseling but also obtaining other services, jobs,
or housing. We originally had planned to make many referrals to outside agencies. As we began to get feedback about the outcome of our
initial referrals, we found that most of the referred clients (if they took
our advice) were rarely dealt with in a way that they felt was helpful.
We began to sense that our difference in values and our commitment to
building an alternate culture made us acutely sensitive to the irrelevance
and lack of responsibility of other agencies to our people. When we did
make referrals — as for abortions or legal aid — we found that we had
to take the initiative to insure that our client received service and to
offer counseling concerning the necessary legal or medical service. As
we began to view referrals as an adjunct to our service, we began to
feel responsible to go with our client and to maintain contact until he
obtained relief from his original problem. We tried to accept responsibility for helping with any problem, to act as a parent or friend would.
In contrast, agencies assume responsibility only for providing a specific

kind of service, so that for example, a psychiatrist feels that he need only do therapy.

We began to deal with many people who had difficulty in breaking free of their parents, getting close to other people, or dealing with the prevailing educational system. We developed a variety of groups, both scheduled and spontaneous, around common themes and issues. Our association with the Free School led us to work with high school students in initiating educational reforms inside and outside schools. When, for example, large numbers of young people told us about difficulties from a single source, we took the initiative to act as ombudsman or mediator on behalf of our clients. More recently we have had a lawyer working with us in the very important and usually ignored area of civil and constitutional rights for young people.

Another service that developed is the residential crisis center. We found that there was no place where a young person could go when his parents were having difficulties or were for some reason unable to take care of him, where a person could work out the transitional period of leaving home to work, for runaways to deal with their problem and reconcile themselves with their parents, and for a score of other difficulties. Usually a youngster in such a situation ended up in penal institutions or a mental hospital, starting a cycle which very soon made him feel either worthless or crazy. The house environment, which is flexible, is still in the process of defining itself. Some of our full-time staff members live in the large house as a commune, and it is hoped that residents will become part of the ongoing community for a stay of up to a month. We try to offer a free and open place for young people to look into themselves and to receive shelter and support for that process.

The Staff

Our staff represents another radical departure from established institutional policy. Basically we found that education or credentials had no relation to intelligence, sensitivity, or ability to help others; we have therefore never looked to professionals for our staff. (We do, however, utilize some professionals as consultants, and in many cases their experience and involvement has enabled us to understand better what we are doing.) We felt that young people who had learned by experience, who had gone through personal crises themselves, were the most suitable helpers for others, provided that they had worked out their difficulties sufficiently to enable them to focus energy on another person. Many of our full-time staff members originally came as clients. The staff consists mainly of high-school students and drop-outs or vacationers from college, with a median age of twenty. Most of our staff members have used drugs, many have been addicts or spent time in mental hospitals, and all of us are in the process of searching for an identity and for meaningful work as part of a movement to change society.

We see working at Number Nine for a period of a year or so, not as a career, but as a stage in our own growth, combining community service with a meaningful learning and growth experience. This short-term and educational aspect leads to the tremendous energy and dedication in the staff's work. Since we constantly incorporate new faces, we hope to withstand rigidifying or loss of commitment as an organization. We hope that we are a school for community leaders in social change. Each of our staff members, as he graduates (without certificate), should be prepared to work in and to form a growth-oriented institution.

The training process is the work itself. A new staff member initially watches others as they work and counsel, and then takes initiative to get involved in one of the projects or to develop a new one. Our whole culture is training, because outside norms are overturned as much as possible, and our staff members must develop a way of dealing with each other that is different from previous ways. Alternative cultures were first artificially created in T-groups or encounter groups for training or growth, and our educational nature stems from the extent to which we can actualize these new values in our culture and help people to overcome personal difficulties that inhibit them from operating on this level. Our meetings are analogous to counseling sessions in that we discuss all aspects of a situation, including our feelings, and then collaboratively reach a decision. Leadership comes from being involved to the point of having the relevant information to make a decision or having the energy to carry it out and take responsibility for it. Thus learning, growth, and leadership are all defined in terms of effective action, which is in sharp contrast to educational institutions whose criteria are largely irrelevant to action.

Our history over the first year can be looked at as an experiment with various styles of leadership. After the first three months it became apparent that the concept of pure participatory democracy was not working in that three of the founders were doing the greatest share of the work and decision-making. This was due to their greater experience in radical service organizations and to the fact that they had arranged for funds which paid them to work full time for Number Nine. Other staff members felt guilty about not working as much, found it harder to initiate action, tended to defer in making decisions, and experienced personal difficulties and outside pressures. The three who were assuming more and more leadership found themselves in the position of therapists to other staff members. As a solution, they became the directors, which concretized the differential in leadership and made the three more comfortable about exercising authority.

As Number Nine grew and found funds to hire others to work full-time, this structure became inadequate. The new staff members began to develop the skills that the directors had, and the structure developed some of the drawbacks of the hierarchical organization. The directors felt that nobody was taking responsibility, while the staff members felt the directors were holding them back. During the summer the entire structure was called into question, and the three directors stated that they wished to be relieved of their responsibilities by the staff, although they would remain in the organization for a further year. They wished to devote more time to looking critically at Number Nine and helping to start other organizations. The staff elected six of the ten full-time staff members to be directors; these were the staff members who felt comfortable exercising initiative and making decisions in ambiguous situations.

Number Nine as a Community

Although we are an institution and an organization, Number Nine tends to think of itself as a community. This feeling is in line with the counter-cultural assumption that working and living should not be separated and that people should be open and intimate in work relationships. In addition, most of the staff members live together, so that social and housekeeping activities are integrated into our service work.

The reason for the emphasis on community and the attempt to include its volunteers and clients in our activities stems from our concept of the "cure" we offer people in difficulty. Traditionally, therapy is focused on adjustment to the usual situation or sufficient independence from the therapist to leave him. Since we are oriented toward rejection of the status quo, we must do more than help the person to some degree of comfort with himself. We try to offer him an alternative society if his growth through counseling leads him to want to commit himself to personal or social change. Since our community is also engaged in this process, "cure" would not necessarily mean that a person leaves us or loses his dependence on us. Instead, we would define his dependence by the quality of his participation. Many clients join the staff, while others hang around while they continue to absorb what we have to teach or offer. As encouragement, we have a fairly firm policy of not asking anyone to leave. We can tolerate the presence of disturbed people because we can accept a wide range of behavior and because we are pursuasive in asking people to examine the effects of their behavior. We enlist support by creating the feeling that we are moving as a community toward goals a young person might share and are asking him to participate. We have less difficulty with discipline than do schools or hospitals, which take few pains to assure that their goals are shared with their inmates.

We have been praised and criticized because at times we seem like a religious community (or a fantasy system). We have "rites" at rock festivals, inspire a religious devotion to our values, and use openness and group pressure to communicate and enforce our norms. Many of our people also use drugs and seek a communal consciousness, and we have frequent intense encounter groups. It is a valid view of what we do to say that we are just changing values, not improving them. Our "religion" seems to be fairly effective in building a shared and worthwhile set of values, while most other institutions are currently failing in that area. We have found that it is this sense of a religious community, where people are close and dedicated, that most often accounts for young people's coming to us in the numbers that they have. The meaning that we represent to them, while partly based on a fantasy, is the reality on which we build their own sense of themselves and faith in their ability to do what they want and find what they want, despite depressing world or home situations. This community feeling is a form of creative energy that seems more powerful than psychotherapy alone for producing personality change.

The fears, avoidances, and depressions caused by trying to live at this level produce crises in our community and among its members, so that we are constantly facing powerful learning situations. A primary function of the directors is to utilize personal and group crises — such as shared frustration stemming from a fear of getting close or retreating because of unresolved anger — as learning opportunities. This effect increases each staff member's comfort with his own strong feelings and her willingness to look at them. There seems to be no better training for counselors. The constant ability at Number Nine to disarm serious crises by resolving them — not in the restrictive sense of making rules to prevent their occurring in the future or establishing informal social norms to avoid such threatening issues, but through actively dealing with what is happening in a way which leads to greater understanding by each person — is probably the source of its great strength and great attraction as a working and growing community.

Number Nine as Social Change

In a political sense, we feel that if a community such as Number Nine can survive and grow, it will pose a constructive threat to educational and social service institutions. First, we will prove to bored and tired bureaucrats that their jobs do not need to be dull or frustrating. We can show that satisfaction will lead to better service. We can demonstrate to community mental health clinics why they lose so many clients and frustrate so many others. We can develop and practice new modes of counseling from a wide variety of sources, such as Eastern religions and growth centers. By letting students work effectively to help others, we can challenge schools to look into their concepts of the maturity and responsibility of young people. We can also educate students to pose challenging questions and propose alternatives to the educational system. And we can educate parents who come to us about the ongoing social changes and perhaps teach them to fear them less. We are trying to be a model for the type of treatment, the kind of education, and the style of life that we want.

Our way differs from the familiar methods of confrontation politics. Although we respect serious political confrontation and many of us feel the need for it, we have decided that for the sake of our own survival and our own values, we will deal with the world differently. Since we see ourselves as a model of the kind of community we would like to live in, we have chosen to relate on the basis of this model to institutions outside us. In our current political situation, violent confrontation seems in many cases to be the only way to obtain redress for the violence perpetrated on us. Our clients are primarily middle class and white, however, and for the large majority of them violence is not and never will come naturally. We do not feel a need to reach those who have already been politicized, rather, we seek young people who are not yet ready to recognize and deal with violence for what it is and what it is doing to the people around us. We see ourselves as recruiting new people to a movement toward massive cultural change rather than working with old faces.

Our contacts with adults have a similar aim. We try to make ourselves visible, and we engage many people in dialogue by modeling our community as much as we can on the outside. For example, in our frequent talks to PTAs, community groups, or mental health workers, we do not lecture. Rather, we try to conduct exchanges, which, similar to our meetings and counseling sessions, deal as much as possible with the feelings and reactions of the people we are addressing. Instead of providing a lot of information which can be misunderstood, we work to lessen the fear and hostility that keeps adults from engaging in meaningful encounters with young people. We practice subtle confrontation; for example, we may send a former patient to address a hospital staff or a high school student to a PTA meeting, or we ask parents who come to us with questions about drugs why they cannot ask their children or read a book. We do not blunt or soften our message for our audience, but we try to offer it in a context of friendliness and basic respect for what our audience has to say. We try to plant a seed of doubt in their prejudices that will lead them to look further into the counter-culture. We are armed with the knowledge that we have more fun and that we are nice people, even if they do not think so at first. Adults who hear us usually come away feeling better about us and themselves.

We try to create a change in each interaction with the community, in such a way that those we contact come back for more. We encourage people to visit us when they are suspicious, and we include them if they come to our meetings. Gently but firmly we hope that people will begin to respond to what we have to say. We offer workshops and seminars for parents and families. When they tell us that they want to get involved in our work, we do not discourage them or put them off. Of course we mention our financial needs — which are considerable — but we also tell them that we would like them to gather their friends for an evening discussion with some members of our staff at their home. In this way we can not only solicit funds, but can also communicate to a small group the meaning of what we are doing. This is community organization at its core. We ask our adult friends to help us by talking to other groups. This is the crux of our method of working for radical social change, and it presupposes that other groups, especially in the political sphere, are working and recruiting actively from people who have worked with us. Ours may be a naive conception, but at an individual level it has been responsible for some powerful personal learning by adults, has informed them about the nature of our critique of society, and has enlisted their aid in carrying the message further.

This essay has looked, in a somewhat oversimplified and naive way, at some of the issues that have been worked on by a community that is trying to develop a cultural alternative that goes along with its critique of the current cultural norms. The hard issues of how to stay alive, how to deal with our own upbringing in a culture that we now resist, and how

to accomplish things with a new set of values have had as much to do
with how we developed as have our ideals and values. We feel that experimental organizations such as ours form a sort of transition stage,
where human potential can be actualized, to act as a concrete message
that such changes can indeed take place. We feel that such organizations
cannot exist only in the laboratory; they must be visible and operate
within the political reality of a community.

B. The Battle For "Free Space" at a Drop-In Center

From the moment Number Nine's crisis program began, everyone
connected with it agreed on the need for a drop-in center for youth. This
center would begin with an open door on the street — a place that anyone
could enter. We felt that Number Nine should be a friendly and open center for members of the New Haven community, particularly street people
and high school students. These two groups usually have nowhere they
can legitimately hang out. Ideally, a drop-in center would be some form
of free space, where young people could congregate and initiate activities.
Our experience in creating such a center gives some idea of the obstacles faced by youth centers in trying to live up to such an ideal. Creating
free space is difficult, because both staff and frequenters find that their
internal barriers and habitual behavior patterns inhibit self-expression
and creativity in such a space. Paradoxically, when the drop-in center
was most "open", the atmosphere was most oppressive, forbidding, and
cold. When it had gained popularity, there were several unrelated, and
seemingly unprovoked, incidents of violence. This circumstance con-
tributed to the intimidation of staff and frequenters, but it also catalyzed
a process of learning about structure which finally led to a more viable
conception of the purpose and leadership of the drop-in center.

This history corresponds with that of many other programs; it demonstrates that our initial concepts were simplistic and naive. Until
many shared norms and group skills are developed it is unlikely that an
open center can exist. A drop-in center requires a redefinition of structure and leadership, the end result being that the whole community of the
center can solve problems and deal with crises other than by the creation of restrictive rules applied universally by authority figures, regardless of whether any rule is appropriate to any individual. It is
precisely this model — the creation of a generally applied system of
rules to deal with specific extreme and unusual occurrences, applied by
clearly distinguishable authorities acting primarily through disciplinary
roles — that young people experience as oppressive in homes and schools.
The drop-in center is one effort at moving toward an alternative kind of
community, where everyone shares in the creation and keeping of order.
Number Nine's history demonstrates that total lack of structure is not
a viable alternative, and while this concept is popular with young people,
it is unable to sustain any kind of program. Similar dynamics confront
radical and alternative communities; our experience may illuminate
similar struggles in other groups.

Background

Number Nine was founded as a hotline and crisis center, staffed
mainly by high school and college students and dropouts. The initial response to our service was considerable, and the place began to be used
as a community center by young people in the city. Scores of them came
and wanted to help out and be a part of Number Nine. While only a few
actually went on to learn the self-discipline and skills necessary for
counseling, they used Number Nine as a hangout where they could relate
to each other. The staff members wanted to define a program. While
many of them resisted the idea of any kind of structure — reacting out of
their negative feelings toward authority and systems which had oppressed
them in the past — others wanted to separate out the crisis center, but
felt that a lounge should be set aside and that staff members should be
less distant and aloof ("elitist") than they had been. Many of the staff
members and regular frequenters felt uncomfortable with any role differences as far as offering and receiving help were concerned. Since
there is almost no disparity in age or experience between staff and clients, the distinction between helper and helped was often dysfunctional
and unrealistic. This group wanted a space which provided access to
information, other people to meet, happenings, and shelter, independent
of artificial role distinctions and any type of formal interactions. They
wanted a place where they could be themselves.

The idea quickly became fact in people's minds, and they began to
plan artistic projects, music, space to make things, and so forth. A
nearby storefront was rented and named the Arts Lab. The energy behind the Arts Lab was one staff member who had the most contact with
street people. Those involved in it organized themselves according to a
schedule, but they did not define any roles or responsibilities for themselves. When this staff member left, the semblance of order disappeared.
While this setback did not deter people from coming, a mood of disillusionment and discontent was evident; eventually despair set in because
the Arts Lab was not getting off the ground. After the summer this
storefront was closed, and Number Nine moved into a three-story building, which contained a large open space on the first floor that could be
used as a lounge. The consensus was that the original program had
failed because of its distance from the crisis center (one block) rather
than because of the absence of authority and structure or because of the
many conflicts over the nature of responsibility and the definition of the
program. The idea of a new drop-in center was still the most powerful,
attractive part of Number Nine's program.

From the beginning it was unclear which particular staff members
would focus on developing a drop-in program. The whole organization
was in flux, and each group involved (the cofounders, new staff members,
volunteers, and frequenters) looked elsewhere for direction. We all expected that the community using the space would coalesce around the
need to define purpose and tasks, at least to the extent of determining
what was suitable and what was not. We hoped for an organic

(unstructured, evolving, undetermined) planning process that would involve the young people using the space, many of whom were unused to
sharing responsibility for defining norms.

As this planning process developed in actuality, it went through
several stages. First there was acute anxiety concerning the space,
which was reflected in the various groups' and individuals' relations
with each other, which were such that the myth of what free space could
accomplish was flatly contradicted. This situation led to extreme forms
of oppression and was aggravated by the center's attraction for violent,
severely disturbed, or profoundly depressed and angry people.

After several incidents of overt violence and exploitation, staff members and frequenters set down some norms on paper, divided up the
space accordingly, created roles for regulars, and proceeded to establish boundaries. This stage was remarkable for its severe conflicts and
for the ambivalence expressed toward constraints on individual autonomy
in excluding people for any reason.

The final stage came when a core staff developed out of the actions of
individuals willing to assume responsibility and to intervene. These
staff members focused on the overt and covert interactions between frequenters and of frequenters and the crisis center itself.

Group Responses to the Undefined Environment

The appearance of the drop-in center was forbidding and uncomfortable, both inside and out. The exterior was boarded up, so that no
natural light came in. Inside there were scraps of building materials,
old and deteriorated furniture, and an open high space without walls or
partitions. There were no obvious clues to possible use of the space and
little that was inviting. Until January we had no heat. Yet as many as
50 people came at any one time, perhaps because of the symbolic significance of free space. Street people, winos, high school students, dropouts, runaways, and drug addicts, all seemed to find each other's company tension-producing but acceptable. Considering the constant high
level of anxiety, the intensity of the need for such a space seems apparent.
The people who came were continually waiting for something to happen
or wanting something vague and undefined from Number Nine. The tone
was that of a Beckett play.

Behavior reflected the atmosphere. People sat around listlessly,
sometimes talking or engaging in active, aggressive, repetitive horseplay. Boredom and aimlessness were apparent. There seemed to be no
core, purpose, creative activity or direction. Any attempt to organize
activity, or even to focus discussion, was met with irritation and resentment. People seemed to prefer inertness, sitting back and watching,
and occasionally forming a small group, for example around a card game.
Slater (1966) and Bion (1961) have described the spontaneous emergence
of basic emotional patterns in groups. Group members defeat their own
desires to organize around a task because of shared fears and assumptions. In the absence of any set task, the drop-in-center frequenters
apparently experienced anxiety concerning the group's survival. The

pattern we observed corresponds to Bion's category of fight/flight. Members of the group fight anyone who is suspected of increasing the likelihood of the group's falling apart or altering, while others chose to withdraw into personal fantasies to avoid the hostility generated by those choosing to fight.

This pattern can be seen in the following example. Several people were sitting around, apparently watching each other. Others played cards. No one talked sensibly. All occasional comments were shouted, and were on the order of "If you don't want to play why don't you get the hell out of here." When a boy approached a girl, as happened three separate times, each one almost immediately asked her if she wanted to leave, while each girl seemed irritated at being approached and looked away while replying in the negative. When a staff member walked through, he was immediately surrounded by several angry men, who yelled, waved their fists, and generally expressed hostility. The burden of their demands was that he take various steps to "get things together." The men were vague about specifics, and anyone listening closely would have been confused.

Whenever someone attempted to gather people in a group, each person had to be invited individually; shortly after the group finally formed, many with a small attention span left. The remainder of the group then attacked each other and the staff members about the situation, or they remained silent. Though plans for the next day were met enthusiastically, no one was willing to assume any responsibilities, and the plans were never carried out. People answered only direct questions and showed resentment at being asked to participate, although when they talked, they complained about the group's not getting together to deal with the issues. Meetings could not even be convened unless one of the central leadership group was present, and it became a common belief that only this trio had the skills to make things happen. No common enemy appeared to focus the irritation and hostility until later.

Individuals relied on personal defensive systems to deal with the normless, structureless environment. Up to fifty people at one time could be seen acting out their hangups almost independently. One man was openly propositioning a girl who was staring into space, oblivious of even his presence. It was obvious after several minutes, that no contact was established; each was reacting defensively by refusing to acknowledge the other's personality. The situation resembled the behavior of mental patients on back wards. Since the staff remained aloof or blended into the action by taking no responsibility, each person was free to deal with feelings through behavior which was restrained by only minimal inhibitions. When it became the norm that almost anything was acceptable, only those who could tolerate the often bizarre and depressive behavior continued to come.

Withdrawal and depression, exploitive relationships, such tension-releasing activities as running around shouting, mock fights, making out, drug use, and drinking, and sleeping — all were methods for dealing with the situation. People used their own primary means of decreasing tension—

drug users used drugs, promiscuous people sought sex, angry people had fights. It was not that the center encouraged these activities; they were simply inevitable. Young people who on the outside were not likely to seek behavioral extremes avoided the center, and a self-selection process brought together some of the most highly deviant members of the community. The center discriminated in precisely the opposite manner of conventional environments, preferring extremes to moderation. When given the choice, disturbed people appear to seek out other disturbed people and collude to create a permissive environment. They always exhibited an underlying, but inarticulate, openness to being helped along with a strong resistance to what we defined as helpfulness. The drop-in center was perhaps the only open space in the area, and it attracted the most marginal and maladaptive people around. But even as they were attracted by it, they felt threatened by it and defended themselves with violence and withdrawal.

Violence as a Catalyst for Differentiation

The second phase of growth — the development of some norms and roles — came in response to several unprovoked instances of violence. In the first case a staff member answered the door of the residence, two miles from the drop-in center, and found two men, one with a gun. He accused Number Nine of having burglarized his home and pistol-whipped the staff member. The man was never identified, but the staff members went through a period of intense fear; they boarded up windows and closed Number Nine for two weeks.

Another incident occurred during a training session. A frequenter, known for multiple drug use and violent explosions, came angrily into the group. A friend of his advised everyone to be cool, that he was just tripping. Out of fear and regard for his psychic balance, everyone remained quiet. He then walked over to someone and punched him in the face, and he repeated the provocation with someone else. He then picked up a crowbar and swung it around the room, until his friends finally controlled him.

The final incident, a week later, was the catalyst for change. Three men came in and attacked the first three people they saw. One staff member had his shirt pulled over his head and then was punched in the stomach as he fell to the floor. The men were later arrested and eventually released. Some staff members wanted to press charges, while others were reluctant for ideological reasons. It was revealed that one of the men was the brother of a frequenter who disapproved of his brother's choice of company.

It was clear that the chaotic atmosphere and the fight/flight dynamics were creating anxieties both within and without the center which prepared the way for the violence. Staff members and frequenters, in community meetings, formed a theater which focused on acts of violence, aggression, and hostility. People would make long diatribes during meetings, and discussions were fixed on any violent individual or incident; evident pleasurable responses were made to these topics. Decisions to limit harangues or violence itself produced conflict in the group, and many took the position on the side of the violent person against any limits. When moves were made to exclude anyone, staff opinions were split, and the decision was undermined. The effects of the atmosphere — for example, the fact that most of the young people for whom the program was intended were afraid of the place — were ignored in the focus on extreme acts. The withdrawal of others provided a silent and tacitly approving audience for anyone who monopolized the center, and it supported avoidance of discussion of issues. People merely repeated that "Things must be done" and left the group. The group dynamics created a theater for extreme aggression.

After the final attack in the center, there was a significant change in the dynamics of the community meetings. People were initially upset and numb after the attack, many of them feeling inadequate because they had not intervened to stop it or just crying in empathy. Minutes later, the community of about thirty met. Support grew for the idea of talking about fears and asking for physical support and empathy from others. Unlike previous meetings, which had been diffuse and characterized by one or two people's acting out feelings for the group audience, this one was focused in a tight, small circle. People remained in physical contact, and many spoke and reacted to each other. The earlier pistol whipping had been followed by long meetings, but instead of mobilizing support and solidarity, the result had been fear and withdrawal. This time people came to grips with the fact that there was not likely to be a recurrence, that they had done what they could, and that they should respond, not with paranoia, but with support. People felt that Number Nine's collective strength was greater than outside oppressive forces.

Pain was etched on the faces of the staff members. They had been terrified, but now they were conflicted over the best response. The obvious solutions presently legitimated by society — force, the use of police, structural restrictions on entrance into the program, and the like — were all rejected on moral grounds, despite the fact that they offered immediate protection. Staff members wanted to solve the problem in ways that corresponded to their ethics. The incidents exposed a deep contradiction in the youth culture concerning ways of dealing with violence.

A discussion a few days later offered one solution. There had been an incident with one of the winos who frequented the center, a black man called Butch. Besides permanently being drunk, Butch was hostile and at times carried guns, knives, and clubs. Although he had never used them his threats were explicit. He pulled a knife on a staff member who was trying to talk him into leaving and drove it into the wall about two inches from the staff member's head. During the subsequent discussion of how to deal with him, it was learned that he had been arrested shortly after leaving the center. Two staff members bailed him out. Butch was amazed that the same people who had consistently told him they did not want him around because he scared people now took this action. In gratitude, he has avoided Number Nine ever since. The feeling of release

among the other staff members when they heard what the two had done
was more impressive. They learned of a concrete action which clearly
reflected the values they believed in though they had doubts about them
and also solved a problem of violence.

The attack overcame some people's ambivalence concerning the
proper response to violence. But continuing ambivalence about the best
way to deal with people like Butch was shared, and bullies got on so
well that staff members felt guilty about intervening in incidents of
obvious exploitation. The resolution took the form of a self-defense
workshop. People shared their feelings about how they wanted to respond
to violence; they engaged in role-playing in situations where someone
was causing a hassle. The staff members formed a leadership group for
the first time; they established rules concerning disturbances and devised a method of enforcing them. The generally agreed-upon rules
forbade dope, liquor, and violence. When the rules were broken, it was
agreed that the offender would be asked to leave. Without arguments or
defensiveness about the rightness or wrongness of the judgment, the request would be backed up physically by every staff member present. If
attacked, a person would try to knock down his assailant and call for
help. Everyone was pledged to respond at once. In the past, staff members had been reluctant to enforce rules because they could not count
on support.

The effort continued to solidify goals and establish norms. The organizers wanted to institutionalize them through personal interactions
with individuals and by the support of other staff members, rather than
by the use of rules, regulations, force, coercion, and police. The moment when they were able to depend on their ability to relate to violent
people marked a significant step in personal growth for staff members.
The violence had challenged their idealism but not weakened their resolve. They began to move in the direction of reducing disorder by
initiating personal relationships with deviant frequenters. Steps were
also taken to cut down the arena like quality of the open space by par-
titioning it into three rooms — a reception room, a lounge, and a large
workshop. The area acquired a more intimate and comfortable look, and
the noise level and audience for individual events were cut down.

A crucial difference came from placing a receptionist at the door.
The newest staff member was having trouble defining her role. Though
she was fearful, she wanted to learn to deal better with threatening situations; she therefore made herself responsible for the door's being
covered at all times. Because at first it was hard to recruit others, she
herself did the job most of the time. This device offered some control
over those who came in and their purpose in coming. We excluded anyone over twenty five because of our inability to deal with winos' threatening behavior. The receptionist was also able to identify people coming
in to use the upstairs crisis center — those needing immediate help,
counseling, or information. The space around the door became a cooling-
out area for diffusing tensions.

Evolution of Task Leadership

In the final stage the staff — the members of the community who took on the explicit task of being helpful — intervened in individual and group situations. (It should be noted that "staff" does not indicate paid full-time employees only, but includes anyone who takes on a role or some ongoing responsibility.) A group began to meet fairly regularly to set up activities and workshops and to take responsibility for knowing what was happening. The atmosphere cooled down down considerably, and staff members tried new ways to deal with extreme behavior. The emotional atmosphere changed from one of fight/flight to one more indicative of dependence on the leadership group. The core group began to meet daily and invited anyone to sit in or take part in the process of task formulation.

What made these meetings different from earlier ones was the decision of five of the regular staff members to attend regularly, and they came armed with issues and ideas for discussion. This behavior established norms concerning direction and participation. While this seems a simple and obvious step, it must be seen in a context in which the ideology of free space and the fear of the results had all but ended sensible action. Frequenters understood that they were free to participate in the work process at any level that was comfortable for them, and they did not view the core group as an arbitrary rule-making body. It seemed that people who had distrusted all authority were learning that some authority could be tolerable when it was offered in an open group process, whose necessity and rationale was evident to all. By keeping the boundaries open and flexible, and because of the community's experience of the need for leadership, the staff members were more comfortable in responsible roles.

Most of the leadership was exercised by women. During the violence and in the period when norms were being set, women found that they could deal with potential disruptions and defuse violence in ways that male staff members could not. Women fit more easily into warm, directive leadership and were more easily able to keep boundaries without falling into win-lose dynamics ("If you step in, I'll throw you out"). Both men and women frequenters felt comfortable in relationships with women on the staff, while male staff members had difficulty talking to other men and found that the seductive energies involved in relating to women frequenters led to more defensiveness than trust. Some men on the staff began to look at their own dynamics and fears in the areas of sexuality, closeness, and aggressiveness, and formed a men's consciousness-raising group to deal with them.

Once the ambivalence about exercising leadership was resolved among the staff members, energy was released for planning sensible structures, and many people came to the daily group sessions to propose additional ideas and to help implement them. This core group was smaller than the community group which had met previously, but the norms it set were supported by almost everyone. The shared sense of order in the community made it easier to ask disruptive people to leave; eventually four of the frequenters who had been the hardest to handle

were banned. Because these still had their advocates, they were not of-
ficiously kicked out; rather, someone always felt responsible to meet
with them outside, take them out for coffee, or get together at one of
their apartments. This tactic kept them in touch with Number Nine and
communicated the message that our inability to tolerate them in the
storefront was our problem, although it had real consequences for them.
Fights declined to zero and belligerence decreased, while exuberance
and horseplay continued to discharge energy and tension.

With a feeling of minimal trust, security and support, the center
developed a minimal program. Art supplies were available, and resource persons came some afternoons to hold workshops. A weekly
movement workshop was held by a local dancer, who was superb in
dealing with people's anxiety about moving and touching without embarrassment. Community meetings became sessions at which people could
tell their feelings about what was happening and what they wanted. These
were discontinued after a few weeks because they demanded large-group
leadership skills, and none of the staff members had the time or the
interest to develop them. A psychodrama group and men's and women's
consciousness-raising groups, held upstairs at the crisis center, were
a step toward integrating the two programs.

Spontaneity did not vanish. People did not respond to schedules. When
anyone started a project, those around would join. The piano was used,
and spontaneous workshops were held in chanting, body awareness, creative writing, poetry, and around problems or things people wanted
to share. The original dynamics did not entirely disappear, and individuals did not stop using the center for their private fantasies. But through
the role playing and discussions, the core group was able to focus energy on particular people who were not active in workshops but preferred
to relate on a one-to-one basis. Staff members began to respond to
people's needs by listening to them, thus offering a concrete alternative
to the previous style of simply acting out needs. They worked on the
assumption that people would act differently if they received nonobtrusive
support. Such encounters were seen as the helping function of staff
members. One time, for example, a staff member noticed that one couple
was deeply entwined while several other people in the room were sitting
alone. The staff member talked to each of these and discovered that they
were all disturbed by the sight of the couple, who made them aware of
their own loneliness. He then approached the two young people and asked
them how they thought their behavior was making the others feel. They
were quite surprised — it had not occurred to either of them that other
people might react to them. When the situation was explained to them,
they decided without any urging to stop what they were doing. In this
way they were spared the feeling that they were being forced into anything and at the same time achieved a new awareness of a level of interaction they had previously ignored.

Goals and Tasks

If the drop-in center was to provide consistent learning experiences,

skills in counseling and group work had to be passed on to the staff and
frequenters. The entire center had to be treated as a sensitivity group
by the leaders of Number Nine. The core work group had been successful
in fixing up the space, differentiating tasks, and creating a sense of order, but the group still lacked a training process. Another group was
formed for those who wished to learn about holding workshops, running
group meetings, and counseling. Trainers also worked with individual
staff members on developing sensitivity to issues; they walked together
around the area, going over what was happening and thinking about possible tasks. In this way sensitivity to signs of distress and to possible
interventions was built.

In addition to providing a space that was free and comfortable for
young people to meet, the basic task of the drop-in center seems to lie
in transforming into learning experiences the kind of personal behavior
which in other settings might lead to rules and restrictive solutions (such
as a blanket rule against all horseplay). This priority necessitated the
development of an alternate model of authority — one that kept order
without being defensive against change. Staff members tried to resolve
situations in such a way that people would take responsibility for their
own behavior and would learn how they affected others. The process was
similar to sensitivity groups. Many times the decision to change came
from the person involved; this was often the first time someone was made
responsible for getting himself out of a situation. Most settings for youth
remove their responsibility for making decisions on the grounds that
they are not mature enough. Consequently young people become dependent
on outside authority to make decisions for them and are unable to act
autonomously or even to define what they want. This situation may account for the tremendous initial reluctance to take the initiative in defining the drop-in center. The growth of the center can be seen as a
deconditioning experience, in which growth, learning, and taking responsibility for leadership all have the same meaning.

The other goal was to make the drop-in center a space where young
people can be open, honest, and direct in their relationships. Again, this
is the ideal; the reality is that some people try to be more open, and
others try to support them. Number Nine is relatively unique in that
there is always someone to whom a person can turn for support. When
the level of support is high, the frequenters report that the drop-in
center is a unique and high-energy space quite unlike anything they have
experienced before; they feel that it represents a concrete step toward
their personal goals of how they and others should act. Some of the
staff members felt that at times the excitement was frustrating and
draining them. Frequenters and even other staff members responded to
the ideology of trust and support by making strong demands on each
other. The training sessions constantly heard accounts from staff members who spent a lot of time trying to "help" someone, only to see that
they had wrought no improvement; consequently they felt slightly manipulated. Such situations usually resulted in part from their need to see
immediate results from their helping behavior. As they relinquished

their need to change everyone they talked to, their experiences became less frustrating.

The drop-in center is in many ways more fully in line with the ideals of Number Nine than are the counseling and crisis center upstairs. It is here that the role distinctions are most often broken down, including that of helper and helped, which creates dependence and discomfort among both staff and clients. Many young people, particularly the younger boys and street people, are not able to articulate a specific "problem", and consequently they do not think of the crisis center as a place where they can find help. They want to create a community which shares resources and offers support, and in this context people with helping skills can be crucial. Such help is not offered as part of an unequal authority relationship. Hellmuth Kaiser (in Fierman, 1965) has suggested that a good psychotherapist can work without the patient's even being aware that he is being helped; a relationship in which people trust each other and are honest is all that is necessary, and a person does not have to be recognized as the official helper to accomplish his ends. Since most of those who frequent the drop-in center would not define themselves as needing help, the setting must meet their immediate need for a place in which to spend time with others and to engage in projects. In that context, the likelihood is strong that those learning experiences that are offered supportively will be utilized. The drop-in center experience has implications that go beyond therapy; they apply to education and community organizing as well.

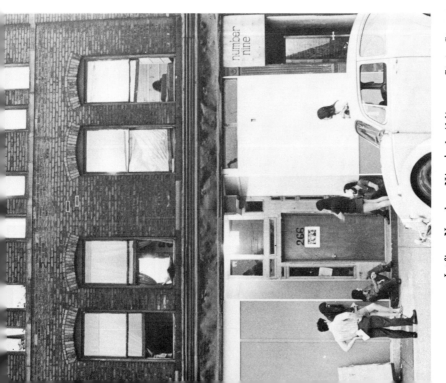

Left — Number Nine's building on State Street. Right — Residential center on Mill Street. (Clark Broadbent)

Top — Number Nine bus at Mill Street in June, 1970. Bottom — The crash pad cottage behind the house. (Bottom by Clark Broadbent)

Dennis and Yvonne's wedding celebration in June, 1970, with
entertainment by the Nine Peace Band.   (Chris Pattee)

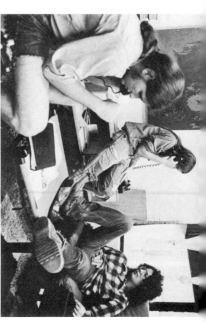

Counseling at the crash pad, on phones and in person. (Clark Broadbent)

Quiet evening in the phone room. (Clark Broadbent)

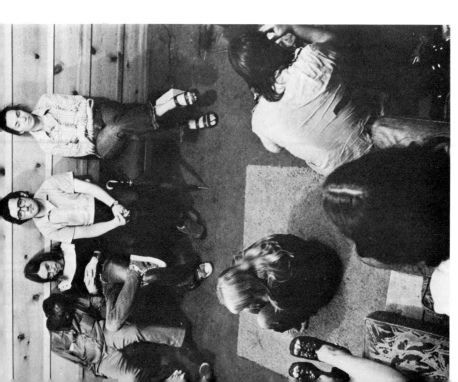

Left — Staff training and role play group. Right — Simulation of crisis center operation for community drug intern program.

(Clark Broadbent)

One of the irregular staff meetings. Top — Tom, Nina, Sheila, Barry, Inez. Bottom — Ginger, Kathy, Fred, Dennis, Sheila's back. (Clark Broadbent)

Sheila, Yvonne, Dennis, and Ted at home, with Kristin.
(Clark Broadbent)

Chapter 6

THE STRUCTURE AND FUNCTION OF ALTERNATE SERVICES

A. The Development of Alternate Services

The 1967 "Summer of Love" focused attention on the Haight-Ashbury
section of San Francisco, where a new phenomenon had taken root in the
youth culture. Hippies were invented, idealized, caricatured, criticized,
scapegoated, and over-killed by the media. News stories detailed how
young people were using drugs — particularly psychedelics — leaving
home and forming new communities, breaking down barriers to other
people and sexual taboos, and trying to live by a new set of values. Public attention took note also of the casualties of this new culture; they
were many and ominous — drug addiction, violence, self-destruction,
apathy, insanity, anger, confusion, pregnancy, VD, theft, and boredom.
Such results were to be expected, because the people involved were
quite young, often on their own for the first time and without means of
support, and experiencing a powerful series of changes through drug
use and other experiments.

Of crucial significance to the alleviation of these casualties is the
string of indigenous self-help social service organizations that sprang
up in response to young people's explorations. Traditional social services were not equipped to deal with the needs of young people in this
counter-culture, since most of those involved in these changes saw traditional services as irrelevant to their needs. The new alternate services
try to operate within the values of the counter-culture. The more than
1,000 such service centers offer full-time or volunteer employment to
thousands and help an uncountable number of young people. Services offered include twenty-four hour hotlines, places to stay, food, information, medical care, friendship, and counseling about drug problems or
personal crises.

These alternate services began when some of the people involved in
this new style of life began to offer help to their brothers and sisters,
not in the traditional, bureaucratic mode, but in a communal, free,
sharing, caring way. They started new services in the awareness that
new values demanded new approaches to helping. Toward this goal they

began a reevaluation and restructuring — on a small, direct service level — of the basic concepts and procedures in providing service. Many of their innovations have been developed to the point where they can be applied in areas where traditional services fail. New values demanded revision of dehumanizing red tape and treatment of clients, lack of collaboration in the goals of the service, long waits and hours inappropriate for crisis needs, fees, professional roles, hierarchical structures, and a lack of connection with the basic problems of the community. Alternate services now struggle to define precisely how to provide help operating on the basis of roughly the opposite priorities.

Beginnings

The Diggers, a counter-cultural group in San Francisco, recognized that the operational test of the hippie love and care ethic lay in self-help groups, sharing resources by a basic barter system. They opened the first free stores, which distributed donated goods and gave out free meals; they organized crash pads, where street people could find shelter, and health services; and together with other groups, such as Ken Kesey's Merry Pranksters (see Wolfe, 1969), they created such gatherings as the be-ins and trip festivals, offering free psychedelics. They promoted their work with a theatrical instinct for the inspirational value of direct action. Their naive, simplistic, do-it-youself-and-do-it-for-free reasoning became the source of a number of clichés; but its simple truth captured the energy of many who were tired of the frustration, delayed gratification, and lack of observable results from other forms of political activity.

Other factors account for the sudden and extensive spread of these indigenous help groups, none of which had the sponsorship of government funding, the impetus for most other community innovations. The first element is that such programs can be set up cheaply, drawing on large numbers of staff members willing to work for minimal subsistence wages. Like the settlement houses of an earlier generation, alternate services were improvised when the need arose and were small and autonomous. The existence of urban parishes and the churches' concern with the problems of young people provided space, made some funds available, and helped obtain community support for what seemed a new and threatening venture. As church attendance fades, ministers look to innovative services as one of their provinces, and the community has essentially accepted their leadership. For example, in the spring of 1967 concern over the influx of hundreds of runaways to Haight-Ashbury was high, and Minister Larry Beggs pursuaded the united ministries to set up Huckleberry House (see Beggs, 1969). This experiment became a model for houses in almost every major city and for government-sponsored group homes and halfway houses. Seminary students founded Project Place in Boston around the same time; it has since grown into an umbrella organization sheltering scores of experimental programs. When, as happened at Place and Huckleberry's, staff members are arrested or the facility is shut down by the authorities, church affiliation has helped

in working through the difficulties and countering negative stereotyping
of the programs, so that they could continue. In many smaller towns
churches offer the only space and funds for looking after young people's
needs, and they can share control over the program.

Meeting Needs

Alternate services respond to the unique and particular needs which
the existence of the counter-culture has created. Young people, many in
their early teens, take summer or weekend migrations, or they run away
from home, and they need to stay in places where they can experience
some degree of independence yet be protected from the more destructive
forms of exploitation. Voluntary poverty, rejection of "straight" jobs,
and the variety of drugs in common use increase the basic needs of young
people whose class origins did not prepare them for such a life style.

In the cases of drugs, running away, and pregnancy, the punitive
stance of society has forced most helping programs to grow up independent of the heavily regulated medical and social service agencies. The
risks of identification or arrest deter many young people from using traditional services. They view such programs as thinly veiled attempts at
moralizing against their activities, and they avoid them because the
agencies show no respect for their privacy, independence, or real needs.
Even when the young people see a counselor or social worker, they still
feel that the professionals' lack of information and difference in values,
and the detachment and stereotyping of their professional role, all hin-
der them from giving the necessary help. Young people have come to
look to their fellows for help and support.

Alternate services also respond to the pressure that young people
face when they find themselves in conflict between their own and their
parents' values. Their early independence, sexual experience, and drug
use exaggerate these conflicts, until many are being "spaced out" or
"freaked out" — confused or alienated. They need a cooling off place
where they can explore their confusion, meet others in similar positions,
make decisions about their own futures, and perhaps reestablish contact with parents without feeling that they have failed in their efforts.
Such places are similar to what Alvin Toffler (1970) calls transition
houses, where people can work through the psychic reaction to great
personal and environmental changes.

A young person cannot simply shed the skin he has grown for many
years, espouse alternate values, and live by them. The patterns of defensiveness and exploitation which he rejects in his family and society
have been internalized as reflexes, which reappear almost automatically
— for example, when he meets a girl or when he needs money and begins
to sell drugs. Such services as hotlines and crisis centers help define
and shape the new culture by helping individuals work through their own
solutions to moral dilemmas and personal pain. Given the tremendous
pressures experienced by young people in such transition situations, the
aggravating conditions of drugs, their prevailing rootlessness, and the
repressive response of society toward them, it is remarkable that there
have not been even more casualties in the counter-culture.

The Effects of Alternate Services

The credit for ameliorating many potentially destructive situations within the counter-culture must go to the life style of young people, which stresses love and support; it produces a powerful trust that often overrides the need and desire to exploit others. The most organized and the clearest expression of this ethic is in alternate services.

These new services have tremendous effects on their clients, as well as on those who form the volunteer and consultant staffs. Both are helped to articulate their values more clearly and to formulate strategies that will overcome internal and external obstacles to their realization. In this way alternate services greatly enhance the quality of life in the counter-culture.

Switchboards centralize and disseminate clear, concrete information on such topics as drugs, pregnancy, venereal disease, and the availability of such basics as food, shelter, clothing, or jobs. They also create a body of knowledge concerning the handling of bad drug trips; this has led to a decline in bad trips as a significant problem, even while drug use itself increases. Rather than turning the care of bad drug trips into a specialized skill, crisis centers experimented with techniques and passed them on to large numbers of volunteers. The eventual result is that most young people are aware of how to intervene in bad-trip situations, thereby decreasing the need for such a special service. Most crisis centers now report fewer bad-trip interventions.

They have also taken leadership in differentiating among drugs. They sift community opinion and determine which drugs — such as heroin, speed, and barbiturates — are causing great harm, and they try to lead young people away from these drugs to comparatively safer ones, such as marijuana and psychedelics. The government, by failing to make such differentiations — it makes negative pronouncements on some fairly harmless drugs, while refusing to crack down on amphetamine traffic by large drug companies, overprescribing by physicians, and unlimited use of alcohol and tobacco — has lost credibility. Crisis centers, conversely, have concrete information about drugs that are being traded, and they share experience-based knowledge of what to do in emergencies; this information is often inaccurate, but at least it is more useful and accessible than the information spread by large clinics.

Alternate services may have even greater effects on their staff members — young people who often maintain contact with both cultures and who are pondering the implications of a commitment to one or another life style. Work or contact with an alternate center helps determine or alter career choices for both drop-out youth, and pre-professionals or professionals. Centers attract those who are dissatisfied with their training or their current work but who are not willing to drift or change until they find other modes of work that allow them to deal with the pain and injustice of our society. Alternate services are a positive response to social injustice, less encumbered by the bureaucratization or pointlessness of many training programs and service institutions. By setting a moral and practical example of work and by dealing with the real basic

issues of providing service, alternate centers force young professionals
to examine their basic assumptions. For staff members, alternate services provide a focus for exploration of themselves and their relations
to others even while they provide services. They respect the fact that
much learning about careers includes personal growth, and they adopt
that growth as a basic goal of the center. Thus, staff can use the alternate
service community as a learning center in ways similar to clients. This
attracts those who have left or are disinterested in professional training,
but would like to learn to be helpful to others.

Types of Centers

The most highly developed and influential alternate services have
grown up in the youth ghettos of major cities. A city may have several
small services, each run by a closely-knit work family who, in addition
to providing service, sees the building of a community and personal growth
as goals. Common services are twenty-four hour telephone counseling
and survival information, crash pads and youth hostels, free medical
clinics, newspapers, bookstores, natural-food stores and information
centers, food cooperatives, craft cooperatives, job information centers
and cooperatives, and drug or group counseling centers (usually for
general problems, but named to satisfy funding sources). Actual drug
counseling projects, usually run by ex-addicts for addicts, such as
Synanon and Daytop Houses, are usually much stricter and more regimented, reflecting the different reality of addicts, and are not dealt with
in this essay. Alternate centers are often the only social service agencies
available to large numbers of young people.

The centers cooperate and share resources informally; at times they
may share staff and facilities. But they operate in small units in order
to develop a community centered on the unit's particular task; this coalescing of a concerned group is one of the most positive organizational
innovations of the counter-culture. In Washington, D.C., for example,
many services are located close together at two "liberated" churches in
the Georgetown area, where young people congregate and live. The beginnings of cooperation among services are signaled by community pot-
luck dinners and intergroup projects and fund raising. Though there are
also competition and undercutting among services, many staff members
are beginning to face up to this major issue of rivalry and to work on
lessening it as they become more secure in their own particular work.

One group SAJA runs a series of group homes which are supported
exclusively by welfare support payments; it also provides a counter-cultural job placement service. The Washington Free Clinic sees about a
hundred people a night; it has its own lab and a large staff of volunteer
medical helpers. The clinic, with its long nightly waiting line, also runs
rap groups and serves as a community center where people can meet,
get food, and share such resources as shelter. These groups use standard
business and organizational techniques to insure the delivery of services,
but they clearly reflect counter-cultural ethics in their stress on absolute
confidentiality, lack of fees and red tape, and informality. Counter-

communities such as Washington's are common but are highly vulnerable
to legal entanglements with the authorities, loss of funding, or attrition
from lack of consistent leadership.

Many suburbs have opened telephone hotlines and community centers
which use the same rhetoric and appearance as urban centers, but are
structurally and procedurally more like traditional professional services.
They represent a compromise between the values of young people and the
standards of the community sponsors. For example, they use volunteers
only after screening and training by an adult or professional director.
They are much less critical of existing services, and often use the program as a funneling mechanism to the traditional services which have
proved unattractive to young people. The control of most suburban centers is vested in a board of prominent citizens who set the policies and
guidelines and limit the program to activities they can understand and
condone. This is in contrast to urban centers, where authority is usually
vested in the staff, who share the concerns and values of the clients.
Since most suburban centers allow young people only to ratify or participate in lower levels of decision-making, they represent the general
community's attitudes toward young people, rather than the counter-culture's attempt to share the decision-making within a small community
which also takes on the responsibility of operating the program.

But in order to retain the support and participation of youth, suburban centers find that they and their clients must have an increasing voice
in policy decisions. The movement to a youth-run program is usually
precipitated by internal conflicts concerning the composition of the staff
or by widespread apathy toward the program. Though such programs
will move toward shared decision-making, they stop short of questioning
the basic social structure and institutions in the community. They adopt
what can be called "sensitivity group values" — the belief that problems
rest with the individual, not the society, and can be solved by recognizing and expressing personal feelings, and by facing reality as a responsible individual. These programs tend to avoid the issue of drugs
or deal punitively with it (firing staff members who are known to use
drugs and minimizing the positive aspects of drug use), and they side-
step the question of sexuality, usually by hiding it or forbidding its overt
expression.

Suburban programs adequately reflect the state of mind of the high
school students who frequent them. These young people are confused and
out of touch with basic social issues, and they are far from confirmed
in their political critique of society or their commitment to their own
attitude toward their community. If they wish a less ambiguous situation,
they will usually leave the community. But suburban centers are often
the only places where young people can take a meaningful and responsible role, and as such they exert pressure for change, if only by contrast with the intense dependence fostered in schools. But they differ
from most of the counter-culture in viewing drug use and sexual exploration as problems rather than ways of growth, and they assign a higher value
to adjustment than to creating alternative realities.

This book focuses on alternate services which see themselves as radically different from traditional services, which operate out of assumptions which young people are beginning to define as a new kind of community. The issues that face a service group which attempts to operate under new values are clear, if difficult. The first is simply survival — finding funds and space, surmounting legal difficulties, and resolving various forms of harassment from the community. A second problem area is the evolution of a "structure" and a process for maintaining it. This includes sharing power and defining the center's work, staff development, use of "experts," and the quality of care and responsibility of the center to clients. A third area is political orientation — the provision of help to clients in such a way that the political and social conditions which contribute to the problem are as much a concern as alleviating the individual misery which is a consequence. Alternate services want to initiate social change, and they are distinguished by a high degree of awareness of such issues and the definition of parts of the program in political terms. A final issue facing alternate services concerns staff — meeting their needs for personal growth and dealing with their conflicts which led them to the alternate service.

Survival

For alternate services, developing independently of entrenched social service organizations, survival is difficult. Even in suburbs, where committees are formed to create programs for drug abuse and youth crises, any new program must very soon face the fact that community leaders have a very incomplete understanding of what young people need. They act out of the preconceived notions that the main aim of any youth program is to control behavior so that drugs are not used, that young people should not run away or defy authority; that controversy is dysfunctional; and that adults are fully absolved from any responsibility for the problems. This attitude is at odds with young people's needs as they perceive them. As a result, the program deals with the community's needs and loses the support of young people; or else the program must look elsewhere for financial support and sanction — among the foundations, churches, and the pitifully small amounts of government funding that inadvertently go to innovative programs.

When competing for funds, the willingness to innovate in basic structure and goals and to share power with clients (youth) is more often a liability than an asset. Most programs have to make do with very limited funds (usually less than $25,000 in seed money extending over only one year) to run a program for which established service agencies could command far greater sums. Community chests contribute heavily to agencies whose right to command funds comes from their longevity, so that, for example, a block-long YMCA which stands almost empty receives large donations, while the crisis center struggles along with seed money from a church and no clear prospect of extended funding. Most crisis centers will not last, simply because they cannot attract funds past the first year, and at that time the community is ready to judge their progress negatively.

The search for funds is accompanied by the struggle to fit into a storefront or building never meant for such a program; it is usually an old deserted building, possibly scheduled for demolition. Programs are always on the move as building inspectors and zoning officials enforce laws without regard to the program's ability to renovate a building which they may use for only a year. An added problem arises with the resultant congregation of young people in the area; and the need for sleeping space, leads to further interest on the part of the police in what they see as a potential drug trouble spot. Currently the police, psychiatrists, and alternate services are fighting for the authority to deal with the "drug area," and young people are rarely allowed to choose their agency. While few programs still face the continual police harassment that big city programs confronted in past years, in fact most staff members do use drugs in some form or other, and sporadic arrests are an everyday occurrence. This circumstance feeds the cycle of community distrust of such programs and tends to negate the "good efforts" of the program in the minds of citizens who see the elimination of drug use as the reason for the center's existence. Chapter 9 discusses some of the difficulties faced by Number Nine in its fight for survival in New Haven.

Structure

Once an alternate service program has provided for its survival, it must define a structure which will provide its service. One of the basic struggles of the counter-culture is the defining of structures and relationships so that they meet people's needs and actualize their values. Since most young people distrust social agencies because there they do not feel treated like people, they will be sensitive to the structure of the alternate service as it is reflected in the treatment they receive. The staff members make the connection between the way they treat each other and the way they treat clients. If they deal fairly, openly, and expressively with issues, they assume that they will take the same tone with their clients. Ideally, the service will become an informal, collaborative, role-free, accepting community in which helping is not sharply differentiated from other activities.

The center is structured around a cohesive small group, where role differences and specialized tasks are usually minimized. The group sees itself as part of a personal and organizational change process, and therefore it aims at the periodic transcendence of its own norms and procedures. It is also a community, in which individuals work out their personal relationships while engaged on a common task. Most groups use techniques of confrontation, role play, and other therapeutic tools naturally, as part of their evolving process. The group is concerned with examining itself and its constituents and in evaluating procedures in terms of the collective goals. These concerns produce a climate that is intense, conflict-ridden, and unstable; it often serves as a crucible for critical emotional issues.

A center must work out its power relations as a developmental learning process for individuals and the group as a whole. Most centers express

a verbal preference for a collaborative authority structure to make policy
and decisions. The difficulty arises when the group realizes that expertise
and taking responsibility for carrying out decisions are not synonymous
with sharing power. Inevitably some people distinguish themselves in
either ability or energy for work, while others find it hard to take action
or are distracted by personal issues. The group must recognize these
realities and develop a structure which is both collaborative and aware
of individual differences. At this stage most centers appoint a single
director or small core group to oversee operations, with a subsistence
salary while he devotes his full energies to the center. It is recognized
that volunteers may not be in touch with all the basic issues, so the staff
as a whole may only get together to share information or at most to make
major policy decisions.

This set-up retains many elements of the traditional structure; the
innovative aspects concern the definition of individual responsibility.
Supervision, which is kept to a minimum, is usually used not to enforce
strict procedures, but to assure a staff member's competence. Since the
counter-cultural ethic favors strict personal freedom with a minimum
of organizational encroachment ("Do your own thing"); staff members are
not prevented by hierarchical supervision from offering help to clients
within any boundaries they set for themselves. There is therefore little
accountability at some centers. In others, accountability arises out of
shared work space, working in teams, and informal observation of each
other, coupled with discussions of particularly difficult situations.

A related structural problem concerns the definition of expertise and
its relationship to traditional standards. In some centers the radical
structure is partially contradicted by the fairly traditional definition of
service and skill. A professional therapist is accepted as naturally competent, and he is allowed to supervise and to set standards without the
usual trial period imposed on other staff members. But most centers
have a fairly precise understanding of the limits and failings of traditional services, and while they accept help from professionals in training
and supervision, they usually select professionals who have themselves
begun to criticize traditional services and who see work at the alternate
center as a learning experience. The alternate service is thus helped
to separate what is the real skill of providing service from the rhetoric
of help which may disguise little constructive action.

Alternate services constantly apply varying degrees of sophistication
and insight to their basic philosophy and the kind of structure that will
support it. Since staff turnover is usually high, most centers are constantly changing their structure or finding inadequacies in their present
synthesis. At times service suffers from constant flux because of basic
criticism and dissatisfaction with partial solutions. Centers may become
personal growth exercises for staff members, or may turn into ideological discussion clubs. But like other stages, this one too is unstable
and usually leads to a reemphasis or rediscovery of service. The opposite extreme is more prevalent. That is, the alternate service attains
a stable structure and begins to articulate clear roles, which are

independent of the people involved, and assumes more and more the reality of the traditional service institution, with only the rhetoric and appearance of the counter-culture.

Political Orientation

The political question for alternate services concerns the relationship of individual help to changes in the basic social conditions which led to the problems requiring help. This concern takes specific forms. The first strategy allows alternate services to make use of their critique of traditional services and force structural and procedural changes in them, while protecting the civil liberties of clients. The second consists of organizing the clients to make basic changes in their life style and to broaden their understanding of and concern with social issues, so that they can relate them to their individual experience and take them into consideration in making personal decisions. The first process is creating social change, the second process is politicization. If either of these can be integrated into the activity of alternate services, they may have a potential for change as great as that of the various mass political movements which have stirred in recent years.

Many possibilities for social change have already been mentioned. The existence of an alternate institution in a community legitimates change within traditional services as their staff members begin to recognize the merit of an alternate approach. Particularly in such areas as role flexibility among professionals, acceptance of growth-oriented approaches to therapy, crisis work with a minimum of red tape, and family work, the example of alternate services has been important. The existence of a place where professionals in training may try out new roles helps to create a climate in which change appears less threatening to traditional institutions. The concrete alternate service in practice is usually less fearsome than the staff's fantasy of its effects. Further, when the staff members of alternate services put their values into practice in dealing with staff members of traditional services they tend to break down the stereotypes of radical mental health approaches and exponents. Rather than finding hostile, negative, ideologically oriented young people, professionals meet open, friendly, dedicated, and questioning young people. All of these break down what institutional change agents have written about as the fear and resistance toward change which prevails in traditional services.

The area of most direct confrontation, where the alternate service is directly at odds with traditional services, centers on the rights of young people, of clients and patients. The traditional model is paternalistic, oriented toward control of behavior and adjustment to prevailing social structure, and tends to favor the desires and needs of the community and the parent over that of the deviant and the youth. Because alternate services tend to view deviance and rebellion as potentially constructive social responses, they support rather than frustrate the individual's right to choose them. Taking a position similar in most respects to that of psychoanalyst Thomas Szasz, they also support an end to involuntary

hospitalization and the mystification of expertise. Alternate services see
the positive aspects of psychedelic drugs — which are growth-oriented
and potentially dislodge a person's previously held truths — but reject
tranquillizers, amphetamines, and barbiturates, which they suspect
as having the effect of promoting acceptance of a status quo which is
objectionable (see Chapter 4).

On these issues, and on the related matters of the rights of students
in high schools or in their dealings with parents, the alternate service is
carving out a role as ombudsman. This role — as advocate of the desires
and civil liberties of the client — is one that social agencies, tied as they
are to the institutions which can also be the source of grievances by individuals, have avoided or assumed only tentatively and in limited areas.
Alternate services see the right to protest, to legal counsel, and to
choice as central to humanity and as essential to individual problem solving. When an alternate service center matures, it not only may support
individual attempts to gain these rights, but also organize pressure groups
and efforts to change basic institutional policies. At this time, because
of increasing support within institutions for such reforms, alternate services stand a chance of promoting a highly successful change movement.

Alternate services support the politicization of individuals, not by
ideological brainwashing, but by the demonstration of a successful strategy of individual change and social action. Staff members who have
chosen a radical life style which also involves them in helping others
are a powerful example to a client searching for a similar synthesis.
Clients can begin to help others as volunteers even as they are being
helped. This device supports change not only in counseling sessions but
also as new behavior. In a traditional service, the client can only relate
in that role, and continued relating is defined as dependence. In alternate
services it is not necessary for a client to leave in order to be considered
"cured," rather, he can become a more responsible member of the community as a way of showing growth and positive change.

Transitions toward new life strategies are thus made easier because
the support of others is available. The message is conveyed that dis-
satisfactions with the way things are should be accompanied by changes
in behavior and concrete action. Clients and staff often begin to live
together in small satellite communities. Increasingly, even high school
students are maturing rapidly and becoming more sensitive to a possible
stifling atmosphere in their families, and they are forming living arrangements with peers. Others establish new schools, job exchanges,
cooperative day-care centers, farms, arts coops, and support communities based on such personal issues as sexuality. The alternate service
becomes a clearing house and exchange for activities relating to changes
in life style and a center where new activities can be initiated.

Staff members of an alternate service obtain an experiential education in the workings of institutions whenever they try to get help for
another client or for themselves. They see law enforcement, courts,
family service, schools, and mental health clinics as they actually operate on people, not as they rhetorically describe themselves. A day

spent in court or observing psychiatric interviews can do more to build
a highly sophisticated critique of society than can scores of books, lectures, and demonstrations. By locating itself in a position where it deals
with the unmet needs of many failing social institutions, and by trying
to develop concrete alternatives to their structures on personal as well
as organizational levels, the alternate service becomes not only a helping service, but also a powerful educational experience.

Staff

   As is true of most situations in the current world, the most certain
characteristic of crisis centers seems to be transience and change. This
is true both for the centers as evolving institutions and as an overwhelming personal issue for staff members. Like the people serviced by the
center, the staff members are usually transient, moving around, exploring, and looking for new ways to live as they try to make sense out
of the array of personal choices and cultural changes occurring around
them. Their work represents a stage in the process of basic personal
development; and this is an experience they share with most of their
clients. Most staff members stay at centers no more than a few months,
a year at most, so that the processes of institutionalization and role-
hardening rarely take place at crisis centers. This turnover makes for
some vitality, because staff members have experience (through observing,
helping, or being helped) of other alternate services and counter-communities. Staff exchange occurs with a regularity that facilitates sharing
new ideas and unleashes a constant flow of new energy.

   The negative side of this process, which Marty Beyer (1971) reports
on in a study of Number Nine, is the fact that many staff members allow
their own working through of personal conflicts with authority, sexuality,
and intimacy to take precedence over service work at the center. Staff
members usually live together, many for the first time being free of their
families or of paternalistic dormitories. The rush of freedom brings a
host of feelings and reactions, and it may take quite a while to resolve
them. This fact is coupled with the circumstance that constant interaction
with the pain and confusion of strangers, and their assumption of the
staff's competence or at least free energy to deal with their difficulties,
is an enormous drain. Staff members may also reject all structure in
reaction to the oppressive presence of irrational authority in their previous experience of school or family. The pressure on staff members
to provide service may thus conflict with the pressure of sudden liberation from external constraints and sudden clarification of internal conflict.

   Staff members of alternate services at times feel the need to make a
choice between their personal needs and the needs of others; this conflict
produces a constant tension in centers where young people in personal
flux hold decision-making power. This tension can be resolved either
restrictively, by curtailing service or denying personal needs, or by
growth toward a more mature and creative synthesis of the two in the
work community. The presence of those with greater experience or maturity can help centers to maintain adequate services though many staff

members are in flux. Many of the greatest success stories of crisis centers concern positive changes in staff members through the work they
perform there. The frequency of this result reinforces the minimal differentiation between helpers and helped and accentuates the sense of a
community working together on issues of common concern. The intense
focus and involvement which can thus be produced accounts for much of
the excitement such organizations can arouse in their local community
during periods when things are "together."

Other than the possible gain in maturity, staff members also find
work at alternate services useful as part of a search for a meaningful
work identity. Many of them come to work at centers part-time as part
of a professional, university or high school course, or full-time as
part of a work-study program. Their initial interest in working at the
center usually results from a tension in their lives between assuming a
professional role in a more or less traditional institution and assuming
a deviant, but increasingly viable role in the counter-culture as part of
a new community. They come to the center to test the choice, to try out
the role of counter-cultural worker, while remaining attached to a traditional structure. They test out whether they can work with integrity in
the counter-institution and they explore how they can apply what they are
learning there to a more traditional setting. This situation creates a
flow and dialogue with traditional service and in professional programs
as such settings open up. As faculty and professionals become aware of
the innovations offered by the alternate service, they may offer
themselves as researchers, as consultants, or occasionally simply as
volunteer workers.

Conferences

The sudden nationwide growth of alternate services, the effects of
staff members' moving around and in and out of more traditional settings,
and self-definition and survival issues have brought some embryonic
attempts to organize and confederate. Funding sources, particularly the
government, have shown some interest in supporting alternate services,
but with their aid have come requests to formulate "guidelines, standards,
and training programs " which have the effect of pushing the innovative
centers toward the mainstream of professional services. This development conflicts with the political and social change orientation of many,
particularly the larger urban centers.

There have been at least three national gatherings of alternate services. Two took place in the spring of 1971, occurring, almost simultaneously in California and Maryland; the third was held June, 1972 in
Minnesota. Although great resistance has been shown to forming a professional organization, with implications of exclusivity and agreement on
basic issues, at the conferences the wide disparities among programs was
less obvious than the area of shared goals and concerns. Another common concern centered on basic identity conflicts surrounding the definition of a center as "alternative" service or "new professional" service,
innovation or counter-culture. As cosponsors of the Maryland conference

we gathered information from seventy operating programs, about two-thirds of them suburban hotlines, the rest urban alternate service centers. In visiting and in helping centers with issues, we arrived at many of the impressions shared here.

The Maryland conference (Jaffe, 1971) was a microcosm for some of the basic structural innovations and conflicts facing alternate services. The planning process, initiated by the suicide prevention center of the National Institute of Mental Health, exposed two different concepts of alternate service. The initiating group saw themselves as professional helpers, and they desired the conference to share what they believed to be a well-defined body of knowledge about training, quality control, funding, and starting a program. The counter-cultural group saw the services and the conference as attempts to open up basic questions about how people could live together, what kind of support they needed, how to cope with change, and how a new culture could be formed with a reordering of priorities.

The conference represented an awareness of this basic tension that pervaded all talk of alternate services, but it was recognized that an exchange might prove helpful. The conference was structured as a loose confederation of groups, with large meetings where anyone could state a need or organize a workshop. There were no extensive panels or professional resource persons, rather, each person was seen as a resource by virtue of his participation in a program. Most centers left the conference with a greater sense of the schizophrenia which seems to infect each individual program, as founders try to deal with the youth culture and youths try to build effective services.

The basic choices facing alternate services concern continued support. If large-scale funding is found, there is a danger that the more innovative programs will be forced into the mainstream, as a body of procedures and lore ends experimentation and direct response to problems which marked the movement at its inception. Professionals are eager to incorporate what they see as the innovations of alternate programs, but they may misunderstand the basic philosophy while they incorporate a new appearance and style. The development of two national networks (The Exchange, 311 Cedar Avenue S., Minneapolis, Minn. and the National Free Clinic Council, 1304 Haight St., San Francisco, Cal.) and unceasing conflict about funding, expertise, political position and basic goals, provides a base for continued development amid constant tension.

B. Two Models of Youth Crisis Centers

This section details the intimate connection between the structure of a helping service, and the way it offers help. That relationship is the crucial insight of alternate services. The emergence of the counter-culture is fueled by young people's discontent with, and distrust of, the established social order, its values, structures, and systems. Young people do not identify their interests with those of the social system they live in. They often experience themselves as alienated, and this experience is rooted in value conflicts between the youth and his society and is concretized in his internalization of society. Those who experience this alienation most acutely will be confused, conflicted, insecure, defensive, and distrustful of attempts to "help" them. While most young people have internalized the belief that social (particularly psychiatric) services are helpful, they are reluctant to go to them with their problems without being coerced. A recent study in New Haven (Reed, 1971) indicated that fully two-thirds of the young people served by social service programs were there under pressure from their family, school, or police. Many youths perceive social service programs as allied with the values of parents, school administrators and the police. They notice that others who are acting the way they do (or want to) are diagnosed as emotionally disturbed. Any other motives for running away, using drugs, or dropping out of school are thus invalidated. As a result, despite the fact that many young people will express a belief in a program's efficacy, they will not seek it out, and when they are compelled to go to it, professionals will find them uncooperative and uncommunicative.

Youth crisis centers have been created in recognition of this failure of traditional approaches to make inroads among adolescents. Despite similarities in form among these programs (twenty-four hour crisis phones; free counseling with a minimum of red tape; walk-in space with easily accessible contacts; crash pads; and young people as volunteer staff), there seem to be at least two basically different models of such a service. Each model begins with a fundamentally different understanding of why traditional programs failed. In the most common type, the basic internal conflict (which is present in traditional professional programs also) between providing help and attempting to modify behavior to correspond with the normative values of society, is ignored. Such a program is, in fact, a threat to young people's integrity and values. These programs assume that traditional methods fail to appeal to young people because they are not "fashionable" or relevant, and consequently they create crisis centers that seem innovative in style and appearance. A second type of program questions the nature of the "help" offered to young people by any institution which reflects only the core values of the social order. In trying to depart radically from existing institutional practices, this kind of crisis center attempts to manifest the different priorities of the counter-culture through its structure and basic conceptions of service, as well as in its style and appearance.

The first approach can be characterized as the innovative professional model, and the second as the counter-cultural model. Here we develop both models to clarify the direction of change in crisis centers which are only groping toward a model of service that does justice to young people.

The values of the "establishment" are to some extent internalized by everyone growing up in this society. But many young people are ceasing to identify emotionally with these values, although they may appear to conform to them in their behavior. Because society's structures legitimate these values, they are not easily dismissed or outgrown. The new priorities of the counter-cultural trend, experienced as emotionally true and personal, are in conflict with the internalized rules. The difference is between "should" and "want", rule and desire, what exists and what might exist. Young people who act on their "own" values will appear to the society as unrealistic or even as severely disturbed. These young people are paternalistically tolerated, and the counter-culture is devalued because it is considered a phase, a fashion conformed to as a part of adolescence. There may even be some truth to this view. When young people attempt to create a program which reflects their values, they inadvertently begin with many of the beliefs, rules, and habits which they have internalized in growing up, and at this point the program can be characterized as innovative professional. As young people gain control of their programs and begin the attempt to actualize their values within the program, they unlearn behavior patterns which do not support these values. A change process begins toward the ideal of the counter-institutional model.

The innovative professional center lays stress on providing a service. As a center attempts to become more counter-institutional, staff members seek radical personal change as an additional goal of the program, which is valued as highly as service. A professional, for example, may leave a traditional program because he dislikes the limits placed on him and may find the innovative professional center supportive of his need for greater freedom and casualness. This move does not require him to undergo a radical examination of himself, his society, his skills, the nature of the helping relationship, or his economic position and life style; nor need he develop a commitment to political change. But if he is to be part of a genuine counter-institutional program, all these processes must occur.

Community Support

Communities generally support crisis lines. This support is usually expressed as a gesture — financial support is more difficult to achieve. While the inexpensiveness of a crisis line is appealing, as is the fact that such a program involves many young people (teens and college age) in responsible and constructive activities, the reasons behind the community support tend to be less relevant to the program and more influenced by the felt needs of the adults.

When the community became aware of the "drug problem", there was general panic. Many people had dismissed young people's discontent with society as a phase of adolescence, something they would "grow out of." The danger of drug addiction made this alienation more ominous. Community leaders realized that orthodox social services did not attract youth, but they assumed that this lack of appeal was due to superficial qualities (red tape, formal procedures, and language which was "out of it") rather than to more subtle differences in values. As the community saw it, professionals could be helpful to young people if they would only be more "with it." When young people turned up wanting to create such service programs as hotlines, many adults saw a two-fold benefit in this suggestion. Crisis lines could help deal with the drug problem, while also providing a means for filtering out severely troubled young people and sending them to professional programs. In the hysteria of the moment, brought on by the drug-use epidemic, community leaders were more open to innovative programs (particularly if they were sold as drug programs) and more tolerant of young people whose behavior, language, and especially appearance were unconventional. They were, after all, closer to the values of the established individuals by virtue of their desire to help through institutionalized means than were the other young people who openly disliked community leadership and other forms of authority.

In fact, the community was ambivalent toward young people. Many adults recognized that moral leadership within this country has come from youth, particularly in race and peace conflicts. To the extent that young people were part of the "cutting edge of social change," liberal leaders wanted to identify with them. On the other hand, the disregard, or rejection, of many social standards and conventions, the experimentation with sexuality and drugs, and the avoidance of institutions and "legitimate" authority (if not the attack against the system and authority) created antipathy. When young people who were clearly identified with the nonconforming element by their dress, language, and unconventional ideas (which these liberal community leaders tended to view as creative and innovative) offered to work in crisis lines, liberals were excited. Here was an opportunity to deal with the drug problem — particularly drug abuse, as liberals refer to it — and a means of bringing alienated youth closer to socially acceptable limits; but most importantly, it was an opening for these leaders to support, and identify with, social change agents. Liberals provided the legitimatization necessary for the establishing of crisis lines and for the search for funding from the more conservative community leadership which almost always has control over money.

Young Leadership

Many crisis lines are run by young people under twenty-five. If they were not active in the civil rights movement of the early 1960s and the peace movement of the late 1960s, they were influenced by the ideological conflicts surrounding this activism. Leaning toward a radical, but not usually overtly political, stance, young leadership brought to the program a dedication to serving their peers. The young people believed that society offers very painful experiences to youth during its development. Almost everybody endured the struggles, but there were casualties. Activist youth wanted to help these casualties and to minimize the number of victims among its peers. These young people also experienced a sense of alienation from their society, and they desired to build an alternative culture. Crisis centers were alternate social service programs, helping young people by offering a service grounded in an ideology or philosophy based on common experiences, not in academically trained professionalism. Young leaders knew intuitively that drugs were not the problem; rather, young people were being "fucked over" by the family as an institution, by the school system, and by the communities they lived in. Yet adults were not the enemy either; rather, they too were victims of the same processes and systems. Their hostility was rooted in a defensive attitude toward change and a fear created out of the narrow perspectives they had learned from their older generations.

The challenge to these youthful, idealistic, but inexperienced and un- trained leaders was immense: not only to build new organizations, but to create a "counter-institutional" structure truly reflecting humanitarian values, at the same time recognizing these values as unarticulated and vague. Furthermore, society was not prepared to facilitate the growth of alternative programs. It reacted defensively to changes based on val- ues that were only dimly comprehended (such as the absence of hier- archy, salaries based on subsistence needs, communal living, and roles which carried no more authority than the individual himself could gen- erate), and it pressured young people through funding sources. As well as the basic structure to support a program, there was the problem of service. Young people relied, especially during the early stages of the program, on the innovative professional model (the psychiatric litera- ture, professionals as trainers and consultants), while experiencing in- ner conflicts and ambivalences about the nature and quality of this as- sistance. They were referring clients to people they themselves would never consult, acting as if they could be helpful while personally doubt- ing and distrusting psychotherapy as such, and legitimating an authority they only recognized as an authority out of their own feelings of inade- quacy and helplessness.

Young leaders took on the dual task of creating an entirely new kind of organization and developing a new form of help, while personally dealing with many of the conflicts, self-doubt, and sense of helplessness and powerlessness their clients experienced. Often new programs were so caught up in the day-to-day process of surviving that no energy re- mained for personal or organizational growth and for the improvement of the offered services. Disillusionment set in, while the feeling of sub- tle resentment and hostility from the adult community grew each day with dwindling funds, mounting criticism, and I told you so's. Many programs closed; others, in an effort to survive, took on the forms most tolerated by the society. They ended up alienating kids in the same way established programs did, while more successful alternative institutions angered and frustrated staff members and "fucked over" kids through inexperience, inconsistency, or misunderstandings and suspicions. Many young people in the community who still identified with their parents took on the atti- tude of their parents (suspicion and veiled hostility), since they lacked any experience with the programs.

If crisis centers (larger, more experimental forms based on crisis lines) survive, they will do so against formidable odds. Probably the greatest strength — impressive to both liberal and conservative leaders in the community — is the sense of mutual dedication among the staff members in crisis centers. This energy is creative, innovations have occurred, and changes have been brought about in more established

social service agencies. The direction of this change process can be
thought of as moving from the innovative professional model to the counter-institution.

Structure

An innovative professional service usually begins with either a com-
munity-based committee or an agency concerned with the problems of
youth, such as drugs. Their motivation seems to be to help young people
to act in terms of the norms of society and to control socially unacceptable behavior. The founders of an innovative professional program con-
ceptualize their problem as a failure to reach young people. They therefore create a more attractive program, with changes in appearance,
language, and procedures. The center is meant to be a supplementary
program, a connecting link between young people with problems and
professionals. Young people who work there are told that being helpful
consists in developing a trust relationship with other young people who
have "real problems," then transferring this trust to professionals.
Young volunteers provide a front for unappealing professional programs
which do not look deeper for the cause of their unattractiveness.

This model defends itself against questions concerning the program's
implicit assumptions. These are that professionals are necessarily helpful to young people and have no vested interest in supporting societal
values that the young person may challenge. These assumptions can be
challenged empirically. Although young staff in innovative professional
programs refer those with difficult problems to professionals, when
asked whether they would themselves seek out a professional for help
with their own problems, they smile in embarrassment at the obvious
contradiction. They refer young people to professionals, not out of any
belief in their usefulness, but out of a sense of helplessness about what
to do with someone's pain. Their reliance on professionals is thus a
defense against their feeling of helplessness, and by not questioning
this behavior, the program attempts to legitimate social norms which
the staff violates. The program thereby defends rather than experiments.

The board holds the power in an innovative professional center, usually as a requirement of the funding source. The board, which justifies
its existence to young people as a fund-raising source, then uses this
power to exact changes in the program. As far as the community which
provides money is concerned, the board acts as a watchdog over the
young people in the program, keeping them in line with the norms of the
society. That is why, despite the fact that the program is intended for
young people, a majority of the board members are always adults. Through
lack of interest or because of liberal fears concerning the exercise of
power, the board may remain aloof from or disinterested in the day-to-
day functioning of the center. But it usually resorts to indirect means of
exercising a controlling function. The dual role of the board creates
ambivalence among the staff members. They feel positively toward the
board because it raises funds but resent the continual, if indirect, controlling force, which mitigates against radical change and leads toward

institutionalization (record keeping, supervisory and administrative hierarchies, and the like). Staff members support the board because they fear a loss of funds, and the community supports the board because it produces a nonthreatening program. The demands by funding sources for a certain kind of accountability makes it hard for young people to move the program in a counter-institutional direction, which would be controversial and unable to justify its effectiveness by the established criteria.

The hiring process is a board's first indirect means for controlling the direction of a crisis center. The director who is hired conforms to two criteria — acceptability to young people and to the board. Since young people are so desperate for programs that any older person who is sincerely interested in them is remarkable, it is easy to satisfy them. Most of the hiring process is concerned with satisfying the board. It usually hires a person who has demonstrated his (reflecting male chauvinist values) ability to conform to socially acceptable standards by obtaining some kind of degree (or is in the process of doing so), or he is an ex-addict (a convert to a religion is always a strong moral example — the board would not hire a person who is known to use drugs). Controversy is considered contradictory to mature leadership. To establish a connecting-link program, a director must be willing to accept professionals as authorities and experts.

Hiring not only selects a person who has demonstrated an ability to be coopted as a militant or radical, but also establishes a deferential relationship between the board and the director. This hierarchy is reinforced by the judicious application of money. The director is primarily accountable upward, not to clients and staff. The board does not have to exercise overt influence, simply because the thought of what they would do "if" is sufficient. The director is the board's agent, and any conflict of interest between the board and the staff or young people must strain the director's integrity. The desire to survive — reinforced with the prestige, financial reward, power, and the like, that are tied to the director's role — eventually leads to a "realistic" attitude and a feeling that direct confrontation is not an acceptable strategy. Obfuscation and mystification of the central issues becomes a necessary defense by the director, the board, and eventually a majority of the staff members. Helplessness and despair are the alternative, since the staff members remain dependent on the director and board for survival and direction (limits and structure). They do not learn how to provide for themselves. Withdrawal from the program (disillusionment) or cooption are the only choices because fundamental change in structure is impossible. Staff energy is dissipated in power games, manipulation, generating ideological confusion, the exercise of "competence, expertise, and experience" as criteria for the prescribing of power.

The creation of a hierarchy is another indirect influence on the innovative professional model which implicitly determines the limits of the program and services of the center. The director's authority prescribes the hierarchy. He has earned it not within the program. but by activities outside it which are not visible to the staff; therefore he is

artificially invested with power. The staff has no alternative, he is a
given. Furthermore, the structure becomes deferential. The director
has assistants, or roles are created and filled with his permission. The
differences in roles, power, and status become associated with overt
activities (gaining experience, authority, expertise) or covert activities
(sleeping with the director, being submissive and deferential, colluding
with the director). The client is devalued because all attention is directed
upward. New, inexperienced staff members begin with face-to-face relations with clients and move away. Clients are denigrated by labels ("really crazy") or subjected to procedures and routines that must be interpreted by staff members. Novice staff members must appear useful by
being directive and assertive, which leads to arbitrary and authoritarian
attitudes and aloofness, disdain, and lack of interest in clients. Given
these conditions, staff members can move up and become part of the
organization; they become administrators or in-house experts (trainers
and the like). If the staff members must focus on scheming within the
organization in order to be valued and to feel less alienated and helpless,
this situation will be mirrored in staff-client relationships. As in all
standard organizations, the structure creates the model for the service
relationships, which form the bottom of the hierarchy.

The professional plays a major role in assisting the board to limit
the center to activities which reflect the core values and structures of
society. The professional as such is not necessarily an integral part of
the innovative professional center; it is sufficient that he exists somewhere, since his principal value is as an authority legitimating the center and its concept of service. Professionals can comfortably give this
sanction, since the concept mirrors their own, as do the structure and
staff hierarchy. Occasionally an individual professional works within
the crisis center as volunteer help. He does not, of course, enter the
organization in the same way a young person does; his entry indicates
his prescribed authority and status. This circumstance implicitly devalues the young volunteer, since what he has to offer has to be demonstrated, while the value of the professional is assured. This dispropor-
tion artificially depresses the staff's confidence, whereupon the professional
can use his prescribed authority and status to increase it again by con-
ferring legitimacy and transferring "skills." Thus staff members become
dependent on the professional for their sense of confidence. He reinforces
this dependency by the role he selects to play. He rarely answers phones,
drives people around, or cleans up the office. More probably he is a
program consultant, acting in an advisory capacity, or a supervisor, who
controls quality and brings the experimental approach in line with community standards.

These roles of the professional are all defensive. He never really
does anything which can be subjected to empirically based evaluations.
He is an observer and commentator, but not a participant. His expertise
is not questioned. If the staff members handle themselves well, his value will be enhanced in their eyes. If not, their disillusionment will be
interpreted to them as dependency. Though valuing the professional is

prescribed, it is also interpreted as dependency (deification); thus any
direction taken by the staff frustrates moves toward autonomy.
The implication that only a neutral attitude toward a professional is
realistic, seems valid in the sense that their three nonparticipant legiti-
mator roles are indeed neutral as regards service. They create roles
that substitute verbal facility for action, objectivity for responsibility,
and academic capabilities for demonstrated competence in relationships.
Since the professional never really acts or overtly commits himself to a
position, preferring covert implications and inferences, staff members
tend to mimic this approach. They begin to use interpretations as a
defense against criticism, as a means of devaluing a person's beliefs
and values. The professional may judge, but may not be judged; the organization has one-way accountability. His role is based on his myths;
he furnishes a defense against helplessness and despair in the staff and
against the community's fears of harmfulness and incompetence. As a
supervisor, he minimizes the community's and staff's fears that their
incompetence will hurt someone. Yet as a professional expert, he establishes the nature of the incompetence and undermines efforts to overcome it through reliance on direct experience rather than established
procedures. As a trainer, he limits the risks the staff members will
take and subtly conforms their beliefs and behavior to the norms of society, which the professional has internalized through his social-group
membership and his education. As a consultant, he assures the community that the new program will function as a social service agency, along
realistic lines determined by social norms.

The basic purpose of the innovative professional model is to institutionalize the core values of society in a seemingly experimental form of
social service and to subtly support the internalizations of the young
people the service meets as staff or clients. The power, authority, and
responsibility of the program remain in the hands of the community and
its representatives. Professionals unintentionally collude with this process, since their roles imply that professionalism is synonymous with
expertise, despite the fact that the very existence of the program is evidence of their failure. The counter-institutional form begins to evolve
when the power of the center moves into the hands of young people,
then no longer disenfranchised and powerless. This happens only when
they learn to raise funds, to determine priorities, and to establish guidelines. These young people move into leadership positions even though
they are distressed by the authoritarianism implicit in such social structures as the innovative professional center and resent the class biases
supported by hierarchies based on unearned power prescribed by the
community. They create the counter-institution not as a supplement to
established programs, but as an alternative. "Nothing is known, all must
be learned" is the guiding assumption, rather than the belief that professionals are the source of expertise on how to be helpful. Although this
position is basically anti-intellectual, much of their relearning process is
in fact based on a reading of the literature, but with a more open mind
to non-normative concepts, such as Wilhelm Reich's ideas about the body
and R.D. Laing's formulation of madness as a form of revolt.

The Counter-Institution

A leveling process in forming the counter-institution leads to structural changes. All must unlearn their basic social reflexes while simultaneously building alternatives. All staff members are fundamentally equal until they demonstrate (and continue to demonstrate) different capacities. The entire staff constitutes a support group, without prescribed leadership or delegated authority. The people are in the group to grow as individuals, to support each other in surviving in an environment they perceive as hostile, and to build relationships (play). The structure evolves from the needs of the organization, and therefore it changes periodically through subtle shifts in the perceptions of the staff. Change becomes a continuous process, unlike the situation in the innovative professional center, where most changes occur in the period before the center opens, allowing only for later adjustments and accommodations "Do it!" — rather than plan and implement — is the guideline, because only through experiment and experience can we learn the consequences. Planning before an organization opens is a defensive maneuver, anticipating dangers which may or may not have substance and creating structures and roles to defend against them. Such planning is slow and careful because it is primarily a strategy of prudence. In a counter-institution planning takes place after a need is felt. The structure allows for risk and experimentation and tries to deal with real needs rather than with indeterminable internal fears and anxieties. The model of authority also shifts from father to children, to brothers and sisters.

Because the running of a counter-institution is a consciously political activity, a nonviolent radical change process within society, it cannot remain isolated and remote from other services, even though its existence often provokes an initial response of defensive anger and fear from the community. While the program utilizes adjunct agencies, such as birth-control clinics — it would rather relate to services that have a greater ideological similarity, such as a free medical clinic. If such services do not exist, the counter-institution must deal with other services in a way that forces them to face up to the humanity and rights of a client and to look at the effects of their structures on service. The staff members of the counter-institution may initially exhibit an antiprofessional, antisocial stance, but as they gain confidence and support for their work, they learn to become a constructive, confronting force acting on other services, rather than an obstructive, argumentative power. The community often takes pleasure in pointing out a center's seeming similarities to professional programs, noting, for example, that the center is becoming more "establishment," but this reaction tends to be a defense against noticing the substantive changes in structure which the center has already attempted as it moves away from the innovative professional model.

The political nature of the counter-institution (in the sense that it models a new authority structure) can be observed in the staff selection process. People are given a period of time to work within the organization in order to demonstrate what they can do. There are no a priori evaluations. Staff members work and live a life style they support through their counseling. Counseling is a political activity, a support activity for the emergence of autonomous individuals who live the values of the counter-culture, an adaption to change (Chapter 7). Everyone participates in counseling, which has a priority second only to community organizing when the program becomes sophisticated enough to work in this area. The staff members perceive needs and accept responsibilities to the end that the organization can survive as an economic and structural base for social change activities. They do not delegate responsibilities; rather, a required task is voluntarily assumed by someone, or assigned equally by lot.

Entrance into the counter-institution is based on what one does within it, not on who one is or what one has done outside. Many dysfunctional individuals therefore become part of the structure. Staff members spend many hours supporting each other toward a more integrated and helpful personality. This process blurs distinctions between clients and staff. Staff members reinforce this merging by denying that they "do counseling" and insisting that they are in fact simply developing helpful relationships. The flexibility an individual may demonstrate in switching from a helpful role to one where he himself needs help, supports this definition. By refusing to establish roles in situations in which individuals must be mobile within a class system, the reliability and quality of the program remains flexible. Volunteer part-time staff members provide the base necessary to maintain the program, since any community has large numbers of such people who desire to serve and be a part of such an institution.

Standing groups or committees rarely exist; groups form around crises. This is an accurate reflection of the attitudes and values of young people, who do not trust planning, stabilization, and institutionalization as strategies to protect their interests. The energy available at any given moment for a crisis is therefore increased, and the steady depression caused by ongoing responsibilities is eliminated. Staff members have a sense of freedom and autonomy, since they have few role-related responsibilities to determine their direction. Their potential for growth within the group is thus limited entirely by themselves. Personal changes as well as real needs (funding, publicity) demand a structure which is always evolving and dying out. While the danger facing an innovative professional center is stagnation and solidification, the dangers facing a counter-institution are an inability to complete the necessary tasks for survival and total resistance to structure itself as staff members externalize their own resistance to internalized values and authoritarian parents and teachers.

Service

Since the counter-institution is a structure intended to support radical change processes, it is not surprising to find the strategy of rebellion offered as a reasonable direction for a young person with difficulties. This does not mean that counter-institutions reject the personal change

strategies of the innovative professional center — adjustment and accommodation (subversion and concealment in some cases) — but that they are
not highly valued. Young people are supported in establishing alternate
life styles as well. Staff members are a living example of the ability
to say no to social norms (rebellion), and their behavior demonstrate the
ability to develop and choose alternatives. Disturbed behavior is not ignored,
but its causes are seen to lie not in the individual but in his social setting
— family and school. Disturbed behavior is viewed as a frustrated, only
partly conscious (verbalized) act of resistance and rebellion. Since the
same attitude is applied to the staff, the person coming for help is a
peer of the staff member who gives (and perhaps receives) help. Help
consists of articulating the sources of limitations and frustrations for the
individual and developing strategies to deal with them. Though this method
is not substantially different from the rhetoric of the innovative professional model, in fact, when the actual strategies are pinned down, the
professional model supports the family and school as legitimate institutions that could use some "changes," while the counter-institution works
at alternatives, such as underground runaway systems and young people's
living and learning in alternate high schools, group homes, etc.

The "client" in the counter-institution defines his own problems, and
the parameters of this definition are accepted by the staff. Her judgment
is not coopted by benevolent intentions on the staff's part ("she really
should go home for her own good") or by superior insight ("his problem
is really ... "). The underlying assumption is that the client is fully responsible for his behavior, and other than for their own protection, the
staff does not want to control or channel his behavior. The unconscious
as a construct is not useful in the counter-institution because the goal
is full awareness of self. Less than full awareness or responsibility is
accepted, but it is not explained away as the result of mechanisms out
of the individual's control. Within the revolutionary model, the prime
evils are exploitation and oppression in experiential terms.

The innovative professional model's bias toward middle-class values
and the interests of the community over the interests of young people
can be examined in its response to the "drug problem". In the first place,
just the attempt to categorize drug use as a problem is a reflection of
how the adult middle-class community views illegal drug use rather than
of young people's attitudes. When a person denies that he has a problem
with drugs, the center has an interest in contradicting him. The young
person gets the implication that drugs are an escape and not a valid experience, without further definition of what is real and valid. Drug use
becomes a symptom in the perspective of the program, if the client continues to remain in the program. Often the innovative professional program demands a cessation of drug use as a condition for the client's receiving help. Staff members who use drugs are continually confronted
with the contradiction between their wanting to help but having a "problem"
with drugs themselves, if they are not dismissed immediately. Most
often staff and client drug use becomes an undercover activity.

Not only does the bias against drugs in the innovative professional

service determine the nature and conditions of service, but the role of
the organization in the community becomes a moral example to young
people, who will learn to condemn and deny the validity of drug use, despite the fact that many of the staff members may continue to use drugs.
The ultimate result of the superficial liberal tolerance of marijuana
smoking in order to cover up moralistic positions concerning other drugs
is the gradual alienation of the program from young people, who prefer
to consider the drug question in terms of useful and not useful, instead
of right-wrong, healthy-sick. Despite its initial appeal, if the program
persists in this position, it will eventually create the same alienation
which was the reason for the program in the first place.

The counter-institution's ambiguity, its lack of structure, and its
concept of counseling as a relationship do not initially appeal to young
people, since the center's orientation supports their internal conflicts
rather than immediately defining some system of rules as legitimate.
It does not immediately help them build defenses against anxiety. After
the initial discomfort, however, the ambiguity allows individuals to define themselves clearly and to make their own determinations concerning
the values they will integrate into their behavior. The counter-institution's
initial effect is anxiety, even resentment, but over a period of time it is
more useful to young people and develops stronger bonds between those
it serves and the program. It will also risk more for a client, based on
less evidence. In the cases of raising bail, fighting legal battles against
parents, helping a runaway find a job or an apartment, or becoming the
legal guardian of a youth, the counter-institution just needs to be asked,
while the innovative professional model resists this involvement and
demands corroborating evidence. This unconditional support by the
counter-institution of a young person's face-value desires and beliefs is
unusual; it often offsets the initial anxiety generated by the program.

The conservative nature of the professional model imposes limitations on the role of staff members, while the counter-institution leaves
the degree and type of involvement up to the individual. The staff member
is also under pressure — generated by the openness of the environment
and the discussion of issues — to be unexploitive and nonoppressive,
and the group draws up a shared understanding of what this means. The
nature of the relationship is considered a risk, and the job is to take
risks which will be meaningful and helpful to both parties, rather than
to structure the relationship to minimize confusion, ambiguity, and
personal involvement. Angry parents (including the staff's), law suits,
difficulties with police and other community harassment, insanity and
hospitalization — all are real risks which come with helping young people
on their own terms: rebelling. The responsibility for a client's actions
is never accepted by a counter-institution, although it is responsible
for developing a contract about how it can be helpful. Therefore, protection of the staff and program need never be disguised as the protection
of the client (as through taping suicidal phone calls, hospitalizing a disturbed person, prescribing "down" drugs to counteract strong emotions)
and in fact cannot be, since staff members do not accept a power relationship toward their client.

In the innovative professional model the stress is on program development, which amounts to a focus on staff-client relationships as role interactions. Learning one's role and working to perfect this role become central issues; counseling becomes work. In the counter-institution relationships are mutual; both people grow through shared experiments. Problems are principally problems of relating. The development of a counseling relationship is part work, part play (in some cases it is exclusively and necessarily play). While training is useful, it is not necessary. Some things are known and can be transferred. There are guides, not experts, and each person must select his own guide through mutual interaction and a shared contract. Relationships cannot become case loads. Staff members of a counter-institution are not evaluated on the basis of the quantity of their counseling relationships. They can choose to become involved, and they determine the nature and extent of this involvement through negotiations with the person who has come to the program. The counter-institution staff members move toward becoming role-free, while staff members in the innovative professional center become skilled in role behavior.

The holistic structure of the counter-institution (a community with permeable borders) is reflected in the kinds of relationships formed within it. The "discovery" is made that while many young people do indeed come for help in the solution of problems, others — perhaps a majority — are looking for deep, intimate relationships and need a supportive understanding, and tolerant (patient) person for a guide. Nothing has to be "done." They just want a place where they can be themselves, and the counter-institution legitimates this desire and tries to be that kind of place, where relating is the goal and end. Seeing staff members as peers, through mutually defined relationships, returns to the young clients a value they lose when they are identified as victims, as needing help, or as less competent at being human.

Counter-institutions see the survival of young people as the principal issue, and their purpose is to support this survival in terms of young people's values. The counter-institution is an advocate of youth's right to rebel; it therefore tolerates strong positions held by staff members which a majority might identify as contrary to the interests of the organization. "Firing", like "hiring", is practically nonexistent. The center moves naturally toward the basic need of organizing young people and toward providing activities for young people to come together — at concerts, festivals, communes, food or job coops, and the like. Controversy is neither sought for its own sake nor avoided on principle. While the innovative professional center is defensive and avoids real issues and radical self analysis, the counter-institution is confrontive. It struggles to identify substantial conflicts and contradictions and to act on them. Obviously no crisis center can completely adhere to such positions, but most reflect these shared basic trends and values.

Since the counter-institutional program is shaped to meet the staff's needs as well as the organization's, their relationships are determined largely by their own intuition and judgment. Since all their relationships are to some extent created according to personal needs, they enjoy a

fairly high level of satisfaction. The repression of life styles in the innovative professional model leads to restrictive norms and ethical limitations within the program. The taboo against sexual relations with
clients is an example of the sexual frustration found in most middle-class
situations. Counter-institutions do not prohibit sexuality with clients.
When such relationships do form, they are often no more or less free of
exploitation and oppression than any other modality of relating, and sexuality is therefore not punished and restricted as such, but is understood
as a natural aspect of relationships. Individuals are free to explore and
learn about their sexuality. Since this freedom is endemic to the counter-
culture, staff members do not find themselves particularly interested in
"exploiting" young clients, since there are enough sexual relationships
available with those not in need of help, and sexuality is no longer treated
as a scarce resource, to be guarded and defended. Sexual exploitation
seems to be a function of life-style restrictions carried over into a program limiting the natural development of an individual to the extent that
insecure and confused individuals become attractive. In the counter-
culture living with another person, having sexual relations with many,
the ease with which sex is introduced into companionship, and the di-
minution on other cultural taboos on expression of feeling and bodily contact of all kinds diminish the need and desire for strong prohibitions
against involvement and experimentation in relations.

If young people are truly emerging as the locus of a counter-culture,
social service models which only pay lip service to this change will
be ineffective and eventually unattractive to young people. A natural
change process is occurring, and given time, young people will choose
programs which offer them different structures and content rather than
merely new styles and appearances. Minimizing real change and sub-
stituting rhetorical and superficial adjustments are a devaluation of
young people's idealism, their needs, and their capacity to define and
implement what they want. This process, as epitomized by the innovative
professional approach to crisis centers, is a further confirmation of the
inability of the system to really change, and it will be experienced as
just another attempt at paternalistic control over young people who are
developing real alternatives and eventually new systems. The dehumanization and depersonalization, which many have commented on, is endemic
because it is rooted in the structure and values of institutions. Any solution which does not address itself to the need for radical change is self-
defeating. Already founders of innovative professional centers are noting
with cynicism the failure of their attempts to be "relevant" to young
people, and they are falling back on more conservative means of control.
Young people are also becoming more cynical and suspicious of any organizational structure. It is not possible to compare the quality of service in each approach, since so many different values are involved within
the concept of service and help. But the innovative professional model,
despite contrary intentions, defends against change on every level and
against information which might suggest change (since it imposes

perspectives and relationships through roles). The counter-institution may also fail to develop into a viable form of service, but it has fewer internal limitations on change. Its future depends largely on the individuals within it, and on their ability to escape from their own internalization of society.

Chapter 7

RADICAL COUNSELING PROGRAMS

A. Crisis Phone Lines

The basic concept of crisis lines — using a phone to call for help — is as old as the telephone itself. Alcoholics Anonymous was probably the first program to apply the idea in any formal sense when members were encouraged to call other members whenever they felt like taking a drink. The Suicide Prevention Center in Los Angelos used a crisis (or emergency)line for people who were thinking about killing themselves. This modification was later enlarged by young semiprofessional people interested in relating to the problems of adolescents. Many who had made friends with young people had found themselves frequently called whenever the adolescents had a desire to talk to someone. The popularity of the crisis-line program has led to the proliferation of this approach over the last four years, to the point where almost every major city has a crisis line.

Whenever such a number is called, a variety of services are available. For people who want to talk, or need advice, counseling is provided by the person answering the phone. Rarely does the caller have to be referred to someone else or to wait. Information about a number of different topics, such as sex or drugs, is available, and anyone needing specialized services is given a referral to appropriate programs. In any emergencies, such as a suicide attempt, transportation, and other relevant forms of help are possible.

Critical Differences for Young People

The basic issue for most young people concerning the existence of hotlines is not, as many might suspect, the quality of service. Young people are more concerned with style. By this is not meant style in the trivial sense of jargon, informality, or appearance; young people want a program that is sensitive to them as adolescents. A program must, in other words, be aware of what the experience of adolescence is like at this time in history. Face-to-face counseling implicitly treats adolescents as if they were adults and does not take into consideration those facets of adolescence which can be summed up by the simple response, "Everybody treats me as if I were still a child." When people are powerless to define their situation, it will be defined for them; young people

151

are powerless, and their situation is largely defined for them. They are therefore not free to act like adults even if they desire to do so. A program which expects them to be adults ignores their social reality. Crisis lines, with their open attitude, have been successful in reaching young poeple in large numbers. (Number Nine reports an average of 6,500 new callers a year). It is therefore useful to see what unique features of crisis lines appeal to young people.

Young people lack mobility; such mobility as they have is generally contingent on their parents' consent (or the youth's ability to conceal his movements from his parents). But phones are accessible. A young person has only to dial a number and he is in contact with someone to talk to. He can call at any time, from any place he happens to be. Phones are easily available and may be used in a way which guarantees privacy. The youth cannot be seen, and whether or not he reveals his name is up to him.

The most critical difference between face-to-face contact and a phone call may be the degree of control the caller-client can exercise over the relationship. A feeling of control gives a person a sense of independence (at an age when becoming independent is a critical issue), of safety (at a time when young people are becoming increasingly suspicious of authority), of freedom (being able to choose instead of having to submit), and finally of maturity (the act of calling is completely the caller's, free of parental influences). This feeling of control is real. The caller can and must initiate the call; he can terminate it at will. The typical excuse is "I have to go now"; but hanging up quickly is common under any disturbing circumstances. Anonymity protects the caller against any punitive acts on the part of the counselor or any attempt by the counselor to gain complete control over the caller. Many young people fear seeing a psychiatrist because he might label them crazy and commit them. Many others fear being turned in to the police because of their involvement in illegal activities.

Young people are much troubled by the issue of authority, and they easily confuse any older person's influence with the kind of control they expect from their parents. Distrusting all adults, they are embarrassed to expose sensitive areas to them, fearing ridicule, censure, or rejection. Phone contacts equalize the relationship. The voice on the other end becomes more human because the projections are less likely to be of parental authority figures and of a sense of invulnerability and distance. Open and direct in peer-group relationships, young people use the equalizing effect to speak to the counselor as simply another person, rather than an authority. The calls can last an unlimited amount of time, since there is no effort to terminate the "session" as is done in face-to-face relationships. Therefore the caller can become more deeply involved in his situation. Callers build up slowly, increasing the likelihood of emotional involvement in what they are saying, since they do not feel that they have to "get everything out before the time is up." The equalizing effect also offsets the caller's often irritating belief during a face-to-face relationship that the counselor is talking to him because it is her "job."

Counselors themselves are more relaxed when talking on the phone; they
expect long calls. They know, furthermore, that roles are excruciating
obvious over the phone, and therefore they try to be less routinized and
formal than they might be in a face-to-face contact, which automatically
seems more businesslike.

Finally, phone contacts are more personal than face-to-face relationships. Just as the availability of crisis lines appeal to the impulsive
urges so characteristical of adolescence, they are also conducive to deep
emotional involvement, which is part of this impulsive quality. It is difficult for a young person to limit or feel safe with his emotions; phone
contacts permit the easier expression of feelings (because the other
person can more easily be fantasized about; because the other is not physically present and therefore potentially able to do something). Embarrassment at crying or at looking ugly because of emotional upsets is less
acute over the phone, while the necessarily subdued tone of the other's
voice is supportive and comforting. With the voice of the counselor next
to the caller's ear, and his body relaxed and safe, the adolescent often
creates involved fantasies about the counselor. Many of these are sexual, but since the phone contacts are safe, the fantasies are easily explored by any phone counselor aware of their presence. In face-to-face
relationships sensitive issues cannot be dealt with directly until considerable time has elapsed to build trust. Because young people's interest flows
faster than their trust, counselors often find that significant issues are
never talked about, and any help the client receives is purely circum-
stantial happenstance.

The Crisis

Young people who call a crisis line may not be experiencing a crisis;
or, if it is a crisis, there is no emergency; or they may experience an
emergency which is not a crisis. Essentially a crisis involves a decision
which must be made although it appears either dangerous or impossible
to do so. Previous experiences appear irrelevant or useless. The individual is confronted by a new set of choices, yet he lacks the necessary
confidence to choose. Because they cause a sense of being blocked or
stuck, crises are usually accompanied by anxiety, panic, depression, or
aggression; this fact contributes to the common assumption that an emergency and a crisis are synonymous. There is always, in a crisis situation, the potential for learning, for going beyond the self. There is also
the possibility of catastrophe.

A crisis develops slowly over time. Often a crisis can be seen as a
conflict between a desire and a rule prohibiting either the desire or behavior which would satisfy the desire. More complexly, a crisis occurs
when I want to do this becomes I want to but I shouldn't or I should want
to but I don't or I want to because I should or even I should want to, so
I must want to, but why don't I feel anything. Despite the time it takes
for a crisis to develop, it usually comes to a peak very quickly. At this
critical point the impasse can lead to inaction and withdrawal, resolution
and growth, or ambivalent, contradictory, or self-destructive attempts
at solution.

A crisis line is fundamentally designed to provide a means of solving
the dilemma during this critical period. Whatever is necessary to help
the individual make a constructive decision is used; this includes advice,
information, conversation, counseling, referrals, or just a person on the
other end of a phone line. The purpose is to expand constrictive and limiting alternatives, create new alternatives which are unexpected or were
previously assumed to be "impossible," or if necessary, supporting a
lesser-evil choice in order to minimize destructive consequences. Many
times it is sufficient to occupy a person's mind until enough feelings have
been expressed to allow him a more balanced frame of reference for resolving his own dilemma.

Types of Crisis Calls

The calls received by a crisis line fall into roughly six categories:
referrals or information; conversation; crises (including any situations
of forced choice or limited or unacceptable alternatives); emergencies
(as in overdosing, suicide attempts, or acute psychotic breaks); regular
callers; and crank calls.

Referral and information calls. The use of referrals to other agencies can
be a basic tool of any crisis line. Referrals are often unsucessful in many
other kinds of service (an estimate of 50 percent, perhaps because a person selects a program for some reason, then is told he must go elsewhere
— a subtle rejection and disregard for the choice). However, young people
call for information, and this information can include the names and
numbers of other agencies, particularly those specializing in such services as legal aid, abortions, and birth control (the three most common
needs). Occasionally a counselor may know some elementary answers to
problems such as birth control or arrests. The percentage of callers
(approximately 10 percent) who use a crisis line for information suggests
that ordinary methods for learning about professional help are inadequate.
The possibility also suggests itself that young people are intentionally
isolated from this kind of information because parents and teachers assume
that telling them about abortion, for example, is a tacit acceptance of it.
Parents assume that a failure to provide information in dangerous areas
is tantamount to preventing their children from exploring, while in fact
it only increases that likelihood. Providing accurate information, and
making resources available, actually minimizes potentially destructive
outcomes, while having little effect on decisions to engage in various
activities. This information must come from a trusted source; otherwise young people will test out its validity through experimentation. Attempts to present information under the guise of "education" (either on
sex or drugs) which prejudges and prejudices the issues are also useless.
Young people are not easily misled. Experience with crisis lines confirms
the fact that moral decisions are ultimately made by the individual. The
manipulation of moral decisions, and the indirect punishment of immoral
(socially unacceptable) decisions is destructive and ineffective. As a
secondary consequence, the manipulation of information to support

implicit moral judgments creates distrust, engenders alienation, and
supports paranoia.

The caller who requests and receives accurate, factual information
concerning sex, drugs, or what is acceptable or unacceptable (question
from a twelve-year-old girl: "Will making out spoil me for marriage?")
is moved toward independence and self-reliance. He is able to make
more informed, and therefore more clearly reasoned, choices. When
youth are deprived of such information, or fed extreme and unsupported
statements ("LSD destroys chromosomes," "masturbation will make you
sterile," "VD always has symptoms"), the opposite effect occurs: dependency, irrational and impulsive decisions, and resentment, distrust,
or paranoia. The extent of young people's misconceptions about these
areas of human experience is astounding. A sixteen-year-old girl, quite
seductive and appearing experienced, described intercourse to a caller
as an entirely anal activity out of sheer ignorance. A fourteen-year-old
caller had intercourse regularly because she did not realize what it was
she was doing; no one had ever related the words to the activity for her.

Conversation calls. The caller who appears to desire a conversation,
without a particular focus or problem, rarely receives counseling. Counselors tend to accept the conversation gambit at face value, assuming
that the caller is simply lonely or bored, as indeed she is. Conversation
over a crisis line is most often an "undercover" problem — perhaps two
kinds of problems. The caller may simply distrust the counselor and may
be using conversation as a means of either testing him out as a potential
confidant or avoiding sensitive issues. Usually the perceptive staff member uncovers an emotionally blocked individual who is unable to relate to
anyone except on an intellectualized and superficial basis. The cheery
and entertaining caller may be starved for intimacy but lacking in means
for achieving close relationships. The absence of problems may mean the
difference between a conflict and the emotional experience of the conflict.

A common type of conversational caller is the overweight girl, under
eighteen, whose girl friends protect her feelings by feeding her self-
esteem with lies. This type of girl is seductive but always avoids physical contact, at the same time hinting that she does want to meet the
counselor. Her weight — a kind of self-indulgence, as is extended (heavily fantasized) conversation — remains unmentioned ("Naw, I don't have
any problems really"), since the fantasy infatuation-friendship would, in
her mind, dissolve if the counselor discovered the "truth." If the counselor can develop the girl's trust while convincing her that appearance,
particularly the appearance of an overweight girl, is no obstacle to
friendship, meanwhile making the erotic overtones clear and unnecessary,
he is in a position to really change such a person's style of relating.

Another type of conversationalist is the immature, slightly hysterical
girl (suggestive, seductive, highly impulsive, and anxious) just coming
to awareness of her sexuality. The conversation is a safe way to become
comfortable with sexuality, and the topics usually include liberal spicings
of giggles and explicit sex talk. As the conversation matures, the girl's

talk will deal less with sex; she will be more sincere (and sober) in her
discussions of it. Many times this type of girl is pressured by a mother
who is hostile toward sexuality, is not given support by a withdrawn
father, and has a high level of intelligence coupled with a low level of
maturity. She will report about many experiences in which she felt she
was embarrassed, or she may brag and show off.

Males rarely call just to talk, although occasionally a boy or immature man will develop an infatuation for a female counselor. When men
do call just to talk, they can be very manipulative, even provocative,
enjoying "playing games with people's heads," as it is referred to.

The difficulty with conversationalists is the time it takes to make any
headway with them. Despite their friendly tone, they have a deep-seated
distrust of people. They call in a moment of loneliness, but contact and
the possibility of talk immediately snaps them out of it. The counselor
must develop a slow but direct and constant style, encouraging friendship while focusing the topics on the caller's especially sensitive areas.
The loneliness of phone duty, coupled with the interesting subjects these
callers can talk about, unfortunately distract the counselor from the
more subtle aspects of the caller's situation. A question to keep in mind
with these callers is, "If they are really so entertaining and friendly,
why do they call a crisis line?" Or, "If my job is to help people with
problems, why am I just bull-shitting?"

Crisis calls. Whenever a caller presents a specific difficulty, the staff
member's interest increases. Results are tangible, and some sort of
resolution is possible within the period of one call. Common experiences
leading to the typical crisis call are loneliness, confusion, anxiety, and
depression, while the typical problems fall under four categories: self,
others (sexuality), parents, school. The following examples come
from Number Nine's phone log.

> 10:00 p.m.   Girl, Jane called. 16 years old. she was very
> lonely and afraid to talk, but wanted to. she says she can't re-
> late to people, and feels withdrawn. She said she feels like she's
> falling off a cliff backwards and can't feel anything. she talks
> about animals and really digs them, but all of a sudden, after
> talking for 45 minutes she just withdrew, and wouldn't talk any-
> more.

We know more about Jane because she had subsequent contacts with
the crisis line. The counselor took a supportive, nondirective role, probably because he was intimidated by the cliff image and its self-destructive, possibly psychotic implications. The girl raised a real problem,
retreated to a safer topic — the animals — but returned vividly to her
problem later in the call. The call at least established some degree of
trust, and was an encouraging enough experience for the girl to call
back. In subsequent calls was learned that Jane is unwilling to talk to
her parents about her fears, since she believes that they would ridicule
her or, worse, think her crazy. She was unwilling and unable to seek

professional help because of her desire to conceal her problems from
her parents. (Her perceptions subsequently proved accurate; when her
parents eventually learned of her difficulties, they minimized them,
refusing to "hear of such silly things" again.)

While Jane had been retreating further each year, for a period of
months she relied exclusively on the crisis line for support, occasional
counseling (including feedback, confronting, and interpreting), and plain
friendship. She had, the counselor learned, been engaging in self-muti-
lation; when she began to realize how seriously upset the staff became
at this, she stopped.

At one time the staff considered tapping her phone (a breach of contract since confidentiality was promised), but decided not to, since her
trust was too important. Experience shows that phone tapping is always
unwanted (unless specifically requested by a caller who might pass out,
or some such) and many times is destructive. Rarely — in our experience, never — is it helpful or life-saving. Phone counseling is not a substitute for psychotherapy, which has different goals, dealing with gradual
personality changes, rather than specifically and only crises. While
the conversations with this girl continued over the course of nearly a
year, they were basically friendly talks, with interventions (deliberate
attempts on the part of the staff to either initiate change or develop insight into the conflicts) limited to crisis situations. Phone counseling
can mark time more easily than can face to face relationships.

> 4:30 p.m.   Girl named Marty called. Hung up about going out
> with an ex-boyfriend's best friend. She still likes the first boy,
> but he won't go out with her now for fear of hurting his best
> friend's feelings. Told her to talk to the present boyfriend and
> make that relationship more flexible than going steady. Then she
> could date the boys she wanted to more easily. She'll call back.
> Phone log July 1970.

The Ann Landers variety of personal problems is the most common
type of a call a center receives. Such calls demand advice, even though
giving advice is against standard psychotherapeutic theory and practice.
Attempts to engage a caller in conversation often lead to the caller's
hanging up angrily at being ignored. After hearing the advice callers
commonly hang up quickly, with a sincere but short "Thank you." The
suggestions which are most effective coincide with the caller's own in-
clinations so a counselor is not so much asked to tell the person what to
do as to support an unstated but implicitly made choice or to argue effectively against it. To avoid being considered wrong or stupid, the caller
states the situation in the form of a question to avoid being held responsible for the decision.

After answering the question at face value — thus supporting the
caller — a counselor might broach the matter of any implicit decision
with a remark such as, "It sounds like you already reached a decision
on your own, or you wouldn't agree/disagree so quickly with my advice."

At any rate, no harm is done by giving advice, particularly of the sort that includes alternative answers, and if the caller disconnects immediately at least he will feel respected (accepted at face value) and positively toward the crisis line ("They tried to help"); the way is thus prepared for a second or for encouraging a friend to call. Building support among youth by dealing with them on their terms first is good business and makes sense in terms of counseling goals as well. The point that it is also honest seems too obvious to mention, but many people assume that inferrences and assumptions are more positive bases for building a relationship (when they are yours about the other) than accepting the other at face value until proven wrong; they do not view this kind of second-guessing as a form of dishonesty; but this response implies that the person is being accepted at face value and then assumes that he is, perhaps unintentionally misleading or deceitful.

The basic cause of family conflicts is the unequal distribution of power. Parents command community support, legal sanctions, access to money, and past contributions to the child's welfare, while young people have no power base whatever except rebellion. The crises that raise issues of the use or abuse of power or of manipulation, indirection, concealment, or deviant behavior (depending on the person focused on in the family structure) are inevitably differences in values and beliefs. Values tend to be translated into actions, behavior, or appearance and imply an evaluation of one set or class over another. The child identifies with his parents and through this process internalizes many of their norms and codes, while creating his own through personal experiences and peer-group contact.

> 5:45 p.m.   Girl called. Said her mother is sending her to camp this summer, but she doesn't want to go. Told her to talk to her mother again, and to let her know how much she doesn't want to go and to try to work out a compromise — to do something for her mother if her mother will let her stay home; e.g. housework, to keep her out of her mother's way. Phone log April 1971.

In this case the counselor is thirteen. Traditional attitudes toward helping and toward adolescents assume that competence and maturity are synonymous, or highly correlated, with age. Crisis lines have demonstrated that remarkably young people have maturity, common sense, and good judgment in emergencies. This counselor's response is simple but practical. Her casual acceptance of the mother's motivation for wanting her daughter at camp — keeping her out of the way — as indicated by her tacking it on the end. This is an example of the universality of adolescent experiences. It is commonly experienced that mothers and fathers pretend to be acting in the child's interest when their behavior is entirely or largely motivated by self-interest. The casual, implicit rejection of the daughter as a thinking, opinionated person, while acting as if she were an object to be ordered about is also common.

The basic struggle is clear. Must the girl's behavior correspond to her mother's judgments (and values), or can she find ways of negotiating

partial acceptance in her own right? In this case the mother recognized
what she was doing, and allowed her daughter to stay home when the full
situation was brought to her attention. The counselor had based her
suggestion on an intuitive (subverbal) awareness of the mother's basic
respect for her daughter. The fact that the mother did basically respect
her daughter only demonstrates how easily parents can move into the
role of parent (boss, controller, arbitrator, and so on) and away from
their own feelings.

> 15 year old, Joan, called in crying, very upset, saying her mother
> and father are fighting now all the time and tearing each other
> down in front of all 5 kids. Mom just found out dad is cheating on
> her. Joan says she can't hack any of it. Phone log May 1970.

Joan was counseled over the phone, resulting in an agreement to see
if her mother would talk to the counselor. Her mother was referred to
a family counseling service for help with the marital problems while
encouraged to come with her daughter to the crisis-line office for an
in-depth session. This approach points up the usefulness of professional
counseling programs for supporting the work of crisis lines. They are
properly designed to appeal to adults and are sometimes effective in
working with adolescents, although in the latter case it is usually a matter of an exceptional counselor rather than a generally helpful program.
Crisis lines are unique services, designed for a section of the community with unique needs.

> 3:00 p.m.   Call from a girl who had called before. She had
> been told to leave home during a heated argument, and so had
> run away. She called her mother, after discussing her alternative
> with us, and things worked out. Phone log May 1971.

Unresolved crises tend to escalate into larger, more critical, situations. Crisis intervention in minor, even absurdly trivial, events often
prevents patterns from continuing to the critical stage and exploding.
Once a person commits himself to an action such as running away, successful intervention is less likely. Crisis lines experience a high degree
of success, but they have specific goals, work in limited and well defined
situations, and can use the strong emotions of a crisis to motivate an
individual to change, if only to relieve the pressure. Changing family
situations is more difficult, and runaways are often better off with alternatives to returning home. In the case of this caller, the parents were
not vindictive or punitive. In another experience the father, when contacted by his daughter after six days and told she was willing to come
home, arrived at the crisis-line office accompanied by three squad cars
and a paddy wagon. Sixteen policemen escorted the fifteen-year-old to
her parent's car, while the father refused to discuss the situation with
anyone, including his deploring wife. Another father, overjoyed at his
daughter's safe arrival after less than a day's absence, beat her severely
in a fit of rage at her audacity and lack of repentance.

The issue of family problems, focused on here as an example of one kind of problem crisis lines typically deal with, raises another issue: fully two-thirds of the clients of a crisis line are girls. Boys tend to have more freedom to act out inner conflicts with less negative results, and therefore seem to have less need of crisis intervention; at least, they ask for help less often. Girls are especially powerless in a family because they have the additional burden of being the victims of a double standards many parents actively enforce. Certain disproportionate arrangements in statistics reflect this difference clearly. Boys more often call for legal help, girls with regard to sexual questions. Rarely do boys call concerning abortion, birth control, family issues, running away (boys run as frequently as girls, however), and dating.

Emergencies. It is the emergency call, or the possibility of one, which keeps crisis-line staffers excited about their work. There is no doubt about the effectiveness and significance of the intervention during a crisis involving life and death. Crisis lines literally save lives, but they do more: they save lives in a way which facilitates the growth of the individual. The police or the hospital will also act when someonw is on the verge of death, but the likelihood of developing any positive, supportive, life-affirming relationships during the process of rescue are slim. Crisis lines rescue people because the staffers are deeply, and primarily, committed to them as people. Police and hospital staff generally relate to disturbed individuals through a role, rather than as people to people. The life may be saved, but the individual's worth is not respected. The unwillingness of many crisis lines to call the police to tap a phone line during an emergency is one example of the trust placed in the caller even during a critical time, rather than treating him as a person without rights or integrity. Callers respect this treatment and will call crisis lines more often in cases of possible overdose, suicidal feelings, drug-related freakouts, and the like, than they would other resources in the community.

A unique problem, with features common to most emergency calls, occurred recently. A telephone counselor was called at his home, by a girl who reminded him of a call she had made two months previously, when she suspected that she was pregnant. His warm, nonjudgmental attitude at that time, combined with his willingness to be helpful, had stuck in the girl's mind — even though her call had escaped his. The situation was unbelieveable. The girl had carried a baby to term without her parents becoming aware of the fact. She was sixteen and had only had intercourse once. At the time of the second call, she was at a friend's house, having just completed a Christmas shopping trip with her mother, who, in turn, was up stairs having coffee with the girlfriend's mother. Meanwhile the pregnant girl had begun to have labor pains; her bag of water had broken. She was crying and feeling helpless, yet neither she nor her friend could summon up the courage to tell her mother.

Rather than expressing cynicism and suspicion, the counselor acted on the face-value statements of the caller, despite their highly unusual nature. He insisted that the girl call her mother to the phone. When

the mother answered (still upstairs, while her daughter was downstairs),
he explained briefly and to the point who he was and what was happening
to her daughter. He concluded with a specific instruction to go downstairs
and take her daughter to the hospital. Then the counselor went to the
hospital himself. The girl had already been admitted to the delivery room,
and the mother wanted to be left alone. However, the counselor discovered
that no social worker or psychiatrist in the hospital would be informed of
the peculiar situation, and fearing for the girl's emotional difficulties in
having to confront intimidating parents (the father put his hand through
a wall upon his arrival at the hospital), he called someone himself. After
explaining the situation to the head social worker in the hospital — who
was grateful that the affair had been brought to his attention — the phone
counselor went into the waiting room, where the girlfriend, a fifteen-
year-old, was sitting shaking. She had been sent down to wait for her
friend's father but had not wanted to tell him exactly what was happening
to his daughter. Despite the man's angry and hostile attitude, the girl
had ridden the elevator up to the appropriate floor without saying anything. Now she was terrified, uncertain about what would happen to her
friend and upset because of her own involvement almost from the beginning. The counselor calmed her down; when the social worker arrived,
he left.

The girl telephoned again the next day to tell him she had had a seven
pound, three ounce boy. Further developments occurred. The counselor
found the girl willing to call and talk with him with more honesty and
feeling than she was able to bring to contact with the hospital staff or
the social workers assigned to her case. He communicated freely with
them about the content of her calls, after receiving the girl's permission
to do so. Her deep and reassuring trust in him grew out of his quick and
decisive intervention. It is doubtful whether any other agency would have
ever been called; no family work would ever have been done, and the girl
would have continued on without any intervention if it were not for this
crisis line. As it was, he continued to give help (always over the phone)
to the girl as she dealt with her grief and her unwillingness to give up
her baby — issues very important in her life if she is to ever trust relationships with men again.

Regulars. Regular callers tend to reveal a basic phenomenon in phone
counseling: the tendency to promote close emotional attachments. Furthermore, regulars demonstrate a desire to rely on the crisis phone
line as a source of stimulation, friendship, and on-going support. A few
create on-going relationships as a means of testing out the trustworthiness of the counselor. "Does he/she really care?" The dependency of
some callers on the crisis line tends to create frustration, as does the
testing. Crisis-line staff members seem to desire excitement and novel-
ty. The consistent caller is boring and makes them feel they are missing
a more interesting call. The constant demands of any dependent individual impose a strain, while the monotony is disheartening. Yet many
individuals are trapped by their situation in a place where their only

outlet is the phone. Housewives, taking care of children and without transportation, often call a crisis line during the day. After crisis staff members express their irritation through tones and sarcasm, these dependent callers eventually get the message. Some are simply hung up on after repeated attempts to tell them not to call again unless they have a really important reason. The attitude toward regular callers shows a perceptive observer much about the attitudes and values of the phone staff toward people with problems. Most are generally receptive and supportive over great lengths of time, and when their limit is reached, they handle the frustration directly and compassionately, while some become irritated and hostile.

Cranks. Crank calls are not popular with staff members, although they offer a chance to be truly creative in relating to deeply disturbed individuals. These callers can do little more at first than to generate ridicule or hostility. There is no willingness to deal directly, because the trust level of these individuals is so low. Expressions of paranoia and sexual deviation make staffers particularly uncomfortable in dealing with these callers — especially older teenage staff members. Young teenagers, both boys and girls, tend to take a masturbator in stride surprisingly easily, for example; they support the sexual urges despite their unwillingness to be used by the person; and they remain clearly willing to relate to the person even if he continues his behavior. Generally this acceptance dumbfounds the callers, who expect rejection and punishment.

Many crank callers are paranoid. A recent example began with a long series of hang-up calls. Most staffers resent these, and when the person called, they told him how they felt. Others were willing to talk to the person without demanding that he talk with them. Eventually this approach worked, and the caller began speaking, but saying only, "I want some beer." Staffers took this either quite literally or as a put-on; the possibility of a metaphoric expression did not occur to them. Eventually everyone was bored and irritated. All their attempts at helping had met with little success. One counselor went so far as to tell the guy to fuck himself. As it happened, a more experienced staff member overheard this remark and his attention was drawn to the calls. He decided to accept the next call himself; he told the caller that he was willing to help him get whatever he wanted, but that he did not understand what it was about beer that indicated the caller's wishes.

The caller hung up, but on the very next call, seconds later, he said, "Beer turns me on" in a very sexualized way. During the few seconds of the following call the counselor explained that he was willing to help the person find a way to be turned on, that he appreciated how depressed the caller felt. On the next call the counselor added that he understood the caller's sexual frustration because he was not able to trust women with his feelings. The following time the counselor wondered if the caller was afraid that the counselor would think him crazy and would try to have him locked up. The caller whispered, "Yes," and hung up. Later the counselor mentioned the possibility that the phones could be tapped, and

congratulated the caller on keeping the time limited by hanging up. On
the next call the counselor said he would help keep the person from being
forcibly detained by accepting the fear that the phones were tapped — even
though they were not — and acting accordingly. Then he hung up with a
quick, "Oh, this call's too long already." Other staff members learned
from this conversation — despite the interruptions, clear communication
had been possible — and became more willing to "interpret" the coded
messages. As they did so, the caller became more trusting and eventually came in for counseling. This move led to on-going psychotherapy
with a friendly analyst who acted as a referral or resource whenever
staffers felt that someone needed in-depth long-term counseling.

Callers' Strategies

The most common strategy young people use with a crisis line is
testing. The caller explores the capacity of the counselor to respond
meaningfully by using a superficial problem or conversation as a substitute for the more painful and risky issue prompting the call. Testing is
simultaneously a means of demonstrating to the caller his power over
the counseling relationship (I keep secrets, I determine when and if, I
judge you before I let you get to know me) and a defense against painful
revelations. Consequently, testing can be used manipulatively. The
caller will hint that he is withholding something and make implicit demands on the counselor, promising openness as a reward. Although this
is a manipulative tactic, it is rarely done in bad faith. The caller is
asking for a demonstration of trust from the counselor. If you will control me when I tell you my secrets (expressing the vulnerability of the
caller's state of mind), I must know how you will deal with me if I control you. How much is the counselor in control? What will he do if the
caller plays games? To what extent can the caller influence the counselor's behavior?

A fifteen-year-old called up and said simply, "Hello." The counselor
went directly to work with an attempt to draw her out, leading to an aimless but slightly conflict-laden conversation. Finally the counselor asked
point blank, "Just why did you call?" "To hear someone say, 'Hello',"
the girl answered. This brought the counselor around, since he realized
he had not said hello to the girl. "HELLO!" he responded warmly. The
girl opened up almost immediately, admitted to being alone and lonely,
and eventually brought up many complicated issues in her life: living
with her mother and six other kids without a father; her mother's implication that she had caused her father's death; promiscuous and indes-
criminate relationships with older boys; and more. This case appears
at greater length in case section (p.191). Note the suggestion
there.

A supportive, slightly confronting and aggressive approach, sensitive to the caller's tones and movement toward or away from the counselor, will usually promote a caller's opening up. Any counseling program must recognize that most of the initial contacts made by adolescents are to test the responsiveness and trustworthiness of the counselor.

Insignificant words or statements may conceal deeply experienced conflicts or emotions. Casual omissions by the counselor may stalemate a
relationship. After many contacts with a young boy, the counselor finally
said that he liked him. This admission led the boy to reveal a problem
that had been bothering him for years. His reticence to discuss had been
based on his uncertainty about being liked. The boy had been afraid of
trusting his own inferences, since he had been mistaken in canier situations. Testing works, protecting the caller against an incompetent
counselor. Community fears that young people will be harmed by openness
are based on a distrust in young people which assumes them to be naive
and excessively vulnerable. Certainly they are more open, but they are
not easily fooled into opening themselves up to more pain than they can
tolerate.

Another frequent strategy is previews of coming attractions. Callers
who use this build up to major revelations over a period of time, maintaining the counselor's interest by leaking portions before they are
ready to deal with them completely. This strategy builds a relationship
and works on the problems simultaneously. Many people seek help as a
means of creating a close and meaningful relationship with someone who
will not hurt them. When this strategy goes overboard, the caller becomes
a star feature each night of the week. Desperately afraid of being rejected,
he manufactures crises to keep the counselor involved. In one case a girl
pretended to be swallowing an overdose of pills. The staffers responded
as if she were really swallowing pills, convinced her to let them come
to take her to the hospital, and went to her house. Shortly before they
arrived (someone remained in contact with the girl over the phone), she
really took some pills to authenticate staff actions.

Another strategy used by callers, especially young girls, is confusion between a counseling relationship (which they ask for initially) and
a romantic involvement (which is what they want). Having failed to find
ways to handle real relationships that can bring them close to someone,
these callers present themselves as helpless in order to gain this end.
Phones are conducive to this sort of infatuation, since they provide plenty
of safety for the inexperienced or frightened girl with strong sexual impulses. Flirtations over the phone are often helpful, since the counselor
is able to help the caller develop confidence, learn new ways to relate,
affirm the value of the girl as a person independent of sexual longings
for her body, talk about the issues concerning relationships, and eventually work out a relationship with a girl which does not end in pain but
simply becomes less needed as time goes on. The counseling-love relationship can be one of the most powerfully helpful transitional experiences between childhood and adolescence. But this strategy can also be
used to seduce a counselor, trap a counselor in a relationship which the
girl suddenly ends (making up for past experiences), or to develop a
powerful hold over the counselor (exposure leading to punishment, threat
of exposure leading to dominance). In its simplest, least helpful modes
this strategy just avoids any real contact between the counselor and the
caller, keeping the relationship in the realm of projections and fantasies.

Both need to want this for it to happen, however, and a good counselor
(someone who remembers that his own relationships worked out best
when they were not based on phone calls) can work things out by merely
being direct and open.

Another common strategy is the use of the <u>counseling call</u> — "Will
you help me with a problem I have" — to find support for undisclosed
decisions the caller has already made but feels ambivalent toward. Less
interested in alternatives, these callers want to have the counselors
recommend and support their choice. Using the moral authority of the
counselor to decide the ambivalence in favor of the caller's own feelings
in the matter is not harmful. In fact it is very helpful since it is a transition between the need to be dependent on someone completely and the
fear of acting completely autonomously. The caller only rarely pretends
that the decision is the responsibility of the counselor. This strategy
carried to absurd lengths becomes the manipulation of the counselor into
acting as the decision-maker in the caller's life, with full responsibility
for all effects and consequences. Furthermore, this usually adroit caller
finds it fun to convince the counselor that by giving advice all the time,
he is being helped. In fact, his strategies become personality traits
rather than transitional phases in the development process. The caller
ceases to strive toward independence, but under the guise of seeking
independence he creates a new object for his dependency. A rather unusual example was a young man in his early twenties, who had previously
been institutionalized (which made him quite knowledgeable about clinical
approaches). He came into a crisis-line center asking for some help. He
needed, he said, to grow out of his dependency and wanted the staff to
decorate a room as a nursery, set up a crib, and come in to rock him
and feed him with a bottle so he could begin working through these issues.
The play almost worked, until one of the counselors asked, "What issues
are involved in being treated like a baby?" The paradox of treating a
person like a baby so he could deal with being treated like a baby, which
was based on his desire to be treated like a baby, which would be fulfilled
by being treated like a baby ... well, the staff made him call a bus company to find out for himself what time he could get a ride home.

The Basic Equation

Having discussed some of the more common strategies of phone
callers, we are now in a position to comment on the fact that counselors
and callers act alike. That is, counselors also use strategies and defenses,
though different ones. Essentially callers and counselors are the same.
Callers act on their own intiative to seek help for their helplessness;
counselors sit passively by (experiencing themselves as helpless or incompetent to be helpful), waiting to be helped by callers wanting to be
helped. Counselors frequently deal with their experiences through the
use of the caller's problems, while the caller deals with the counselor's
problems in the area of helping. Many times crisis lines find that their
own staff members need to be called as often as callers need to call.
Sometimes staffers call their own program or, when possible, call
another program in a nearby town where they are not known well.

The fallacy in regard to a crisis line is to assume that, because the roles are different between a counselor and a caller, there is a difference in quality between the two people's emotional or social skills and well-being. Many times the caller is more able to handle critical situations than are staffers. Supervision and screening are structured attempts to weed out individuals with serious problems, or to prevent them from answering the phone, but seriously disturbed people call with about the same frequency as they try to work in the program. Crisis lines have experienced the paradox of helping some people more by letting them work as counselors than they could have by letting them be callers. The proportion of staff members with problems is approximately the same in the population who call; screening only encourages people to be scretive about their conflicts and disturbances if they want to really be accepted as staff. Trying to work with staff as entirely responsible, mature, and stable personalities is as misleading and incorrect as trying to assume that all callers are helpless, confused, or disturbed.

When a crisis line begins to realize that the staffers inside are an accurate reflection of the kids outside, having the same problems, the same incapacities, the same disturbances, two approaches can be used: rejection (screening out the ones demanding too much time and energy), or supporting counselers in the same way callers are dealt with, without rejection or punishment. Being responsible for callers does not allow a program to allow just anyone to handle the phones, but a careful distinction should be made between people who are kept off because their personalities annoy "more together" people and those who are kept off because of their genuine inability to handle phones.

Perhaps the best approach to the problem is too view staff members as individuals who do not know how to ask for, or use, support, despite their varying needs for help, and to see the people who call as able to deal with any of the varying degrees of crises they may be facing. In other words, callers usually cannot act in a crisis, but they can recognize and deal with this inability — they call for help. Counselors usually can act in a crisis, but they cannot (to varying degrees) recognize and deal with their personal inabilities to function or to feel good about themselves. Callers can initiate a counseling relationship but often cannot easily respond within one. Counselors often rely on roles to support them in relationships, but given this structure and at least a potential reason for the relationship, they can relate well. There are many parallels: counselors and clients complement each other quite neatly. They are only complete individuals when they can learn to freely move from role to role, developing their potentials as helpers (an autonomous individuals) and victims (dependent on others) in a way which overcomes their own internal divisions.

Crisis lines can build this role reversal into the program by setting up staff groups to deal with personal problems, by encouraging staffers to use the line whenever they want someone to talk to, and by minimizing the stigma attached to callers. Whenever counselors joke about a caller, for example, they might be reminded that they do similar things.

Furthermore, programs can drop the pretense that helpers are qualitively
superior individuals and develop empirical means for screening instead
of using subjective reactions to potential counselors. By opening up staff
positions to competent individuals while recognizing that they may not
necessarily be "together," the crisis line will develop a staff accurately
(even if obliquely) reflecting the community it serves. If screening tends
to confuse competence with how well a personality conforms to socially
(determined by those in power) acceptable standards, then the program's
staff will be made up of a distorted, and probably rigidified, role-oriented,
suppressed group of people. A crisis line the author is familiar with has
a staff member who is recognizably good with people over the phone, but
who for the last few months has been psychologically unable to use her
hands. She was dismissed because of the image of the program — "What
will people say" — after a few months of dedicated service. The routini-
zation of a staff occurs shortly after the staff is standardized. Interpersonal relationships become limited to likeminded people, which creates
a tendency to respond automatically rather than critically to crisis calls.

The Phenomenology of a Crisis Call

The basic issue for training and supervision in crisis-line programs
is the continual confusion of the subjective with the objective, with staff
members often disoriented as to what in fact they are doing. Matters
become extremely ambiguous, and staffers respond by trying to write
things down — particularly instructions which are so contradictory that
they would be funny if they were not held so seriously: Do not give advice; do not give instructions; do not tell people what to do. All are
predicated on the assumption such activities do not help people to learn.
One would hope that staff members notice that these attempts to teach
rely on precisely such methods as they are told to avoid.

To begin with, a crisis call is a phone call. This plain fact is often
overlooked. Put another way, a contact in a crisis-line program is exclusively based on sounds and noises. Hearing, listening, are the only
way a caller and a counselor relate to each other's communications.
This is a substantial change in the way we are used to relating to other
people's communication. Most of us depend on visual cues (such as body
language, or the context of the conversation as determined by the room,
the temperature, and so on) to qualify our understandings of the literal
meaning of someone's words. Literal meanings are rarely accurate. To
the extent that we do depend on visual or tactile sense data to interpret
what we hear, we are distorting the content of our hearing. We are so
used to this process of interpretation that our minds substitute images
and fantasies for missing visual data. Phones create a fairly automatic
though unnoticed response in most people; a reliance on fantasy, images,
and visualizations of the caller as a means for interpreting what the other
is feeling or saying.

The extent of this mechanism can be determined by the number of
times a counselor finds himself surprised at the appearance of a caller
or finds himself using his eyes during a call. Eyes will seek out data

in the room to distract the listener from the gap created by lack of visual
contact with the caller. The primary defense of a counselor over the phone
will be his use of his eyes, or his movements to avoid emotions and feelings created by the contact with the caller. A person's skills in listening
to sounds and using subvocal sounds as cues to determining what a caller
is saying or feeling are developed when he stops watching and seeing,
turning into what he is hearing.

Training programs can use blindfolds (even before participants meet
each other) to simulate the phone-call situation, stressing in role-play
situations attention to every sound and its possible meanings. Sighs,
groans, small choking sounds, swallowing, musical backgrounds, movements, changes in stress, tone, and volume, are all important cues often overlooked in training situations. Going further, the novice can be
made aware of how he uses his eyes to distract himself during a call and
how searching movements can clue him into his own feelings of being lost,
not knowing what to do next.

Beyond sounds, calls basically exist in the mind. There are no ex-
ternalizations of sensations or feelings, as in any face-to-face relationships. When I talk with someone I see, I can "see" unhappiness is in
me; the other person's emotions become subjective experiences for the
counselor, with no object outside the mind to focus on. We depend on ex-
ternalization to create barriers between our own feelings (attributable
to our thoughts or experiences) and other people's feelings, which we
can empathize with but which clearly exist as an outsider's. In phone
counseling the caller and the counselor often get caught up in an intensely personal, highly emotional relationship because of the fact that
identification is almost impossible to avoid.

The intensity with which a counselor and a caller can mutually affect
each other is astounding. By sound alone deep emotions can be catalyzed
in another person — sexualized loneliness or eroticized excitement, to
mention two common experiences. Many counselors remain emotionally
suppressed (they ignore themselves almost completely in their attempt
to maintain their sense of self) during crisis calls, thus creating unusual
degrees of alienation and separation. Fears and anxiety can be generated
easily, since fantasy production is stimulated by the absence of all communication except by sound. Training programs can use fantasy trips
and supportive group environments as means of accustoming counselors
to dealing with their own projections, fantasies, and emotions. Talking
on the phone is similar to talking with someone late at night, after the
lights are out. Almost anything goes, and the experience is highly per-
sonalized. This emotional involvement is an issue in supervision, since
a counselor may have great trouble communicating such a personal experience. One is reminded of the fact that confessional booths prevent
visual contact between the priest and the congregant, encouraging the
subjective intensity of confession and the revelation of a private and
anonymous individuals deepest fears and failings.

The third major insight into the nature of phone contacts is the tremendous reliance placed on the use of words to express virtually the

whole of human experience. An effective phone counselor must be a highly talented translator. He or she must cut through mundane speech and trite expressions to reach a profound understanding of an individual's most painful experiences. This process is complicated by the fact that many young people are practically inarticulate, relying on jargon and colloquialisms to express a wide range of information, emotions, and experiences. Counselors must learn how to develop an experience so concretely that they can easily infer and articulate how the other feels, and what conflicts he is subject to. Putting the problem into words is one of the major contributions a counselor can make.

A girl called up, aged thirteen (although at the time she claimed to be sixteen). She had a "problem." The counselor understood from the tone of voice and the way she stopped short that in this communication "problem" meant a decision to make, as opposed to a situation to get out of, or the like. To the question, "What is it you are wondering about doing?" the girl replied, "Going out tonight." "Going out" is a slang expression for dating or being with a boy, but it also means just going out, going out with the gang, and so on. Since the girl seemed to be conflicted about the situation, the counselor assumed her decision involved boys or a boy. "There are these five guys ... I'm supposed to meet them." The counselor heard anxiety and assumed the five guys had an arrangement with this girl which was to some degree sexual. The girl was having second thoughts. "They want you to do something with them," said the counselor, using an ambiguous term that could be taken to refer to either sexual or social activity. "Yes, but I've done it before with four of them." The girl had either picked up on the implication of sexual activity or had something else in mind. In this syntax, "it" usually refers to intercourse. As the call continued, the counselor discovered that the girl had agreed to a "gang bang" and was having second thoughts. However it would have been both emotionally and linguistically difficult for her to express herself, without the counselor's constant translation.

Concentrating in training programs on listening to what is heard, recognizing one's own subjective experience of the call for what it is (based on fantasies, projections, and the like), and learning to translate the words, tones, syntax, pauses, coughs, silences, and so on, into a meaningful and clear communication process is the essence of phone counseling. Considering that it must all be done in a situation where there is little the counselor can do to minimize the effects of bad judgment (such as the caller hanging up and not calling back) and where the counselor must shift into a style of communicating much less rich and complex than a visual-auditory-tactile one, phone counseling is more difficult than a face-to-face relationship. Here interpretations can be checked out for accuracy by watching the other person's expressions, if nothing else. Over the phone a caller may use body defenses quite unknown to the counselor who cannot see them, leaving no indication at all in the sounds he makes. Unfortunately most professional models of counseling are based, implicitly and often unwittingly, on the assumption that the client is seen by the therapist. Therefore many techniques useful in one-to-one relationships are not relevant to the phone call context.

Goals in Crisis-Line Counseling Programs

There seem to be four basic goals which are realistic and relevant
for any crisis line program: contact, building relationships, being helpful, and growing. These are goals for the individuals within the program,
for the leadership of the program, for the organization, and for the service offered in the program. They are simple yet complicated; possible
yet often seem impossible. Other goals which often assume primacy include survival, personal needs as against program needs (in programs
where stress is placed on work-oriented staff roles which do not leave
space for individuals), affluence, power, prestige, and the satisfaction
of unfulfilled personal needs as against the recognition and support of
other people's needs and wants.

Contact is the unmistakable experience of having touched someone
deeply, personally, and in a way which affirms each individual's unique-
ness and individuality. Contact can also be trivial or heroic; being there
when someone calls to talk because she is bored, being there when someone calls because he is drawn to death. Contact is in meeting the eyes
of another staff member; recognizing how far away one has grown from
one's ideals and feelings. Contact is touching, seeing, listening and
arguing, even fighting. Making contact is the first step in any relationship,
and the avoidance of contact is the first step toward depersonalized, routinized, and meaningless role-playing.

Building a relationship means supporting, accepting, and initiating
contact in more ways, on different levels. Listening to people's stories,
cutting through their bullshit, casting the I Ching with them, or remembering what is important in their scheme of things, are all means for
building on the first contact. Being bored, turned off, cynical, unaccept-
ing, critical, judgmental, rejecting, withdrawing recognition of other
people's presence, denying that other people have effects on oneself, all
are ways of taking apart a person who is fragmented and divided.

Being helpful means acting in good faith, being supportive without
conning the other into being dependent, listening when people want to talk
but not giving up oneself in order to do so. Being helpful means doing
for others sometimes, and not doing for them at other times. Being helpful means remembering that the other is a person, not an object; a de-
cider, not a puppet; and a feeler, not a robot. It is also helpful to be oneself, as a process, and not a static and changeless person who implies
by immobility that she has reached a state of bliss and perfection.

Growing is an organic, natural process with its own direction, energy,
and meaning. Growth does not have to be encouraged, it comes naturally.
What is not natural is being told all sorts of rules to direct growth, being
punished for growing in the wrong direction, and being rejected as an
ugly weed that has no value except as a complement to prettier flowers.
Growth is fun, not work. Furthermore, growth is pleasurable and does
not require suffering. Most often when a person is working without having
fun, is learning without enjoyment, and feels that he only changes when
he suffers, there is a basic misunderstanding in his life about what is
natural and what is conditioned. Crisis lines have the eternal problem of

overcoming conditioning in order to remember how to just be natural, but at least these programs are aware that that's the problem.

B. An Alternate System for Counseling

The reform of counseling is not the development of new techniques. Counseling takes place within organizations whose structure reflects the basic norms of our culture, and people bring to the counseling system a set of expectations and a definition of their problems which also reinforce and maintain these core assumptions. As in any dynamic system, a change in one section usually sets up opposition in other parts, and the net result is a return to equilibrium. Attempts to change norms and structure at the level of the client-helper relationship must therefore also be matched by work at redefining the whole system, from mental sets of clients to structural support for counselors; otherwise the alterations will most probably be undone by the reaction of other parts of the system. The innovative counselor whose ideas are opposed by his colleagues and who is ordered to produce hard data justifying his position, subverted by the rest of his staff, or is finally forced to move to a new job where others share his concept of work, illustrates some of the system's conservative reactions to change. The development of an alternative must work at several levels and must include structural and interpersonal, as well as technical, innovations if they are to "take."

This essay has been the most difficult to write because it is about a process of definition which we have only begun. It is the outline of a journey to come. We are trying to look at the entire system in which counseling is practiced and to redefine it in the light of humanistic values and political sophistication about the nature of social change. The basic assumption is that meeting human needs is the shared responsibility of a community and that presently there is a need for a remedial institution with such a task. Traditionally this task is called therapy, counseling, or social welfare, and tradition rigorously limits the role and responsibility of the helper. Our work calls such limits into question and tries to work directly from needs presented in a situation of minimum expectations and minimum definition of the nature of the response. Through such a process we hope that the counseling we practice will become a radical therapy.

An alternate theory of counseling begins with a redefinition of the nature of the need. The clients' dilemmas are seen as consequences of their positions due to oppressiveness in the society, and the solution is to develop a personal theory of social change which will allow people to meet their own needs. Rather than adjustment to the objective situation, the goal is to develop a sense of movement, so that the environment can be adjusted to fit legitimate human needs. The mental health counseling system acts to neutralize and mystify personal strategies which might aid this change process; the current system supports and reflects the root causes of the clients' dilemma. The traditional system of therapeutic practice has not caused social problems, but it reflects the basic structures which produce them and therefore its practices do not allow the discovery of a way out of them. The system is effectively closed.

Alternative counseling models begin with a new definition of the dilemmas and perspectives of the helpers. The way they go about their work and see their role determines whether they can be of help.

Individual Dilemmas

Counseling begins when someone seeks help. Much of this book has dealt with the situation of young people today, and why they need new institutions to help them. An alternative service must begin with a new definition of the basic needs, moving from the stated needs to a way that the institution can be helpful to them. Whenever an alternate service opens in a community, large numbers of young people immediately come for help. An examination of the reasons for this appeal is the first step in the search for a response.

When someone seeks an alternate service, he usually has some awareness, however limited, that professional counseling will not meet his specific need. She has chosen a service which is nonprofessional, has a different appearance, and a looser structure and definition of itself. People come in expecting help which does justice to their experience, and they expect that this is more likely to happen at an alternative service. It has been mentioned previously (Chapter 6) that many clients have had previous contacts with professional counselors and have learned to distrust them or to suspect their intentions. They seek alternate counseling because it is less likely to define them as sick, a patient, needing help. They either do not see themselves in this way or do not want to. Many come with a less clear idea of what they need, they just want to hang around. Young people perhaps have a clearer view at first of what they do not need than what they want. They want something that they vaguely sense is fair, that deals with where they are, that does not play power games with them about who is right, and that respects their personal limits and freedom. They will say that they want to share and to grow with others, despite internal and external obstacles. The decision to choose an alternative service, then, is based on a limited rejection of established services because of a vaguely defined fear and distrust, and on a search for a more helpful process. In other terms, it could be said that young people seeking alternate services have an awareness that they are oppressed by society and its major institutions, but they are not sure of the oppression's sources and how to overcome it.

Their personal dilemmas can thus be restated in political terms and connected to their own experience. The linkage of political and personal perspectives is one way an alternate theory of counseling diverges from standard practice. Internal contradictions and pain are rooted in the experience of everyone, and those who are aware of it are not considered the most disturbed and in need of change, the worst off; rather, they are at a stage of awareness when they may be ready for a decisive change. The alternate service connects with people who are ready to change, who are in touch with contradictions and oppression in their personal lives. The task we suggest for an alternate counseling center is to help those who come in to define more precisely the nature of their situation, recognize mystification and internalization of situations they would like to reject, and then to act on this new awareness. By this definition, counseling has as much in common with education and political organizing as it does with counseling as traditionally practiced. While there is much overlap between each of these areas, and though a good counselor would be good as an educator or organizer, counseling deals specifically with the interaction of an individual's history and particular current sources of stress, and therefore complements the efforts of education and organization.

More specifically, people come to alternate counseling centers in crisis or confusion about their inability to move within their environment or because they experience great pain in doing so. The counselor's first impulse is to help them flee or extricate themselves from the relationship or institution which seems to be at fault, but such dilemmas are much deeper and more complex. From a lifetime of inhabiting such oppressive structures within family, school, and community, a person internalizes their norms as social reflexes and responses, so that she recreates those patterns, and the self-image which that environment has communicated, in every new situation. The new culture has found it difficult to flee the neurotic games of its parents, the confusion over learning of the schools, and the economic exploitation of the society, because these are so deeply ingrained. Alternate counseling deals simultaneously with oppressive situations and people's internalizations of them. Dealing with internalizations while creating a new environment is the task of a counselor and an alternative center. For example, when intervening in communes or acid trips, we found that these stress situations exposed the deep fabric of the self at points where the facade of a new culture was breaking down. People desperately trying to create something new with each other, or to win a new sense of themselves, have gotten into all sorts of sexual rivalries and confusions or have found life to be a never-ending search for parental recognition or acceptance displaced onto other authority figures, though they had left old institutions far behind. For younger people on the verge of such changes, internalizations make the process even more painful, as the task of separation of self from institutions which attempt to control almost all aspects of life is even more acute.

Some of the more concrete ways that this dilemma is presented have been alluded to in early chapters. Young people discover that their goals conflict with an internalized "should" and do not know how to deal with or even recognize this conflict. For example, a young girl who wishes to use sex to express closeness and communication with someone, comes into conflict with her parents' concept of sex as a bad activity. Her parents refer to a friend of hers as a slut, little knowing that their daughter acts in similar ways. She thus acquires a sense of wrongness, which makes her doubt whether her parents love her or only their image of her and makes it hard for her to express her real self to them and to

her peers. When she does get into a sexual relationship, it is often exploitive or depressing because of the conflict between her internalized
"should not," which countermands her own explicit goals. Similarly, internalized goals of college, career, and security conflict with a desire
for change and with the observed meaninglessness of some of these pursuits, producing most often confusion, depression and inability to act
in either direction.

Young people also have limited and self-defeating strategies for obtaining what they want. Strategies for social change are often mystified
into limited attempts to strike out at oppression without an informed strategy of the outcome (see Chapter 2). When the desire to be different has
as its outcome a self-defeating action, or when a first strategy does not
attain its goal, the result is frustration and cynicism more often than a
realization of the limited nature of the attempt to change. Many tell alternative counselors that they have found all activism or change to
be meaningless. They turn inward, away from any type of change that
involves others, not because they have gained new knowledge, but because they feel that they have failed. They remain depressed and unable
to act further, caught up in society's evaluation of their activism and
without the energy to envision new strategies. This "burn-out," common
to people in all areas of counter-cultural work, seems to result from a
conflict between the frustration of change and the internalized devaluation
of such work in the old culture. While many years of hard work can be
accepted in a traditional task, people are more easily frustrated by and
disillusioned with alternatives because they need quick reinforcement of
the new work's usefulness in order to compensate for their negative internalization of it.

Conflict over power and authority is the most pervasive dilemma,
showing up in staff debates as well as the presented situations of clients.
Young people fear and hate power, with the result that their power conflicts tend to be mystified and overt seeking of power is often seen as
inherently oppressive within a group. Alternate projects often discourage
any self-initiated actions as "power trips," inviting subtle manipulations,
diluted group consensus, or simply inaction. Such ambivalence toward
power is a result of the way power has been presented in socializing
institutions, the family and school. The rationale for authority is that it
is "for your own good," or that it is an effort at "teaching the way the
world is," and it tends to devalue any responsibility or initiative among
nonauthorities. Thus power is the property of a few and submission and
obedience is the property of the mass; this situation is a mirror of the
society. Expression of dissent, or even an internal feeling of disagreement, is defined in such institutions as mental illness or problem behavior (see Chapter 2).

When a person seeks a more authentic and autonomous mode of dealing
with power relationships, feelings associated with previous treatment
will inevitably enter the situation. Distrust of oppressive authority becomes distrust of any authority. Unresolved anger and self-hate generated
in such situations as a result of frustration of initiative are brought to

crisis centers. The limitation on creativity and self-expression of many people in crisis is a residue of previous authority situations. For example, relations among families, where the youngster is growing up but is not recognized as a legitimate or autonomous person, is a common crisis, and the resolution involves both political and personal learning about the nature of power relations. The structural debate within an alternative project over leadership and power-sharing also frequently leads to hassles on issues of mystified authority in staff members' past institutions.

People are fragmented and objectified by others, and when young people react against this dynamic, they form support groups to create a kind of closeness and intimacy which they desire but must learn to experience. But the most extremely fragmented and objectified people, who are labeled psychotic or extremely alienated, have such strong shells that support groups can only remove them with long-term care. Alternate counseling centers are often presented with such casualties, in extreme or limited form, and an accurate diagnosis of madness as a result of extreme oppression does little to correct the situation. Such extreme reactions to our culture can only respond to a sheltered, consistent, and revitalizing environment, and alternate counseling centers most often fail to meet this particular need. Much theory about the roots of madness, and the creation of such experimental communities as Kingsley Hall (see Chapter 8), have not led to many similar communities, primarily because the demands of such a place are beyond the commitment of most people. Crisis centers often turn to hospitals as the only environment which can shelter such people; the crisis center will offer the supplementary care and contact which can help these people get out within a short period.

When a directly oppressive situation is presented at an alternative center, there is greater hope. The client does not feel free to move within a current environment, and he seeks counseling to find a way out. The previously mentioned mechanisms make separation or rebellion from oppressive situations difficult, and centers often have to create a support network to help someone change. Women's groups, which often facilitate moving out of the nuclear family and out of oppressive sexual relationships, are the best example of support for separation and change. Leaving school, finding alternative vocations, or finding a growth environment to supplement the present living situation, all involve the creation of alternate but simultaneous realities.

The Political Context of Therapy Systems

The dilemmas of young people involve the effects of oppressive institutions on them and their internalization of these effects. The mental health system has not been too helpful in resolving these dilemmas because it mirrors the dominant assumptions of the other institutions and offers additional mystifications of the difficulties brought to it. As a system it purports to serve clients, but structurally and empirically, it can be shown that its basic mechanisms are more for the purpose of

reinforcing certain power relations in society, for socialization rather
than for personal growth. The areas where mental health systems ally
themselves with oppression and against social change include social
control, reduction of morality to health-sickness distinctions, economics,
authoritarianism, and sexism.

    An alternative model of a counseling system must be an alternative
to this entire system; it cannot simply adapt a few techniques which can
be utilized for more effective accomplishment of socially dubious ends.
The structure of a center, and the way it relates to the other dominant
institutions of society, determine which strategies and mechanisms it
will allow its clients to utilize to resolve their dilemmas. A structure
which does not allow change and growth among its staff will not allow
similar behavior for its clients. If counseling is to deal, not with individuals, but with the social environment and context of distress, it must
analyze its whole system according to its values. Therefore, the development of an alternative starts with an investigation of the social basis of
help and a perspective on the institution before proceeding to styles and
techniques of help.

    The use of therapists to limit and control deviance has often been
noted. Recent concern over the civil liberties of patients committed
to custodial care in hospitals, the use of psychological tests and psychiatric advice in job decisions, the control of active school children
through prescription of psychoactive drugs, the routine of lavishly prescribing tranquillizers, and, in Russia the treatment of political activists
as mental patients, have all brought out the dimensions of this practice.
Szasz (1970) has written most comprehensively about this trend. His
thesis holds involuntary therapy to be the root cause of many of these
abuses. Szasz shows that when the rule of law becomes cumbersome or
sticky, the rule of medical expertise can accomplish the same task of
scapegoating a problem and removing it from public view without the
need to establish a person's criminality. Alternate centers are constantly
in need of psychiatrists who will testify for the defense of someone who
is in danger of losing his freedom by psychiatric fiat, usually as a result
of actions taken by parents or educational authorities "for his own good."

    In the area of morality, therapists exercise an even more powerful
influence toward adjustment and social control. Theories of behavior
which include normative values for health and sickness essentially
make moral judgments about the goodness and badness of behavior. Since
such judgments are disguised as medical diagnosis, dissent by laymen
can be denigrated as scientific ignorance. Thus society is equipped with
a handy way for avoiding moral justification of its values, since this approach labels and discredits behavior and judgments which society does
not like. Hence, psychiatrists are called to judge political leaders, dis-
senters, youth services and any other person or situation where it
becomes useful to discredit nonconformity. The reduction of the morality
of student protest to adolescent rebellion may have done more harm to
legitimate dissent than have the unsuccessful trials of activists. Critics
couch their fear and disagreement in attitudes of superior morality and

ultimately superior scientific name-calling. This tendency is not only
a conservative tactic, it is also used by liberals to discredit militarists
and tendencies they disapprove of, creating a precedent for others. The
treatment of delinquents as social problems, forcing them to accept treatment, is no more benevolent than is locking them up, since the result is
the same, as are the effects. The disguising of punishment as treatment,
irrespective of whether the subject actually benefits from it, mystifies
and disguises genuine oppression. When deviants are not rehabilitated
by such benign programs, they are accused of lack of motivation (as is
seen currently in the formulation of policy regarding drug addicts), because they will not accept punishment as being for their own good. The
link of certain values with health does not stem from any ability of therapists to help people change, but from the need to reduce dissent to sickness and from the consequent justification of punishment as treatment.

Mental health social control agents have been well-rewarded for
their work. This further solidifies both their power and their motivation
to continue to preach rather than cure. Within the prestige and power
structure of the medical profession, a noncorporate monopoly, positions
of power and authority have been monopolized by physicians; clinical
psychologists and social workers take on the heavier case loads and
lower salaries of the welfare and school bureaucracies. Although there
is little empirical justification for calling therapy a medical subspecialty,
to do so has many economic advantages. The first is inherited expertise
— the virtual infallibility and lack of accountability which has been granted
physicians — as well as a certain standard of living. Legislation and research operates under the auspices of the Department of Health, and
medical schools subsidize psychiatric training. The provision of low-cost
care in community mental health centers actually subsidizes the training
of high-priced private practitioners. Eventually they will treat exclusively
upper-class, usually female patients over long periods of time, with no
guaranteed results, or they will operate private hospitals which harbor
unwanted children and relatives. Their monopoly on community care
creates a hierarchy composed of physicians on the top; they view community care only in the form of medical psychiatric models. The next
level has the physician dispensing expert care to individuals, and the
bottom layer is made up of auxiliary, purposefully untrained, functionaries
who help out. This is an ambiguous and oppressive model of service to
people who derive little benefit from it. Society derives increased social
control over middle-and lower-class misbehavior, and this control is
gladly practiced by physicians in exchange for free training in pseudo-
skills.

The rigidly authoritarian practice of therapy is the result of the lack
of demonstrable results. This does not mean that some of the more
theoretical and personal efforts of therapists have not been helpful, but
rather that these efforts are largely divorced from the justification that
they must be physicians and from the structural nature of the mental health
system. The established frameworks of psychoanalysis and drug therapy
have been no more effective than has the helping relationship of alternate

approaches, yet the standard modes are subsidized for their economic
and social control benefits. The justification for continued use of traditional therapy, in the light of lack of results, rests on the authority
of its practitioners. They convince the patient that she is receiving help,
that he will do worse outside of therapy, but that the therapist is not responsible for any specific results, although he is competent to make decisions about a job, institutionalization, and schooling. They achieve
credibility largely through the institutional trappings of their role rather
than through observed proofs. This imposes a complementary role for
the patient, which is submissive, passive, dependent, and subservient.
This role is the preferred one for survival in many institutions, but it
does not correspond to the role that such theorists as Maslow have suggested as leading to personal growth. Hence therapeutic authoritarianism
serves to reinforce a character type which adjusts to a role rather than
promotes growth. Therapy is similar to the other socializing institutions.
All its actions follow from the assumption that the therapist knows better
than the patient, and what he knows is part of his skill in dealing with an
illness which is nonspecific and interminable.

Recently, women have begun to figure out that they provide the majority of patients to therapists, who are for the most part male. The sex
bias of Freudian therapy — its lack of positive image and concept of the
female — plays right into the social conviction of women as a lesser
class which should be content with a dependent place. Thus, channeling
of women's anger into self-hate, depression, and guilt at the culture is
the unconscious aim of the therapist. By focusing on the self rather than
on the social conditions, the effect of therapy is often to turn emotions
inward, creating an involution which makes decision-making, action, and
social change less likely to occur. Therapists can have the same effect on
angry men, but the effects on women have been greater. Eventually a
"good" patient works her feelings into a healthy blandness — unless she
becomes eternally depressed and confused, a self-obsessed therapeutic
failure. As women form support groups among themselves, the contrast
between the effect of therapy and of such groups has become more pro-
nounced. Psychoanalytic theory would argue that after analysis a patient
is more likely to have energy free for social as well as personal change,
but empirically there is evidence both for and against this contention.

We have maintained that the structure of the mental health system
and the role it plays are more helpful in maintaining the dominant values
of society than in helping individuals change. The way it is practiced
makes therapy a maintenance function of society, a resocialization process when family, school, and community fail. Our premise is that there
is a task which can be called therapy or counseling which meets important human needs. This is a less extreme position than Fanon's, himself a psychoanalyst. He maintained that neurosis was a direct result of
oppression and that revolutionary action was in itself the resolution. We
feel that resolution is a more complex phenomenon and that a radical
counseling practice deals with oppression by mobilizing the energy which

has been trapped by such mechanisms as mystification, internalization of oppressive stereotypes, and reduction of dissent to triviality. The rest of this essay is concerned with building a model of therapy which structurally and theoretically support substantive change.

Destructuring Therapy

Alternate therapists must first demystify their role and remove the authoritarian, moralistic, and pseudomedical components. This new attitude does not deny that counseling is a skill, which demands learning and authoritative practice. Demystification involves removing the indirect power of the therapist to command obedience and aquiescence, such as the power to cꬴerce a decision or the ascribed authority of a professional status. Counseling is not necessarily helpful, and a demystified relationship supports the client in defining for himself whether he is being helped. All counselors are not identically helpful by virtue of their skill, and the client should not be deterred from determining the helpfulness of the process. This dynamic makes the parameters of the role more mutual; the counselor should be less likely to rely on a specific role, such as the rigid psychoanalytic stance, and instead make a mutually defined contract with the client as to the methods for help. Demystification thus involves the self-validating demonstration of his skill by the counselor, combined with a free choice by and a mutual contract with a client. The gap in knowledge and status between client and helper is reduced, and the possibility of fallibility, mutual self-disclosure, and uncertainty is programmed into relationships. The therapist is thus less responsible for change, and the shift of emphasis is from the therapists' knowledge to the quality of the relationship between helper and client. The focus shifts from the individual alone to the dynamics of the relationship, of which the helper is as much part as the client.

Client control is an important concept, with implications for all institutions. The argument is that, no matter how much skill a role demands, it is still possible for a layman to evaluate the results, especially when he is their recipient. This dispute takes place in mental health centers, where communities are not allowed to set service priorities; in school systems, where administrators dispute over power with school boards and deny power to parents; in classrooms, where students are never called on to evaluate the quality of their teachers; and in the conduct of foreign policy and war, which citizens are continually asked to leave to experts. The thrust of most radical efforts is in the direction of control over basic policy and priorities by those affected and limitations on the power of the experts. In counseling, the use of jargon to devalue criticism and the secrecy with which its practice occurs (confidentiality) make it especially difficult to improve limits or controls. By emphasizing the free choice of the client and limiting any power the helper might have over the client, the balance of power can flow back to the person who is helped.

An alternate counseling practice stems from a learning-growth model of man rather than a health-sickness one. Following Maslow (1962) and others, the person is seen as having an innate capacity to grow and choose correctly, in the direction of his own unique potential. The task of the counselor is to aid in this self-discovery by removing obstacles and confusion from the path, not by curing a social mistake. This task is closely allied to, if not identical with, experiential education. If the metaphors used to describe change are to transcend the oppressive constraints of classical practice, they must allow the person to take precedence over the society. Counseling theories have in the past been inherently conservative because they propose normative rules of progress and historically bound developmental models. Freud, and most analysts since then, have sought to remove therapy from history into the realm of pure science (although in his later work Freud sought to write history as myth independent of events), thus neglecting the role of the individual in relation to change. Erik Erikson's studies of Gandhi and Luther have begun to correct this defect, but others have not applied so much sensitivity to the role of the individual in change, and they tend to write psychoanalytic justifications for every action rather than providing psychohistorical analysis. Education focuses on integrating the environment and acting on that knowledge for greater control, and educational metaphors describe that process in such a way that the learner can pursue it independently of the educator. The two theoretical demands — a proper role of the individual in relation to historical change and a learning process which the individual can seize for himself — should be components of an alternate theory of counseling.

The demystification of the counseling role and the application of learning metaphors can take place within the context of a private practice; but only with difficulty, and it does not often happen for several reasons. The alternate model implies corresponding change in the life and attitude of the counselor. Helpers have also been raised in a destructive environment which they have internalized as basic assumptions that they read into all their relationships. They cannot therefore be expected to move instantly into a new role. For that reason alternatives are largely developed at centers or by groups of people who derive support from each other. Following a learning model, the alternate counseling center is a learning center for counselors. It can also provide a shared economic base, so that the practice can transcend the difficulties of fee-for-service work and several people can share income from several sources. The center is also a community where counselors can move beyond their own concepts. An essay by Bill Torbert (1972) begins to clarify the rationale for a support group as an alternative to independent innovation — as an action science — in that the support group allows the innovator personal intimacy as well as the opportunity to break free of culturally determined boundaries. Very few accounts of counseling explore the personal experience of counseling for the counselor, and yet the emotional exhaustion of such work is a primary reason for its rigidity. Many times the counselor deals with the intensity of the work by building strong defenses against others' experience, which he cannot help but carry into his private relationships. The alternative support group or center allows

counselors to look at the consequences of their experience and to learn
new mechanisms for dealing with its pressures. There is no reason why
clients cannot also participate in these explorations, even moving out of
the client role to become part of a community of shared concerns. The
change process begins with the counselor and proceeds to the clients after a shared change process triggers the task of critically examining
basic assumptions and defining new models, directions, and action.

Helping Relationships and the Rap Center

The simplest and most common alternative to traditional counseling
is based on the work of Carl Rogers (1961). Because of its directness
and simplicity, his model has spread to cover most nonpsychiatric professional counseling, as well as the new youth programs. Although
Rogers' model does not in itself define a new system or structure for
counseling practice, it does offer some useful guidelines for the individual relationships in counseling which demystify counseling and operate
out of growth model of man. While alternate counseling must go beyond
the helping relationship, it provides good basic guidelines for a helping
service. Radical therapy can add to them, but it cannot neglect them.
In addition, this model accurately describes the practice used at most
youth service programs, after they dissociate themselves from psychiatric practice.

Rogers defines counseling as a highly personal form of shared experience, in which the counselor is helpful by virtue of his empathy, con-
gruence of words with emotions, and acceptance of the client. Counseling,
then, is a human quality, and a good counseling relationship is no different from any good interpersonal relationship. A good counselor is
simply a healthy, warm, open, accepting human being. Counter-cultural
groups, which work toward sharing, expressiveness, openness, and the
erasure of hierarchical distinctions in relationships, have adopted this
definition of their work. Counseling is redefined as "rapping," establishing rapport and sharing experience without preconceptions, expectation
of any outcome or structured roles.

The Rogers model reacts to the tendency in psychotherapy to extend
the impassive, rigidly defined role of the psychoanalyst to all forms of
therapy, regardless of the needs and expectations of patients. Alternate
counseling centers all reject the notion that counseling is a technical
skill alone, which can be practiced like a chess game, independent of the
quality of the interaction between therapist and client. The psychoanalytic
role offers a handy defense to a student who has been isolated from direct contact with people in medical school and who fears the craziness
and intense needs of patients. The spread of the helping relationship
represents a backlash against this trend. Counter-cultural changes have
increased therapists' frustration with the traditional distance and have
led to a willingness to adopt a more interactive and responsive style.

Rap centers, hotlines, and crisis centers usually take the helping
relationship as their first model. They select counselors who are warm,
genuine, accepting, and empathetic. This choice creates a highly

supportive and tension-reducing environment for people in crisis or pain.
These centers find quickly that they tap very deeply into a great reservoir
of unmet human needs. Many of these can be met simply — by supplying
medical aid or housing, by talking someone down from a crisis or by
making contact with isolated people and forming support groups to deal
with common issues, for example. Since helping relationships reflect
human qualities rather than learned skills, rap centers assume that
competence is distributed among many people, who can form the staff
regardless of prior expertise, which at the start is rarely respected
or built in as a hierarchical structure. The distinction between client and
helper becomes blurred; help is a quality of the ethos of the community
rather than a skill practiced by a limited minority. This approach lessens
the expectations of the client; they do not look for cures or expertise but
search out helpers for their common humanity.

The helping relationship is based on the assumption that when a person is allowed to follow a natural bent, she can help someone else. When
an alternate counseling center utilizes the helping relationship, several
guidelines and values seem to follow as common goals and guides.

Rapport and trust. The first issue in counseling is to make contact with
the client. It is not assumed that because the person has come to the
center or has telephoned, that he will absolutely accept any help that is
offered. The help must be justified, and the justification comes from the
helpers' immediate attempt to create trust in the client, being willing to
share information about himself and the center, and being open to hear
anything the client has to say and to the conditions for relationship set
by the client. This process of establishing contact, the quick communication of shared feelings, is rapport; it determines whether the helping
relationship will be formed.

Mutuality. The helper does not expect the client to share unless the counselor is willing to take risks and share also. The aim is a dialogue,
where the helper-client dichotomy, as well as other ordinary social roles,
break down quickly. Clients who make great demands, or who expect a
great deal of authoritativeness from helpers, usually experience difficulty
in rap centers. Others, who have been frustrated by the impassivity or
lack of exchange in traditional therapy, are refreshed and find themselves opening up quickly in a mutual helping relationship.

Client control and responsibility. The client is not sick, irresponsible,
childish, or in any way less of a person than the counselor. There is
therefore no reason for the helper to make decisions or exercise control
over the direction of the relationship or to make decisions for the client.
Agreements and contracts are arrived at openly, and no arrangements
are made behind the back of the client; such as for example, the helpers
do not talk to other agencies or the client's family except at his request.
There is a high value on freedom and a reluctance to accept institutionalization as a solution, as well as an unwillingness to take care of the
client by doing things for her out of an assumption of her helplessness.

Expressiveness. Helpers try to be sensitive to the client's feelings, and they express their own. Inner experience, which is highly valued, is a frequent topic for exploration in all relationships. Many helpers use non-verbal exercises like deep breathing, hitting a pillow and body awareness to help create awareness of feelings.

Refusal to judge. There is a high value on tolerance of others. While opinions and suggestions are shared freely by helpers, there is an atmosphere of acceptance which makes these different from evaluative, norm-setting, punitive, and "put-down" responses which imply an external value system for behavior.

Orientation to Problems. Sessions are usually directed toward defining and resolving a problem. There is some pressure on the client to clarify his wants concretely. Otherwise, the process must be redefined as rapping or friendship. This tendency is strong in rap centers, even though it contradicts some of the other values. Helpers commonly give advice, offer suggestions and resources, and try to point out hidden assumptions and implications. Concern is usually focused on the present situation, with very little emphasis on history-taking. Since most helpers have had little formal study of theoretical frameworks, they approach each situation experientially, relating it to their own experience and looking for reasonable explanations and solutions with the client.

Flexibility of responses. There are no prescribed durations for sessions or any restraints against informal contact, visiting, or further involvement with clients. Relationships can therefore develop naturally and grow beyond the strict helping situation. There is a continuity and lack of differentiation between staff member and client at a rap center, and anyone there is likely to see himself as staff. Further, counseling is not strictly limited to talk; helpers can, for example, go with clients to get professional help, put them up, or, put them in touch with other people who share concerns.

Confidentiality without secrecy. No names are required and few records are kept; the client is thus assured of confidentiality of a sort. But there seems to be little concept of priviledged communication or secrecy. Helpers treat conversations with clients as they would those with friends, and they feel free to share or exchange experiences with the same restraint or openness that they would show to a friend. This course is not usually resented or unexpected, because clients seem to have a few special expectations that their conversations will be treated with strict secrecy unless they specifically ask for it.

Little accountability. Through defensiveness and lack of confidence, and because counseling is seen as a human quality rather than a professional skill, there is a reluctance to examine critically the goals and results of helping. Staff members see themselves as autonomous and independent in their work, and they feel that good intentions are synonomous with good work. There are some safeguards and forms of accountability, such as counselors working in teams and logging work, but there is also a reluctance to share information and check up on what others are doing.

The rap center based on the helping relationship is a pleasant, direct, simple service offering support and human contact. Its effectiveness is due mainly to the lack of these virtues in larger, depersonalized mental health systems, where technique and staff efficiency have replaced compassion. The tremendous response to rap centers is analogous to a vote for a third-party candidate — a protest rather than a solution to difficulties. There are many crises, however, which respond very well to contact, expression of feelings and support, and these difficulties are increasingly dealt with by rap centers. Rap centers take advantage of the natural human capacity to spring back from difficulties; they do so through encouragement and through a refusal to define the client as disabled or incapable. They also validate such solutions as may have been independently arrived at which need to be reinforced by some nonthreatening support before they can be put into action. Many people who come to rap centers already have a way out of their dilemma; the helping relationship merely reinforces a client's reliance on himself. The other basic need to which the helping relationship addresses itself effectively is the need for people to get together. Much anxiety and defensiveness is the outcome of isolation, of the belief that others do not share one's fears and that consequently they must be hidden. Maturing increases the number of such hidden fears, and a group with norms of support and acceptance deals with them as well as does the intervention of a professional whose technical skill can do no more to convince someone of the universal nature of her difficulty than can a group of helpful friends.

The helping relationship represents a view of the purpose of counseling in society very different from that of the mental health system. It makes a limited advance by breaking free of some assumptions about skill and professionalism. But it is a limited model for personal and institutional development. People do not change a great deal as a result of human contact; rather, the result is often just a rush of good feelings, a "positive thinking" which is unconnected with and unreflective of the client's original situation. The helping relationship, overly simplistic in its view of relationships, is primarily a-social in that it does not recognize the rigidities of situations. One cannot easily practice humanity within an oppressive family, in a ghetto street, within a corporation, or at most schools. That issue is a structural one which youth programs must recognize constantly. The helping relationship offers a few guidelines to the basics of setting up a relationship, but it does not presume to be a theory of personal and social change, nor a model for accomplishing it. The alternate counseling center must soon move beyond the helping relationship, though few centers have actually yet been able to do so.

New Therapies

What does it take before a rap center can evolve toward a viable alternative to a mental health system which limits and frustrates change by its clients and its staff? There is no shortage of new therapeutic techniques to choose from, but they must be understood in the context of dealing with personal crises caused by internalization of oppressive social structures and the struggle to move beyond them. The past few years have seen the rise of various personal growth centers as well as popular variations of therapy, which have sold widely as books. Transactional analysis, gestalt therapy, bioenergetics, and now primal screams have been billed as solutions to all sorts of pain and difficulties. They have increased public awareness of therapeutic games and jargon, and they have greatly reduced the fears and stigma attached to therapy. While hospitalization still retains the stigma which leads society to treat former patients as untouchables, going to a therapist has become as acceptable as going to graduate school and is indulged in by the same populations. Another effect of the popularization of therapy is to create a clientele for any new counseling or growth center. People call up to find encounter groups of any kind, looking for freedom from an undefined bondage, which seems to consist of boredom, lack of immediacy and contact with others, and confusion about their future and the purpose of their existence. These are primarily religious dilemmas, and Back (1972) has pointed out that the encounter movement represents an impulse similar to past anti-intellectual, religious searches and pilgrimages.

Is the alternate counseling center destined to be another therapeutic fad, preaching its own version of the gospel, as a theory of how to connect and participate in immediate experience? In Chapter 3 we linked the growth center phenomenon to other promising pursuits called the counterculture. This section looks at what the alternate counseling center can learn from the new therapies, and how much of its aura and practice it will incorporate. Since the model for alternate counseling stems also from education, and from political and community organizing, it will combine encounter techniques with a critical analysis of society and experimental structures for meeting other human needs. The result has the possibility of attaching the ahistorical, non-(not anti-) intellectual, and transient benefits of the new therapies to the parameters of the helping relationship, and finally to the social and political concerns of its community. An alliance of political and psychological radicals is much needed, even if it has not so far led to much integration.

The new therapies have in common several aims and techniques important to a community counseling project. They include:
1. focus on immediate experience and feelings;
2. expressiveness of interior experience;
3. powerful, positive support from a small, face-to-face group;
and   4. a socializing forum for the redefinition of social norms, values, and behavior toward new forms and boundaries.
Pilgrims to weekend groups find freedom to get in touch with parts of themselves which they have not experienced before, in a setting which programs new experiences and allows for exploration. The group essentially creates a free space for new ways — it is a good learning

environment. People do exercises to explore their interior through focusing awareness, touching, working on expression of specific feelings,
exploring the structure and sensation of using the body, redefining sexual
practice, questioning the nature of interpersonal attachments, and engaging in confrontation about topics ordinarily avoided or defended against.
These tactics open people to new dimensions toward which they can
grow.

As with drugs, where there is an inevitable return to earth, the group
-goer must return to his social situation. These uncovering and expressive therapies are in the end conservative because they do not deal with
an actual situation, offering instead secluded blow-out centers for dammed-
up feelings, with little practical thought to change within anyone's actual
life system. Experiments of encounter-group veterans in living their
values after the group have often been disastrous, as the movie Bob and
Carol and Ted and Alice satirically demonstrated. People seek groups
for escapism and release because they do not know how to create extended change outside it. There are obvious and glaring exceptions to
this generalization, which applies mainly to those who attend centers,
rather than to the often visionary and powerful leaders who live in them.
Groups have taken on a commercial flavor and marketing mentality as
leaders search for a quicker and more effective rehash of the basic
format, and centers collect fees with little thought to the economic structure they create and the needs of the people they attract.

Alternate counseling centers must bring the culture of growth centers
to the community and apply it to people who do not come prepared to be
true believers. Their real dilemmas demand more than awareness and
feelings. In cities, awareness can be a disaster as well as a liberation
if it is not turned into concrete strategies for survival and change. Centers deal with internalizations — the recreation of old patterns in new
situations. Encounter groups have many techniques to demonstrate the
existence and pervasiveness of these internalizations. Gestalt therapy
does this quite simply, and transactional analysis has a conceptual framework of life scripts and analysis of common games which is durable and
adaptable to alternate centers. The Radical Psychiatry Center in Berkeley
has adopted transactional analysis as the framework for a radical therapy
center.

A Counseling Model

The task is to develop a theory of alternate counseling which builds
on the helping relationship, the new therapies, and the oppressive situations which clients bring in. The model can be expressed as a matrix,
in which three modes of action are combined on three possible levels of
intervention. Alternate counseling is an integration of the three basic
tasks practiced on the relevant level.

The modes of action are:
1. contact (support, helping relationship);
2. awareness (expressive work, encounter, gestalt); and
3. strategy of action (understanding, change relationships).

These combine with the appropriate level of intervention:
1. alone (drug use, religious disciplines, individual therapy);
2. support group (weekend laboratory group, therapy group); or
3. network (family, couple, work group, friends, institution).

The first requirement for any kind of counseling is support and human contact. Rap centers achieve this by offering empathy, giving help in solving dilemmas, and taking care of legal, family, and institutional problems. Support and contact involve being with a person through a difficulty, and eventually helping that person find a group or network of people to provide this contact and support in the future. This is the basic service offered by the helping relationship; it is effective for short-term changes when the person knows the direction in which he wants to go.

The second mode, awareness, includes all the new expressive and sensory awareness exercises, as well as a certain intellectual awarenesses of such realities as the inherently repressive nature of many social structures, along with the belief that change can only come about after both internal and external barriers and constraints on personal development have been faced. This is the point where awareness of the many layers of internalization is important and where the writing of such authors as Haley, Berne and R.D. Laing have exercised such a powerful influence . Rather than prescribing an expressive therapy Laing simply writes about the experience of being knotted up in social networks, many of which have the aim of reducing or invalidating personal experience. The reaction is mystification, a lack of awareness of the difference between one's own and other's experience. The practice of expressive therapies along with exploration of relationships with others and their meaning to oneself is the therapeutic task of creating awareness. This mode is the most common among new therapists, and the combination of expression techniques with clear perceptions of social reality is an important part of a new style of counseling. This is usually incompletely done by alternative counselors, who tend to concentrate on one or another form of awareness, neglecting to develop a holistic examination. Since short-term counseling can only hope to focus on a portion of the whole, alternate therapy must begin to see itself as partly an educational process, to be pursued by a small group over a large period of time, in order to fully become aware of the social and experiential situation which one inhabits.

The expressive awareness-creating mode is closely joined to that of action, creating new strategies for behavior. This is the stage of substantive change, and the awareness and support which one gets over time is crucial to the outcome. This is the time in which the person being helped, aided by counselors and other peers, reinterprets reality and thus obtains new degrees of freedom within which to act. The chronic rebel who learns to act within a strategy for changing society (see Chapter 2) is an example of a person who has changed through this mode. The helper provides a new conceptual framework which allows for the growth of new patterns and styles of response based on the new awareness.

The three modes of helping — providing support, creating awareness, and acting on a new interpretation of reality — are the task of helpers at an alternative center. This goal demands a fairly high degree of growth in staff members, necessitating a support network, awareness, and interpretation done by other people on the staff. Everyone must go through the process; the preparation for helping others is the process of being helped, with the added focus on ways in which the forms of learning can be transferred to others. Training moves from the learning of the staff group to an exploration of how this learning can be transferred to others.

The level of help starts with the individual. He can work alone, as some people do with psychedelic drugs, or she can proceed with a helper to clarify and reflect back the work. Alternately, a group of relative strangers can come together to support and help each other on the three modes of counseling; such a group may or may not have a formal leader. Finally, the most relevant set for personal change — and one in which growth centers and traditional counselors fail to feel comfortable — is the social network. This is made up of the relevant people who constitute the social situation of the person seeking help. Laing points out that in families, for example, one person's behavior may make no sense unless it is seen, and ultimately dealt with, in the context and the presence of the other family members. At crisis centers it is often the friend who brings the person in, or the other member of a couple (in the case of suicidal feelings), or the child and parents together, who make up the troubled network. Seeing one person alone may clarify some aspects of the situation, but in order to bring about change, the whole network must be involved. Networks also include the major institution with which a person is affiliated — family, school, work group, or organization. Some interventions require facing institutional authorities. The struggles often resemble, and indeed are, political conflicts, interest and power struggles. By dealing with the network as well as the individual and a support group, counselors can unravel the interpersonal bonds which have become twisted into mystified or confused internalizations.

Case Studies

Little has been said in the preceding pages that can be applied easily by someone working at a center; and many of the concepts presented are merely outlines for future development rather than a working model. But our work is backed with some experience, and the following case studies show some of the ways we have tried to go beyond the confines of a rap center to deal with unraveling of difficult knots among people and within individuals. Each intervention focuses on one or two of the possible levels — for example one session alone and two with the family. Each intervention also incorporates aspects of support, awareness, and action; the elements of a successful change. The first few illustrate aspects of developing awareness of the relevant situation, mainly in one-to-one counseling. Finally, there are some examples that include the whole network, whether couple or family or friends.

The Struggle with Good Parents

Elle is a fourteen-year-old girl from a suburban town, who came to Number Nine to accompany a friend. She is an attractive, clean-cut girl with a conventional style of dress, a steady beaming smile, and bright brown eyes. In the casual conversation with both girls, the counselor (who goes on the assumption that anyone who comes into Number Nine wants some kind of help) began to interest himself in Elle's background and listened very carefully to what she was saying.

Elle described herself as constantly happy. It was suggested to her that such a statement might be an indication that she did not want to talk about some of her less "acceptable" feelings. She glanced at the floor and neither denied nor agreed with the hypothesis, although it was clear that she was willing to go on with this train of thought.

The counselor then asked Elle to sit in front of him on the floor, so that both their attention would be focused on her and their interchange. He drew her out by vague speculations about what might be troubling her in her relationship with her parents. She nodded and said yes or no; it was not until he hit on a sore spot that she began to contribute information. Focusing on the girl, changing the seating arrangement to one of close but non-threatening opposition, speculating about the few hints she had given the counselor — all these are various ways of encouraging a person to share herself with a stranger.

Elle began to talk about a dream she had had in which she was afraid she would die owing some unidentifiable person something, but she did not know what. The counselor asked the girl to take the place of the other person in the dream. It became evident that the girl was not blaming herself for withholding something from the stranger; but she was afraid nevertheless. He suggested that this fear might come from the nature of what she "owed," and he began to ask her what her parents wanted from her. She said that her mother wanted very little, but when she mentioned her father's expectations she froze a little.

He asked her to pretend that she was telling her father that she was afraid she would die before paying him. Then, when she played the role of her father, she responded as the dream figure did. The demands her father makes upon her seem reasonable. Remarking upon this, she said, "He is always reasonable." The counselor noticed the emphasis upon the word "reasonable" and detected a touch of anger. He went back to her mother and asked how she acted with her mother when she got angry at her. She said that she argued with her mother and that her mother argued back. But, she went on to say, she could not do this with her father, and her mother could not argue with him either.

As he explored this area, thinking of several basic factors — such as her feeling that she owed someone, probably her father, but could not pay him back — he began to wonder about the nature of her real response to her father's indirect expectations ("Be a good girl, do what you think you should but don't disappoint us"). She admitted that he aroused her anger at times, but she was unable to express it because he never grew

angry himself. She did not know what to do about this anger, so she hid
it, causing stomach aches, nightmares, and the like.

During the conversation she began to cry, and at other times she
squeezed the counselor's hands very tightly as her anger came out. After
the session she felt much better and more secure. It seemed to her now
that it was all right to feel anger at her father, and she said that she
thought she could even tell her father more about how frustrating his
lack of expressiveness is. By finding the sore spot, offering quiet understanding and unjudgmental, uncritical acceptance of her feelings, and
holding her hands so she could talk through them as well as with words,
the counselor was able to help express feelings which are not able to
come out in other situations.

Pressured

Ginger is an attractive sixteen-year-old, an above-average student
in a suburban high school. She does not use drugs except for an occasional
experiment with marijuana. She is a girl who does well in everything,
smiles a lot, and is well liked. She happened to visit a Number Nine
training group. The leader mentioned she looked depressed, and while
she denied it, she seemed willing to talk if the leader was interested.

After a little coaxing Ginger described herself as feeling that "I don't
really exist." Everything she did was for other people — although, she
quickly added, what they wanted was the right thing, so she did not mind.
She said, "I would probably do them anyway, but they won't let me decide." She described her parents as genuinely concerned but very co-
vertly making demands on her, at the same time denying that they were
making demands.

She talked about her Sunday-school group, how kids in it were wasting
time, not doing anything in particular, and how she felt that she could
not make them change. Essentially, Ginger felt powerless with both her
friends and her parents, fulfilling their demands, living a life over which
she had no control, unable to be angry because she was only being asked
to do things that were for her own good.

Ginger's twisting a piece of paper, her expression of sadness which
her face assumed when she did not know she was being watched, her helplessness, all disappeared when she began to express her anger, resentment, and frustration — feelings she had never felt comfortable in expressing because they seemed "wrong" and "I feel guilty because they
only try and do what is right for me." As they talked about the ways her
parents gain (in pride, satisfaction) from her successes, she began to
see that their statements of selflessness were not entirely true, and she
began to feel that she could now express more of her resentment at their
pressures upon her.

Ginger beamed genuinely after the conversation and went home. Two
weeks later she came back and happily told the counselor how she had
gotten her Sunday school class to listen to her criticisms, and how they
had respected her and made some real plans to do something. She said

she felt more comfortable talking to her parents about the way they encourage her to get good grades and restrict her social life by their expecting her to be perfect.

The issue of resentment and demands continually occurs with young people, who often bury their anger because they feel guilty about it, as Ginger did. Demands are often covert, understood, or they are covered over with disclaimers of any gain for the person making the "legitimate expectation" demands. However, with Ginger and many others, the inability to comment directly on demands made on them creates a general state of confusion and helplessness, and often a vague feeling of emptiness, of being a form existing for, and comforming to, outside pressures, with no existence within itself.

Two Different Paths

Mike is a handsome, thin boy with long hair and a distinctive style of dress, though he would not stand out in a crowd. He is talented artistically, a student in a local high school, and has parents with whom he gets along rather well. When he came to Number Nine it was to help, and he proved to be both sensitive and mature, contributing much of his time. In fact, he became dependent upon the organization to meet social needs before he also indicated that he would like to discuss a personal problem.

Mike is about sixteen years old, and has had a number of sexual relationships with boys, including one boy to whom he was particularly close. As their relationship developed, he called it love with only some embarrassment when he was with the boy. Shortly before Mike came to Number Nine, the other boy moved to another city; although he indicated that he wanted the relationship to continue through the mails. This event created a crisis for Mike, who had great guilt about being homosexual and had many questions about his feelings for girls, which were also strong.

In three individual counseling sessions Mike discussed his age; the commoness of homosexual relationships among this age group; his feelings for girls, which were becoming stronger; and the lack of reasons for feeling guilty. He became more sure of himself, wrote a letter to the boy in Boston, broke off the relationship, began seeing more girls — to whom he related fairly well physically and emotionally — and accepted the feelings he had for boys as part of himself. He stopped feeling that he had to act on them instead of remaining a nonphysical friend. This adjustment to his "bisexuality" has been rewarding for him; he could not have made it without outside support of both kinds of feelings.

Just to Hear a Friendly Voice

Myrna, a fifteen-year-old girl, called up one night just to hear a friendly voice. When the phone counselor responded in an open way, she relaxed and chattered about school, home, and generalities. After about half an hour of apparently aimless conversation, she began to discuss boys; she hinted that she was having trouble handling their expectations of her — a disguised admission that she went too far too often.

After discussing this at greater length, she ended the conversation by agreeing to come to our storefront. About a month later she finally arrived, bringing with her several other kids from school, to see what Number Nine was all about. The counselor, who remembered her, expressed happy surprise to meet her in person at last.

Another long period passed before he heard from Myrna again. This time she called because she was in trouble with her mother. She wanted help, and she trusted Nine. Her mother was alarmed because she was seeing a twenty-year-old college student. The counselor talked to both the girl and the boy, and it was agreed that she would accept counseling about this crisis, since she was obviously confused and upset, caught between wishing to maintain the relationship with the young man and wishing to spare her mother hurt.

In the course of counseling he learned more of her history. She had lost her father at a critical age. Perhaps as a consequence, she essentially distrusts men, suspecting that they are not genuinely interested in her. If they pursue her sexually, she submits willingly and even enjoys the experience; but the man is then degraded in her eyes, and she rejects him. In one sense her relationship with the college student was an aggressive and hostile one; she taunted him with her promiscuity and her desire for other men, and in general brought him down by attacking his masculinity.

At the bottom this crisis was precipitated by Myrna's inability to grieve for her father; consequently she engaged in a relentless search for the attention, support, and acceptance normally supplied by a father from the boys she met. By unconditionally accepting Myrna, counseling broke down her defenses, allowing her to cry and in particular to talk about her fears and resentments connected with her father's early death. A nonseductive but physically supportive counselor (he puts his arm around her when she cries, for example) is able to supply her with affection and concern free of sexual overtones.

As she expresses — rather than just talks about — her deep and suppressed reactions to her father and his absence, Myrna becomes more aware of the self-destructive nature of her methods for dealing with her feelings, and she grows better able to accept both the traditional limitations imposed by her age and the limitations of her personality, which at the present time prevent her having a truly intimate and reciprocal relationship with a man.

Junkie Kid

Jim is a highly intelligent young man of sixteen who became a junkie for six months, taking three to six bags a day. To true addicts this is "kid stuff," since most of them graduate to fourteen or fifteen bags a day. However, Jim's physical withdrawal took over a week, and the psychological withdrawal (intense depression and related phenomena) lasted for another week. He had associated only with drug users like himself, who spent much of their time stoned or talking about being stoned.

Jim's father is a successful professional, and his family lives in an upper-class neighborhood. His mother is a housewife; he has a brother and a sister. He has had many advantages, including music lessons. Jim was introduced to drugs at his local high school.

Jim was first brought to Number Nine by two of his straight friends, who were alarmed by his drift into heroin use. He had been gradually disassociating from them as his habit increased. Interestingly enough, Jim was unaware that he was an addict because his supply had been so plentiful that he had always gotten enough and had never paid for it or gone without. After a discussion with one of the staffers, he began to realize where he was heading and stated that he wanted to "come down." He was ambivalent, but the honesty and lack of pressure left him free to decide for himself.

After making the decision, he and a staff member talked with his parents, informing them of their son's problem. They were shocked but understanding and wanted to know what to do. Jim was removed from school and went off "cold turkey," with Number Nine supplying twenty-four-hour care for a week and intermittent care for another week.

Many of these nights he sat up and talked for hours in an effort to keep his mind off heroin. On such nights he would stay in our crash pad. His friends helped by staying with him most of the time, learning how to help keep him from going back to heroin. He wavered back and forth, never really sure if being clean was what he wanted, but the encouragement, support, and even the restrictive setting helped.

For several weeks he stayed off heroin completely as he was counseled alone and with his parents. Jim was encouraged to spend time at Number Nine and to seek some kind of long-range intensive psychotherapy, which he eventually did. Jim sniffed heroin once again, after several weeks of this effort, frightening his parents and creating a sense of helplessness in them. The counselor became quite angry at him, and he promised to never do it again. Since it is not unusual for an ex-addict to occasionally return to heroin for a one-shot deal, nobody became alarmed. Weekly counseling sessions and monthly family meetings continued.

At the end of three more weeks, however, Jim was discovered high by his parents; he admitted to having snorted once more, even refused to promise that he would not do so again, because he had a craving for the drug. This attitude alarmed his parents, and his father, although he was grateful for Number Nine's work up to that point, felt that his son was exposed to bad influences among some of the people he had met there; he began to wonder if some other program would not be more helpful to his son. He threatened the son with institutionalization.

Up to this point the situation remained within the confines of standard crisis intervention. A boy had a decision to make, although he was not presented with clearly acceptable alternatives. He could continue with drugs, or he could give them up — for what? He was given information concerning his habit and his future. Number Nine offered support if he wanted or needed it, as well as allowing him membership in its community. He thus had a chance to do something meaningful. The intervention progressed through several levels, such as therapy, counseling, discussions with Jim's family, and outside activities for him to engage in.

But his return to drugs on two occasions presented us with a dilemma. Could we rest content with this incomplete success? Could we sit back and watch this young man end up in an institution? Or was there something we could do to change the pattern of his life? We still had the alternative of network intervention surrounding a critical situation following a crisis intervention; this seemed a risk worth taking, though it would demand a lot from us. Dealing effectively with a crisis creates some degree of trust. A pattern of crisis, such as repeated heroin use, brings out many of the same feelings; but in a situation of this type, it is not enough that a decision has been made; the behavior pattern must also be changed. What can be done when the pattern has produced a sense of desperation on the part of the parents and resentment on the part of the son?

Traditional approaches are centered on long-range pattern changes, usually of the client's personality. These require long-term investment for both the client and the therapist (an increasingly impractical requirement, given the small number of therapists and the growing number of patients). However, this situation had also demonstrated to us the limits of crisis intervention. We took a leap of faith and decided not to relinquish the boy, his family, or his situation until we felt that our own efforts had been adequate. We would go beyond our fairly conservative practices, we would become radical, focusing on the deepest aspect of the problem — the relationship between a sixteen-year-old boy and his parents.

Three experienced staff members made an appointment to meet with the family, in their home, one evening shortly after the second episode with heroin. These two men and one woman had not consulted with each other about what they would do beyond thoroughly exploring the family structure and system of interelationships. They entered the home respected and trusted to an extent, because of our organization's previous work with the family, and because the parents were desperate, afraid, and angry, looking for a kind of help they had never received.

They sat in the living room in an informal casual circle, created by the position of the chairs and couches. The session was to last some three hours. It began casually, as if there were not a deeper level of concern among the six people present. Jim began to rationalize his use of drugs, saying that it was his business. He felt he had a right to do what he wanted, as long as he knew of the possible effects of the drugs. He said he did not know whether he would use drugs again, but there was no attempt to promise. He left the possibility clearly open.

After half an hour of Jim's displaying this kind of defensiveness, an irritating disregard for the feelings of his parents, an arrogant self-

centeredness, a subtle intellectual game being played of overt reasonableness camouflaging a deep disinterest in anyone but himself. The counselors began to feel more confident about what was going on. An example
is sufficient. Jim wore his hair shoulder length, and frizzed out, and he
was often mistaken for a girl by his family's friends, to the embarrassment of the parents. They had tried to point out the pain he was causing
them (humiliation, embarrassment), and he had listened to them carefully, saying he would take what they had to say into careful consideration; then he let his hair grow even longer. This irritated his parents, but
they depended on reason to communicate and to convince. His father was
a liberal, who felt that reason was the only appropriate way to deal with
the situation. His desperation came from the sinking feeling he got when
his son played at being reasonable but continued acting in a selfish way,
which hurt his parents deeply.

As the session focused on the parents' feelings, the counselors began
to treat Jim as a four-year-old, interpreting this to both his parents and
to him as the only appropriate way to deal with his actions and his defensiveness. He denied he was being defensive, but the counselors cut him
off several times, telling him to be quiet, they were talking to his parents.
As his parents talked, their feelings of helplessness were clearly evident. It was interpreted that Jim seemed to have all the power in the house,
able to do whatever he wanted, even if it hurt himself or them. The counselors refused to believe that it had to be that way, pointing out that they
did not let Jim control their behavior by either threats or actions.

As the threat to his means of power became clearer, Jim became
uncomfortable and attempted to threaten the counselors: "This isn't
helping," "I'll probably take drugs just to show you I don't have to do
what you say," "Who are you to come in here and do this?" Finally he simply
got up and walked out, saying, "I don't have to put up with this bullshit!"

The counselors told his parents they were adults and did not have to
take this form of abuse from their children, that rights are earned, not
merely granted. The son was using the father's reasonability to his own
advantage, manipulating him through an overt appearance of cooperative-
ness but a covert use of anger, resentment, and hostility behind his
every move. Their son was telling them he would do anything he pleased,
whether it hurt them or himself, and by their refusing to intervene except by arguments, which, Jim proved, could not convince him, they were
allowing him to use drugs.

Jim's father began to realize how powerless he was and how his son
was blackmailing him with threats and gestures. As his son got up to
leave, he looked at him with both anger and helplessness. One of the
three counselors, however, got up and went to bring Jim back regardless
of what he wanted to do.

At this point several facts clicked in the father's head. He was the
father; he was the one with the power; he could prevent Jim from growing
his hair long or from taking drugs; he was the boss. And he had surren-
dered all of this, threatening only to send the boy to where someone else
would be powerful and would make him mind. He could also see Jim's

incredible anger and resentment, how it was directed at himself through drugs and indirectly at his parents through his hair and his drug abuse. Jim's father got up and went after the counselor and Jim.

For the first time the father used physical force to bring the boy around to doing what the father wanted him to. He realized that, if the boy could not act in a reasonable, adult manner, it was absurd to treat him as an adult. The boy was acting like a four-year-old; so the father tried to pull him back, though he was still indecisive.

The second counselor walked over to where the three were struggling and picked the boy up and carried him back, where he sat quietly. The father then decided that the boy must cut his hair. Immediately the boy protested, saying he must talk to his father alone. The clear implication was that he could control his father, but not them — something the father could not miss. He refused and insisted the boy cut his hair to a respectable length. He said to Jim, "You have been punishing us with your hair, and we are merely stopping you from continuing to do this." After his hair was cut, by himself, with no use of force, Jim ran out of the house. His father ran out after him. He had only walked a block away, to see if he still cared. He returned without a struggle.

Jim's father had learned that he had to set limits and, more importantly, that he had to enforce them. By being strict with Jim he gave Jim an opportunity to act like a little boy, which Jim needed, expressing anger through swearing, crying, and yelling, instead of shooting heroin. As Jim acted in this new way he was able to relax more, and his personality began to change.He became much more friendly, convincing, open, honest, and stopped playing games. He was a different person. The pattern of trying to reach his parents through drug abuse stopped, and was not resumed, since the behavior of his parents toward him changed.

Since this time Jim has not used any drug, nor has he been in any way a discipline problem for his parents. "I have decided I have to do what they say, even if I don't agree with it." At first he resented Number Nine, but as he said himself, "I guess it's only therapeutic anger, and I will come back when I get it out." Jim is proud of his father for being more of a man and less of a pushover. His own sense of masculinity has been strengthened, and he is more secure in his home. He is continuing helping other kids at Number Nine. He recently supported a decision of a parent to spank his sixteen-year-old daughter because "she is acting like I used to, as a four-year-old, and she needs someone to stop her, since she can't stop herself."

A Generation Away

When Marge ran away from home, her parents, feeling helpless, allowed her to stay away for two weeks. Cindy, the older sister, decided to take a hand and brought them in to Number Nine. Marge is an exceptionally sophisticated fifteen-year-old; Cindy is seventeen. Mrs. X is very open to her daughters but is unstable herself. Mr. X, a businessman, is reserved and conventional. He did not like Marge's life style, as a hippie, very much at all.

Marge, who cries periodically for no reason, has a distinctly withdrawn side and is conflicted on many levels. In our first intervention we
arranged for her to be seen by a private psychiatrist, for an adjusted
fee. He wanted us to attempt to create a less stressful home environment.

In talking with the four principals, the counselor at Number Nine
discovered several basic sources for the stress. The first was the mother's position as a confidante to the girls, supporting them in fearing the
father and acting as advocate when they had a request. She was weak and
used the father for limit-setting, threatening to tell him any impropriety
although she never did so. Constant interpretation reversed this balance,
bringing out the father's concern that he had to be overly strict and the
daughter's that they had always been afraid of him. When this basic
game was changed, allowing the father to be more human, his basic dis-
like for the girl's life style became more acceptable and appeared less
threatening.

The girl's efforts to manipulate rather than negotiate were also demonstrated, interpreted, and controlled. The parents' feelings of frustration and of being used therefore decreased, and they became more tolerant. Instead of Marge's having to conceal her feelings, she found support,
and tensions decreased markedly. On a thirty-day followup, this
continued to be the case. The parents were content with their daughter's
progress in psychotherapy as well.

The Lonely Acid Trip

Mary is a fifteen-year-old girl from an upper-class professional family. She goes to a private girl's school, where she gets a B average. She
is attractive, well dressed, and pleasant. Before her "bad trip" she was
sullen, depressed, withdrawn, and uncommunicative. She felt that her
family distrusted her and, worse, didn't care. When they went away on
a vacation, leaving all the children at home, and were going to be away on
her birthday, she dropped five hundred mics of LSD to see what would
happen. Her older sister, left with the responsibility of all the kids,
called Number Nine when she discovered her sister laughing and crying
and her sister's friend in hysterics.

The staff members who came to the house told the other children
immediately, describing accurately what the effects would be, how long
they would last, and what they could do to help. They decided the others
would be better off out of the house and had them sent to their older
sister's apartment. As they left, their sister Mary was yelling and running around. They called for assistance, and two more people from Number Nine came over.

After restraining her until help could arrive, they put her in the living room of her house, a familiar place for her to be, removing anything
she could hurt herself with, and formed a line around her with themselves.
She undressed in this living circle and ran around naked. She attacked
the line but was supported gently, being neither held nor pushed away.
After several hours of this behavior, she collapsed on the floor. The
counselors gave her orange juice to drink and warm towel baths. Holding

her hands whenever she tried to hurt herself, they kicked back when
kicked and slapped her when she hurt them. Most of the time they responded supportively. After several hours of being cared for — including
having her back massaged, her hair combed, her hands held silently, her
body covered — she began to express strong sexual feelings which the
counselors converted into pseudo actions with cushions and other physical
objects.

While two people worked with her, in the presence of her sister, another member of our bad-trip team stayed with her brothers and sisters,
clearly explaining what was happening and helping them talk about their
fear and anger. Furthermore, a member of the team went to meet her
parents as they got off the plane, to tell them what was happening. Her
father, a doctor, knew about the possibility of her being given thorazine,
a major tranquilizer, but rejected this as presently unnecessary. Their
daughter had been tripping for over four hours, but they trusted the team
and wanted to know what they could do to help. They went to see their
other children first, comforted them, and then returned to their home.

As they returned, they were told in detail what to expect, so they
would not be caught off guard. This also diminished their anxiety. They
were helped to understand what they saw when they met their daughter,
and the counselors interpreted the conflicts she was expressing with the
help of the drug. Presently they began to understand that a bad trip is
merely a very emotional act of self-resentment, fear, and sexuality. As
they listened and talked with their daughter, she revealed many of her
personal secrets, which her parents had been unaware of, including her
feelings about being mistrusted, rejected, uncared for, and so on. Mary
went back to the time when she was four years old, and they held her in
their arms and talked softly to her. As she "grew up", they went through
many of the experiences she had been through, none of which they had
ever talked about. The trip was similar to Sara's (Chapter 4).

When Mary reached the age of sixteen, her birthday, they sang happy
birthday to her. After ten hours of this trip Mary relaxed enough to
sleep, awaking six hours later. The family and the team held a session
the next day at which everything was gone over. In this session Mary's
father cried, and so did Mary for the first time in a long, long time.
Since this bad trip Mary has been much more communicative with her
parents, has been given more trust, and has not taken drugs again. She
is more outgoing, trusting, and generally happy, spending more time
with other people than she used to.

An Incredible Triangle

Candy is an unusually attractive nineteen-year-old who is steadily
dating a boy named John and living together with him and his friend,
David, who is very much interested in Candy and is more responsive to
her needs than John.

They originally came to Number Nine for help in finding an apartment
and for a place to stay in the process. Candy presented herself as

confused and unsure of where she was heading. In a conversation with one of the staff members, she admitted to a very unhappy home life. Her father's death she believed, was blamed on her; he had been an alcoholic. She fled from this guilt and horror into a withdrawn period, which her mother aggravated by being hostile, unpleasant, suspicious, and continuously dissatisfied with Candy. Candy regains some of her self-esteem through being able to attract men and then cut them off, with a very conscious castration impulse behind her flirting.

John is a passive, withdrawn, insecure man of twenty, very much like Candy in background and personality. He is insecure and afraid of becoming dependent on Candy; he makes many demands on her, as she does on him, but he rejects hers out of a fear of being totally dependent. This leaves her feeling more unlovable and more angry, so she turns on David, the third party.

David is unlike either of them; he is a replacement for Michael, a boy Candy felt was "going with John," and she disliked him immensely. Candy had persuaded John to give up his friendship with Mike, who was, Candy said, "influencing" John. In fact, Candy wanted to control John herself, to obtain satisfaction for her needs from him.

After seeing Candy separately, John and Candy were seen together. Discussion revealed that John was intensely jealous of David but felt he could not compete, that his relationship with Candy was only a matter of time.

The counselor pointed out that neither of them was able to look at the other because too many soft feelings came out which frightened both of them. He also pointed out that they talked to each other through him and, he suspected, through David as well. They admitted the truth of this observation; neither one of them was happy with the situation. John asked if he should ask David to live with someone else. The counselor pointed out that it was unusual for a man to invite someone trying to make his girl to live with them; it was equally unusual to make sure his girl wasn't receiving the kind of attention she needed to keep from turning away.

John and Candy accepted their insecurity and self-defeating feelings and struggled to see each other as they were, instead of as projections of their own unfullfilled needs. They decided together that David should go, although John stated the decision directly to Candy; John also said that he was going to tell David when Candy was not around. Candy smiled and said she felt more like a woman.

In the following session together, ways of mutual support were discussed, as well as ways of meeting their own needs without depending upon each other. Interpretation of their demands and how they are making them on each other revealed to each their mutual distrust and also their intuitive feeling of love for each other. They learned to give and take affection without trapping the other in the embrace.

The Future of Alternative Counseling

We have mentioned that counseling can be conceived of as both a skill and a human quality. We conceptualized the task of an alternate

counseling center as dealing with support, awareness, and creation of
strategies for change, and we related that task to the context of a radical
restructuring of society. The final question is of the ultimate role of
therapy in a society and the location of the required skills. At present,
alternate counseling centers are struggling to demystify and deprofes-
sionalize a human quality which has become reified as a detached series
of maneuvers by the traditional practice of psychotherapy. The skill
is associated with medicine and belongs only to a professional elite which
has no accountability for its work and pursues detachment and greater
skill often to the exclusion of counseling as a whole human relationship.

It was suggested that alternate counseling starts with a rediscovery
that humanness heals more than do detached skills. But this simple
formulation also required a theory of society and ways to deal with the
oppressive social structure and people's internalizations of it. Some
possible ways to do this were sketched, and case studies were offered
from our experience at Number Nine. But are we again manufacturing
a skilled profession, and will radical therapy also be practiced eventually
by an elite which mystifies its skill and loses touch with the people?

There are several reasons why we think not. The first is that there
is much less ego invenstment in the identity of a skilled counselor once
the process is demystified. People from varied backgrounds, who intend
to go in various other directions, take the time to acquire this skill at
an alternate counseling center, but with the intention of growing in the
process and then moving on. The skill is then disseminated to whatever
living and community groups that person has contact with in the future.
Further, clients who have received help which is no longer mystified
but a product of group support can use the support group as a template
for forming other support groups in their communities. Thus the skill
of counseling is not secret and hidden away in schools but becomes part
of the process of delivering service to others. Eventually training and
help will become intertwined, and the skill of counseling will, like a
new gene, become a part of the new social structure of the community.
In essence, an awareness of internalization, and the way beyond
it are essential qualities for any community which is not to become
calcified within a structure whose meaning has become mystified by
overly long use. The skills broadly mentioned in Chapter 3 as necessary
to the counter-cultural change process are the skills which are specifically developed as an alternative counseling center grows. This dis-
semination and codification of understanding of psychic process is in
the end a more important product of the center, than its personal successes or its advocacy battles with recalcitrant institutions. If people
learn to help each other and this skill is distributed around the community, coercive therapy institutions will simply wither away as government funding runs out and people stop paying for what they can receive from each other. This is a highly utopian speculation, but it is
important to hold such a future concept in order to check periodically
on one's own personal progress in developing a style of counseling which
reflects these new priorities. Only if his clients can ultimately put him

out of a job can a counselor feel that he has passed from traditional to alternative counseling, and only if a center has that concept of its function can it lead to genuine change.

Chapter 8

THREE EXPERIMENTAL THERAPEUTIC COMMUNITIES

In Chapter 3 we dealt with new communities as the basic structural unit of a new culture and with the need for transition groups to help people move from one life style to another. This chapter presents case studies of three communities that deal with extreme forms of transition. Each of these communities includes people coming from one of our society's most repressive institutions — the mental hospital. Such hospitals are gathering places for those who have not been socialized in the most minimal of survival skills or those who were subjected to such intolerable stress in their living situation that they had to seek refuge. The concept "mental illness" implies that the experience of such people is crazy and that it has to be straightened out to conform to that of other people. Yet those in the counter-culture know that such experience also has many elements of a far clearer perception of the way things are, and that in a supportive environment people can go directly from "mental illness" to great personal insight and a synthesis of their experience which enables them to master their environment and live well. Such is the goal of the communities we describe.

The three accounts are all by Dennis Jaffe. Each is from a different perspective because he had a different relationship to each community. The first is his diary of the initial months of Number Nine's residential center, which served both as a home for young staff members in training and as a place for young people who needed a temporary space while they "got their heads together." The experiment represents some quite traditional concepts, such as formal helper and director roles, outside counseling, and fairly directive limits. The diary shows that the consequences of these structures are dysfunctional to the goal of helping people gain a sense of who they are and what they will do. The second account is compiled from taped interviews with all the residents of a halfway house for people leaving hospitals and students, two kinds of people in transition. Dennis, who was a resident there during its first year, has remained close to the house as consultant and friend. The house has worked through some of the issues which caused difficulty in the Number Nine residence and seems to work toward its goals rather than being at cross-purposes to them. The third account grew out of a visit to London's Kingsley Hall, which was started by R.D. Laing and others who questioned the entire relevance of the category "madness" as a personal defect or a pejorative term. Instead they saw "going down" into madness as a growth experience, and they tried to create a residence to allow for this process. This account is an interview with one of the Hall's notable successes. It reflects an early stage of the development of a kind of community which presupposes a great deal of cultural learning and growth before others can duplicate and expand on it.

While many experiments have been called halfway houses, most do not go beyond the structure and assumptions of the hospital itself. They do not confront the hospital's placing a high value on what is "real", nor do they question whether madness is a defect and whether society's norms have validity or are merely training grounds which socialize people into "correct" behavior. The communities in this section are more concerned with the expression and understanding of inner experience, regardless of whether the results are conventionally valued. The evidence of such communities, when taken with the almost total absence of "cures" in conventional treatment centers, suggests that these categories are indeed relevant and crucial. A community which explores such distinctions is, then, necessary to a more balanced understanding of the processes of madness and of sanity. The social transitions described previously make one less eager to rely on conventional categories, and the need to explore alternatives forces us to take seriously and respect the reality of those who rebel through mental illness.

Small communities like these are cheap, functional alternatives to the custodial, oppressive care offered by mental hospitals. They utilize the concept of a self-help community rather than the notion of powerful doctors using expertise to cure the sick. Not surprisingly, it is the economic argument which is causing this model to spread as large custodial institutions try to form small outside communities for long-term patients. The issue which these and the communities described here must then face is whether the outside world is in any way preferable to that of the hospital. Perhaps the changes which might take place within hospitals will relate less to getting people out than to creating small colonies and intimate groups within them. That task would be even more difficult than getting people back into the world. Laing and his associates seem to be moving toward this concept as the incongruity of the world to even mad people becomes apparent. A withdrawal impulse in the face of the "normal" world becomes an understandable part of the search for alternatives. The questions of permanence and isolation have been on the periphery of each of these communities. The pressure to get people out and make them self-sufficient turns into a proliferation of supportive communities, where the graduates of these houses live together. People from each of these communities have gone on, not to the nuclear family, which each found stifling, even maddening, but to an extended support group.

In each account the role of the helping person is crucial. The strong need for helpers is illustrated by the quite different roles of Joe Berke in Kingsley Hall, Koren in the halfway house, and the outside leadership of the Number Nine house. The possible helper roles range from director to guide, authority to peer, parent to sibling, confronter to accepter. There seems to be no limit to the kind of stance that is helpful, but some characteristics appear throughout. The role must be genuine and flexible, it must involve a sharing of experience, it must be noncoercive and at ease with deep personal experience, and it must offer some protection from external stress. The helpers usually live or have lived in the community. The inference is that such qualities are those of the good community member, and also the good counselor. Experimental communities like these demonstrate that healing power is more a matter of humanity than of good technique.

A. Diary of a Residential Crisis Center

This section consists of a diary kept by Dennis Jaffe during the first three months that Number Nine's residential crisis center and staff house was in operation — from May to August 1970. Dennis was one of the directors and participated in all aspects of planning and activity, although he did not live there. The house was renovated and purchased under a grant from the New Haven Foundation, to be used as a residence for staff members of Number Nine and a short-term residence for young people in crisis or in need of shelter. The diary has been edited only by correcting grammar and adding some background details. The aim is purely descriptive, narrating what happened without interpreting, evaluating, or inferring what is going on inside people. Some interpretive comments were added retrospectively; they are set off in parentheses.

May 6 — This week the first floor (kitchen, dining-meeting room, bathroom, two bedrooms) has been finished, and the second (living room, three bedrooms, bathroom) is on its way. The staff members — Ralph, Stuart, Nell, Bud, and Dave — have moved in. At a staff meeting Monday we decided that Ralph would be joined on the house staff by Nell (the newest staff member), probably Stuart, and Dave, who was in charge of construction. At the meeting the decision was taken to have Joan become the first official resident of the program and move in after leaving the state hospital. Ted and I, two directors, had known her when she lived at other hospitals and at the halfway house, and we recounted what we know of her past — how she had been repeatedly punished and not treated adequately at hospitals, her violent and fearsome family history, and her forced abortion. Nell was especially anxious that Joan come to Number Nine because they had been friends when Nell had been at the state hospital. She was also fairly tense about whether things would work out.

I have been working with Ralph and Nell especially on defining the structure and goals of the house. It will be available for stays of up to a month for people in acute crises or needing a place to stay because of various emergencies. Residents will work two and a half hours a day on tasks specified by the staff, in return for their room, board, and participation in the program. People hanging around the storefront all day, who are not taking on staff tasks, will be offered a chance to join the house program also. Although the group and counseling program will be optional, we will select residents partly on the basis of their commitment and interest in the kind of self-exploration we plan to do.

The program will include house meetings Sunday nights for everyone, to settle business and housekeeping issues. Mondays and Fridays from 10 a.m. to noon, counseling groups will be held which will include talk about where people are and decisions they have to make, confrontation, psychodrama, and other exercises. Dennis and Jack — a Yale student who has done it under supervision — will join the house staff at these groups. Jack will also offer psychodrama training to staffers. There will be weekly staff encounter groups, and supervision meetings with Dennis and Sammy, a clinical consultant, to deal with counseling issues. Each resident will be offered family counseling and one-to-one counseling if desired.

Joan became the first resident. She attended the weekly community meeting at Number Nine's apartment crash pad (not the house) and was quiet and seemed tense. Nell asked me the next day how to handle Joan's wish to use drugs this weekend. We agreed that we wanted her to retain her freedom of choice but still to know that we were concerned enough to want to keep communication open on the issue. Her aim in staying at the house is basically to set herself up to stay out of the hospital and to undo some of the destructive effects of her previous treatment — many years' confinement in various hospitals. When I interviewed her that evening, I found her guarded and noncommital, answering questions in short phrases. I feel this is the result of learned distrust of people who are trying to help her. She also expresses some of her doubts about being able to make it on her own. I explained our program, with particular stress on the fact that she was free to do as she wished. I said we would be available and hoped she would seek people out. She was quiet and seemed afraid. Since I knew she was seeing Ted for counseling, I did not press the point. I also explained that she was free to make decisions about drugs (outside of the house!) but that I hoped she would be able to talk to us about it.

Today the staff, myself, and Dick (another clinical consultant) interviewed our next prospective resident, Mary, who arrived with her social worker. Like Joan, she was coming from several years of hospitalization and was trying to make it outside the hospital and outside her family. She too knew me from before, a fact that helped the interview go smoothly. She said her plans were to get a job and an apartment or perhaps to go to the halfway house. She also wants to make friends,

and she was enthusiastic about both the counseling program and the prospect of family meetings. Ralph did most of the explaining of the program,
and Mary agreed to move in on Sunday.

We also talked to Bill, a high school student who first came to the
storefront at 2 a.m. on Monday night. His transcendental meditation
checker (he was learning this technique) brought him because he was
having an acute anxiety attack. He dates these attacks back to several
bad trips, but he has a history of two short hospitalizations. He finds it
hard to talk to people, and greater fluency is one of his goals. We offered
him the possibility of participating in the day part of the house group
program, while living at home, since he is currently afraid to go back to
school. He seems to like the program, especially its informality, but
is pessimistic that it will relieve his anxiety. He is in therapy at the
mental health center and wanted to drop out, but I urged him to go through
the final weeks to official termination. I agreed to talk to his therapist
with him about our program and to work with him and his family as he
wished.

When I had seen him late Monday night, sitting huddled up and shaking
on a couch, he said that he simply could not get out his feelings or thoughts,
and they seem to create an almost intolerable pressure within him. I was
very active, in order to draw him out. We did some exercises to get out
anger — which he participated in stiffly, with little relief — and a short
psychodrama. He talked little about his parents and felt that sex played
little part in his problems, but I felt that he had some tremendous tensions in both these areas and that a program like ours could encourage
him to trust other people enough to begin to express his feelings.

May 10 — On Friday I picked up Bill at the storefront, and we drove to the
house to attend the first of the morning counseling-groups. It began about
half an hour late, with Jack directing a session in psychodrama. Joan
was out working, Mary had not yet moved in, and only Nell and Stuart
from the staff were there, so the total participants were five. First we
did an imagination exercise of what we would save if the world was destroyed. Jack picked up on a pastoral setting of Nell's, and I doubled
with her for a walk through her imaginary scene, which was devoid of
people. I added someone to the scene, but she went on creating a fork
in the road to avoid meeting him. We talked about feelings we had about
being alone and about the implications of choosing not to be with people.
Jack closed Nell's scene with Nell meeting herself in twenty years.

Next a scene of Stuart and his father fishing was set up. I alternately
played Stuart and his father. We got pretty far into that, dealing with
what he wanted from his father and some feelings about growing up, and
ending with some less heavy scenes of Stuart being taller than his father
and meeting him in a few years as an equal. (Both dramas were well
designed and carried out, in that they focused directly on central issues
for each of the people and created space for them to "come down" and
reintegrate their experience at the end, which some encounter leaders
forget or are uninterested in. This concern forms one of the core values

in our work.) People then shared similar experiences or feelings with
the two protagonists. Bill felt he could not get into a scene with anybody
besides himself, and he felt pretty tense, as he usually does.

Everyone seemed in high spirits during the weekend. Joan helped
out some, with Nancy, and seemed more comfortable. Dave raided a
deserted house and got a TV antenna and some piping. There seemed to
be some tension about Betty, Bud's girl friend who is living at the house,
and some anger was evident. Sunday night was the first full house meeting. It started with some Frisbee throwing while people waited for Stuart
and Bud to finish eating. I talked about the reasons for the house meeting
and suggested that it be compulsory, so people who had issues would not
be tempted to skip it. I also suggested that the focus be on house business
but that other issues between people were by no means excluded. Dave
was very active, talking about many things to do with structure and construction, sometimes out of context of the rest of the discussion. It was
clarified that Dave was in charge of all building, with Stuart (who has
the only car) helping to get materials. Ralph agreed to supervise the
housework for this week, to set up duties for residents, and to allocate
the other tasks. Joan and Mary were quiet, and it seemed from their
jokes that the process and talk about duties and schedules reminded them
of institutions. This made me uncomfortable, because I shared their
perception. Nell and Bud (representing Betty, who was not present) got
into a hassle about cleaning bathrooms and dishes, but I interpreted the
issue as probably being about something else, and that closed it.

May 18 — The morning group began the next day at 10 with Frisbee throwing while Stuart and Nell got up. Stuart had to fix his car, so only Ralph,
Nell, Bill, Joan, and Mary met with me. We started with one-to-one
encounters; each person went to one other who made him most uncomfortable and started talking about that. I wanted to follow up the theme from
the night before of me, Mary and Joan all feeling like the place was
another institution. Nell went to Bill, Mary to Ralph, and Joan to me.
After about half an hour, it became apparent that the staffers had, in
effect, interviewed the residents. I suggested a role switch, and residents
interviewed the staff. There followed some talk about trust in the group
and about hospital practices that put people off and keep them from expressing anything. Everyone seemed to feel pretty good after the session,
as if some of the tensions between people had been lifted.

Sammy and I met with Nell and Ralph that afternoon. Ralph felt down
about the slower pace and less rewarding counseling at the house. The
shift to being part of a community, rather than remaining just a
crisis-intervention center at the storefront, was discussed. Nell brought
up the bind she felt in at having to be nice to Joan and not getting angry
at her which she felt was her problem and not a demand of her staff role.
The guilt created by Joan and Mary, who are used to a hospital and thus
do not trust easily and have a lot of residual feelings, was discussed as
a lose-lose proposition for the staff. They will feel bad no matter how
we respond, because institutionalized people are used to passively hating

their jailers. Our own need to make the house different and our consequent defensiveness, as well as our own feelings about institutions, were
mentioned. We feel that we have to be helpful to the residents, which
makes us not genuine and not able to form a collaborative working community. The slow pace of the house, and the need for clarity in our tasks,
was discussed.

May 15 — The week has been quiet, and my own feeling of aimlessness
and diffuseness seems to be echoed in the house, although others seem
less depressed about it. I cancelled the Tuesday staff encounter, feeling
that I had no desire to go to a meeting and that others, too, were fed
up with meetings. I wanted to stand back and see how things worked out,
how people created a structure. (Retrospectively, this depression and
later similar ones seem to come from the great amounts of directive
energy I had been expending and the feeling that my concept was not
shared by the staff, so that, rather than working toward collaboration,
the whole structure would fall apart without direction. I have never suc-
ceeded in creating a training process or recruiting people whose energy
and commitment to this type of thing matched mine.)

On Wednesday, after spending a night with her parents, Mary called
to say she would not be back. Nell felt bad about it, as did I, and when
we talked, we began to rationalize that perhaps it was good for her to be
able to leave, even though our feelings told us we had somehow failed. I
saw her briefly that afternoon, and she said she wanted to get out of institutions and not have to always think of her hassles. She said she felt
good, and she appeared more animated than I had ever seen her, so I
agreed that it was good for her to try to make it on her own, not questioning whether living at her parents' house was being on her own. Nell
had told me the day before that Mary had said that, while she liked our
place, she felt that the things that were said in the group came too fast
for her to get them. She was confused by it all, and I felt that another
reason she was leaving was the high expectation (in the area of health)
that we had for her. She wanted to get away from feelings right then, not
go into them.

As a group we began to feel that perhaps we had erred by taking in
recently institutionalized people, and that we should focus on people who
had problems with their families or other hassles that they wanted to
work through. We should have only a minority of people at any one time
from institutions, because their demands and the pull toward being dependent will be too much for us to handle. A feeling was growing in me
that perhaps we were just reinventing the hospital, especially in view
of our growing defensiveness and our feeling that, since our treatment
is correct, people had better like it. It seemed that perhaps people were
seeking our center because it was accessible and an easily available
shelter, and that they were willing to put up passively with our intro-
spective trip. I talked to Ted, and he agreed that we were having a tendency to copy existing institutions, rather than trying to redefine the

whole concept of what we were doing, in order to eliminate the kinds of
dehumanization and alienation that we were opposed to.

A bunch of people from the Clearinghouse at the University of Massa-
chusetts came to visit with a videotape machine, and there was a lot of
fun and excitement as we experimented with filming what we were doing
and creating situations. By Thursday well over a hundred people were
around, and a number of high-energy discussions took place about our
role and the coming summer. The idea came up to make the house into
a commune of people who were working on community projects, supporting them to do their work, and using the house as an energy center to
share the projects. (A unique aspect of our work seems to be that we are
always open to redefinition of what we are doing, even on basic levels.
This might make us rather flighty at times, but at critical moments it
seems to free us for really creative work on ourselves.)

The other use for the house that was suggested was to use it as a
center for workshops and weekend seminars in the new culture for teachers and others who want to learn with us. The workshops would be free
and would hopefully attract lots of people, perhaps all from a single
place, who would then go back to their systems and work for change. This
idea excited us as a more viable use for the house than a crisis center.
I was beginning to feel acutely the limitations on us by the kind of demands for consistent structure and purpose that we were getting from
our first residents. For young people who are feeling dead, confused,
or out of touch, the need might be for a more structured and orderly
place than we provide. It felt good to us that we were not locked into a
single rigid mode, and we hoped that the best purpose for our place
would somehow manifest itself out of our conversations.

The rest of the staffers seemed to lean toward the commune-work-
shop center as a model, but no explicit conversations on how to do this
have been initiated. Why not? There seem to be a variety of reasons for
our not generating any practical consequences from our ideas, not the
least of which is our recurring tendency to fantasize rather than act.
The style of generating ideas at Number Nine seems to be based partly
on a synectic model. We generate a lot of energy at group brainstorming
sessions, which crop up from time to time at regular meetings (we are
usually pretty loose, except when under a lot of stress because of avoiding covert issues). When a director, or occasionally another staff member, takes on the burden of organizing something or taking responsibility
for seeing it through, it happens. While we seem to have a somewhat
shared decision-making group, I feel a greater burden for carrying out
our programs; this seems to be one of the greater defects in our practice.

The ambivalence toward the work is shown by staff members' neglecting to follow up leads for new residents. A girl whom Yvonne (the
third director of Number Nine) had seen at the hospital, and who had
been to the storefront before, has not been seen again about moving in,
and I finally told Ralph to do it. There is a heavy dynamic around enforcing work norms; people seem to expect me to do it, and they wait,
but then they resent it when I do. This drains me.

Another problem we are facing is that our self-image as an alternative to professional care is not always seen or appreciated by those who come in, who are used to con jobs. We are a little too eager for customers, and there is really very little reason, other than our appearance, to feel that we are more honest, trustworthy, or helpful than any other group. A girl, seventeen, who had run away from a home for disturbed girls, came in, saying she wanted freedom. Since she also said she wanted to learn to understand herself and her feelings more, I told her she could stay with us. Since she wasn't eighteen, she needed her parent's permission to stay. She was afraid to contact them, but when we made it plain that there was no other way she could stay, she called home, and her mother convinced her to return. She said that things were okay, and she would come back if she wanted to stay. Again, like with Mary, there was no reason to believe we had failed, but we couldn't escape the feeling that perhaps it was something about us that made people shy away.

Wednesday night Joan was really upset, and Dave took time off from his work to stay up with her most of the night. Dave had come to Number Nine one night when he was looking for a place to crash and to withdraw from alcohol. He found that the best way to keep away from drugs was to work all day, and he had an incredible array of skills in engineering and construction. He had taken a similar role under similar circumstances at one of the Daytop drug-addict communities, and his concepts of relating were therefore based to some extent on confrontation. He used this approach with Joan, talking about her hurting herself by using drugs, and he pushed her on how she showed in her behavior that she hated herself and couldn't cope. He told me the many ways he cut into her games and how he got the message through to her that if she did not pull herself together, she'd had it. I told him that he seemed on target and that he had done as good a job as anyone could have under the circumstances.

On Friday night another minor freak-out occurred. Nell's friend Janis came, and a group of us went to the Sunshine Festival, smoked some hash, and drank a lot of wine. Nell left Janis alone for a while, and her friend felt rejected; this brought up a host of other feelings concerning the collapse of her marriage, her Southern sexual repression, and her feelings of sexuality and anger toward her parents. Once again, Dave was helpful in guiding her through it, aided by Bud. They felt later that Nell was angry at their intervening in her friends' trip, because Nell has been upset since then. But Janis felt incredibly relieved after the experience. She had never had such an upheaval, and was glad others were able to bear with her. By the next day when I came by, Nell, Janis, and another friend all seemed in good spirits, so I assumed things were okay. I suggested to Ralph and Janis that she feel free to participate in the program while she was visiting and that she come to house meeting on Sunday. I felt that that meeting could help clarify her role at the house, so people would not feel tense about how to treat her.

A new resident, recently discharged from the state hospital and sent to us by his social worker, was scheduled to come for an interview. The

staffers handled this without me, and when I met him he seemed to be
a pretty passive chronic-patient type, helpful and obliging but not looking
for the type of encounter we wanted to offer. He went to the halfway
house for supper, and we decided to encourage him to move in there and
find a job. He talked to me later about working at Number Nine, and I
told him that he would be fine if he wanted to be a volunteer, but that he
would have to find another kind of job to support himself.

May 23 — A week ago Jerry and Ron, who had just left a small prep
school for "slightly emotionally disturbed kids," began hanging around the
storefront. They described the place as fairly free and benevolent, as
well as expensive, but Jerry feels that, now that he is eighteen, he has
gotten what he can out of it and needs to leave to find motivation before
he can go to college or settle down. Ralph has become friendly with Jerry
and proposed that he stay at the house for a month to pursue this journey.
His parents seem to support his staying with us, because he says that
they do not understand him and he cannot bear to be at home. They are
near enough to come for a family session, and Jerry agreed that such
a meeting would be helpful. He wants to use the month at Number Nine
to go into himself, find a job and an apartment, and see if he can find
meaning in the kind of work we do. Everyone seems to like him a lot;
he is easy-going, good-looking, cooperative, and articulate. He seems to
be the first really gratifying customer for our service. A couple, Candy
and John, who need a place to stay for a week while they find an apartment are also at the house.

The house meeting, held in the newly finished and fairly comfortable
second-floor living room, was attended by all the staff except Nell and
Dave, who were in Provincetown, and by staffers who wished to move
into the house. The need to get the building finished as quickly as possible was stressed by Ted, and there seemed to be a feeling that things
were getting done. A work party was scheduled for the next day for every
available man. Priorities for the upstairs and cellar were made. Bud
will decide next week whether he and Betty will move out. Nell had told
people she too was unsure about whether she would stay. Sue, a long-
time volunteer who had been living at home but was switching to full-time
work for the summer, wanted to move in, so there was doubt whether a
Yale student working for the summer, could move in too. Many housekeeping issues were discussed, such as eliminating meat for health
and financial reasons, which was carried over Ralph's strong objections.

May 30 — The work party did a lot of cleaning and little fix-up jobs. That
night, Dave and Nell returned from Provincetown. Dave was feeling
very spaced out; he said it was partly due to his medication getting lost
there and partly to his interaction with Nell, which he characterized
as hard at times but very interesting. We talked a lot the next day. Since
we had just hired another Daytop alumnus, we talked about the parallels
of his work at Number Nine and Daytop, and the differences especially

along the lines of Daytop's incredible intrusion into your head. We also talked about Dave's partial disintegration during the weekend, and I tried to help him reintegrate. This he related to his feeling of marginality on the staff. I realized that I had colluded in this because of my doubts about his ability as a counselor, but he had convinced me in his interventions last week that he had some ability and interest in this. We had not been paying him, since he felt that having money would tempt him to get back on alcohol. I told him that he was entitled to a salary of $15 a week like everyone else, and I tried to deal with his fear that we would dump him when the construction was done. We then talked with Ralph who was planning a workshop for high school students on "Alternatives to College."

That night the staff meeting dealt with house issues and with who would live there for the summer. My anger at people's not doing anything and then getting mad when I pointed this out was brought up. People focused on Bud, and Ralph wanted to confront him. Bud agreed that he hadn't been working and said that he felt that Number Nine was getting too big to deal with his problems. Ted felt this was a cop-out. It seemed to him that Bud no longer showed the kind of commitment and potential to Number Nine that had made people want to deal with him personally, but that now he mostly withdrew. Ralph, who had been feeling less close to him since he went back with Betty, asked to talk to him downstairs, and from time to time Dave and Yvonne joined them there. They focused on their feelings about tensions they felt around his relationship to Betty, and Bud's and Betty's personal games in which they involved others. Bud got angry and said that he would deal with that alone with Betty, with an outside psychoanalyst-consultant, as moderator.

Upstairs, the issue of who would lead the house came up. It was pointed out that Ralph had expressed his interest in such a role, similar to Charlie's at the storefront. The need for leadership was seen as a solution to the fact that not even rudimentary work things or counseling was getting done. Stuart who was absent to run a family session, had been in charge of work for that week. People said that, despite Stuart's steadiness and competence, leadership was not his forte. I pointed out that it seemed like some sort of collusion about the work had been in force when he was appointed to head it. Nell said that she felt she could be the leader of the house. She reminded us that some previous efforts in that direction, like calling meetings, had not come off despite universal agreement that they were a good idea. The need for legitimation from Ted or myself was discussed as seeming to be necessary to get others to do something, and people hoped this would not continue.

The next day I met with Ralph, Jerry, and his mother. The meeting was very low-keyed, skirting deep issues, talking about Jerry's reasons for coming to the house and our program. His father had not showed up, and his mother was obviously tense and angry. I suggested that Jerry's lack of motivation was due to some deep feelings he had about his father and his family's rejection of him, and that some fairly deep, directed counseling concerning these issues was needed. In a private conversation with Jerry afterward I learned that nobody had talked to him regularly, which made me angry. I suggested that some sessions were needed with his family; Jerry wanted these, and he also wanted his work at the house to be more structured.

We were to have a short meeting before the regular Number Nine community meeting, and I came in quite angry, since I felt that the staff was not doing very much. (In retrospect I see that our lack of shared goals, coupled with my tendency to be self-righteous and not really hear what was being told to me by the staff's not working, probably made me ineffective.) I decided to exert fairly rigid control over the meeting, to go over what people were doing, and to make plans to do things that were not getting done. The staffers were all late. Each person told what he was doing, and then we went over the fact that things like coordination, work on the house, and finding residents jobs and places to stay for residents were being neglected as people spent time in the more rewarding tasks of family work and planning workshops. I gave examples of neglected chores, such as arrangements for seeing that Jerry's needs were met and checking that a new resident, who had been referred by Charlie, was settled. I said that I wasn't interested in assigning blame. We worked out a list of necessary tasks, and I told them that I didn't want to continue to exercise daily directive leadership. Nell was active and helpful, Ralph was angry, and Stuart was quiet, which illustrated to me their respective tones in the house. The community meeting that followed was incredibly intense and complicated. The focus was on people's dependence on the directors and their anger at them, and the tremendous need for support that this demonstrated. Ralph, who continued to be especially upset at how he was treated, got out a lot of feelings.

On Thursday the staff had two meetings to coordinate tasks, neither of which I attended. Little John, a young street hustler and member of Number Nine's new band, had been busted a few weeks before, and we had helped pay his fine. To pay us back, he was to be hired for three weeks of hard work, plus extra work to pay for his room and board at the house. Since he had been experimenting with heroin recently and was notorious as a hustler, the staff decided that for him the house should be as structured as Daytop, and Dave would supervise his work and forbid him to go anywhere where he could get drugs. Also at that meeting, Bud announced that Betty would no longer work at Number Nine; he was going to move into an apartment with her that week. That weekend, Little John began to con us; he burned himself so that he couldn't work on Saturday, but he was still able to jam with the band on Sunday morning.

Most of the staff was gone Sunday evening, and feeling that there was no need for a house meeting, I rapped with Ted, Dave, and Stuart about work priorities. Since we had difficulty finding volunteer manpower, the staffers had the major burden. Next week Ralph will spend 5 days as an observer at the Emergency Treatment Unit of the local mental health center. This is part of an embryonic exchange program, which will form part of the staff training if people feel it is useful. (It also shows how much our program was tied to the professional treatment model.) I talked with Dave about Little John's games. He had called tonight and asked if he could stay out until tomorrow morning, and was told no. I told Dave to go as far as he felt comfortable in confronting John. There was to be a meeting the next day with his family, his lawyer, Yvonne, and Stuart, and I suggested that the meeting would be a good opportunity to set the contract with him straight. Dave said that Little John liked to talk about dope a lot while working, but that Dave had told him to cool it when the other kids were around. I suggested that John obviously had qualities that made him a leader, and that we should try to get him on our side by enlisting his aid in helping the others.

June 3 — When I arrived for the Monday morning group, again everyone shared my own ambivalence about getting together, and we did not meet. I began to feel that my own lack of confronting the issues, and my offering insufficient support to the staff in defining their roles, was playing to their own fears. This seemed effectively to keep the atmosphere from getting too intense. Ralph came back later from the hospital and told how they spent incessant hours meeting and don't deal with their own issues at all, and I found myself hoping when I heard this that people would begin to do things differently as a result.

Tuesday afternoon, when Ralph returned, we had a house meeting, with a full house. There was a new girl, who had come in the night before, after a referral from the police. She had called them, and they called us to ask if we could put her up. She had just split from a drug treatment house in another state. Her father called that morning after she had contacted him, to find out what was happening. He wanted her to go back to where she had been. She had left after a serious suicide attempt, feeling that the place was not giving her enough care. She wanted to go to a special unit at the state hospital, where she felt she could get better care because she knew some of the staff. She also felt that she could perhaps stay in New Haven and get a job and some therapy at a local clinic, but at the meeting didn't seem too strong on that possibility. We interviewed her at the meeting, and Dave knew some of the people at the center where she'd been. She wanted a family session, and Dave was given the job, his first family session, supported by Stuart. They had it that evening, and the decision was made that she should go to the hospital.

The agreement with Little John had been clarified, and he was back at work with smiling reluctance. They have agreed on an 11:30 curfew. Jerry said that he was feeling better, and that he and Ralph would meet with his father soon. The guy that Charlie had referred to the house is never around, and I suggested that they get together with the two and clarify what he was doing here. Nell reported that she had decided to join the Freedom Harvest in Georgia and would leave for the summer. Sue would move in and take her place on the house staff. Nell has become almost indispensable in the time she has been here, and the change in

her since leaving the hospital is considerable. I told her that I hoped she
would return. Jack, the psychodrama leader, was back, and I said that
perhaps the groups would get more serious now, because I was having
trouble getting to them consistently. I thought that the staff should start
to get comfortable running the sessions themselves if neither Jack nor I
could attend.

June 4 — I learned this afternoon from Ralph that little John and Jerry
had come in last night tripping and that Dave and Nell had joined them.
What happened is unclear, but it seems that John, defying the ban on
drugs in the house and on giving them to residents, conned Jerry and the
others into joining him. He claims that Jerry asked him for some acid
and he didn't want him to get bad stuff; I did not press the matter of how
the others had gotten it. It seems that he pulled a power switch on his
supervisor Dave and made the house staff look and feel rather foolish.
I told him that we couldn't do much about his own drug taking, but when
he impulsively acts to fuck up another kid in the house, he has violated
our trust at every level; I added that the next time it happened, I would
beat him up. I told him to grow up faster. I warned him that Dale, who
would be moving in, hoped that she could become less confused and less
dependent on drugs, and that if he got to work on her, she could become
a junkie. I told him to try to influence her away from drugs. Dan feels
properly humbled, and Nell said she will do her tripping in more appropriate places. Jeff went to see a girl he thinks is pregnant, so he
could not be reached today. The issue will be brought up at the next
meeting, because I feel that drug use should be an open issue if dealings
at the house are to be up front.

Dale is nineteen; we have been helping her on and off since January,
when she came in upset after a family session at a clinic. She has been
to every agency in town. She comes from an orthodox Jewish family.
Her mother faked a heart attack to get her to come home and has called
up and screamed at almost every staff member. We have had some family sessions. The original contract I made with her was to help her get
out of her house and then deal with her guilt about it. She has moved out,
but in the process she has slipped into drug use and frequent sexual relationships. The original contract is still in force as regards her living
in the house, with the added hope that her self-destructiveness and immaturity can be worked on. She is one of our regulars; they are around
a good deal but are not regularly counseled or seen; rather, they get into patterns of acting out, in order to get us to deal with them on crises
they feel obliged to create. We have not done well by her so far. Her
being near Little John will be a constant problem.

The Number Nine staff has a weekly psychoanalytic group with Dr. Jack
Sheps. At his session this morning Nell talked about her plans to work
with blacks in Georgia. Everybody felt she had grown a great deal, and
Yvonne and Jack spoke at length about the sexual and human implications
of the South. They felt that Number Nine offered a much more healthy

and helpful environment for growth, and most people said clearly that
they don't want her to go. There was also discussion of how Dr. Sheps could
be more useful, and the idea of adding another group for more recent
staffers was raised.

Laura will also be moving into the house, after a stay at the state
hospital for about half a year. She had come to us months before, after
she had fled from her first night at a girl's halfway house. One of our
staff was able to establish a quite intense relationship with her, and they
began to explore the fact that she had been afraid of her homosexual
feelings. She is quiet, and agencies feel she is very hard to work with,
but she liked us most of all and asked to come stay with us for a while,
until she can get a job and move into the Y. We are resisting the pull
from hospitals to become a transitional residence, because there is a
tendency for people to be dumped on us without any plans for their future,
but we took Laura because we knew her and liked her.

June 5 — There are now five residents, and each night several people
who crash for a night, now that summer is near and people are migrat-
ing. Jack was back and began the psychodrama program again. We split
into two small groups and discussed ways in which we were different
from each other. Jack picked up on what was happening between Little
John and Dave, and got them to replay a discussion they'd had after Little
John got a call and wanted to go downtown to buy some acid. Dave had
let him go. I was doubling for Dave, but I became the third focus when
both of them mentioned that they hadn't wanted me to know. Each of us
then placed ourselves to spatially demonstrate how we related to each
other. Then we discussed the incident, and Little John gave his account
of it, and I was moralistic and told him that he could not have possibly
thought he was helping Jerry by giving him acid. Dave talked about his
guilt about the incident, and Nell talked of what had happened on her trip.
I suggested that a more responsible way to trip was to plan it ahead and
make sure a guide was around to be helpful. I pointed out that Dave's
guilt had made him have a bad trip anyway.

I asked Dale what she thought of the whole thing, and she said she
was confused. She said Stuart had told her not to use drugs when she
was staying at the house, but that she had gotten stoned last night. I said
that this incident told me that it probably wasn't too realistic for us to
expect her to stay away from drugs entirely, since clearly she needed
them to deal with her tensions, and that perhaps a better goal was for
her to talk about it when she was stoned or wanted to use dope and try
to get at why she needed to get high, rather than feeling that she had to
sneak away to use drugs. She said that she felt that she could relate when
she was stoned. I said that I hoped that drugs and sex would not become
underground issues but would be dealt with openly, as some of the ways
people relate. But I reiterated that I did not expect any staffer to give
drugs to anyone, and that no drugs were to be used in the house; but the
decision to use drugs outside had to be up to each individual. Little John
was talking about how he had been rapping with Dale last night, and that

staffers came in and looked at him as if he might be trying to make her, and now he felt guilty about talking to her. There were some giggles about sex, and I asked if John thought he might make it with Dale. She said she was going steady already.

June 13 — Jerry's friend Ron and Patti, another young girl trying to break free of her parents, are new residents, as well as several assorted friends and crashers. Ralph came back from his weekend of observing at the mental health center with many recommendations. He suggested a lot of informal team counseling and daily staff meetings early in the morning, although neither plan was followed up consistently. Many volunteers are around, and the house is usually crowded, which means that a good deal of construction is being done. Sue has moved in and joined the house staff, and Lenny has moved in and will be on the storefront, where the other half of the staff works. Jack has been doing psychodrama sessions three times a week and has created a lot of excitement over that, as well as offering a fair degree of clinical skill on a daily basis, which frees me up some. Jack Sheps has moved suddenly to New York, leaving a gap for the staff in meetings to discuss personal issues.

Ralph had what he felt was a tremendous family session with Jerry and his father; they talked about expressing affection and did so in a direct way that they had not done before, even in many years of family therapy. They did a nonverbal exercise. Ralph felt that the similarity between him and Jerry had made him able to facilitate the exchange. Yvonne and I are getting married tomorrow, and we are using the house to do some of the food preparations, and another group is working on the bus in front of the house. This has made the house a center, but Sue has noticed that the residents, especially the girls, are feeling neglected and out of it, and their anger and tensions have not been dealt with.

On Friday there was a meeting with Sammy to discuss the issues of split commitment to fixing up the house and counseling. Ralph felt that the others weren't living up to their commitments to the residents. Sue talked about feelings she had about the work's being done and about decision-making, from which she felt excluded at times. Ralph talked about how he, sometimes with Stuart, had shared decision-making and had excluded others because of a feeling that the meetings weren't working out. Sammy pointed out how easy it was to get away from dealing with the conflicts in sharing decisions. Reasons for not having staff meetings were discussed, and everyone shared the resistance to them. Stuart felt there were no issues, and Sue expressed to me later that she felt that he and others were refusing to deal with the problem of leadership. The problem posed by some of the guests at the house in that they were becoming a nuisance was settled with a decision that those individuals be talked to. Ralph proposed again that he have a role similar to Charlie's at the storefront, and this was not really taken up, but obviously leadership and taking responsibility for the program are big issues. People discussed feelings about Nell who had not yet made a definite decision about leaving and who is somewhat withdrawn from the work now. Pictures of the meeting were taken for a newspaper feature. The staff had a meeting afterward with Lenny and some of the residents, to try to bring up some of the issues that had been discussed before, but people told me it was frustrating and inconclusive. All the issues about leadership and support and shared goals, as well as additional issues about closeness and particular tensions and rivalries between people, do not seem to be getting resolved.

June 28 — We got married on the 14th, in a field in the country. Everyone came, and the newly painted bus and Number Nine band had their premiere performance. People danced and shared in the preparations and celebration, and the community seemed to be at a high point of energy and excitement. We took off for a few days. When we came back, we found that things were very confused at the house and that the place had not really been cleaned yet. Nell had returned.   Mark, a friend of Dave's had been crashing and working an incredible amount on construction. Little work or attention seemed fixed on the residents — Laura, Patti, Dale, Ron, Jerry, and Dick, a black youngster who was having family problems whom Ted had been working with. Yvonne was angry and said that if the place wasn't cleaned up, the house would be closed down. We scheduled a meeting for later, but it was postponed several times before everyone could get together.

   Yvonne and I had several talks about how we could work together without undercutting each other or being split off. We decided that Yvonne would organize the housework and cleaning for a week or so, and I would concentrate on the counseling. We both felt that some fairly directive leadership for defining tasks would be helpful. The question of how to offer leadership without telling people what to do preoccupied the staff for the next week. There was a definite confusion around the house, and Ralph and other staff members seemed isolated and distant, or else angry, most of the time.

   On Sunday night we came after the house meeting, and I found Ralph giving Dale an angry lecture about how she had broken a rule she herself had made — that she would not use dope in the house — and now she was tripping. She alternated between giggling and feeling that she would not be understood, and Patti was there trying to defend her. The whole scene seemed to be a parody of the parent role, as if Ralph were trying it out, and it made me very uncomfortable because I wondered if I seemed that way when I was in the house. I finally asked why a confrontation like this was happening, and we had an inconclusive discussion, because Ralph did not feel I was right to be so permissive about drug use.

   The next day we came after the psychodrama session, which had been going on regularly. Yvonne spoke of having been to a commune that operated by setting up accepted role divisions between men and women, and she suggested that they try that system for a week, because the other ways were not working. She assigned jobs to each of the girls and spent time shopping with them, while the men were responsible for cleaning up the house and heavy cleaning. Stuart and Sue spoke against this system, saying that they had already assigned roles the night before, but Yvonne asked that they try it her way.

In the afternoon the house staff met again with Sammy. A lot of anger at Yvonne, who was not there, was discharged. The staff felt that she had implicitly called them failures. This feeling aroused a lot of depression. Sue was upset and also felt sick, and she went home. She said that she felt like quitting, because there was so much tension that she felt that her style was not needed. There was some talk about the basic aims of the house, with Nell and Ralph emerging as representing different counseling styles, although it was hard to understand what the explicit differences were. It seemed like a conflict in personal styles, and people were unsure whether the two could coexist.

The next evening was the regular house meeting on interpersonal issues. Ted, Yvonne, and I attended, coming in late. When we arrived, Stuart was talking to each of the residents about what they were getting out of the house. The focus was on Ron and Jerry, who had many levels of rivalry. They faced each other and talked about what they liked and disliked about each other, and Ted made some interpretations about how Ron seemed to be relating to Jerry. A lot of feelings came out, including also some of the ways they used each other to act childishly; we examined what each of them was getting from the relationship. There was a lot of resistance from the residents, and the staff and the directors had to run the meeting directively. (Did we really have to?)

The next morning everyone was asleep, because they had been up all night rapping about the meeting. There seems to be a tendency to stay up all night and be tired all day, and I wondered whether the informal gatherings, which I had very little knowledge of, were perhaps more useful than our structured program. At the meeting almost everyone had specific plans to look for jobs, find places to stay, and hold family sessions. A lot of the staffers were sick. After the meeting Jerry and Ron rapped, and there were several confrontations between them concerning a girl they both liked and who was playing them off. On Friday morning the meeting focused on Dick, who had been working closely with Stuart. It was a very quiet session. It focused on his political views and feelings about how the community was not truly collaborative, and we agreed and tried to focus on ways to change that would be agreeable to him. Yvonne and I had a long session with Jerry and his family, which led to a decision that he should not go home, despite the fact that he wanted to, and that he would have to get a job quickly, because his time at Number Nine was almost up.

July 7 — The week began with another mass tripping episode; all the residents and Dave took some acid and went to a local music festival. At the Monday morning meeting just after everyone was coming down, they all seemed a little embarrassed about it. The group focused on Ron, who was smiling and acting as if he were still tripping and was not responding to questions. I said that I felt that he was trying to avoid dealing with what was happening to him by freezing in place. The tensions and feelings were too much to allow the group to stay together; the group broke up, and I talked to each person individually. I talked to Ron and Jerry for a while. Jerry was about to leave, and Ron was crying, and we talked about how tripping brings up all sorts of feelings that had to come out.

Dave had been using drugs more and more, and that evening he became totally hysterical. Yvonne and I talked to him, and he became coherent enough to express anger and fear, stored up from his childhood, toward the house for not respecting him and toward a girl whom he had recently broken up with. He wanted to get his feelings out in a long marathon meeting (scheduled for Wednesday), especially his reaction to Ralph's bossiness. However, Wednesday morning he was so spaced out and sick that he had to be taken to the hospital, and the doctors prescribed total rest for a few days. We took him to our house. When he returned during the weekend, he began drinking again, and Nell confronted him about it. She said she was pissed at him and had heard him say hundreds of times he was quitting, and now it was getting to the point where he was hurting himself and setting a bad example for everyone in the house.

The marathon was to be a long encounter session, which would be led by Dennis, Ted, and Yvonne; it was held so that people in the house could confront the issues among themselves. We used a fairly consistent interpretive model, explaining what was happening in terms of the games and strategies people were using to avoid their feelings and to obtain power in the group. We hoped this exploration would get at the leadership issues. We especially went into how people used interpretations and getting angry as ways of manipulating others. We tried to keep people to the topics they were discussing, and we did not allow people to discuss their feelings about us, since this was to be a meeting to deal with house relationships and since we felt that we were taking a good deal of real but projected feelings from the others. In this case we felt that it was more relevant to deal with the feelings and frustration as if they were coming from the others. The staff was there, as well as two researchers who were observing. The residents were downstairs, playing noisy music and asking why they couldn't have a marathon. I told them they could if they wanted one. Jack, who did psychodrama, came in late after taking Dave to the hospital.

People talked about their feelings about Ralph's role and especially what seemed to be an undertone of anger in it. The suggestion was made that, since groups and other means did not seem to resolve his anger, it had to be directed elsewhere, most probably at his family, and that probably the only resolution would come when he resolved it there. Some of the ways Lenny used silence and working alone as ways of obtaining power in the group were looked at, as was people's need to define turf for themselves around Number Nine. Jack elected to remain silent because of his anger at the tape recorder; I confronted him about what he was doing, saying that I reserved the right to set the ground rules for groups I ran, just as I paid him that respect in psychodrama, and that the tapes would be kept confidential. We both felt better. Howie, one of the observers, gave the group feedback about his observations of the past weeks, which generally supported the group's feelings that the directors were the cause of tensions. I reflected how his feedback worked into the general dynamic around leadership.

In the afternoon we gave the group the task of planning the rest of the week, without our leadership. We interpreted some of the task blockages, such as the failure to ask relevant questions, refusal to deal with nonparticipants, forgetting to look ahead for priorities, and lack of criteria for evaluation. We scheduled meetings for every day at which planning, training, discussions of the house community, and evaluation would take place. We talked a little about how the program could develop without trying to blame specific people for fouling up, focusing instead exclusively on the future.

The next day Sue decided that she had to give up her work at the house for health reasons but that she would continue to work part-time at the storefront in her original job. The pace had been too much for her, she said, and she moved out. She seemed upset by the featurelessness of the house and the lack of explicit demands or planning.

The three girls moved out on Friday, to stay with a friend while they waited for an apartment for all of them to live together. Yvonne helped them look for jobs, but they were not very successful, probably because of a combination of external and internal factors. Ron moved out on Monday, leaving Dick as the only resident. Another girl, fifteen, with a confused and colorful history on the streets, moved in under Ted's supervision, but she felt that her contact with Ted was restricting her unduly, and she split. On Friday the bus and band had their public debut at an outdoor concert at Powder Ridge, where we made some money and entertained a few thousand.

The planning meetings are moving along, with Nell back in a fairly consistent leadership position and trying to devise a long-term plan for buying and using food. The third floor and the cellar are shaping up, and another work party this week should finish the big jobs. I gave out some articles about communities, and we will discuss them at a meeting. In about a week we should be ready to take in more residents.

July 10 — Some visitors from the halfway house began to attend our training meetings. Stuart began the morning meeting by saying that the previous meeting had left off during an examination of areas of ambiguity concerning our policy, about our tendency to make arbitrary decisions. These center on drug use and going out of the house. I asked if the problem was that there is a need for policy in these areas or that an ambivalence about enforcing it exists. Stuart said we were totally inconsistent with Dale about drug use, the feeling being that I had said it was okay and others had said no. We went over how the messages had been distorted and how we had not checked stories out.

The question turned to how you can stop kids from using dope. Stuart told how last week all the residents had said they wanted to trip at the festival. They said it in a group meeting, and they wanted to do it

together. We discussed whether allowing kids to use drugs — for example, helping them when they tripped — encouraged them to trip. I felt that
strict guidelines were unworkable outside of the house and would only
serve to make drug use a covert, unspoken issue. Mark suggested that a
clearer and more explicit intake procedure would lessen the ambiguity.
Mark has moved from construction into a role as a very active house
staff member.

I pointed out that Jerry had needed limits and they were set forth in
an intake, but they were never applied, and this had undermined what
we did. Stuart said the two and a half hours of daily work is too vague
and too small an amount for residents who are not working at outside jobs,
and that perhaps people should be given an area of responsibility as their
job. The visitors spoke of the similarities between these problems and
those at the halfway house. There was talk about Dave, and how people
felt about imposing strict limits on him concerning drug use. People
talked about how to influence him away from drugs and how to deal with
his incessant raps; the decision was that he should be treated as if he
were at Daytop until he pulled himself together. (He did not take to this
treatment and eventually left the house.)

July 13 — Lenny partially presented the results of the interviewing he had
done with staffers about what they considered the goals and norms of the
house and how they should be changed. He found conflicts between personal and house goals and a split over whether the house would be a commune that helps people or a crisis center. Ralph and Nell talked about the
staff-resident split at the house, and Stuart sensed a conflict over what
they expected from the house. I asked what people wanted to happen.
Ralph said that the widespread resistance to counseling made it hard to
do it. Jack said that Ralph was perceived by residents as threatening.
Jack said that he felt tons of anger from the residents in groups, but
found that he could relate to them quite easily alone, and he had done a
good share of counseling. Nell said there was a feeling that we were ig-
noring them except when we were punishing them. Ralph said we shoved
them in the direction of the goals of the house, whether or not they wanted
to go. I felt that the anger somehow seemed inevitable in the situation we
had set up, and Jack talked about how the counseling is threatening to
everyone.

I noted that people were talking as if we were a clinical crisis center,
and I wondered if this meant that we had decided not to be a commune.
Nell suggested going around to collect their ideas of what they wanted the
house to be. I thought that a house community of staffers was primary,
because if they weren't together, they couldn't begin to be helpful. Ralph
said that he could not work without a community feeling. Jack said, although he didn't live here, he thought the happy-hippie house was a good
idea, where kids could get what they didn't get from a family and learn
to be self-sufficient but responsible to others. Stuart asked how the house
would integrate with other parts of Number Nine, and then we took a
coffee break.

I recalled the meeting by asking to hear from quiet or controversial people. Mark said he felt the staff should work together, that he saw the problem as a lack of confidence in the staff. He felt that sometimes it was as if they were just a bunch of people hanging around. Ralph saw two issues — the intake procedure and people's adjustment to the house. Mark said that the house has to be together physically and seem orderly before more residents can move in. There should also be a consensus about how things should be run. Herb, from the halfway house, felt we were struggling with a problem of definition — were we a crash pad or did we exist for longer stays. He felt that we were looking for who we are and were beginning to find out how draining a situation like this can be, especially if we run the house as a crisis center. I clarified by saying that for many reasons the limit of one month for a stay should be adhered to. Mark and Ralph felt this was too long for a crisis center and too short for real changes, and so people had to leave just when they became comfortable.

Nell said that in her opinion the choice should be either intense very short stays or a whole month. She did not like the suggestion of a structured two-weeks-long intensive personal growth program. She wanted an experiential environment, where kids could deal with their feelings, needs, and wants. She felt we should start with a fairly rigid structure, which after a resident was here a week or so would gradually dissolve. Lenny thought that we should take the school as a model rather than a house, that we could become the Berlitz School of Self-Awareness Crash Program. He felt that we should prepare people with a lot of preliminary counseling before they move in.

I said that a highly structured program will always arouse lots of resistance and hostility toward the staff. I suggested another model — the community owned by the people who have as their ground rule total sharing, a real commune. Jack said that if we did that, we would have to deal with each other when we weren't measuring up, and this was threatening. Nell said we never were together to begin with. I talked about the need to begin where we were at, and I said something about how demanding the commune model was and how the development of structural distinctions was a way of avoiding anxiety about issues.

Stuart suggested that we have a place that focuses on developing the residents' sense of self-worth. All interpretations and suggestions would focus on the ways that people show they don't like themselves. In a month we could plan activities around that theme, like working on meaningful projects which build up a sense of accomplishment over time. I felt that emphasizing the positive side of people and not working so much on personality change and problems is a more viable model for us. I did not feel that we were competent at or very effective in promoting personal change through confrontation, and we were creating a lot of bad feelings in the process. I felt there were enough positive elements going for us without going into negatives, except in a supportive way.

The diary documents a fairly complete cycle of experience, learning, and reflection. Though we were trying to develop an alternative model of a crisis center, the account shows how deeply we identified with professional models. When faced with the tensions of living together and the responsibility of dealing with the difficulties of the residents, we all fell back on structures and defenses to protect us from the immensity of our task.

Retrospectively it appears that several major problems faced the community which were not resolved during the period of the diary:

1. A lack of clarity and consensus existed concerning the goals of the house.
2. Skills were not adequately transferred from the directors to the staff.
3. Staff members were ambivalent about their roles and their positions of authority vis-à-vis the residents. As Mike Vozick put it, the staff members were trying on parent roles for the first time.
4. The leadership was inconsistent and unclear.
5. Personal needs and goals among the staff were not met.
6. Decisions and evaluations about competence and ability were confused, mystified, and largely punitive.

B. A Halfway House Community

The New Haven Halfway House was founded in 1967 by a group of Yale undergraduates as a cooperative residence both for people recently discharged from mental hospitals and for students. The community of sixteen is located in an old two-story wooden building. The inclusion of students from nearby colleges as paying members of the community, the absence of paid staff other than the director, the democratic nature of the operation, and the fact that, aside from an initial grant of $20,000 (to buy the House), the House is self-supporting, all make it a unique and noteworthy venture in community mental health. It is an attempt at consciously creating a new type of institution, in which many of the unintended drawbacks of hospitals, schools, and traditional aftercare residences (insofar as they exist at all) are avoided, and where some of the new structures that its larger parent institutions are struggling to realize can be tested.

The aim of the House is to be a community where a resident can learn about himself and grow, either to accomplish the difficult transition from the hospital back to the community or to have an experience of involvement with people far removed from the university. To accomplish this end, each resident has a responsibility for taking part in every decision that affects the community and for helping to carry them out. On issues that do not pertain to the community as a whole, each resident is free to regulate his behavior as he sees fit. The House director (the only employee), the students, and the other residents help each another as friends, companions, and counselors; occasionally they intervene to mediate disputes. By offering a supportive community which allows experimentation with strategies for making friends, getting jobs, and coping with conflicts, the House tries to create conditions for growth in all its residents.

Nearly every resident feels that the House is helpful to him, and of the approximately seventy discharged patients who lived there during its first two years, only about ten have had to return to hospitals for short stays, and only five are currently in hospitals. In this section I would like to convey an idea of what it is like to live in the House and how the community differs from many conventional hospital and aftercare commuties. Since no single participant can adequately describe what goes on in a social situation, and since most accounts of psychiatric institutions are biased in favor of the professionals associated with them, I have tried to go as far as possible in the other direction. The House is described by the ten former hospital patients who lived there in March, 1968, as related in taped interviews.

The interviewer was the consultant to the House, who knew each of the residents prior to the study and who had lived there as a student the year before. He was thus familiar enough with the residents and the House's operation to ask meaningful questions and to seek out concrete details; he also developed a high degree of trust and rapport during the interviews. The discussions asked people how they get along in the House — the pressures they feel, the problems they have, and the values they hold, as well as the way they see the House and the others in it. The values and behavioral norms reported in the interviews were supported highly (over 70 percent agreement on behaviorally defined values of group support, responsibility, personal growth, self-control, and openly expressed conflict) in a questionnaire administered a month later, as part of a further study.

Future Projection and Definition of Mental Health

The interviews included questions on the residents' view of themselves, their future plans, and their definition of mental health — all of which presumably point the direction in which they want the House to help them develop.

The self-description seems to show a generation gap in the way residents regard themselves as changing and capable of growth. The six residents who were under twenty-three were able to pinpoint both positive and negative qualities in themselves and could speak of very specific dimensions within which they were attempting to change. They valued change and growth, and they saw self-change as a self-initiated process. They were almost universally concerned with becoming more spontaneous; they wished to be more connected, involved, and integrated with other people. Three of them had specific goals for the future, while the others did not want to project themselves so concretely but wished only to concentrate on their immediate problems.

Some of the phrases they used were:

> — I hope to keep on growing for the rest of my life, because when you stop growing you die.

— I want to be more spontaneous; I don't want to be mechanical.

— I have a lot of dreams I'm capable of fulfilling. I'm very aggressive, and you have to be. It's hard to say it, but at bottom I'm pretty satisfied with myself. I'm not intent on changing it.

— I am weak, unsociable, egotistical at times, and childish. I would like to change the granite like quality in my action and decisions. I want to feel more and work more, and be more integrated with people. My future is still shaky. I do all right, but it's tough.

— I want to meet people and find love, within them and myself.

— If you're looking for a way to express yourself, come to the House.

The older people in the House see themselves much less actively. They aim at trying to accept themselves and what they have become and to work out whatever solutions are available to their fears and uncertainties. The tone of their replies is much more one of acceptance, and their ideals are in the area of learning to control their feelings rather than the more active self-development voiced by the younger residents.

When asked to define mental health, only one resident gave a cynical, social definition — "Act cool, calm, and collected, not be bothersome, don't show anything odd." By contrast, the other definitions seemed almost like the religious ideal of the morally good man — selfless, understanding, having only good feelings, living without illusions about oneself and others, involved, moving out toward others, and attaining satisfaction and enjoyment in life. All felt that the House was at a level far below the ideal, but that this was to its advantage, because it allowed residents to learn to deal with people as they really are.

The Hospital Experience

The residents came from four nearby hospitals, two of them large state hospitals where there is little or no psychiatric care other than medication, and two of them Yale-run hospitals, in which both the quality and intensity of care is about the best available. In all but two cases the length of their stay exceeded five months. The only generalization that can be drawn from their accounts of the hospital is that the only positive experiences resulted from rapport with an individual therapist who was perceived as having concern and empathy with their problems. Care in the state hospitals was reported unanimously to be horrible, and it was compared in almost all accounts to a prison. Those who had been at the Yale-run hospitals were quite ambivalent about their experience, in most cases feeling good about having had a chance to get away from outside pressures and to work on their problems, while at the same time feeling that this dependence and the experience of being cared for did not especially prepare them to make decisions or to find support and strength on the outside. While none reported having been sent to the hospital against his will, all the residents said that the initial suggestion to enter the hospital came from another person, such as a social worker, who noted their obvious distress and advised hospitalization. Most reported that breakdowns or acute crises led to their hospitalization.

In the cases where changes or insights were reported during the hospital confinement, the insight usually consisted of learning to take responsibility for one's own problems. Some of their comments were:

> — People were dependent and asked for too much at the hospital. They said, "Tell me when to do everything." They can't do that. They can only get to the problem, they can't make you into a new person. This is up to you.
> — The hospital has a purpose that is demeaned by being taken care of. But it's a safe place when you are pressed by the world.
> — The hospital wasn't helpful because it pampered me too much and tried to protect me from the outside. I needed something realer.

Their resentment against the hospital was shown by such phrases as "They are there for punishment, not treatment," or "The hospital stunk, I got no care or help" and by reports of fights with staff and patients, restrictive rules (a limit of six cigarettes a day, for example), and being tied to a bed or thrown naked into isolation cells during an upset spell.

Entering the Halfway House

The residents first heard of the Halfway House from a therapist, social worker, or, in two instances, from another patient. While professional people can suggest the House, the prospective resident must deal with the House himself. If space is available, the candidate is asked to visit for dinner or a weekend. The decision to come to the House must be made by the future resident on the basis of his visits. If he would like to become a member, he must then be voted in by the entire House community. This vote is usually a formality, since House members consider that anyone who has nowhere else to go and wants to move into the House, should be given a chance if there is room. Only one resident objected to this criterion, opting for a more careful selection in order to screen out those who might be violent or create disturbances. No residents felt that the director should be the one to make decisions about who enters the House, although all expected the director to make some sort of preliminary screening at the time of the initial contact.

There are several reasons why a prospective resident chooses the House. He usually has few, if any alternatives. If he has a family, the resident may feel that it would upset him too much to return to it; he is old enough to want to start out on his own. Coming out of a hospital, with few friends or connections to the community, he has great difficulty in living alone in an apartment or finding roommates. Because it offers a group that shares the same problems and can accept one as someone who may have deep personal problems and yet can make it outside the hospital, the House is also attractive. Only two gave their reason for selecting the House as merely "having no place to go."

Some of the ways residents came to the House, and their reasons, are:

— I figured I could best make it on the outside by having some people around to converse with, not really serious conversation, just to have several friends.

— My biggest fear was of being alone, on the outside. The summer before last I was due to leave and broke down, due to the prospect of living alone. I figured I'd play it safe this time.

— I wanted to pay people back who were nice to me, by helping others who needed it after I left the hospital.

— I was anxious to get out of the hospital and heard about the House from a friend. She had read a newspaper article about it, and I got the phone number and called when I was in town. The doctor had told me the week before that I would probably be there all my life, but I didn't worry much because I heard that he said the same sort of thing to others who had gotten out. I put on a good impression for the doctor and convinced my father. I was allowed to visit the place, and I got in. I considered it a place to go where there would be other people like me, and you wouldn't have to lie and fake your way through these things like you do with people who have never had any experience with this sort of thing.

— My doctor suggested the House, and at first I wasn't too impressed. I expected it to be another thing, like a house I had been in before I went to the hospital. The doctor said this one was good, that there were both sexes and less rules, and I trusted him. I was tired of rules and being psychoanalyzed — they were usually wrong. I could have gone to a foster home or worked on a farm, but I decided to give this a try.

— I wanted a chance to make my own life. I didn't expect much from the House, but I thought it would help me.

Residents' initial impressions of the House are not very different from those of anyone entering a new environment. They wonder how they will be expected to act and how they will get along with those who are already there. The move from the highly structured hospital makes the House seem even more unstructured than it is. One resident said, "My first impression was not very good. Something adverse struck me, a looseness of makeup in the House bothered me. I'm used to being thought about and told what to do by doctors. There seemed to be a lack of backbone in the House, no structure. The fact that you can go anywhere and do anything appealed to me very much, but it also made me uneasy." The initial contact with the House seems generally to be very cautious. Most residents have learned through long, painful experience not to be too trusting too quickly. The new resident must come and visit, and she must then present her reasons for wanting to join and tell a little of her history at a House meeting or to each of the residents privately. She is then voted on for membership. This is most people's first experience of this form of openness and democratic decision-making, and it seems very threatening to some. Also noteworthy is the fact that the procedure for membership is identical for students and residents, although the reasons they give for wanting to join the House differ.

Some comments on moving into the House were:

— The hardest thing about getting into the House was going to the meeting and saying why I wanted to live there. I couldn't throw on the brown sugar, and I was a little afraid to be honest.

— I was initially curious, gentle, trying to understand what was going on around me. They seemed to be saying, "There's a new member, I wonder what his problem could be." They began to dote on me and show me respect, which I had never had. I had never accepted help before, and at first I wasn't used to it.

— I thought the House was just a boarding house when I came in, but I found out that it is a community. I was shy at first and then began to like it more and more.

— I was very nervous and anxious about getting out. I worried about everything and was afraid something would happen to make me go back. I didn't expect the House to be so sympathetic to me, so I kept to myself until I knew people better. It wasn't too hard to adjust.

—I was scared of the House at first, but it worked out well in that the person who I thought disliked me most I got along well with.

A person does not feel pushed or forced into a mold as he enters; he is left free to negotiate his own role and relate in his own way and at his own pace.

Working

Everyone at the House is expected to have a full-time job or to attend school. The residents strongly feel that working is a necessary condition for making it outside the hospital. Living at the House is regarded as a privilege which has to be earned by self-sufficiency. The new resident must show that she has made provisions to pay rent and board of twenty-five dollars a week; this usually means that she has been promised a job or can show that there is a reasonable expectation of getting one. Paying the rent is more than a therapeutic issue for the residents, since they all are aware that the House has no outside source of funds; rent must therefore pay all expenses, the mortgage, the director's salary, and upkeep. A situation in which more than one or two residents are unable to pay or fall behind in their rent would spell financial disaster.

The residents realize the difficulties a former patient faces in finding a job, such as prejudice, lack of skills, or having to account for the time spent in hospital; but since the other residents have found jobs, it is expected that the new resident will also manage. Five residents have found jobs through the state employment agency, one attends college full-time, and two others are taking courses and plan to finish school while they work. Most find their jobs satisfying; they work at television repairing, as an IBM trainee, with retarded children, as a lab technician, a draftsman, a teacher aide, and a telephone operator. When someone loses his job, as happens from time to time, he gets help and support from the others, but he also feels pressure to quickly find another. If he falls more than a few weeks behind, he faces expulsion from the House. This eventuality became reality one or two occasions, after a decision by the community.

The House Community

"Often a role is assumed, but you don't have to go along with it if you don't want to," a resident notes. The director, some students, and some residents have a very explicit conception of what type of community they would like the House to be. For example, they would like every resident to feel that the others in the House are people they trust, can count on for support, and can be open with. All rules must be agreed upon by the community, by consensus, and there are various pressures to take on some of the responsibility for running the House, making decisions, helping others, and responding to overturees of friendship. Conflicts are close to the surface, and if people cannot resolve them without the interference of others, the matter may be mediated by the director or brought up at the weekly meeting. The pressures and problems a resident faces at the House are not so much authority problems, problems of dealing with a structure of rules and demands, than they are those of getting close to people, living together, and making personal decisions about the future and about methods. The burden of handling himself and getting along with others is placed on the resident, and he can neither blame his past, his illness, restrictive rules or external circumstances for his own failings in the House.

Following are excerpts from accounts by each of the residents about what the House is like and about how people get along. The community is the sum total of the way each member sees it, and these accounts show that the same atmosphere can be perceived very differently.

— People are supposed to unravel some of their problems. This is supposed to be a community, so you're not supposed to be evasive. Maybe people can help you if you come out of your shell. Most people try to work on their problems alone, but they find they need an understanding person to listen. The House gives people a responsive attitude to themselves, to know there's another life when they leave here. They're learning to accept other people, so they can go out and accept others. The House is a lantern to show the way out.

— You go to the hospital because you feel nobody needs you and say to hell with life. I couldn't develop a relationship and didn't feel wanted. Here I find I can contribute, so relating is a two-way street. People listen to me and sometimes they accept it. It makes me somebody because they need me.

— You act like yourself here. You don't have to be phoney. I don't feel I have to put on shows or acts. Like if I get mad, I won't be threatened with being put back into the hospital. I feel no pressure, strain, or anything.

— You have a stigma after leaving the hospital and lack

confidence. At the House you find people with worse problems. You say, if they can make it, so can I. They give you a shot of confidence.

— I've had enough therapy and I have it now. I want to come back here and learn the rules of life. I come back here for conversation, social interaction, and friends.

— The House offers a temporary shelter against the outside world. People let me be and this is what I wanted at first. It's helpful not to be poked or pushed.

— It's nice to know there are people around, whether they are lukewarm or enthusiastic about your friendship. It's nice to have a group.

— Living here, I have changed in the way I am with people, in handling everyday hassles. You learn what people are like in a real situation, not just a hospital.

— I feel a pressure to be here and to talk to people, which comes from everyone. If some people scare you and you don't want to get close, you shouldn't have to.

— There is too much of this group therapy, openness stuff in the House. You should not be forced to be open. I feel this at times from the director. There's too much of a mental-healthy atmosphere and interpreting what you do. There is banter about "your problem" which makes you watch what you say a little bit. That's not all the time; you can enjoy yourself a lot. It's there, but if you know how to handle yourself, it can't damage you much.

— Everybody puts on this thing of how they love people, a kind of make-believe altruism, how everybody else, which may be true in some cases, but I can't quite swallow that, this thing about everyone should tell everyone about themselves. There's something very fishy about that.

— At first I was really withdrawn and alone, but now I realize I have to be with other people. You have to pay attention to people, talk to people, not reject them, and like them, and talk to everybody, or people get annoyed and say you aren't getting anything out of the House. I get annoyed sometimes, but the House really has helped me. It's real; you can be yourself here, and people are. They do what they want to do.

— The impression I get is that the House is sort of a community. Everybody takes care of everybody else. I don't like that idea too much. I care about people, I'm just not in love with people. I didn't dig it when the director told me I'd have to communicate with people here. In a way I have and I haven't. It's good that way.

— If somebody gets into trouble, I think the House is willing to back them up. I've never had that before. It's always been me against everyone else.

These statements are important also because they reveal the tension that exists between expressed values and their actual implementation,

between the commitment asked for and the commitment received, and
between the director's hopes and the residents' reservations. The important point is that the tensions do not exist underground, discussed
privately among residents but never questioned openly in meetings or in
the director's presence. The values and ways people get along in the
House are constantly challenged or reevaluated. The extent to which a
person wishes to be open and pressure from others are always issues
under discussion in the House. In general, a resident enters the House
feeling distrustful of others and jealously guarding her personal privacy.
This seems to be a residue of the hospital environment, where openness
and responsibility are not valued. Sharing feelings is threatening, and
most residents have little experience with close friendships; the process
of becoming open and taking responsibility in the House is therefore a
gradual learning process, rather than a simple yes or no proposition.

Making friends and helping others is for most residents both the
hardest thing for them to do and in many ways the most rewarding experience in the House. When they can trust someone without being hurt,
it is usually one of the first positive experiences in their lives. They
say:

> — I find it hard to make friends. All my former friends were
> not really, they just used me. I trust people, but maybe I shouldn't.
> But you have to taste the pie to see what it's like.
> — This is the first time I've ever made friends. At first I was
> very cold and showed no emotion and was indifferent. I try to
> make friends, but then the other must make the effort. Living
> with many different people who are unlike me is great. Help here
> is reciprocal, sometimes people help you so much, you recipro-
> cate.
> — Being free of "prison" and being able to do what you want
> has helped me to become more loving. It's hard to make friends,
> that's why it's hard to get love.
> — In the House I've learned how people and I get along to-
> gether, not as concepts but as a feeling. I've become more
> flexible and more feeling toward people here. I know there are
> good people in the world, so I'm not so hostile. I feel like it's
> worth while making a contribution. Being with people at the
> House caused this.

Rules and Responsibility

Freedom in the House can be limited by rules that are set by the
community, as well as by the environmental necessities of cooking,
cleaning, obeying laws and statutes, paying the rent, getting a job, and
accommodating a roommate. There are no written rules in the House,
and any rule can be reconsidered at any time. Residents in effect agree
to the following rules: (1) pay rent regularly and on time; (2) do assigned
chores (though less regularly); (3) keep one's room presentable; (4) no
unprescribed drug-taking inside the House; (5) no friends staying over
at the House for long periods; (6) no physical violence; and (7) no making

love (although there is disagreement as to whether this rule is or should
be actively enforced if the love-making is discreet).

Feelings about taking responsibility for handling problems and making
decisions are generally positive. All residents feel that they have a say
in making decisions, and all but three feel that they exercise that say
whenever they wish to. Most feel that much of the personal problems and
the counseling should be, and is, handled by the House director. On the
question of whether personal problems should be handled by the community, disagreement exists. A few residents are bored by House meetings
or feel that personal problems should not be discussed publicly but should
be handled privately by the director. Most others feel that the House does
and should operate democratically and that they both enjoy participation
and feel that it changes them for the better.

A representative sampling of their opinions follows:

> — I believe in democracy, and I believe the House is the most
> democratic thing I've ever been in, because the House is a society
> in itself. Anything that comes up is voted on. It's a beautiful
> thing to see it actually practiced. An example came the week I
> moved in, when the first thing that struck me was that people
> could express disagreements, even with the director. In the end
> the majority voted.

> — Each person has a responsibility, which gives them a
> chance to learn that they are capable of living on the outside. No
> one stands with a hammer saying, do this, do that. It's up to the
> individual. He can make his life a bed of feathers or a bed of
> nails. If he chooses nails, he's going to be pretty uncomfortable.

> — My problem was keeping away from the drug people that I
> knew from before. The House didn't tell me I couldn't do this, but
> rather gave me a chance to use my will. You can't always be in the
> House, so you have to learn to be responsible for yourself. If
> there were rules here, you wouldn't learn. I take drugs now, but
> in moderation.

> — I don't want any say in handling people. I don't want that kind
> of responsibility. I'm content to leave it to the director. I am
> against disturbances by anyone, and it's hard to escape getting
> involved in decisions.

> — I'm sort of indifferent to how the House is run, so long as
> it doesn't run me.

> — Decisions are made by majority rules, and everything is
> discussed, even personal hang-ups, either in private or with
> others. But if you don't want to talk, you don't have to.

> — I was always outwitting authority, and then I came to a House
> without rules. It's a pleasure here because people work together.
> You want to do things here.

> — Anything that concerns the other people in the House is dis-
> cussed, and rules are made about it. Even when a rumor starts,
> it gets talked of openly.

> — I am sometimes bothered by the way that the cleaning

doesn't get done, but I don't take it on me, I get sick of doing it too, so I guess I can't really complain.

Meetings

The core of the House's operation, and its only formal gathering, is the weekly House meeting, at which attendance is mandatory. All decisions are made at that time. Anything can be discussed; and there are no designated leader, agenda, or rules of procedure. However, some people feel that the director has a good deal of influence — but "not in a bad way, because what she says is to the point and good." "The meetings are times when everyone is together. Lots of times you don't see people or never have a chance to talk. People get a chance to see you, and if you're not making it or playing games, they get a chance to express it. Sometimes it drags on or becomes a battlefield, or it may upset me." Decisions about housekeeping and about people who are lax in rent paying or in doing their chores are made; people who wish to move in present themselves and are voted on; and any conflicts or situations that a resident wishes to speak about or which affect the whole House are dealt with at meetings.

All but two residents report that they participate regularly in the meetings and feel that they have a say in decisions. One resident described the meetings as a bore; he felt very strongly that he did not want to discuss everybody's problems of be the subject of discussion himself. The reservations expressed by another resident tell a lot about the process of the meetings:

> — The meetings are sort of criticism sessions, where everyone would go around the room and make lists of demerits against your name. I don't like that. When somebody is upset and feels insecure, I don't think it's helpful to go around the room and get an expression of affection from everybody. I've never been upset myself, and don't know how it would come across. I think I'd be angry as hell. A lot of the expressions of affection are only partially backed up by feeling, but not wholly. People are very hesitant to go against what looks like a good cause. I don't participate much; I say what I want to, but I don't want to embroil myself in trivial issues.

The Director

The director, Koren, is seen by most of the residents as a counselor and advisor and as a warm, energetic companion and friend. About half the residents say she is one of the people in the House they are closest to. She is never seen as a person who tells people what to do, although she is said to give sharp and honest advice; her expressed point of view is that people should be open about their feelings and problems and take part in the community. Though some residents disagree with this, she is not seen as forcing her views on the House. She is also seen as being responsible for seeing that housekeeping jobs are taken care of if the residents in charge of them begin to slip. She makes the initial

contact with prosepective House members and acts as liason with social
workers, therapists, and agencies.

Some of the residents' impressions of her are:

— She guides the black sheep into being white. She knows when
to yell, when to pamper, and when to talk sense.

— We have a good relationship. She tells me about Esalen Institute, but I'm a Freud man. I don't appreciate her analysations
but like her personality and feeling. She doesn't overdo it or get
mawkish or sentimental but is down-to-earth.

— She is the coordinator. She has to make sure people get
along and help people face things to the best of their ability,
which is a lot to ask a human being.

— She's a friend, not an authority. She doesn't use power
things, she's not like a shrink. She tells people where they're
at, if they're playing games. You can really respond to her because she doesn't act like she has the power.

The Students

Students from Yale and Southern Connecticut Universities are also
allowed to become House members, usually for a semester, and to
participate in the House in a kind of a helping role. Their status and
their role is, however, undefined, and they often experience much greater problems of adjustment than do the other residents. The students have
in most cases had no direct experience with hospitals, and they come in
with the same prejudices as the rest of the outside community. If they
have been exposed to patients, it has usually been through a staff or
volunteer position, which is far from the direct and genuine involvement
that House residents demand. Finally, for a college student involvement
with other people and taking personal responsibility are often as difficult and confusing as they are for the other residents. In the students'
case, the initial strategy for defining their involvement in the House is
to remain distant by trying to get to know what the others are like, in the
generic as well as the specific sense. This attitude can be seen as somewhat patronizing, and such distance usually evokes a negative reaction.
If the student adjusts to living in the House successfully, he develops
a more genuine involvement, participating with his own feelings and
experience.

Some of the ways in which residents see the students are:

— Students come to the House as a stepping stone to a career.
They wish to learn about the problems of people, to better know
what they're feeling and facing in life. Sometimes students are
just as mixed up as some of the residents. It helps; it's like
saying we're not the only ones.

— Students ask different questions. They want to know each
one's trouble, and sometimes it's too much for them to cope with.
I want to feel human, not like a vegetable to be studied. The students now are more courteous and won't delve unless asked.

They're closer to their feelings and more reserved, and I like that much better.

— The students contribute their sanity, so this place is not just a home for ex-patients. Some have more problems than us, and some don't thrive here.

— I can't stand the attitude of "I'm going to come in and help the poor unfortunate people." We want honesty, not toleration. And you have to be able to laugh.

— Their professed purpose is to learn about life or something. I like talking to them, and they add an air of stability to meetings and stuff. When they come, they have a medical air, to learn psychology first-hand. Usually they discard that after a while and settle down and become House members.

— I wonder how those students, with their Board scores and IQ's, can come and be friendly with the people here?

There can be no doubt that the House accomplishes its purpose of getting former patients out of the hospital and that it offers a community that all residents feel is comfortable and worthwhile. It tries to erase the distinction between staff and patient, and it expects the former patient to take responsibility for governing the community, controlling himself, caring for others, and helping those who need help. The founders of the House feel that performing such a role, usually assigned to a staff member in a traditional psychiatric setting, is the most useful, easiest, cheapest, and most efficient way to deinstitutionalize a former patient. By any criteria, the experiment seems successful, and perhaps this model is adaptable to larger institutions and centers of psychotherapy.

C. Kingsley Hall: "The Floodgates of My Soul Are Open ... "

Kingsley Hall is an old East London settlement house which was leased by the Philadelphia Association (P. A.) from June 1965 to June 1970. It was one of several households that were set up so that people who had been labeled by society as "sick," particularly those who were said to have "schizophrenia," could live freely, the way they wished. People who have not been labeled sick are also allowed to stay there as residents, but inside the house there is no distinction made between patient and staff. The community, consisting of fourteen people, decides who can stay there and sets rules. The rules that have been set are the minimum allowable for harmonious cohabitation; such things as mealtimes, expectations of social intercourse, and friendship are felt by many at the Hall to be obligations which often have been imposed upon them by family or treatment center with destructive consequences. The residents are free to seek encounters, or even traditional therapy, either from other residents or outside, and a few do.

Kingsley Hall is often criticized by categories that apply to a treatment center, which it is not. It is simply a place where people who have been coerced and oppressed by society may live in whatever peace they can find within themselves, without the intrusion of others. As such, the category which fits it best would be a monastery or contemplative community, rather than a hippie commune, to which it has also been compared. It should be noted that the encounter between Mary and Joe is the exception for residents, most of whom are literally sick of being helped and unwilling to engage in such an intense relationship, and this freedom is respected.

In its first four years, 113 people lived at Kingsley Hall. Seventy residents had been classified as patients before their stay, and forty three had not. About three-quarters of the residents were male. Eleven of the residents have gone to hospitals at some time after leaving Kingsley Hall (none of them for the first time). Most residents are between the ages of twenty and thirty-five. The Philadelphia Association has set up several other households in the London area similar to Kingsley Hall and intends to set up as many as possible in the future.

One Person's Experience

The second time Mary Barnes was mad, she learned to paint out the turmoil within her on the walls of Kingsley Hall. First, she used her own shit, then she used crayons to draw black breasts, announcing her lack of inner nourishment, and finally she poured watercolors and oils on huge canvases, first somber and later bursting with color and energy. They portray the Saints and the Bible, the life and passion of Christ, interior landscapes with dazzling intensity, frightening conflict and ecstatic reaffirmation, final unity and inner peace. They chronicle her death and rebirth through madness.

"In her painting Mary puts outside herself, with the minimum mediation, what is inside her," writes psychiatrist Ronald Laing in the catalogue of her 1969 one-woman exhibition in London. "They are embarrassing. They are too raw for our liking. We are inclined to condescend .... She does not go as far 'out' of herself as propriety and artistic convention requires. We cannot meet her, anywhere else than the place in nowhere, whence she paints. There, I recognize her, in myself, and I am disturbed in myself, by her."

Twelve years previously Mary had another period of madness, but that time it was labeled a "schizophrenic breakdown," and she was "treated" in a mental hospital with tranquilizers to damp the flow of crazy thoughts and psychotherapy which further buried what was inside her, in order that she "readjust" to her job as a nurse-tutor in a hospital. She then spent ten years living a normal life of confusion, depression, and unhappiness which the hospital described as a "cure," until she met Laing, who was about to open Kingsley Hall.

Her second journey into madness led her back to before she was born, through childhood and adolescence, and to the discovery that painting made her experience intelligible to herself and others. Her experience and the community which allowed it to happen have revolutionary implications for the current practices of mental hospitals and psychotherapists.

Her door has a tree painted on it, with the roots flowing up through the trunk and out into branches in a continuous red and brown motion.

Inside the small, windowless room, one of thirteen similar "cells" in the Hall, she smiled up at me as I walked in, from inside a pile of blankets, clothing, and stuffed animals which are arranged on the floor to form her bed. The walls were once white but now form a collage of fiery-bright paintings, darker, more somber ones (some hung and some just painted on), quotations, scribblings, and one of the black breasts which first announced the urgency of her inner needs.

There are some orange bursting fruits on a blue background which are more recent depictions of the same theme, but now the breast-figure is healthy and inviting, rather than barren and ugly. There is an orange sun and a small picture of multicolored streams erupting from a core, at the bottom of which is the explosion of her madness. Behind where she sleeps is Christ on the Cross, almost a stick figure, his face suggesting both his agony and the serenity of his soul, in a style reminiscent of Roualt.

Mary herself is a striking contrast to the violence and passionate intensity of the walls. She sits small and quiet in one corner, wearing a scarlet bathrobe. I sit first on a small stool facing her, but later move in amid the clothing and blankets, next to the pile of papers which are the manuscript of the book she is writing. She looks about thirty, with a mysterious smile that could either mask the ingenuous shyness of a child or the ironic enlightenment of a Zen master. Her eyes support the latter impression; they are blue and intense and give an impression of an age far in advance of the rest of her body. Her hair is straight and long, carelessly arranged as a college girl might wear it to classes.

It is a shock to find out that she is forty-six, because in some ways she is closer to the age of four, which is her age dating from the onset of her madness and rebirth. Her movements are fluid and unpremeditated like those of a child, and when she speaks she slurs her r's with a common childish speech defect. She feels that she is very much in the middle of her growth process, having through art largely integrated the inner aspects of herself. Now she is able to move out to other people in the community, responding to them without fear or reservations and helping them take similar trips.

She was one of the first to move into Kingsley Hall when it opened, along with Laing and Joseph Berke, an American psychiatrist who has been with her through the whole process, although at the beginning neither had the slightest idea where it would take them. It was he who responded to the message of her first painted breasts by feeding her with a baby bottle and who first gave her crayons to draw with, something she had never done before.

The months before she moved in had been agonizing. After her first breakdown she went to a university to get a teacher's diploma. "I kept my madness tucked down inside me by keeping busy, always being on the move, never having a moment free. If you had asked me at the time I would have said I was depressed, but now I know that was my anger, particularly toward my mother. I had words to understand myself then, but they were only intellectual. I read voraciously to keep my mind off myself, so that I didn't have to look at what was happening to me. I got a hospital teaching job and I got frantically involved in anything I could, I was so frightened inside," she told me. She knew she needed psychoanalytic help, but nobody would take her on.

She remembered her first breakdown, when she was twenty-eight, and knew that it could happen again. She had been sent to a state hospital, where she stayed for almost a year. "I felt like I would have become a chronic patient, because they weren't able to help me and understand me the way I needed. They treated me with shock and drugs. I loved to go in the padded cells, where I could lie in a foetal position and be alone. I was like a baby in a cell, which I know now was for me a womb."

After eight months she was taken to a psychoanalyst, the late Dr. Theodore Werner, who saw her for therapy and who helped her get out of the hospital. "He saw that I was below the level of speech and he thought the only thing I could do to get better was to push it down and live on top of my troubles. It was like walking on ice. This wasn't a very good or very permanent solution, but at least it got me out and back to work, even though I could feel how fragile I was," she explained.

She began to feel more and more hollow inside, as she sensed that there was very little that was really hers in her life. She turned to the one thing that she was certain was hers — her religion; she entered a Carmelite convent. She had converted to Catholicism while working as a nurse in the Near East and had been in a convent once before, just prior to her first breakdown. She entered the convent again, in another attempt to keep out the hollowness she felt engulfing her and to attain spiritual wholeness.

"It is really a great tribute to the convent that they were able to lead me to this, to make me begin to go mad. Before that my whole life had been almost unreal and I never had any real contact with myself. In the contemplative life you have to begin to make contact and usually the experience is quite beneficial. But the mother prioress realized that I was spiritually divided in a way that they could not help me with, that I needed special help," Mary said. Fortunately, the prioress had read a little of Laing's work and got Mary in touch with him.

She was especially hopeful because he agreed to see her together with her younger brother, whose suffering and confusion are similar to her own. He recently moved into Kingsley Hall, after spending four years as a "schizophrenic" in a hospital. Mary is very excited about this and hopes that he can begin to trust her and Joe enough to go through a similar process.

"Ronnie met me nineteen months before Kingsley Hall opened. He said that I couldn't let go now, because I needed a place to do it, where I could get help. He said when I could go down into myself, I would become like a baby and that if I behaved like that outside, I would get locked up. He told me to try to hold it in, not to speak to anybody except to him and his colleague Sid Briskin, until they could get a place for me to move in. The next year was the hardest of my life," she recalled. "I had to go through the motions of work and otherwise hold my real self in, so that the madness couldn't come out. I saw Sid regularly and he helped me get out some feelings. Sometimes my anger was so much I could not move away from the door of his office and his secretary had to help me out the door."

Kingsley Hall was meant to be a place where people, especially those who had been diagnosed as schizophrenic and sent to hospitals, could go through severe psychotic episodes, to the greatest depths and to their natural conclusion. Residents would be free to live there as they wished and experience their madness not as a symptom of an illness which they had to learn to cover up in order to be fit to return to society, but as a revitalizing psychic experience. Laing and his associates point out that such intense symbolic death and rebirth experiences are a feature of many primitive and non-Western societies. They provide release and re-integration for those who otherwise might be alienated from the culture. Our culture has become so frail and fearful of man's inner core that it devalues madness and ecstatic experience to the point of defining them as sick. Thus the possible routes to overcome widespread alienation are cut off, because they are called the disease itself.

Madness, especially the form known as schizophrenia, is seen by members of the P.A. as a response to a family or other interpersonal situation where contradictory demands make the person feel that no re-sponse he makes is right. The schizophrenic child has lived in fear of irrational, punitive behavior by his parents and feels prohibited from pointing it out. Such a person never is able to feel at home in a world which is perpetually fearsome and inconsistent. At best, the child learns to face the world with a false self of either rigid conformity or bizarre eccentricity which shield him from destruction by the hostile world. But when life gets too stressful, the fears and desires that he has been holding back burst out; he breaks down and goes mad. Support for this theory has come from several quarters of the United States.

Laing and his group see madness as a natural coping mechanism in an intolerable living situation, much as a fever is a sign that the body is combatting disease. The mental hospital, by simultaneously treating the patient as if he is sick, by not allowing him to experience the in-tegrative possibilities of his madness, and by trying to stop the process with drugs and social reinforcement techniques to reduce the "symptoms," further cut off the patient from experiencing things which are his own, not the expectations and demands of those around him. The patient thus is once again in a situation like that of his family. His madness is usu-ally an attempt to assert his autonomy by fleeing a family which has never allowed him any experience that is his own, by always telling him what to do.

At Kingsley Hall the individual's rebellion is supported, and he is allowed to experience his autonomy. There are no rules, and nothing is prescribed as conventional. There are people available to help one go through the experience, but only if asked. The hope is that undergoing a period of madness, in a place where one is helped not to fear oneself and where others understand and sanction the process, can often lead to a natural resolution. This happened for Mary Barnes.

The Philadelphia Association obtained a five-year lease on Kingsley Hall, and immediately Laing, Berke, Briskin, and some other P.A. members moved in and invited Mary, and others who needed a place to go mad, to move in with them. By the time the lease ran out (and was not renewed because of the unpopularity with the neighbors), over 100 people had lived there, many of them changing almost as dramatically as Mary.

At first Mary did not feel comfortable enough to let herself go and began to forget why she was there. She worked days, commuting two hours to her job, and made all sorts of demands on the others. She asked for a special flat on the roof and felt that she should be paid for living there — all of which were ways of testing whether the others really did care for her and really would allow her to do as she wished. After a time she remembered that she had come there to have a breakdown, and suddenly she allowed herself to go down into madness.

In an account written for Morton Schatzman (1971), another American psychiatrist who lived in the community for a year, Mary describes her life then:

"Life soon became quite fantastic. Every night at Kingsley Hall I tore off my clothes, feeling I had to be naked. Lay on the floor with my shits and water. Smeared the walls with my feces. Was wild and noisy about the house or sitting in a heap on the kitchen floor. Half-aware that I was going mad, there was the terror that I might not know what I was doing away, outside of Kingsley Hall. The tempo was increasing. Down, down, oh God, would I never break."

She resigned from her job and was able to devote full-time to her regression. Schatzman described how the community reacted to the odor of her shit coming from her room, which was opposite the kitchen. They decided that she had to be allowed the freedom to go down as fully as she could into her experience and did not interfere with her. She continues her written account:

"In bed I kept my eyes shut so I didn't see people but I heard them .... Touch was all important. Sometimes my body had seemed apart, a leg or an arm across the room. The wall became hollow and I seemed to go into it as into a big hole. Vividly aware of people, I was physically isolated in my room, my womb...." She created other wombspaces, as she had in the hospital pads. She found a great wooden box in the cellar, where she would play with her dolls and teddy bear.

She would sit huddled in her room, not able to talk at all. She had to be fed, clothed, and changed like a newborn baby by Berke and Laing, who were the only ones she would trust to be near her, so great was her fear.

"Then I began to grow up. It was not what you would call a normal childhood, because I had to unravel myself from all the past twisted feelings and holding it in," she remembered of the first months after her "birth". "During this time I spent almost all my time in my bed here. I was still inactive physically, but I began to feel together a bit more, after the huge regression back to before I was born. Now I could talk again, but only to Ronny and Joe. I was terribly dependent on Joe, as if he were my parents, and I couldn't bear for him to leave my side even for one minute. When he had to leave he would say, 'I am going now, not to punish you, and I will be back.' Being like a little girl I was still always upset at this and in a rage. Later on I began to draw these feelings."

"One day Joe gave me a tin of grease crayons. 'Here, just scribble.' I did, on and on. Suddenly a picture emerged, a woman kneeling with a baby at her breast. That was when it all started. At first my paintings were dark or were figures with no background. I painted what was inside me, especially in my anger and my rages. I still didn't talk to others. I felt the paper would come in on me. I felt that anyone could see what was inside my by looking at my pictures, so I didn't feel I had to say anything," she said. She found tins of paint around the house and some wallpaper backing paper and began to paint them while they hung from the walls. She painted at fantastic speeds and on anything she could find, until almost every wall in the house was covered with her work. Members of the community began to get annoyed and tore some of them down.

In her rage, and her fear of what she might do to the others in such a state, she again went down below the level of speech and for another three months would not leave her room. "I felt I was going to pieces, it seemed to be me coming off the walls," she remembers. "I felt really bad during those times, but Joe was always there to help me, to reassure me that I could get through things. At this time, and this is a phenomenon that many other people go through when they come to live here, little incidents triggered enormous anger and fears. You feel everything in the house has to do with you. If the bell is broken you wonder what you've done to cause it. You feel that nobody wants you here. During this period I had to have the whole security of my room, because I was afraid I would go out and kill people."

She grew to be able to talk again and move about. She continued, "Other things about me changed during that period. Before then I had always wanted to wear black and all my clothing was black. When I came out of bed after that period I wanted new clothes, with colors. Even now I don't wear black. I also began to discover more color in my paintings and to add backgrounds to the figures." Her paintings were living outwardly everything that was going on inside of her, and she began to be able to talk about some of the feelings inside her, and understand them. She began to write little stories to go with her paintings. At first they were rambling and obscure, then they became more compressed and intelligible. Here is one she wrote for Ronnie's birthday in 1967, in which she symbolizes her rebirth as that of "The Hollow Tree."

> There was once a tree in the forest who felt very sad and lonely, for her trunk was hollow and her head was lost in mist. Some times the mist seemed so thick that her head felt divided from her trunk. To the other trees she appeared quite strong but rather aloof, for no wind ever beat her branches to them. She felt if she bent, she would break, yet she grew so tired of standing straight. So it was with relief that in a mighty storm she was

thrown to the ground.

The tree was split, her branches scattered, her roots torn up and her bark was charred and blackened. She felt stunned and though her head was clear of the mist she felt her sap dry as she felt her deadness revealed, when the hollow of her trunk was open to the sky. The other trees looked down and gasped and did not quite know whether to turn their branches politely away or whether to cover her emptiness with their green and brown. The tree moaned for her own life and feared to be suffocated by theirs. She felt she wanted to lay bare and open to the wind and the rain and the sun, and that in time, she would grow up again. So it was that with the wetness of the rain she put down new roots, and by the warmth of the sun she stretched forth new wood. In the wind her branches bent to the other trees and as their leaves rustled and whispered in the dark and in the light the tree felt loved and laughed with life.

She continued to paint. "Through the spring of 1966 work poured out. All my insides were loose. The painting, like lightening, was streaking from the storm of me. Joe suggested, 'Paint the Crucifixion.' I did again and again. Hungry for life I wanted the Cross," Mary writes in the catalogue of her London art show. "That Christmas Eve Ronnie came to see me and I talked to him only about the Crucifixion, for a long time. In his replies he used the same word again and again 'resurrection ... resurrection ... resurrection.' Next morning I really began to feel it," she told me about how she began to paint religious scenes.

In her work the theme of the Passion becomes infused with the almost sexual ecstasy that Mary feels at this point in her new found wholeness. Her inner experience flows out naturally into her life and onto her canvases. She paints now with oils, still with the same furious, automatic urgency. She begins by tacking a huge canvas or paper on the wall and abandoning herself to an inner logic which emerges as the finished painting. "They develop quickly," she explains. "Usually I have an idea of what they are, like a feeling I would like to paint about St. John, and then I let it just happen. The longest I ever spent on a painting was when I began a large one one day about two, while standing at the top of a ladder, and didn't finish until ten in the evening, when I got to the floor."

At first she used a brush, but now she uses only her fingers, as if even the brush would interfere with the spontaneity and intimacy she enjoys with her work. Her hands are several shades lighter than the rest of her skin as a result of the constant abrasive scrubbing to remove the oil stains.

"My dreams are helpful to me and form the substance of a lot of my painting. I understand them now and they now contribute to my wholeness. I was fighting myself before, but now something is free and I am whole in a natural way, so getting in touch with my unconscious is natural rather than frightening and fragmenting," she says. "I never see myself returning to my former job, because that just isn't a part of me now. I see myself painting and writing, that is my vocation, and I am fairly certain that I can find support doing them." A book about her experience, written with Berke is the first account of a psychotic break in which the story is told by both the "patient" and the "doctor."

Her new vocation gives clear experession to her intensely personal religious feeling. She often paints the lives of Christ and the saints, including a thirty-foot-long mural consisting of fourteen scenes from the Crucifixion. The faces and forms of the saints are evocative rather than clearly defined, and in many of the simultaneously tortured and serene faces, one sees echoes of her own serene bearing and it‿ tumultuous interior. She can also be whimsical, as in "Dances," where a series of figures become like stars twinkling, with arms and legs becoming indistinguishable. And there is Christ washing the enormous sunburned foot of a leper, a foot which covers half a canvas.

She stores her work in the large downstairs of the Hall, which was formerly the chapel. As we turn up each painting, her eyes light up and she smiles as the personal meaning of each becomes apparent to her. She feels like a vehicle for a tremendous religious expressive power that has been released through her by her madness.

"I often paint the mother of God and stories from the old and new testament, always expressing the continuity between the two to connect them up," she said. "I know there is a lot of myself in the painting, but I don't think myself in them that way. I know that I paint my anger and my feelings when I have them, and you can see in my work the progression of how I dealt with anger. My first paintings were tight and somber and less free and expressive, whereas now I paint things that flow out easily and freely, like this new one of a volcanic eruption, which is the rush of feelings and free explosion of anger, but in a creative and unobstructed way, because I know why I'm angry and how to release it."

She see Kingsley Hall as a religious community, because its ideals and the experience it values are in the deepest sense religious. The community has helped her to regain contact with the inner truths and feelings from which she was cut off. She sees this as a personal crucifixion and resurrection which has made her as whole as any person can hope to be. She sees a commonality of expression in all religions, and in the psychological journey facilitated at Kingsley Hall, as humanity's universal search for salvation, which can also be seen as a search for the split-off parts of the soul which some call the unconscious.

She speaks of how this inner core is only superficially the fearsome, destructive, animal-like impulses which are usually considered to comprise the unconscious. The deepest levels also contain a tremendous store of love and creative energy. "The floodgates of my soul are open, and the water of my life flows out, into the the endless sea of light," Mary writes. She has seen other members of the community on the verge of despair and seeing nothing worthwhile in life because they were cut off from this core. They rediscover themselves through the care and trust of others, in a way analogous to the psychedelic journey (Chapter 4).

"I feel like it has literally been my entire lifetime that I have been living here. I no longer feel that I have to paint all the time, like I did

when I was working things through, so I feel free to be more interested
in the others. I feel strong now and I'm no longer threatened by other
people. Now this place is becoming a real community for me and I find
that I can satisfy the desires I have to get back to nursing by helping the
people here. I find that I can do things like feed someone who I know is
going through the same thing I did when I first came. I understand and
know how to help them," Mary says of her life now.

Structure of the Community

Now PA members and other parts of the "network," like Mary, are
all living in separate places more suitable, since some of the PA members would like to live together with their families. Joe Berke and Morty
Schatzman formed the Arbours Housing Association and founded a new
house.

The makeup of Kingsley Hall changed markedly since its inception,
although the basic philosophy remains unchanged. The community does
away with all distinctions between helper and helped, doctor and patient.
Since the medical relationship is conceived of as one in which the doctor
possesses information which enables him to change something which is
unperceived by the patient, it is clearly inapplicable for the "cure" of
madness. On the contrary, the psychotic experience is one in which only
the patient can possibly have information about what he is going through
and what his feelings mean.

What a person needs is a place to be free to experience his own madness. Therefore, all social conventions, which are pressures from outside, are as much as possible eliminated in Kingsley Hall. One resident
tells how irritating it was for the community to have a doctor living there
who insisted on saying hello every time a resident walked by his room.
This was felt as a distraction. Other residents use their freedom to dance,
make noise, act oddly (to outsiders), and do anything which helps them
to understand what they feel inside. Indeed, the first experience of any
visitor to the Hall is intense nervousness, because many of one's conventional categories of politeness and order are upset there.

The need for helpers in Kingsley Hall is tremendous, but what they
do is far different from the role of a traditional therapist. First of all,
since many residents come in highly fearful of anyone and at times are
unable or unwilling to perform such day-to-day tasks as cooking and
cleaning, there must always be people who are willing to help others
and take care of the community. If someone is not willing to work, he is
not labeled lazy and begrudged his lack of interest in what is essentially
not very rewarding work. But in order to survive, there must be a minimum number of people who do these tasks.

Another role for helpers there, as exemplified in Joe Berke's relationship with Mary, is to listen, trust, care, and not be afraid of the
journey another member of the community may be taking. If there had
not been people whom she trusted, for her to talk to and to be with her,
Mary could never have gone as far as she did. Being such a helper demands more skill than traditional therapy and more time, dedication,

and intense physical involvement. The members of the PA, whether they were living there or not, have always been available as friends and listeners to members of the community. Frequently a PA member will drop in for an informal conversation with whoever wants to talk, or for a meal. Help is available, but it is not given unless it is expressly asked for. Thus, members of the community can take their time in learning to trust people who may help them and do not have to "degrade" themselves by admitting to sickness in order to get help.

The community was founded so that all members would have the opportunity to go down into themselves and experience madness. Thus far, the members of the PA and other helpers who have lived there have not had the opportunity to go down this deeply into themselves, largely due to the many outside pressures and the great distress in other members of the community. But Laing feels that the ideal community would be one in which those who have gone through madness will help those who are just beginning the journey. Madness is not just for those who have found living intolerable thus far, but may potentially be an enriching experience for an otherwise completely stable person who can find the freedom to let go of himself and take the plunge.

At first there were many organized meetings, social events, regular meals, and a much more orderly structure. Members of the PA organized seminars and lectures for people outside the community as well as in it, including founding the Anti-University of London (which subsequently moved to other quarters) and tried to catalyze an active life inside the Hall as well. Mary feels that this kept people in the community from getting into themselves as deeply as they could have. She was able to do it because she was impervious to such distractions. She feels that the slower pace now, with few organized meals and no scheduled meetings, provides for a much more flexible arrangement of informal contacts. One can be alone much of the time, and yet there is always someone available when one has a pressing need for companionship. Residents are also tending to stay longer and spend more time introspecting rather than in community activities.

There are no rules or obligations, although when someone acts in a way that interferes with another's freedom, the community can meet and try to eliminate the conflict. Usually the community looks for the meaning behind the offending behavior, so that if possible the behavior can be made unnecessary. Dr. Schatzman, in his essay, tells how a resident who threatened to start fires went through people's rooms and disturbed girls late at night with requests to light his cigarette, was found to decrease the annoying activity when he was confronted with its underlying meaning of sexual fear and guilt.

The community has had to cope with considerable hostility from the neighborhood outside and everything from outright obstruction to indifference from the medical authorities, who support almost all of Britain's psychiatric care. The children in the neighborhood have broken all the windows in the front of the building so often that Kingsley Hall has given up trying to replace the glass, which causes considerable discomfort during the winter. The medical authorities have tried to close it several times, citing masses of regulations concerning "proper" operation of boarding homes and ex-patient hostels. This makes it hard to establish similar communities.

But the inability of mental hospitals, with their arsenal of rules, clean buildings, tranquilizers, shock treatments, lobotomies and therapeutic communities, to "cure" psychotics, argues that such experiments must continue. The hypothesis of PA members is that mental illnesses are the projected fears of the "normal man," who by "treating" patients seeks to eradicate what he fears within himself.

Schizophrenia was regarded by Freud, and the vast majority of his descendants, as incurable. But even with the tremendous amount of research into schizophrenia, the number of people who have gone through madness to feel as whole and integrated as Mary, are very few. Might it perhaps be that this massive failure is due to faulty premises? The creation of communities like Kingsley Hall, which respect and tolerate mad behavior and cease to regard schizophrenics as ill, may be the most promising way to redeem the millions of souls facing the torment of suppressed madness. It seems that in many cases the cure offered by mental hospitals is less palatable than the disease.

Chapter 9

THE "FOREIGN POLICY" OF NUMBER NINE

At first glance this chapter may seem like little more than an arrogant, angry, cynical put-down of people in the community who have done their best to try to help us. We hope this first impression gives way to another view, because we tried to offer a sober account of the outer workings of a new project, the ways in which it obtains support and takes its message to the community. We have, of course, felt some disappointment as we confront the gap between the community's rhetoric about change and its actuality, but underneath this reality is the basic fact that we have survived in that environment, relatively healthy and certainly wiser. The result of our survival has been a greatly increased understanding of the liberal pluralistic myth of a constantly changing society and of the actual fact of a scared, timorous, short-sighted community of well-wishers whose actions, while well intended, end in stultifying and undercutting efforts at innovation from any quarter. We feel that innovation is not impossible, but to make it happen demands a kind of practical astuteness and understanding of community dynamics which is seldom discussed in print.

While there are many accounts of the inner workings and development of a new service, rarely are the outer workings examined and clarified. The reasons are obvious. Most new projects have an internal rhetoric of honesty, openness, and trust, but they feel forced to operate on the outside by using political wiles, dilutions of their aims, and manipulation of relevant figures. The contradictions are often shared privately, in informal meetings and conferences, but rarely openly or in print. This chapter is an account of this process for Number Nine, with all its ethical relativity and community manipulation.

The alternative institution is testing basic hypotheses concerning the relationship among social change, individual conflicts, and social service programs. It is therefore precisely the radical departure from established norms and practices which is the most significant feature of any alternative institution. Alternative institutions need public support that does not infringe on the integrity of their programs. Any alternative institution depends on public support for legitimacy and economic resources. The individuals and institutions which supply both kinds rarely share the

basic values, perspective, or experiences of the counter-culture. Therefore the success or failure of an innovative program's struggle to survive and grow depends on the nature of the relationship between the program's leadership and the empowered community leaders.

The ways we work with funding sources, local authorities, radical
and freak groups, psychiatry, social workers, drug programs, and
schools are more than survival mechanisms. We have a message for
each of these groups or institutions, and we relate to them also in order
to obtain services and civil liberties for our young clients. Our goal is
influencing change within these groups, even if that activity endangers
our survival; in fact, such a defeat has not happened. Learning to deal
with community groups without compromising basic values is of tremendous use to other groups facing the same moral dilemma. Number Nine's
differences with community institutions give us a clearer grasp of what our
values and procedures are in practice; not merely rhetoric. In conflict
we are forced to define ourselves with greater clarity than we obtain
to among ourselves, where everyone appears to accept our divergent
views and procedures, whether they fully realize them or not.

In the interaction betwen the program and the community, changes in
the program's form and content usually occur. Considerable pressure is
brought to bear on the innovative program to make changes in the direction of socially acceptable standards. The program's goal is the reverse:
the alternative institution wants to create changes within the community
— in the broadest sense, making the community more tolerant of change;
in a narrower sense, influencing established procedures in social service programs and the like. The community has many vested interests
in keeping the established system justified and ongoing. The community's
defense against change — particularly innovative changes which are not
expressed militantly — is cooption, the process by which the community
pressures a program into socially acceptable limits. Such pressure is
covert and disguised.

The success of alternative institutions reflects both the capacity of
our society to allow for innovation and the skills of the youth leaders in
resisting cooption. The failure of innovative programs primarily affects
young people, who see these programs as models for a kind of change
they can identify with, even if they do not personally use the services.
If they see a program's values undermined by the community, their
cynicism about the possibility of meaningful social action within the
system will be strengthened.

This chapter discusses how Number Nine developed a strategy for
dealing with outside groups — in effect, a "foreign policy." The management of dealings with outside groups is in a sense even more critical
than a program's inner dynamics. An alternate project must survive by
using outside resources, and it must translate its message into terms
the broader community can understand, if it is to have any substantial
effect in producing change in the larger institutions, which are responsible for the problems the alternate service deals with.

A. Dynamics of Funding and Legitimacy

Cooption and Criticism

Number Nine was greeted enthusiastically by liberals within the community. It promised change in an area in which the community had many felt needs: drugs. While many offered support, few turned this support into funds. It was assumed that any worthwhile program will receive financial support from existing government sources. Indeed, communities often link the value of a program to its success in raising funds. As time passed, we became aware that support was conditional. Our interaction with the community was initially for the purpose of raising funds and legitimating our efforts in their eyes. In return for this support, we learned, there was a price, and this price was usually that Number Nine change its program to conform to socially acceptable, traditional limits. This process of implicit threats backed by covert pressures — of cooption — is society's defense against change.

The cooption process began with the way people in the community looked at our efforts. Initially they idealized our program. That is, without looking at it or talking to us about it very much, they understood our program as the potential solution to the frustrations they felt with their own work and programs. For example, young psychiatrists seemed to expect that Number Nine would instantly develop the structure and capacity to meet the needs of young people. Because they "understood what Number Nine was trying to do," they did not feel they had to spend much time gathering direct information on our work. It seems that they relied on a stereotyped ideal fantasy of a youth program, which led them to misperceive many of the actual facts about our operation from which they could have learned. Despite declarations by us to the contrary, many community leaders referred to Nine as a drug program. These people experienced drugs as a problem for youth, and they assumed therefore that Number Nine was an attempt to deal with drugs; in turn this belief kept them from getting the direct information of how and to what extent young people seeking help perceived drugs as a problem. This tendency to avoid direct information about new programs, relying instead on fantasies and rumors, provokes much polarization, false confidence, and difficulty in a counter-cultural program.

Community supporters, acting on their idealized image of Number Nine, then began to predict that our program would fail unless we took "certain steps." The advice which followed usually seemed divorced from the experience of Number Nine's staff members, and it consistently underestimated the amount of risk that the new program could successfully take. We were told to be less provocative; to have many professional consultants to legitimate our program, to avoid lawsuits from parents by refusing to deal with anyone under fourteen without permission; and so on. This advice seemed to come from their own experience of working within a system of constraints, constant frustration, and little personal responsibility for taking risks and initiating change. One psychiatrist in a community clinic advised us to do only referrals, so that when our clients went to other programs, there would be objective evidence of our success and our program would not be faulted. Obviously another consequence of this method would be the reinforcement of existing programs, and the mitigation of whatever potential the new program had for innovation. Our reason for starting Number Nine in the first place was a rejection of the "work-within-the-system" ideology. Since we saw the large -scale failure of traditional institutions to help young people, we could hardly become so quickly dependent on and accepting of them.

When such value differences became apparent, the community began to use subtle pressure to enforce its advice. People acted hurt when we rejected their suggestions, feeling that their authority, expertise, age, and honorable intentions made their advice "objective and useful." We began to hear (always indirectly) that they felt misused, not respected or listened to. The community regarded Number Nine's program the way they regarded young people in general — to be guided, directed, and controlled, but not to be learned from. Disagreement was attributed, not to discussable differences in value, but rather to adolescent rebellion, and it was considered a hang-up of our leadership. Number Nine was given the choice of either accepting the community's benevolent paternalism, and with it support and funds, or "having it our way" and going it alone. The possibility of exchange and collaboration is not considered; the usual result is a growing polarization of the new youth program and the community, which must eventually be ended if the program is to survive.

This polarization results from negative rumors about the new program, which are generated by the differences in value and procedure, as well as the real difficulties in setting up the program. Rumors had a powerful effect on Number Nine's position and reputation in the community, because people supported the program because of what they heard about it rather than because of direct knowledge. For example, funding sources base part of their decisions on community sentiment — which in effect means rumors which professionals hear and do not check out. Unless the alternate institution steps in and deals directly with some of these negative rumors, people simply assume that they are valid. Such assumptions affected both young people, who did not know what to believe, and the service agencies Number Nine had to deal with in order to provide help for its clients.

Negative rumors usually infer that the program has had a destructive impact on some people, leaving them sicker or more disturbed than when they came. More credence is given to these rumors than to similar stories coming out of established agencies. Critics act as if the mere existence of such information invalidates the program. Rumors usually center on areas where there are clear value differences and when acting on the alternate value is seen by the community as destructive. Number Nine was turned down by the local Community Chest because several professionals mentioned a rumor to the effect that couples were sleeping together in the residence and that some girls had even become pregnant. The implication was that the young girls were improperly coerced, that

they were harmed, and that such activities took place as part of the
"treatment" or counseling. In fact, sexual relations between counselors
and counselees are discouraged at Number Nine, although there is no
moralistic prohibition against sexual activity among clients or among
staff members — an attitude that grows out of the values of the counter-
culture. What matters, though, is that such assumptions on the part of
the community were used to cut off funds to Number Nine and that the
staff was not called in either to verify or deny the rumors or even asked
to reply. The whole dynamic concerning rumors in the community is
that neither the source nor the object of the rumor are ever brought together to talk out or confront differences and the probably distorted information on which they are based.

External signs of disorganization or unpredictability are also used as
evidence of the program's inadequacy. When Number Nine's building was
messy (because of lack of funds or of staff temperament), or when different staff members represented Number Nine's position differently or
failed to follow up contacts consistently, this was evidence against us. The
community expected us to develop a structured hierarchical organization
controlled by a few individuals, because such a process was considered
the only valid way to organize service. This expectation placed us under
pressure to cease experimenting with new structures, shared responsibility, and collaborative authority, and to adopt the limiting solution which
other agencies had failed with. In a sense, we were penalized for experimenting and were asked to stop and adopt the traditional course.

Democratic pluralism, Robert Wolf (1968) has pointed out, exerts a
braking influence on social change through many of these mechanisms.
The actual process of "free competition" of innovative programs within
funding and legitimating channels systematically eliminates thorough-
going change because anything new must submit to the power and social
judgment of interests preceding it, which have a vested concern in their
own unchallenged survival. After a new program becomes a "success"
(usually by being funded for or lasting a second year) it is rewarded for
movement toward less controversial positions, and at this time previously existing programs grudgingly make room for it. The veiled hostility of existing interests took the form of cynical predictions of Number
Nine's failure at reaching its aims and the belief that anything we tried
would still end up "establishment." Radicalism, it was implied, was
naive, impractical idealism or, worse, a personal neurosis on the part
of the leadership. Community judgment thus stated that a radical stance
is incompatible with a program realistically dealing with the problems
of society. This position made it difficult for people to take youth and
youth-initiated programs seriously, and their paternalistic response was
frustrating, despite its overt warmth, because it minimized the value
and effectiveness of new projects.

A final response of the community to innovation among youth comes
when it becomes clear that pressures for change toward social norms are
having little effect. The community then can get together and form an
"alternate youth program" of its own, controlled by community members

through a board and funds. When young people, adults, and funding sources are confronted by two projects, one run by "freaks" and another by respectable adults and perhaps one long-haired social worker, the adults opt for the program which they feel comfortable with, despite evidence that many young people perfer the other one. In New Haven no fewer than three crisis telephone lines developed to compete with Number Nine, which was perceived as "soft" on drugs. Each was completely dominated by the "community", young people being involved only on the lowest levels and under adult supervision. (These hotlines were the models for our description of innovative professional programs in the second part of Chapter 6).

The Funding Process

The application procedure for many types of grant builds in changes in structure, rhetoric, priorities, role definitions, statistical record-keeping, and heavy inputs from professionals in training, consulting, and supervisory roles. Alternate services tread a delicate path in locating funds and trying to avoid giving away their program in the process. Foundation and government funding sources make the assumption that a program's ability to raise money indicates its value. A good program has no difficulty being funded. Seed-money grants for a year or two are commonly given out by foundations in the belief that at the end of this time a program will be strong enough to obtain funds from more restrictive sources; this assumption more often leads a youth program toward the pressures described above. The conflict of interest between an alternate institution and the rest of the community actually suggests that its success will make ongoing funding extremely difficult to obtain. Funding sources have placed constant pressure on us to limit the more controversial aspects of our work.

Funding sources usually ask a new program to make structural attempts to insure its continuity and responsibility. These consist of placing professionals and community leaders on the board and in supervisory positions in the program. That the impetus for the new program is the fact that professionals have been failing to attract youth was not considered to contradict the assumption that these same professionals would be useful in advising the crisis center. Ostensibly they would know and be attracted by the innovative aspects of the center, but the funding source generally avoided mention of the creative aspects of the program and focused its justification of a grant on the traditional procedures and structures within the program. Insisting on community members' making up the board, relying on the social responsibility of the program (its public image), suggesting changes in structure, budgets, record-keeping and policies, all transform the alternative institution from an experiment to a toothless parody of professional services. Number Nine received seed money based on its neat building, statistics from its first three months' work, its creative use of professional consultants, and letters of community support, rather than on the basis of the calculated risk of creating an alternative structure and service process.

Another assumption made by funding sources is that financial scarcity
is a spur to the development of innovative programs. "You shouldn't get
fat ... you'll loose your energy." Innovation and change is thus equated
to deprivation, justifying the community's reluctance to provide sufficient money to really develop a program. In effect, the program's staff
members are frustrated and in despair; the situation encourages them to
stop making changes which disturb and alienate the funding sources. To
obtain long-term funding offered by usually conservative sources, high-
risk programs must often drastically reduce the effectiveness of the program.

Funding sources make the program accountable in an upward direction, rather than expecting it to be responsible to the clients it serves.
The two groups have completely different interests, and any attempt to
satisfy both leads to an internally divided and conflicted program. Funding
sources reinforce hierarchial structures with low risk factors and turn
innovative programs into conventional institutions. The skills involved in
writing proposals, dealing rhetorically with funding representatives,
creating a paper organization which meets the felt needs of the community leaders, are all rewarded. Skills which are useful in providing service to the client population are not useful to the leadership of any organization where survival is critical. Leadership in innovative programs
eventually moves from the charismatic innovator (who raises seed-money
for his new vision) to the bureaucrat who raises ongoing funds with low-
keyed, consistent, unimaginative, but socially acceptable leadership.
The quality of the program suffers; but eventually program staffers may realize that the funding sources have no direct information concerning their
program; they receive money based on their personal and community
image, and this can be manipulated easily by recognizing and appealing
to the basic dynamics. The realization that the quality of their work is
irrelevant arouses extreme despair.

Empirical research and program evaluations are also used to coopt
an innovative program. The bias of these studies consists in the factors
selected for study; within the limits of the methodology, the findings are
in themselves accurate. But any social scientist who accepts the pluralistic hypothesis that a program cannot be a genuinely innovative experiment,
can select factors which are basically similar to conventional programs
and minimize or ignore factors which could show substantial differences.
Funding sources which rely on statistical comparisons, attitude studies,
and fixed-response questionnaires inadvertently emphasize conventional
responses within innovative programs. Energy is diverted into forms
instead of content, as when strict accounting procedures minimize the
flexibility with which a program can use funds.

There are some changes which would make the funding process more
responsive to alternate institutions and to projects directed at social-
change in general. Rather than passively waiting for proposals, funders
could actively seek out and observe new programs. Grants could be
offered to individuals to initiate or develop promising projects, and
long-term funds could be recognized as meeting the needs of particularly

innovative programs. This would free the programs from much of the
cooption process and allow them greater focus on the problems of their
clients. Funding officials would have to get into the habit of doing in-
person, on-site evaluations of short proposals rather than relying on
reams of proposal paper.

Funding sources can also expand their role in relation to projects.
Leaders of innovative projects could function as hired consultants, to be
drawn on by newer programs. Travel among projects could be encouraged,
as could conferences for sharing experiences. Finally, funding sources
could use their political, social, legitimating, and lobbying powers to
help innovative projects to vitiate the cooption process. Legal and accounting support could be offered from a central source, minimizing the
collective costs to new programs. Evaluation of projects should be based
on consumer-oriented studies rather than on the opinions of authorities
and professionals, who are often out of direct contact with the client
populations. Such evaluations could be connected with collaborative program development for several programs.

Number Nine's Response

Pressure from funding sources and the community were the context
in which Number Nine had to formulate a "foreign policy" which would
insure its survival, growth, and influence. We defined who had power
over the project, how to educate the community in the possibility of new
values, and how to raise money. This section offers a quick outline of
those decisions, particularly in reference to fund-raising, while subsequent sections detail our relationships with various community groups.

Our earliest decision was to assign exclusive legal control over the
project to the full-time staff of Number Nine. Many youth programs use
well-known members of the business and professional community as a
board of directors. This practice helps create a base for fund-raising,
and insures a group that will provide continuity and hire new staff members if the original workers quit. But board members have legal control
over the program and thus share its risks; they therefore tend to be reluctant to commit it to new and potentially embarrassing areas, and they
act defensively in the face of community criticism. For example, a community board would have found it difficult to accept Number Nine's policies on sexuality and on absolute confidentiality to clients regardless of
age.

We felt that, even if we could find a few community leaders willing
to shoulder the risks, this move would separate power and responsibility
from the staff, who were in the best position to define and carry out
innovations which might seem dangerous or unwise to a board. At the
start, for example, there were questions about the legality of a nonprofessional counseling operation, and the founders wished to assume
such risks personally. We felt that community supporters did not need a
legal tie to Number Nine in order to support it and help raise funds. The
staff became the legal board of directors, following the counter-cultural
belief that responsibility and power should not be divided.

We placed a high value on educating the community to our efforts.
This was due as much to our own inclination as to the need to keep on
top of efforts at cooption and criticism. We realized that many of the
community's defensive fears could only be maintained in the absence of
concrete information about our program. In response, we made ourselves highly visible and were informative in correcting rumors and misunderstandings about the nature and results of our work. Our stances
on sexuality and drug use (namely that it is an individual decision at any
age) and our absolute confidentiality were misunderstood as covering up
harmful aspects of our program or (as several psychiatrists put it) as
well-intentioned but counter-productive policies. Our community education effort was aided by the staff's experience in working for other
youth agencies in the city, our ability to translate our work into the
language of professionals, and our patience. These efforts helped us
weather the harassment that many youth programs face when they try
to exist independently of social sanction.

Fund-raising proceeded by several methods. Originally we hoped to
obtain money from those who used the service or who related to its values,
or through some enterprise that would turn over enough profit to run the
program. The ambivalence and inefficiency of the youth culture around
money is well known enough to make the drawbacks of the first possibility
obvious. Further, we disagreed with the premises of the fee-for-service
basis of most agencies, and mainly our clients consisted of people who
did not have independent means of support. It seems that the second possibility will be important to long-range survival, particularly if Number
Nine becomes more of an advocate or more politically involved, and it
is the most feasible way to remain independent and responsive only to the
community we serve.

Our first donations came from psychiatrists, and our salaries from
the United Church on the Green and a local federally funded drug program. Number Nine opened with almost no operating costs, in a free
storefront loaned by the redevelopment agency. Within three months we
had built a program attractive enough to obtain a seed-money grant from
the New Haven Foundation. We were able to obtain an exemption from
their informal rule that community projects have a board of prominent
citzens. For many of the reasons cited above, continual funding has been
problematic for us. Because of a combination of ineptness and the controversial nature of our work, we have not built up enough community
support to pay the $35,000 per year that Number Nine's crisis program
needs. We receive some contributions, honorariums for speaking en-
gagements, and consulting fees, but these sums cover only a fraction of
our costs. Recently a young conscientious objector doing alternate service, who also works at a local bank, has begun to help us raise funds
without altering the substance of our program.

By default we have sought public support. For many projects this
has been a perilous path, leading either to the loss of a responsive or
innovative nature or to public denunciation when they strayed beyond
what is tolerable to a publically funded agency. We find that distant public

monitors, who rely on cost accounting and written evaluations, are sometimes easier to work with than local sources, who have access to rumors
and undercutting attempts by other agencies. If we comply with program
guidelines, and if we always cultivate several funding sources, we can
keep our integrity by simply doing more than is outlined in the proposal.
By doing things which are not specifically prohibited and by regarding
our program as flexible — consulting our own lawyer in case of doubt —
we have been able to set our own course. Although most of the dynamics
which take place in the community are duplicated within foundations and
public-grant sources, we have found some genuinely innovative subgroups
which control small sources of funds and attempt to offer grants to programs which innovate on more than a rhetorical level (see Moffett, 1971).

Future funding lies in a combination of self-sufficiency and public
support. We have been able to sell the expertise and research-writing-
consulting-training skills of certain members of our staff. Because
these skills are of value to other programs, they justify fees and grants.
If we command salaries of over $12,000, and consulting fees of $100 a
day for doing useful work with other projects, and if we live on less than
half that amount, the rest is available to the program with no strings
attached. This surplus can fund new programs and hire additional staff
for more controversial work. Since it is easier to account for huge professional salaries than to justify expenses for a controversial program,
this method of accumulating funds by selling expertise is attractive. It
embodies the danger, however that we can fall into the professional trap
ourselves and begin to act as if we know, thus coopting, controlling, and
limiting the projects we undertake to help as "experts." We have formed
the State Street Center as an entity for consultation and research whose
profits go to running Number Nine and other youth projects in our network. Number Nine and the State Street Center share ownership of the
building, personnel, and a corporation, and the work done as part of the
State Street Center has so far helped to develop new directions and assets
for the service program.

Local Authorities

In operating an agency within a community, the phrase "working
outside the system" if taken literally becomes a joke. But its metaphori-
cal use has meaning in that, because of Number Nine's moral and political position, the way it proceeds must come under constant critical
examination. Number Nine operates within a framework where compli-
ance with certain laws is in question, and it reserves to itself such potential options as noncompliance, protest through political or legal channels, and overt acceptance but covert noncompliance.

In addition to contact with authorities for legal sanction, Number
Nine also deals with them when representing or working with a client,
and the same options are presented in these situations. Staff members
experienced a great deal of personal agony in making decisions about
how to deal with local government, police, the courts, and the law. The
resolutions seem to represent the demands of "Realpolitik" rather than
our philosophical temperament.

Number Nine's first corporate act was to retain a lawyer. One of the founders knew a young attorney who, though quite understanding and sympathetic, also had an impeccable position within one of the most prestigious law firms in the city. His situation has in many cases helped as much as his legal abilities, and he deserves a great deal of credit for helping Number Nine obtain such valuable advantages as a tax exemption. As a poor community group, Number Nine was also eligible for legal assistance. As an auxiliary lawyer, and as a lawyer for many of our clients, the more activist legal-aid lawyer was a great help, particularly in court proceedings.

We soon recognized not only the existence of the law, but also its incredible comprehensiveness. We learned the ways regulations work to stifle or inhibit new ventures, particularly those without means and resources. For example, at the start Number Nine was unsure of its legal standing if staff members were to be sued for malpractice or for impairing the morals of a minor. The founders decided that, since they had very little money of their own, they could afford the risk, and in fact there has been no trouble in this area. But the possibility of such suits has made other crisis centers decide to thoroughly regulate their activities.

Number Nine has also had to find insurance and to conform its building to the various codes of the city building department, fire marshall, and board of health. Most of these regulations are prohibitive for a new group, but they can be altered at the discretion of the officials. To receive an acceptable ruling, Number Nine has learned to work closely with public officials. Groups such as Number Nine have an affinity for old buildings — it is usually all they can afford — and these were not built to meet new codes. The founders know of many groups, some of them with considerable funds or enjoying much greater social sanction, that have lost their buildings or been closed down altogether. Negotiations in this area, therefore (and the concomitant raising of funds to meet the cost of repairs), has been Number Nine's most pressing and most critical task.

The best way to ease the burden and assemble the power to survive, once these hurdles have been surmounted, is the purchase of land. Number Nine's top priority once it opened was to own first a house and then a larger guilding, and it has reached both these goals. Once one goes to the trouble of fixing up a building, it seems obvious that one should be prepared to stay there; but with redevelopment sweeping through New Haven, there was little chance of a safe, permanent rental. The additional advantages of ownership are considerable. There is no landlord to be upset over whatever publicity a group gets. Once the building code is met, there are no further renovation expenses. If a large space is bought, it can be shared with other groups and thus become a center for change-oriented activities or political groups within a community; bringing groups together produces solidarity and exchange, and such a center is often the only place more controversial groups can join. The tax advantage to Number Nine, the relatively lower cost of a mortgage than of rent, and the additional tax savings on mortgage interest, are all helpful

in cutting expenses after the initial outlay. For example, Number Nine's
house costs less than $250 a month to run; it also represents collateral
for a loan.

De alings with police forces poses another difficulty. In other cities
there has been a great deal of friction and repression, particularly concerning crash pads and drugs. Some crisis centers, though they have
church and community sponsorship, have been closed or busted on
trumped-up charges; though these were eventually dismissed, the harm
had been done. Local young people have an exceedingly distrustful and
paranoid attitude toward the police — justified by the practices of the nar-
cotics squad in particular, which is well known for its harassment of individual addicts and long-haired drug users. In New Haven there are
several cases of undercover agents operating both in the freak and in the
black community; their activities are believed to have led to a murder
as well as to more than a hundred busts of politically active young people,
almost all of whom were subsequently acquitted.

Number Nine decided against seeking out encounters with the police,
either negatively or positively. If an officer came to the house looking
for someone, staff members were polite; in turn, the police have never
asked to search the place, which is kept drug-free. Staff members encounter policemen at drug panels or meetings, and at these times they
always respect police work (with some reservations). Those members
of the force engaged in community relations are expert at listening and
politeness — which makes these gatherings pleasant but also non-
productive, since nothing ever changes. But, incredibly, Number Nine
seems to receive some police support; there have been only isolated cases
of visible surveillance, and at times the police have referred and brought
people to the crash pad. This has been a tremendous victory for Number
Nine's legitimacy, and it has allowed staff members to breathe easier
concerning their legal status.

Another aspect of Number Nine's dealings with police, the courts,
and the judicial apparatus consists of taking the part of young people in
difficulty. Help in this has come from a dedicated and alert legal-aid
office, which is responsible for our minor successes in the courts. When
people known by Number Nine are in jail, staff members try to get them
bailed out, in many cases using their own money to do so. This has always been a good risk. The legal issues concerning the civil rights of
young people are quite ambiguous, particularly in actions against or
without the consent of parents. Number Nine has tried to help out in
these areas, particularly with runaways who strongly desire to remain
independent of their families. In one case Number Nine was given cus-
tody of several runaways, over the protests of their parents. Some staff
members hope to help initiate group homes for young people in similar
situations.

Radical and Freak Groups

Number Nine is part of an expanding social movement for restructuring social institutions. All the founders came from other parts of the

movement — civil rights, peace, community organizing, and educational
reform. While various sectors of the movement have never set any record
for collaboration or for agreement on the aims of the struggle, Number
Nine has set as a personal goal the unification and collaboration for
change with other groups. This goal translates into a policy of unconditional
support for other radical groups and patient responses to their criticism
of our work. Initially radical groups regarded Number Nine with suspicion or hostility , seeing it as "a wipe-ass liberal effort" or, in the case
of a local underground newspaper, possibly a police plot, however un-
witting. The founders patiently explained their work, and as Number
Nine outlasts most of the groups who were initially suspicious, it continues to be subject to both accurate criticism (for lack of service to
some parts of the street community and lack of response to such issues
as the large drug bust), but also some grudging respect. Number Nine's
policy of trying not to undercut the efforts of other groups and sharing
resources like the building , bus, and sound system, are respected. Support of the Panthers (loaning them the bus for a rally) resulted in the bus's
being busted twice, but this only increased Number Nine's credibility.

During the summer of 1970 Number Nine was swamped with people
moving across the country and was in tune   with both the radical and the
freak community. Some staff members outfitted an old school bus and
did several shows. A large rock festival was planned at nearby Powder
Ridge, and Number Nine was hired for bad-trip services. The festival
was cancelled by an injunction, but thousands came anyway, though the
promoters left with the money. Staff members worked valiantly, but
there was little they could do except to struggle with as many bad trips
as they could. Frustration by everyone led to bad feelings among the
staff, some of whom saw the bad-trip work as more glamorous and
gratifying and as more relevant to their feelings of solidarity with young
people than day-to-day crisis work. The founders and many regular
staffers saw neglect of everyday services as self-defeating because it
undermined Number Nine's consistency in the local community. A split
of sorts occurred, and although in the summer Number Nine was most
visible and on-the-spot, it also incurred criticism. Service was not too
well organized, and frustrated young people, who expected Number Nine
magically to help "get them together," got angry when it appeared to be
no more together or organized than they were. Number Nine had created
a myth of its competence, and when the myth was tested, it proved somewhat illusory.

In the following year Number Nine began to work with other service
groups in the community on the common issues of fund-raising and creating a network of essential support services for the freak community. We
worked with a food cooperative; helped with gifts of money to our neigh-
bor, an arts cooperative faced with eviction; ran music nights at the local coffee house; and conducted a series of personal growth workshops.
Because the street community is small, and as a consequence of the
large bust and the move by many people to other places, this collaboration has been only a limited success, despite its small scale. This

direction is exciting to many new staff members. Now that Number Nine owns its building, it can be a free space where many groups can meet and gather, as a local church is; these can include a community resource exchange, student union, and a free school. Number Nine hopes to become an increasing focus for such groups, working on a day-to-day level rather than in the confusion and anarchy of one-shot events like festivals.

B. Psychiatry and Social Welfare

Advocacy and Psychiatric Backlash

Number Nine's most extensive and most conflict-laden relationships are with local psychiatric and social welfare institutions. Many staff members have themselves been hospitalized or have had bad experiences with such institutions, while others on the staff wish to pursue careers in this field. Two of the founders of Number Nine received clinical training at the local mental health center, but both left in frustration. This ambivalence leads Number Nine to expend much energy dealing with psychiatric institutions and to see change in them as an important goal. The presence of Number Nine as an existing alternative raises issues concretely which formerly could only be dealt with by debate. Some of the basic questions which Nine has tried to keep open are:

1. Is psychotherapy a skill which people can be trained in, or is it a quality of human relationship?

2. What sort of choice should those who seek help with personal problems have over what they get?

3. Are psychiatrists necessary and competent to make decisions which can cause a person to lose his freedom?

4. Is intervention in a client's social and political situation an alternative way of dealing with personal pain?

The founders intended Number Nine to be an advocacy group, a social experiment developing out of its own experience directions in which other helping institutions can move. This role is important to many who join the staff, and is one source of Number Nine's attraction for professional helpers dissatisfied with their work. Number Nine has been criticized for violating traditional professional neutrality in its combined advocacy-alternative model. But psychiatrist Seymour Halleck (1971), who has worked in prisons and college campuses, argues that the so-called value-neutral stance of therapists in institutions puts them actively on the side of the political status quo, of acceptance rather than active or rebellious responses to oppression, and of conventional wisdom rather than social change. Since the impulse of many young people is for change, the founders of Number Nine felt that an advocacy organization would approximate their interests more closely than would a neutralist one; it has been one of the aspects that make Number Nine palatable to young people who would otherwise avoid helping groups.

This stance has led as much to misunderstanding as to fruitful dialogue with psychiatrists. Just as some young people tend to stereotype institutions as parts of the establishment, psychiatrists have tended to

dismiss criticism from Number Nine as arising out of personal hang-ups
rather than as based on work experience similar to their own.

A good example of this process occurred when the medical magazine
Hospital Physician (March 1971) wrote a long and quite accurate article
about Number Nine. In the interest of controversy, the headline read,
"Are Help Houses Better Than Doctors For Young People's Problems?"
The bulk of the article consisted of quotes by Number Nine staff members attacking specific abuses in their experience with psychiatric treatment. But this left very little space for the kind of work Number Nine
actually does every day.

In response to this article many physicians cited the "anti-establish-
ment" stance of Number Nine as interfering with its work or marring the
possibility of its being accepted. They implied almost unanimously that
to criticize psychiatry was to be against it, and that when young people
did so it interfered with their potential for useful work. They assume
that being critical means that a group is against or avoiding meaningful
contact with professional groups (which is clearly not the case with Number Nine), and that, rather than helping Number Nine to function better,
being critical of established practices makes us less likely to institute
useful reforms. The staff of Number Nine sees such defensiveness on
the part of professionals to be an excessive preoccupation with our
style of criticism and a lack of interest in answering our criticisms
or examining Number Nine's alternative suggestions. This defensiveness
is backed up also by a community study (Reed 1971), which shows that
criticisms of Number Nine are seldom backed up by direct experience,
such as a visit or talks with the staff, but are based on hearsay or stereotypes conjured up by Number Nine's appearance. This attitude in turn
angers and frustrates Number Nine's staff and leads to win-lose arguments rather than profitable exchanges. In fact, contrary to its alleged
antiprofessional stance, Number Nine staffers have initiated and maintained contact with all local professional programs.

Nor is this an isolated example. When the second part of Chapter 6
appeared in the American Journal of Orthopsychiatry (Vol. 42, No. 4,
July, 1972), it was followed by a commentary, "Service in the Season of
Discontent" by Drs. Quentin Rae-Grant and Saul Levine. The editors considered our article so controversial that a reply should appear with it.
The professionals' tendency to overreact to criticism was shown by
their exaggerating our positions, and then attacking those extremes. The
authors find themselves "bored by [our article's] arrogant assertiveness
and with a sense of dismay at the prospects of this kind of alternative."
They then respond as if we had said such things as that we "have found the
magic answer from within," without any previous learning; that we "always, totally, under all conditions" look for political solutions to personal problems; that we issue a "blanket condemnation" of the professionals who are most like us; that we have a "messianic assertion" of
one "Royal Road to cure"; and that all our views are "presented in the
context of anger, self-righteousness, and above all, self-indulgence" —
an example of "pretentious, unrealisitic, twisted logic." Then they accuse

us of bombastic rhetoric and unconstructive criticism, although at the
outset they claim to be open to criticism from the young, provided that
it is not naive Woodstock or revolutionary rhetoric.

   Their major basis for calling counter-institutions irresponsible and
self-indulgent is that staff members see meeting their own needs and
exploring personal issues as coequal with service. This attitude is quite
threatening to professionals, as is the assertion that in innovation all
aspects and assumptions of service must be questioned. That kind of
analysis strikes professionals as destructive because it attacks some of
the root assumptions, not of their rhetoric, but of their work style. Such
extreme anger, and defensiveness leading to a total misrepresentation of
our integrity are what is in store for those critics who strike at the core
of professional service. The liberal openness to criticism and alternatives
breaks down when the critical judgment strikes at the practice rather
than the good intentions. Even when the questioning is done reasonably
in a professional journal, and in a moderate tone, such points can still
be misread, and publication is no cure for stereotyping and misunderstanding. Our response is to continue writing and to answer carefully
such attacks, but we feel that they reveal more about the fears and defenses of the attackers than about our own work.

Evaluation

   Interaction with mental health professionals also occurs on the issue
of evaluation and quality control. The entire burden of proving the ef-
ficavy of the new program is placed on Number Nine. Mental health programs are normally evaluated merely on the basis of a certain number of
people's receiving a certain type of treatment from professionals, many
of whom are in early stages of training. But a new nonprofessional organization such as Number Nine must find other ways to demonstrate the
value of its services. An added predicament is that Number Nine's situation makes it difficult to keep records, and nearly impossible to do follow-up studies. These pressures have forced the founders of Number
Nine to become active in developing a theoretical framework for their
work, evaluating it with professional support (Jaffe, et al, 1971), and
to be articulate in explaining themselves. This has been helpful in that it
has caused them to be more self-critical and to develop communication
skills, but it has also deflected energy from the actual work of counseling
and supervision.

   The usefulness of evaluation studies for mental health services in
general is an open question. Reginald Carter and Philip Marcus have
completed a study that demonstrates that such research is either used
as justification for policy decisions already made or is dismissed out of
hand by criticism of its methodology. Evaluations of mental health programs are difficult, not only because of the sensitivity of the questions,
but also because the direction of improvement is an issue of value, which
cannot be empirically determined but is subject to long and ambiguous
debate. The previous section mentions how the selection of research
hypotheses concerning Number Nine reflects an ideological preference

for or against pluralism. Since there is not yet a clear understanding of what happens in the process of treatment at Number Nine or in an established program, and since evaluations of established programs have been inconclusive at best, it is too early to ask whether any new program is effective or not. It should be clear that there is a need in this area for greater experimentation and for description of different programs. By stressing evaluation, psychiatric professionals tend to stifle diversity and induce premature closure on basic questions. Number Nine has been drawn into a fruitless cycle of self-justification on meaningless issues of evaluation, in an attempt to justify its legitimacy as a valid and helpful service. This has tended to limit discussion of exactly what it is that Number Nine is doing differently from established programs as Number Nine staff members attempt to prove that their program is "just as good."

Coercion and Ethics

Number Nine's stance on the ethical and political uses of psychiatry, which is similar to the views expressed by Thomas Szasz (1963, 1970), is the source of some friction with mental health groups. Number Nine sees counseling as a voluntary contract, in which one of the parties is explicitly expected to be helpful. Number Nine diverges from Szasz in seeing payment for this service as setting up obligations and mistrust which can be avoided by providing the helpers with an alternate source of income. Staffers try to be helpful in every interaction, and for this reason Number Nine has a tendency to equate the skills of counseling with being a receptive and open person. Chapter 7 showed why the coercive power of institutions, the use of drugs as if they were cures for specific diseases, the stigma of mental illness, and the mystification of skill by medical therapists, are all dysfunctional and politically dangerous to young people. Since young people enter treatment most often under coercion from their parents and/or school (Reed, 1971), Number Nine sees such treatment as more often an attempt to get them to behave in a certain way rather than as a voluntary agreement. Number Nine also sees their confidentiality violated as a matter of course in speaking with their parents and in sending evaluations to schools, and objects to ways that such judgments are used in deciding competence for school, work, or power in the family. Therefore, Number Nine's interpretation of its responsibility toward a client is different from that of other professional programs.

An instance of this conflict of values concerns a woman of about twenty-five (who looked and acted about fourteen), who came to Number Nine, afraid, because she did not want to go back to the hospital, where she was put on medication. A staff member who tried to get a clear idea of what she wanted from Number Nine and the hospital found her to be so ambivalent that she could switch positions in mid-sentence. But she decided that she did want to call the hospital and tell them where she was. On the phone the nurse told her to come back, and she became hysterical. The nurse then asked the Number Nine staff member to bring her back; she became angry when he said that he could not do that against the girl's will but that perhaps the nurse could come down to Number Nine and talk with her. The nurse agreed reluctantly and angrily. When she arrived, she talked with the woman and with another Number Nine staff member. When the staffer asked questions to find out what kind of medication was being given and whether the patient had the right to reject it, the nurse refused to answer. She showed no inclination to give the woman time to decide what she wanted; she alternately threatened and convinced her to go back and hereafter do as she was told. The Number Nine staff member felt that the girl had an observable problem in making decisions, which was reinforced by the nurse's behavior. In later conversations with hospital staffers, the Number Nine staff member explained that her resistance was not to the girl's being hospitalized, as they assumed, but to the way she was treated as immature and not able to think for herself. The hospital staff members saw this as an example of Number Nine's immaturity and antiprofessional bias and felt that this contact undermined the hospital's program.

Number Nine's staffers are learning to suppress their anger at such incidents; they patiently document their moral and legal objections to coercion at every opportunity. In this case they explained that, even if Number Nine wanted to force this girl to return, it is legally not allowed to do so, and that Number Nine's nonprofessional status makes its members' judgments doubtful. This stand against making decisions for others is precisely the position of classical psychoanalysis, but coming from Number Nine, it is seen as radical and antiprofessional. We try to keep communication open by cultivating sympathetic professionals who seek out Number Nine. Several therapists now work on Number Nine's staff, often without letting clients know their professional status. When they literally put themselves in Number Nine's shoes by divesting themselves of their role, they report that they feel freed to experiment with new ways of helping and to learn much about themselves.

The most fruitful exchanges between Number Nine and professionals occur in collaborative work. When Number Nine staffers make referrals to professionals, they either turn directly to someone they know personally or accompany the client to the clinic for the initial interview. While some psychiatrists are uncomfortable about Number Nine's intrusion on the traditional private relationship and about being observed and held accountable by Number Nine staff, this procedure more often develops into a shared understanding and even collaboration. Nine staffers also colead therapy groups with professionals at some local clinics; this collaboration further breaks down professionals' fears and distortions of Nine's work. There is a group of therapists, including professionals and Number Nine staff, who meet weekly and are trying to form a center which offers longer-term therapy and trains therapists to deal more with the social and political contexts of clients. The Number Nine staffers who associate with professionals seem to learn from them an increased sense of responsibility and following through on someone's needs, as well as some theoretical basis for the helping process.

Social Workers

Number Nine's relation to social work agencies, such as welfare and probation, focuses on different themes. Social workers are in a kind of limbo as far as professionalism is concerned — they are considered less competent as therapists, and they are so overloaded and confused by their work that they feel harrassed and depressed. Unlike therapists, they are responsible for intervening in a client's life as well as his personal issues, and their heavy caseloads make them unable to do much intensive work. For these reasons they deal with Number Nine by trying to relinquish responsibility for their clients to its staff.

As a result, Number Nine could very quickly be swamped with young people in great need of intensive involvement but with a lesser crisis and commitment to immediate help, though such crisis is the lever for change used most often by the Number Nine staff. They are often shunted to Number Nine by the social worker rather than coming on their own initiative. When they come on their own, Number Nine staff members can help them as they would anyone else, with the responsibility for defining the problem residing in the client. Social workers deal with Number Nine as if it has some authority over clients, and they expect staff members to freely share confidential information. Thus, the welfare department consistently asks Number Nine if it is seeing certain clients or if we know where runaways are. When Number Nine explains its position, they are upset and define it as irresponsibility. In their own heavily regulated environments they find it hard to conceive of the client's having power and of help as being collaborative and voluntary. They want Number Nine to guarantee service, while Number Nine asks that the client request it in person and take responsibility for getting it himself. For example, Number Nine will counsel parents about their own problems but will not agree to see their kids or even call them up unless they come in voluntarily; and the reverse is also true. After a while agencies understand and respect that Number Nine can only work with a client who takes the initiative.

Number Nine relates more successfully to social workers as trainers. Social workers feel helpless and unprepared to deal with what is dumped on them, and they are willing to spend much time with Number Nine in learning about young people by talking to them. One of Number Nine's major efforts is to train and support social workers whose institutions oppress them as they do patients. Those who become intensively involved with Number Nine usually reevaluate their own work and may change their work style or even their job. Several have come to work at Number Nine.

A Weekend in a Hospital

What happens when the style of work and relating which we try to use within new projects like Number Nine is transported to the rigid, large institutional reality of a large state mental hospital? Can Number Nine effect change? The possible outcomes lie along a scale ranging

from extreme hostility toward anyone who acts according to a heretical
style within the institution to renewed openness and shared exploration
of new possibilities. Several Number Nine staff members had an opportunity to find out what would happen when we were invited to spend a
weekend at such an institution.

A member of the research group there invited several radical mental
health groups to come, with the support of many key members of the hospital staff. The invitation was just a part of a period of increasing awareness of institutional reality and of community action to transcend it. The
hospital had been humanizing itself, and in contrast to other state hospitals, this one seemed almost benevolent. There was a modicum of free
speech among patients, and a key part of the change process was getting
together with an ad hoc patient group, consisting mostly of younger people, who were concerned about their civil rights, as well as with changing
some of the more oppressive policies of the hospital, particularly in the
area of arbitrary punishment and overuse of medication. Several key
staff people shared these goals, as did some of the nursing staff.

The invitations went to us at Number Nine, as well as the staff of
the Radical Therapist journal, the Mental Patients' Liberation Project,
and some individual radical therapists. None of us had worked together
before, and few of us were even acquainted before the weekend. We were
told that the staff had invited us and were aware of our visit and that a
patient group had been formed and was also cooperating in planning it.

We had no concept or plan. The only similar intervention we knew
of had been undertaken a year before, when members of the Hog Farm
traveling commune visited another hospital. They were a traveling
theatre inspired by the Merry Pranksters (Ken Kesey's group) who
specialized in forming an experience which gently pushed each member
of the audience into participating and which broke down some of the formal
sets and expectations about appropriate behavior. During their afternoon
they had chronic patients doing such trust games as jumping out of windows into a blanket, Keystone Kops style; they also featured balloons,
shaving cream, noise, music, dancing, gentle ribbing of stiffer onlookers,
and a complete disregard for any hierarchical restrictions or rules of
decorum which were usually the sole reality of the hospital. There was
a strong backlash directed at the administrator who had invited them.
but there was also a large minority of converts or those who welcomed
that sort of experience as one way of freeing them for greater change.

We were not as comfortable in the theatrical mode, and we felt that
any intervention in a large system had to be more long-term and must
offer inputs comprehensible to the people they were aimed at. Because
outsiders were regarded with suspicion, and because of the substantial
inside support for change, we felt that a carnival-festival might confuse
more issues than it clarified. We wanted also to break down customary
sets and roles and to make the time we were there a kind of open space
in the community, where new structures and ways of seeing the possibilities would be tried out and possibly carried through.

We ourselves were unsure of exactly what to do. We had almost no

information on what the community was like, and we did not know what
each visiting group expected or was prepared for. We expected that our
first task, for each of us to do individually, would be to gather information
and share it with as many people as we could. Sheila and Phil came on
Friday night, and after meeting with the research people and the others
who had traveled in, they each spent the evening on a different ward. The
first act of most of us, then, was to become, symbolically at least, part
of the community by living in it and experiencing the realities of being
part of it. They each got to know several people fairly well — mainly
patients but also some staffers. This was a fine way to get into the community, because it was not a public event. Where a meeting might lead
to posturing and impersonality, even to polarizing on issues based on
misperceptions of what people were actually advocating, the first night
was able to set a tone of personal contact and reality testing.

One of the most deadly pitfalls of interventions in large systems soon
became apparent. In fact, not all the people in the hospital community
supported, or even knew, the real purposes of the weekend visit. Some
of the nursing staff and senior medical people felt that the visitors were
there to criticize them. The word among staff was, "Treat them politely,
but don't tell them too much." Evidently not much clarity had been created
about the purposes or background of our visit. We were seen as people
who had no experience working in institutions, whose sympathies were
only with freeing patients, and who consequently would not listen to the
staff and were not to be trusted. The nursing staff had the most to lose
by any change. Many of the nurses were dependent on their jobs, and reform efforts have traditionally begun with the firing of lower-level staff.
They did not know whom it was safe to support, because supervisors and
some staff told them one thing, while others told them differently. The
ones that genuinely wanted to see reform were similarly afraid of being
fired. One young aide who really felt the need for the kind of change we
advocated felt that he could not speak in any of the open meetings we
initiated, for fear of retaliation. The staff had recently formed a union,
and that group was only at the early stages of fighting for certain wage
and time packages and had not yet shown interest in the general quality
of life in the institution. Our reception by the nursing staff quickly made
it clear that gaining at least their partial support, and some lessening
of their fears and distortions of our role, was a necessary task for us.

We also had terrors of our own. Few of the visitors had dealt with
their own fears of "crazy people" and the strange institutional climate,
and as a result there was a tendency to clump together, to stay with each
other, and to seek out meetings rather than really deal alone with the
hospital community. We learned vividly why people trying to change institutions retreat into structured roles and meetings, rather than working
quietly and individually. There were humor and shared analyses of the
situation, when we might have better spent our time in learning.

As time went on, we began to work more closely with the group of
young patients, although a few of us spent time with staff members, particularly those who invited us and were receptive to our ideas. As is true

in any total institution, the patients had an informal culture; they were subjected to a stripping process which was designed to promote obedience and discourage any signs of initiative. Our task was quickly defined as opening them up to a sense of possibility about taking action, organizing, and then getting key staff people to work with them. In the canteen we began to discuss such possibilities and became loud and excited, until the canteen supervisor brusquely asked us to leave. This almost led to a symbolic minirevolt, but then we left, having a clear example of the institutional pressure against any group doing something together. The difficulty with organizing soon became clear — once one began to show initiative or learned not to fear the authorities' arbitrary action, one was cured. Unlike prisons, hospitals could quickly rid themselves of troublemakers. This led to the idea of an ombudsman as a key demand and of a center for a patients' organization to work out of. Since the hope of being discharged was enough to keep any organizer from taking action, the ombudsman position and patients' organization could be staffed primarily by recently discharged patients coming in as volunteers, or perhaps even as paid workers. A lawyer in the visiting group supported this notion and agreed to help find legal aid.

The climax of the weekend was a Sunday afternoon open meeting. The topic for this session of the weekly community meeting was our observations and developing a plan for action. But no meeting could accomplish that — most staff members were off duty, and most patients had learned that such action could lead nowhere; a major task therefore was convincing key people to come to the meeting and to speak at it. Attendance was good — over a hundred came, including many staff members. Phil, the moderator from Number Nine, called on each person to say what he had experienced as wrong with the hospital and what could be done about it. The process was energizing — young and old came out to talk about how they saw the community, why they did or did not want change (many older patients as well as staffers felt threatened by it), and what they could do in their individual roles. Like much of the weekend, there was no heavy input of suggestions from the visitors, but rather a reinforcing of the idea of possibility, the belief that change could happen, and that it could be brought about by a simple and human process which could rise above the self-contradictory atmosphere of the hospital.

The outcome of the weekend is unclear. A backlash was caused by one of the visitors' getting drunk with a patient, clearly breaking a taboo. He was used by threatened staff members as a receptacle for all their opposition, and the research staff had to spend many hours defending and apologizing for their intervention. The patient group has remained together and has grown, and the few patients who became close to visitors and were subsequently discharged have kept in touch. The way is still clear for further, more focused interventions.

By itself the weekend proves nothing about the relevance of the innovations of crisis centers like Number Nine to large, recalcitrant systems like state hospitals. What it did for us was to remove our own prejudice against working in such systems. Large systems — even high schools,

as is discussed in the following section — are at first impossible and
fearsome to us, because our own experiences within them have left us
frustrated and angry and not very interested in being helpful. But the
creation of limited spaces within a large institution, which are analogies
to the structure and practice of our own center, offers a potential starting point for crisis centers to move into large institutional change. We
did not simply leave this hospital, because people there know about our
own and other centers, and their contact with us left them able to seek
us out and spend time with us in the future. Perhaps the model of our
structure can relate to changes in large institutions and can try out
methods for accomplishing drastic change within a system that resists at
every turn. That is, in part, the direction for our future work. The weekend illustrates a positive confrontation, in which we made clear to inhabitants of a large institution our differences in value, structure, and style
of work. It shows that such direct communication — by doing — is possible
and is an alternative to the method of people from different systems
merely getting together and talking about their work.

Drug Programs

Number Nine's drug policy is outlined clearly in its informational
brochure:

> All use of nonprescribed drugs and alcohol is prohibited on
> our premises and residential center. We are fairly aware of how
> to spot drug traffic, and for our own survival as an organization
> have had to be quite observant of our premises. For example,
> known drug sellers are not tolerated and are asked to leave if they
> show up. We have for this reason not had a single arrest for drugs
> on our grounds.
> We also realize that a great number of young people, parti-
> cularly young people in difficulty, will turn to drugs in an attempt
> to solve their problems or at least forget them. We have found
> that there is nothing we can do to prevent drug use, until the
> client is able to arrive at a constructive other way to handle his
> problem. Thus we have found that when we do not moralize about
> drug use, but attend to the problem that the client presents to us,
> he tends to decrease his use of dangerous drugs. When we find
> out that a client does use drugs, we follow a policy of strict con-
> fidentiality, and we will share this information with no one. This
> is necessary to build trust with our clients, and is a common
> ethical commitment of a helper. We neither encourage nor dis-
> courage drug use, but find that with our efforts young people tend
> to decrease drug use of their own accord.

Underlying this statement is Number Nine's discovery that there is a
split between young people's definition of their drug use as a problem and
the definition used by adults and most "drug programs." Basically, Number Nine will not attempt to deal with someone's difficulties by limiting
or controlling his behavior; this is the preference of most young people,

who resent the often thinly disguised moralizing that underlies many
drug treatment and education programs.

Number Nine's advocacy of civil and legal rights in drug cases, and
its refusal to adopt a punitive or controlling attitude toward drug use,
are seen by many local communities' drug task forces and committees as
condoning the use of drugs or as at least not helpful to their efforts. The
make-up of these community groups adequately reflects community opinions and fears of drug use, which are simply not supported by evidence
or by the behavior of young people, who use drugs. The basic distortion
perpetrated by such groups comes from drawing conclusions, on the basis
of a few extreme cases and the prevalence of drug experimentation in
young people that things will worsen unless such use can be prevented.
They usually feel that the only feasible way to prevent such use is by
presentation of arguments against drugs, providing involuntary treatment to those known to use drugs, and vigorous law-enforcement efforts.

This attitude makes it hard for Number Nine — which is usually perceived as a "drug program" by the community — to participate in their
forums and activities. Such groups usually resist even talking to young
people who try to present evidence contrary to their fears, and they grow
angry when Number Nine suggests that perhaps the extent of the problem
does not warrant such measures. Since the great majority of the members of Number Nine's staff and of those who come in for help use illegal drugs without greatly aggravating their personal problems or
causing damage to themselves, Number Nine has on principle disagreed
with the harsher proponents of antidrug legislation. In a poll of young
people, Number Nine found that almost all of them, not just drug users,
feel that drug use is up to the individual and that society should not try
to interfere; this is the traditional conservative laissez-faire moral
position.

The other facet of Number Nine's interest in the drug area is in
collaborating with the local federally funded demonstration drug program;
we try to help in extending its limits and taking a more active role in
drug law reform. Particularly in the area of psychedelics, which most
programs do not understand very well (although young people do), Number Nine has helped educate them in their positive aspect.

C. Intervention in High Schools

Because of varied social pressures and an ethic that dictates the
avoidance of conflict, high schools are inherently defensive. However,
both staffs ans students genuinely want and need help. The result, as
with other community institutions, was ambivalence toward Number Nine.
This ambivalence was heightened by Number Nine's role both as advocate
and ombudsman for young people's rights and in our developing programs
in schools where young people are full partners in working for
change.

When Number Nine opened, the founders contacted each local high
school about the new program. First they met with the principal, if they

were lucky, or with a guidance or social worker. Usually the school official was sympathetic but claimed that he did not have the authority to bring Number Nine's staff before student groups. Either "all assemblies have been scheduled" or Number Nine's program was "too new and unproven" (which was later changed to "too controversial" when Number Nine was no longer new), or they simply asked Number Nine to come to so many meetings with teachers and supervisors that we despaired of ever getting to the young people. Two schools allowed Nine to put up posters, and none let us pass out descriptive material, claiming that such permission would set a dangerous precedent.

In one suburban school where the principal was contacted by a former student, he made an appointment to see her. When she was ill and another Number Nine staff member came for the appointment, he refused to see him. That school's PTA asked Number Nine to speak shortly after we opened, at a parent's suggestion. The organization then had misgivings and decided it would be better to have a psychiatrist familiar with Number Nine speak about it, along with psychiatrists from other programs. The psychiatrist suggested refused to speak for us. The date was set and then postponed, allegedly because Nine had not properly confirmed it, and finally the whole program was tabled indefinitely. This is how many communities demonstrate their ambivalence about Number Nine.

In another school, with a reputation for being progressive, Number Nine was allowed to have a meeting after school, attended by over a hundred students and about twenty faculty members, including the principal. We began to talk about Nine and quickly switched to the kinds of problems felt by people in the room; this led to high-energy discussion among teachers and students about their frustration with the school. This in turn led to Nine's creating a student-faculty sensitivity group which ran as a demonstration for a month, consisting of four groups of about fifteen each. The outcome was that a group of students in the groups got together and proposed and implemented an experimental program for themselves in school, a faculty group began meeting and seeking ways to depolarize the split that existed between newer and older teachers, and several students learned group-leading skills and started work on Nine's staff and ran a similar program with Nine at a local private day school.

The following is a case study of that series of workshops, which began as a response to a visit to a school, without any expectation that a program would result. It gives a good example of the minimum conditions necessary for an effect on schools; it is also a hopeful case in that it demonstrates at least the possibility of open free discussion in schools. The workshops avoid the civil rights and power issues which are at the root of school systems, and as such they have a basic defect. They illustrate the style and results of the kind of work that many crisis centers are doing in institutions and represent an alternative to the frustrating and pointless avoidance of contact which many centers adopt toward schools.

High School Workshops Program

Starting in November 1969, Number Nine came to a local high school
to run an after-school workshop about our operation and its relation to
ths school. As is our custom, we did very little prepared speaking, focusing instead on the information the students and teachers had about each
others' concerns. The discussion quickly touched on the frustrations of
trying to express oneself in the school. Number Nine pointed out some
of the ways by which adults and young people shielded each other from
information about how they felt about each other. For example, we pointed
out the irony of an institution composed largely of young people, a school,
having to call in outside speakers to tell what students are feeling. The
absence of a mechanism in the school to facilitate and deal with communication problems, and the lack of a forum for in-depth and highly personal discussion of issues facing the school, were noted. The energy
level and involvement of everyone in the room grew, until people were
literally bouncing in their seats to get out their feelings.

Number Nine pointed out the relative openness and willingness of this
large group to discuss such issues, especially when compared to other
schools, and we suggested that such discussions somehow be made legitimate in the school as a whole. Small group discussions with trained
leaders were suggested as a concrete way to experiment with improving
communication. The principal had asked Number Nine to draft such a
program. With this in mind, we suggested that small groups of students
and faculty meet alone for two weeks and them come together for another
two weeks to deal with common problems. These groups would meet for
not less than three hours per session and would have consultants from
Number Nine to point out how communication problems were arising and
to help build an atmosphere for free exchange of feelings and ideas about
education.

The rationale for a small-group program as a way of dealing with
young people's problems, and other schoolwide issues, lies in both recent psychological research and in education practice. Specific problems
of youth can partially be traced to a widespread distrust of and alienation
from the large institutions that govern their lives. No problem, such as
drugs or sex, can be isolated from the more fundamental problems of
building an identity and relating to schools and families when the solutions
which worked for the older generation no longer suffice. Indeed, Number
Nine has found that young people use both drugs and sexuality as a means
of solving their problems of loneliness and disconnection from each other.
They adopt these means because other solutions, such as relating to
school or family, have failed for them. To reconnect them leads spon-
taneously to the abandonment of this very self-defeating behavior — the
misuse of drugs or sexuality. Schools must therefore deal with the more
fundamental issues of communication and connection to institutions and
families. This is the problem; drug abuse and other problems are its
manifestations.

A program which deals only with a symptom may miss its mark

entirely. For example, a program of drug information probably only re-
peats what young people already know themselves, and further scares and
alienates adults, who remain just as far from being able to deal with a
young person who uses drugs as they ever were. A 1969 cover story in
Newsweek on high schools cites the failure of drug information programs
to deal with the problem. Information is only one small portion of what
is needed to deal with a problem, to which must be added a common commitment by all parties to action, a mechanism for realizing that action,
and the freedom for all parties to decide together what is to be done.

Group Style. With the present proliferation of small-group programs
used to facilitate learning or change, it is necessary to specify more
concretely the type of groups here involved. To begin with, they were
not designed for personal growth of the group members. The Number Nine
consultants therefore steered the discussion away from such personal
topics as "Why I am the way I am" toward the more specific "How I act
in the school." Thus personal issues were considered only as they related to the school; group therapy and the more intense forms of encounter group were avoided. However, because a group must be able
to express ideas and feelings freely before its members can work well
together, a certain amount of group time was devoted to building a close,
friendly, personal, and flexible structure. This focus was felt to be
the way to create small groups which could work best to deal with school
problems in such a way that all individuals involved were protected from
psychological harm.

To accomplish these aims, the Number Nine staff had to be fairly
active and directive. They did this, not by setting up an agenda or rules
of procedure for the group, but by commenting on what the group seemed
to be doing at any time. The reason for this procedure is the fact that
groups, especially those in organizations, are not usually doing what
they say they are doing. Pointing out discrepancies has been shown to
be a method for improving group effectiveness, and it has spawned the
whole field of organizational development consulting. Groups are often
unable to solve problems or keep to the point; rather, the group process
can frustrate members by either wandering aimlessly or stifling itself with
rigid rules and procedures. Recent research, leading to the development of self-study or T-groups, has found that this happens because
groups have not dealt with members' feelings at the moment, particularly
feelings of anger or frustration. Only after they deal with them can
groups that are blocked get to work. Pointing out of the group process,
especially on a feeling level, is one way to build better communication.

A second obstacle to group communication is a person's need to
have a fixed and coherent image of himself, an identity which fits his
feelings. Again, this manifests itself in a contradiction between words
and behavior and leads to self-defeating and frustrating activity. Students
and teachers often find that the self-image of themselves that they must
preserve prevents them from really talking. A vivid example of this was
the difficulty for teachers who saw themselves as "progressive" to look
critically at their failure to live up to a philosophy they admired. The

group leader can help the group deal with the issues before it by keeping such contradictions in focus.

Besides pointing out feelings and interpreting contradictions between words and action, the Number Nine consultants had another important function in these groups. They could convey information which would help group members to make the experience relevant and duplicatable in other contexts. The group leaders tried at every stage to explain why they acted as they did, and how this type of leadership could be used in other groups, including classrooms, to focus on underlying issues. They could also furnish information on alternative ways of doing. For example, when it was asked what other ways were available for dealing with discipline problems or parent complaints, the Number Nine staff members were able to share their own experience of many other schools, including a large number of experimental programs, and of family and group counseling. Another way that information about alternatives was offered was in the periodical demonstration of structured exercises.

<u>Senior High Group (first two weeks)</u>.   The senior high school group concerned itself in the first two meetings (first week) with feelings of powerlessness; the apparently irrational, and therefore unpredictable, behavior of the administration; and the deep distrust of the latter. These perceptions created a fatalistic and skeptical tone. The group insisted that nothing could be changed and that therefore there was no need to try. The contradiction between this attitude and the fact of being in the group was pointed out, and the group members admitted to their secret hope that something could be done. They then complained about the frustrations they had been feeling over a three-year period and about the limitations placed on them for clearly (to them) crazy reasons, and they concluded that if college were like that they would not want to go.

We discussed risk-taking and agreed that there was little to lose by trying to see what could be changed before they graduated. There was also a feeling that they could not depend on the teachers, since they had been given many exciting expectations which were never realized. The leader agreed that there was little reason to hope for major changes, but perhaps some smaller improvements could get accomplished with an effort. At the next meeting one of the members proposed a model high school. The idea developed that they might be able to push for a small experimental group experience for graduating seniors or at least for those in the group. Talk centered on guilt, elitism, and specialness because they were so bright. However, the group continued to discuss the plan and to become excited by it.

Because of habitual patterns of behavior, such as dependency, and an unawareness of the techniques of planning and organizing, the group forced the leader to take an active directive role. Constant interpretation of this gradually took hold, and by the final meeting the students were contributing leadership, using the leader as a resource person. Each of the students, without collusion, had independently asked his parents for their reaction to the proposal and had argued until agreement and support were obtained. When this came about, it provided for more group trust and support for the idea.

The conclusions evident from the development of the group are that many of the teaching methods presently used in this school create high expectations and much dependency and work against students' ability to solve problems and demonstrate their abilities and confusions through activities. With a knowledge of group dynamics and techniques useful in forcing the group to accept responsibility, teachers would be more helpful to students in developing independence, problem-solving skills, and an ability to work together on projects.

Ninth and Tenth Grade Group (first two weeks). This group dealt primarily with confronting the members' own feelings about how they act among themselves and what they are doing with their lives. There was a concerted effort to deal with their feelings rather than the politics of the school. The main themes were trust and their lack of control over their lives.

In the first meeting it became clear that some members were not participating; the question; "Why do people have a fear of speaking in groups?" was discussed. The members wanted to lessen that feeling in this group. It seemed as if they were deciding whether to trust each other and to trust the two group leaders. The division of the student body was discussed, as well as the types of students who joined the group and those who did not. Trust was brought up in conversation about teachers. The session ended with the students' seeing teachers as subject to many of the same binds in school as themselves.

The group dealt with the students' role and its emotional effect on them. Much anger and frustration was expressed over the fact that they continued to fill the role. This realization sent the group into a deep depression. After this experience, the group started to come together. They questioned such phrases as "when you grow up," "what are you going to do in life," and "drop-out," because their use implied that they were not yet living and that to not go to school was to not be in society.

The final group meeting was spent examining their feelings about meeting with other groups. This inquiry brought out a somewhat angry response to the effect that they were going to speak out and not be afraid, as they had been at the start. They wished to deal with feelings rather than politics, and they did not want to be pushed into doing this, as the older group was. It ended with everybody hugging each other and feeling good.

Faculty-Administration Group (first two weeks). The faculty-administration group met twice for six-hour meetings before going into mixed groups with students for the remaining half of the program. During the first meeting the participants met in two small groups, and for the second week as one large group.

Group I was composed of teachers, two administrators, and one guidance counselor. It began with introductions and exploration of possible goals, followed by an abstract discussion. The trainer then asked for a replay of the tape, which enabled the members to listen to how they sounded and led to a focus on more concrete issues. A feeling of closeness and identity as a group was developing when a late member, the principal, joined the group. There was much discussion of his

commitment in terms of time allotment to the group, as well as teachers'
reactions to being in a group with administrators and vice versa. They
discussed everyday life in the school; their relationship with other faculty
meetings; and confusion in their roles as teachers, advisers, and dis-
ciplinarians.

The other small group began at a similar level and quickly reached
the feeling of not knowing where it wanted to go. There was a discussion
of their frustration at trying to be innovative and democratic in the
classroom and not being able to make students accept their efforts. The
question of relating lessons to the students, and of the extent of this
practice was posed. The second half of this session was taken up with a
workshop as group members asked for an experience of working together.
Two teams each spent an hour making a sex education program and then
debated the merits of their proposals to a mock board made of the trainers.
This exercise was followed by a discussion of how the teams worked together, but this latter effort never aroused much enthusiasm.

Both groups merged for the second week, focusing on issues of discipline, expectations of faculty and administration of each other, the
school's philosophy, personal philosophies of teaching, and how to set
in motion aspects of relevant change. An incident of a teacher's trying
to stop a group of girls in the restroom from causing unnecessary noise,
and his subsequent reliance on an administrator to enforce the ruling,
led to a role play which allowed the investigation of alternatives to present methods of discipline. The issue of behavior in the halls was seen
as students' asking to be accepted as adults and trying to have a place
of their own, even if only in the ladies' room. The group discussed
faculty's and administrators' functions with respect to curriculum, discipline, community, and school spirit, and explored the causes of differences between the two roles. Number Nine pointed out the various
ways in which the faculty and administrators could work together to
create an environment of trust and collaborative change. The participants went into the needs of teachers to be liked and, in this group, to
be seen as progressive. They ended by questioning whether they were
ready to meet with students or wished to continue meeting by themselves.
They decided to do both.

Mixed Groups (last two weeks). There were two six-hour student-
faculty groups, held after school in two consecutive weeks. The week
before the first one, there had been a power failure followed by some
disturbances on the West Campus (lower school), and the reaction to
that incident was pretty much the major theme of that group. The East
Campus group (older students) was concerned with the proposal for an
experimental school. The afternoon began with a meeting in the cafeteria,
to split into groups. Since each campus seemed to have a specific issue
to focus on, Number Nine made the decision to split into separate campus groups. The West Campus students protested this decision, which
they felt was imposed on then, but the staff convinced them that the
group was too large to meet together.

The East Campus group began by deciding to postpone presentation

and discussion of their proposal until more faculty members were available, and spoke about their relationships to the faculty. It was noted that
these students were very close to some of the faculty members present
and had little conflict with them over the issues of educational reform.
The discussion was general and abstract and touched on ways of making
educational change effective. After a dinner break it was decided to
present the proposal. The faculty members who were present all considered it a worthwhile idea, and discussion focused on how to present
it and on what portions were likely to be controversial. It was agreed to
write it up for presentation to the administration.

The West Campus group began with a general discussion of discipline
and of how teachers and students got along. It was noted that the teachers
and students were sitting on separate sides of the room and that students
were finding it very hard to talk. A teacher brought up the fact that she
was not sure how to react to a student who had taken a cigarette from her
and was smoking in the room. This touched off a discussion of discipline
and the relevance of some rules and some courses, which was carried on
largely by the faculty. People began to feel that the group was not moving
fast enough, that people were not getting close. Nonverbal exercises
were suggested. One of the group leaders suggested that the students and
faculty switch roles in a effort to see how the other half lives. The students were asked to go out and prepare two lessons, one as they felt
teachers should behave, and one as they saw them actually behaving.
There was enthusiasm for the idea, but the students found it very hard
to keep to the teacher role, and by the end of the exercise everyone was
being a student, while one of the trainers was haranguing the mock class.
It was fairly easy for the teachers to simulate students' behavior. By
the end of the exercise there was some boredom and anger; people discussed how it felt to be a student and the fear that a teacher felt when
faced with the prospect of a class.

After the dinner break the group began to talk about the disturbances,
especially the ways students and faculty had reacted. One student admitted his complicity, and the reasons for this form of protest were
discussed. Various responses by the administration were discussed.
Dealings with parents and the reaction of tightening discipline were also
examined. People wondered what to do about the popular feeling that discipline should be stricter. It was pointed out that schools with very tight
discipline seemed to have even more disturbances, and that this should
be brought to the critics' attention. The Number Nine staff made a number of suggestions about other ways to handle crisis situations.

The following week the entire group met together to fill out evaluations
and discuss the program in general, and the proposal by the East Campus
students in particular. About forty-five people were present, including
some faculty members who had not attended previous meetings. The
proposal was sent around for faculty signatures, and objections to it
were raised. The elitist nature of the program, the types of learning,
the hours of required school attendence, and the methods of evaluation
were justified. There was general acceptance, and it was felt that the

proposal would pass the administration. There was a feeling of community in the large group, which was all together for the first time. The participants wanted to continue in the large group after supper and end with a workshop which would be more intense and personal than the discussion thus far and would increase their closeness.

To satisfy all these conditions, the trainers divided the group in half. One group met for an hour and was observed by the other group. Then there was a ten-minute break, at which one member of the observing group offered feedback to a member of the group which had met. Then the observers met as a group, with the other group watching, followed by another feedback session. This cycle was then repeated. During the meetings the only rule was that people should try to deal with their feelings about each other as they happened. The trainers tried to show how people use defense mechanisms to protect them from their feelings; gradually they built an atmosphere in the room so that people were in touch with their own feelings. In this short workshop people who knew each other were able to bring out some of their feelings about each other and to see that many of their fears of self-expression were not warranted. Students and teachers looked at the ways they avoid reacting to each other in the everyday classroom situation, and the program ended with the question, "Why must we hide from each other, when it is so easy to get to a point where we can express ourselves to each other and feel good about it?" It was an appropriate ending.

Evaluation and Results. When working in a living system, there is no sure way to say whether a specific intervention, say a T-group, had a specific effect, such as personal growth. It is very hard to speak of changes in a school; even if changes can be demonstrated, we cannot say for certain that they came about as a result of what was done. Change within an individual — learning — is even harder to gauge. Our best measure is to ask a person if he has learned anything; if he can describe what he learned, we can assume that something must have happened that was useful. We have found that people in the program reported changes in written evaluations, and we can see changes in the school since the program. We thus have a fair justification for concluding that this pilot project had a positive effect.

When signing up for the groups, everyone was asked to write down what she considered the most pressing issues for the groups to deal with. The students wanted to get to know the teachers as people, to talk about changes in discipline and curriculum to make them more responsive to their needs, and to communicate some of their feelings about their treatment. The faculty members expressed concern over the negative image they felt students had of them, the need for more self-expression and community in the school, distance from administrators, frustration with trying to change the school or teaching methods, desire for new teaching techniques, and finally a desire for communication with students whom they knew to be angry and distrustful. Everyone painted a primarily negative image of their relationships, but it must be noted that an ability to criticize openly and a commitment to deal with the problems is usually used as a criterion of organizational health.

Before the final six-hour session of the program, all participants were given an evaluation form, asking for general critical comments on their experience. There was a lot of resistance to completing the forms, especially among the students; this can be interpreted either as residual anger at being treated impersonally in a document supposedly asking for personal reactions, or as due to the difficulty of really describing a learning process in writing. The completed forms, however, showed, a high interest in the program and a hope that it continue in some form. This high commitment was also demonstrated in the attendance, which was over 75 percent — remarkable, in that the program was completely voluntary and took up a whole afternoon and evening once a week for a month.

The reactions of faculty members to the program focused on four areas. (1) There was a chance to meet students as real people, to get at the substance of what was bothering them, in an atmosphere free of the distrust and cynicism that is prevalent elsewhere, and a chance to see them as a group with concerns and difficulties that overlapped with the faculty. Most felt that this new recognition carried over into the classroom and in outside dealings with all students. (2) Teachers saw the possibilities of using the dynamics of the group in discussions and as a way of understanding behavior in faculty meetings and classes. The groups were pictured by one as a "community where students and teachers could talk together with amity and trust, a perfect model for a class." (3) Teachers attained a greater awareness of themselves and others; they reported an increased ability to perceive blind spots and point them out constructively, to look critically at their own behavior and its con- sequences, and to spot and examine the feelings that lie behind a situation. (4) The faculty saw the groups as a start in getting together to talk over general issues of school philosophy, expectations of each other by stu- dents, faculty, and administrators, and building a genuinely responsive decision-making structure to clarify viewpoints, make decisions, and implement them.

The faculty wanted meetings between students and faculty to continue on a regular and expanded basis. They felt the need for general dis- cussions with students about all the aspects of school behavior and policy. They also desired further training in group dynamics and in techniques useful in the classroom. They felt a need as well for further work with faculty and administrators in dealing with their differences, clarifying expectations, and setting up a new mechanism for decision- making. The present mechanism seems to lead to frustration in all the participants, and the feeling is that much intensive work needs to be done before school policies can be clarified and improved.

The students' responses were much more personal; they saw the effects of the group mainly as a greater understanding of themselves and how they act in school. They spoke of learning to look critically at their student role and how it relates to learning. In one group this led to the drafting of the proposal for an experimental high school, which would offer the type of educational and personal experience that they desired.

They also felt that their teachers had similar problems with the school and expressed some of the same feelings. They felt the groups to be a chance to encounter teachers as people and as a good model for further attempts. All would like such groups to continue, and they want many types of students to participate. This feeling is especially strong in the wake of disturbances that occured during the program.

It is much harder for us to make an assessment of what changes have come about in the school as a result of the groups. The most obvious change is the proposal for an experimental school, which to our know-ledge is one of the first such programs originated entirely by students. It represents some of the most concrete critical thinking done by students, and it shows the high degree of sophistication of today's students. It is significant that the students who originated this proposal, in contrast to the faculty-administrator group, all had prior sensitivity training and were thus able to coalesce quickly into a work group. These students also had an opportunity later on to apply their newly acquired group skills as trainers in a large group workshop at a boys' private day school. The students went in pairs and ran small groups with the students there; they used this experience for their own critique of education. Many of the students in this group are also now working as counselors for Number Nine.

The faculty group decided to continue to meet separately in addition to meeting in the mixed groups — again showing the high need for and commitment to such groups. To our knowledge this group has continued to meet. After the disturbances in the school, some faculty members held small meetings with groups of students to discuss them and to ex-amine ways to prevent further actions of this type. They had a concrete idea of how this could be done in a small group, and they felt comfortable in undergoing such a difficult and demanding situation. Several teachers have also reported using group techniques in the classroom, in coun-seling and family conferences, and in their dealings and debates with other faculty members. The teachers in the program expressed a great deal of concern over the fact that the people who volunteered for the groups were seen to be ideologically united, while those faculty mem-bers with whom they consistently had differences saw no need for such groups. Some suggestions on ways to deal with this polarization have been tried out, and teachers feel that since their group experience they have been a lot more constructive in how they handle differences. Fur-ther, Number Nine was asked to visit an experimental English class, which was working together to devise a new curriculum, to talk over some of the dynamics of the group; the possibility is open for this re-lationship to continue or to expand into other class situations.

This experience taught the Number Nine staff that the kind of free space and open discussion that had been created at Number Nine's store-front could be recreated in the community. However, the sensitivity of schools to controversy resulted in a subsequent incident, from which Nine learned the great necessity for tact and caution in school programs. Two students who had been in the original group program began to work full-time for Number Nine after their graduation. They conducted some workshops in the school which were less carefully planned and did not include specific contracts and sponsorship by the administration. A member of a conservative parents' group heard that at one of the workshops there was "partial disrobing" (taking off shoes), "breaking of school rules" (smoking), and a total absence of faculty members. Number Nine had to publicly apologize for the incident and was banned from the school. In a satirical newspaper cartoon, drawn by a selectman of the town who was opposed to the school bond issue, Nine was caricatured as an example of what permissiveness and increased spending were bringing the schools, although Nine was never paid for any of the workshops. The opposition of even a few parents can cause a program to be dropped, while the support of many people is not sufficient to create a new program. That is the dilemma public schools face when they try to innovate, educate, or end racism.

Number Nine learned from this situation that intensive programs over a long term, with explicit contracts made with both faculty and students, offer the greatest promise. One-shot discussions, while useful in informing students about Number Nine, are a lot of trouble to set up and do not allow enough time for students to be able to distinguish Nine from other social agencies because of their great distrust of anything they hear at school. Nine has begun to concentrate on an inner-city school only three blocks from our building. Its administration, which is the most informal of any school Number Nine has encountered, is amenable to our visiting classes when we are invited and passing out material, provided it is done by the teacher as part of the classroom assignment or done outside school grounds. In classes Nine staffers have been able to demonstrate their group-discussion skills to both students and faculty, and as a result, they have been invited to do in-service training workshops for some new teachers and to teach a drug education class. Nine has spent time in the cafeteria and in talking with student leaders, and it has made its most extensive contact with black and Puerto Rican students, aided by some Number Nine staffers who attend the school. We hope that a more extensive program involving students and faculty can grow out of these initial efforts, without the kind of backlash which marred Number Nine's earlier effort.

Civil Liberties and Ombudsmen

Number Nine conflicts with high schools, as it does with psychiatric institutions, on the question of civil rights — in this case, the students'. Nine's primary task is to serve young people in ways they themselves define, and most of its staff members are young people. Almost always its constituents are in basic conflict with the schools. For example, boredom (not drugs or permissiveness) is the most prevalent problem young people perceive, and they attribute much of this to school. Schools also regularly deprive young people of due process in disciplinary matters, and they are quite arbitrary and rascist in the application of rules, which are enacted without the consent of young people. Number Nine

has dealt with administrators, some of whom were also in one of
our sensitivity groups, in matters concerning students whose rights
were violated. For example, one of the few blacks in a suburban school
had her pocketbook searched, and some pills she was holding for a white
friend were taken from it by a teachers. She was later arrested in the
principal's office, without his informing her of her rights. Number Nine
saw this action as not only unfair and illegal, but also as a clear example
of unconscious racism (the girl was seen by the teacher and principal
as potentially troublesome because her brother had quit school years
earlier). Number Nine helped her resolve the issue and supported her
in her decision to leave the school which had typed her; she now has a
scholarship to a prep school.

Although Number Nine has not made many effective moves in this
area, its role seems to lead clearly in the direction of a civil rights
organization for young people or in helping an already constituted reform group of students to win changes in their school. This trend contrasts with the "neutral" stance implicit in working with both faculty and
students in forming acceptable programs within the school. Number Nine
has done workshops for some student radical groups, helping them to
clarify their goals and strategy, and it has started a high school newspaper. There are also several experimental private and public high
school programs, and in each of these, students have initiated courses
which enable them to do volunteer work at Nine and to attend seminars
and encounter groups as learning experiences. This aspect of Number
Nine will be expanded, and if teachers and parents wish to participate,
they will be invited to attend these programs at Number Nine, rather
than attempting to get them cleared as part of a school program. When
such discussions and learning groups can happen at Number Nine, but
are not permitted in the school, the defensiveness and recalcitrance of
schools toward change becomes quite clear.

BIBLIOGRAPHY

Aaronson, B., and H. Osmond. Psychedelics. Anchor, 1970.

Abramson, H., ed. The Use of LSD in Psychotherapy and Alcoholism. Bobbs-Merrill, 1963.

Back, Kurt. Beyond Words. Russell Sage, 1972.

Barnes, M., and J. Berke. Mary Barnes: Two Accounts of Madness, Harcourt, 1972.

Barr, R. "Are Help Houses Better Than Doctors For Troubled Youth." Hospital Physician, March, 1971.

Beggs, Rev. L. Huckleberry's For Runaways. Ballantine, 1969.

Berne, Eric. Transactional Analysis in Psychotherapy. Grove, 1961.

Beyer, M. "Nature of the Staff," in Jaffe et al.

Bion, W.R. Experiences in Groups. Tavistock, 1961.

Blewett, D. The Frontiers of Being. Award, 1969.

Brown, N. O. Love's Body. Vintage, 1966.

Capouya, E. In New American Review Number 12. Simon and Schuster, 1970.

Clark, T., D. Jaffe, and others. A Field Study of Drug Use and the Youth Culture. HEW Contract Number OS-72-12, 1972.

Cleaver, E. Soul on Ice. Delta, 1968.

Cloward, R., and L. Ohlin. Delinquency and Opportunity. Free Press, 1960.

Cohen, Sidney. "LSD: Side Effects and Complications," in J. of Nervous and Mental Disease, Vol. 130 (1960).

Erikson, Erik. Gandhi's Truth. Norton, 1969.

———— Young Man Luther. Norton, 1962.

Erikson, K. Wayward Puritans. Wiley, 1966.

Fanon, Frantz. Wretched of the Earth. Grove, 1966.

Fierman, L., ed. Effective Psychotherapy — The Contribution of Hellmuth Kaiser. Free Press, 1965.

Grof, S. Agony and Ecstacy in Psychoanalysis. Science and Behavior, 1972.

Haley, J. Strategies of Psychotherapy. Grune and Stratton, 1969.

Halleck, S. The Politics of Therapy. Basic Books, 1971.

Harman, Willis. "The Issue of Consciousness Expanding Drugs," in Main Currents of Modern Thought, Vol. 20, No. 1 (1963).

285

Jaffe, D., M. Beyer, T. Clark, S. Cytrynbaum, D. Quinlan, and H. Reed. Number Nine: Responses to Youth Problems at a Crisis Center. Monograph, 1971.

Jaffe, D., Report of the 1971 Eastern Hotline Conference. Monograph, 1971.

——— "Young Radicals and Life Style Counseling," in Radical Therapist, Vol. 2, No. 1 (April, 1971).

Jerome, J. The Postgraduate Community, pamphlet, 1970.

Kantor, R.M. "Communes," in Psychology Today, July, 1970.

Keniston, K. Young Radicals. Harcourt, 1968.

——— Youth in Dissent. Harcourt, 1971.

Kornbluth, J., ed. Notes from the New Underground. Ace, 1968.

Laing, R.D. The Politics of Experience. Pantheon, 1967.

——— Politics of the Family. Pantheon, 1971.

——— Knots. Pantheon, 1971.

Lefcourt, R., ed. Law Against the People. Vintage, 1971.

Lifton, R.J. "Protean Man," in History and Human Survival. Vintage, 1969.

——— Thought Reform and the Psychology of Totalism. Norton, 1963.

Maslow, A.H. Toward a Psychology of Being. Van Nostrand, 1962.

Moffett, Toby. The Participation Put-On. Delta, 1971.

Mungo, R., Total Loss Farm. Bantam, 1972.

Radical Therapist, Vol. 2, No. 3 (October 1971). Special issue prepared by the Radical Psychiatry Center in Berkeley.

Radical Therapist Collective. The Radical Therapist. Ballantine, 1971.

Reed, H. "Survey of Community Attitudes," in Jaffe et al.

Reich, Charles. The Greening of America. Bantam, 1971.

Rogers, Carl. On Becoming a Person. Houghton Mifflin, 1961.

Rosen, J. Direct Analysis. Grune and Stratton, 1953.

Rossman, M. On Learning and Social Change. Random House, 1972.

——— The Wedding Within the War, Doubleday, 1971.

Roszak, Theodore. The Making of a Counter Culture. Anchor, 1969.

Ruitenbeek, Hendrik. ed. Going Crazy, Bantam, 1972.

Savage and Stolaroff. "Clarifying the Confusion Regarding LSD-25," in J. of Nervous and Mental Disease, Vol. 140 (1965).

Schatzman, M. "Madness and Morals," in The Radical Therapist.

Sechehaye, M. Autobiography of a Schizophrenic Girl. Signet, 1968.

Slater, Philip. Microcosm. Wiley, 1966.

——— The Pursuit of Loneliness. Beacon, 1970.

Spergel, I. Street Gang Work. Anchor, 1967.

Szasz, Thomas. Law, Liberty and Psychiatry. Macmillan, 1963.

——— The Manufacture of Madness. Delta, 1970.

Tart, C., and J. Creighton. "The Bridge Mountain Community," in J. of Humanistic Psychology, Spring, 1966.

Tayler, Maurer, and Tinklenberg, "Management of 'Bad Trips' in an Evolving Drug Scene," in J. of Amer. Med. Assn., July 20, 1971.

Terkel, Studs. "A Conversation with Daniel Ellsberg," in Harpers, March, 1972.

Toffler, Alvin. Future-Shock. Random House, 1970.
Torbert, William. "Personal and Organizational Challenges in Post-
    Bureaucratic Life." Manuscript, 1972.
Van Dusen, W. "LSD and the Enlightenment of Zen," Psychologia, Vol.
    4 (1961).
Wolff, R.P. The Poverty of Liberalism. Beacon, 1968.
Wolfe, T. The Electric Kool-Aid Acid Test. Bantam, 1969.
Zinn, H. SNCC: The New Abolitionists. Beacon, 1966.